GOVERNING CANADA

Governing Canada
INSTITUTIONS AND PUBLIC POLICY

MICHAEL M. ATKINSON
McMaster University

Harcourt Brace Jovanovich Canada Inc.

Toronto   Montreal   Orlando   Fort Worth   San Diego
Philadelphia   London   Sydney   Tokyo

Copyright © 1993
Harcourt Brace Jovanovich Canada Inc.
All rights reserved

No part of this publication may be reproduced or transmitted in any form or by any means, electronic or mechanical, including photocopy, recording, or any information storage and retrieval system, without permission from the publisher.

Requests for permission to make copies of any part of the work should be mailed to: Permissions, College Division, Harcourt Brace Jovanovich Canada Inc., 55 Horner Avenue, Toronto, Ontario M8Z 4X6.

Every reasonable effort has been made to acquire permission for copyright material used in this text, and to acknowledge all such indebtedness accurately. Any errors and omissions called to the publisher's attention will be corrected in future printings.

Canadian Cataloguing in Publication Data

Main entry under title:

Governing Canada: institutions and public policy

Chapters based on papers given at a conference held at McMaster University, Oct. 1991.
Includes bibliographical references and index.
ISBN 0-7747-3213-X

1. Canada – Politics and government – 1980 –
2. Political planning – Canada.   3. Public administration – Canada.   4. Policy sciences – Canada.
I. Atkinson, Michael M.

JL108.G68 1993   971.064'7   C92-094107-9

Editorial Director: *Heather McWhinney*
Acquisitions Editor: *Daniel J. Brooks*
Developmental Editor: *Dianne Horton*
Editorial Assistant: *Penny Case*
Editorial Manager: *Marcel Chiera*
Editorial Co-ordinator: *Celène S. Adams*
Production Manager: *Sue-Ann Becker*
Production Co-ordinator: *Denise Wake*
Copy Editor: *James Leahy*
Interior Design: *Dave Peters*
Typesetting: *Bianca Imagesetting Limited*
Assembly: *Louisa Schulz*
Printing and Binding: *Best Gagné Book Manufacturers*

∞   This book was printed in Canada on acid-free (or recycled) paper.
      1 2 3 4 5   97 96 95 94 93

Preface

For the past several years Canadians have been in the midst of a great institutional experiment. In the early 1980s, a gathering of latter-day fathers of confederation succeeded in patriating the Constitution and adding a Charter of Rights and Freedoms. What some thought was the end of the constitutional marathon proved to be only the beginning. Since 1982, Canadians have been on an almost endless quest for institutional solutions to political problems. At first it was a game reserved for politicians, but since the Meech Lake debacle, ordinary Canadians have found themselves reluctantly drawn in. Committees, commissions, and task forces have produced mountains of documents, each one an effort to address outstanding grievances. Canada has experienced the bittersweet taste of a national referendum. Problems that had been subject to the push and pull of ordinary politics have become constitutionalized. Canadians seem to be convinced that their problems are such that they cannot be solved simply by debate and the mobilization of interests. Canadians require nothing short of reform in the basic design of their institutions.

But what is the effect of changes in political institutions? In particular, just what effect do institutions have on public policy? This book helps answer these questions by closely examining the institutions of the Canadian state in conjunction with major realms of public policy. For a long time, Canadians have tinkered with their institutions without giving much thought to the implications that institutions have for public policy. Canadians have experimented with new institutional designs without either theorizing or actually examining the role that existing institutions play in the policy process. It is true that many of the changes to the Constitution have been symbolic in character, but most participants in the great constitutional debate have harboured some hope that new institutions will better equip them to cope with old problems. Is there any reason to think so?

The Introduction and Chapter 1 both imply that it is high time Canadians thought more systematically about what institutions are and what they can reasonably expect to achieve by institutional reform. The next five chapters are devoted to the structure of the Canadian state. These chapters are not simply descriptive or historical essays about key political institutions. Although students will find careful analyses of the prominent features of parliamentary government, federalism, and the judiciary, the principal concern of these chapters is with the connection between the institutions of the state and public policy. And while the Canadian Constitution has changed remarkably in the past several years, these basic institutions remain integral to the Canadian state.

In the four policy chapters, the authors reverse the order of analysis. They describe the major features of their policy areas and then ask what role Canadian political institutions have had in the evolution of policy. Naturally, institutions have not been the only factor shaping policy developments, but these chapters are concerned to show the significance and the limits of institutional design in policy areas that are critical for the well-being of Canadians.

The idea for this book came to me during a sabbatical spent at Duke University in Durham, North Carolina. While I was supposed to be doing something else, I kept wondering whether anyone in Canada would be interested in a project that would knit together some of the most contemporary thinking in the area of public policy. The response to my queries was more than gratifying. Editing this book has been one of those rare experiences in which esteem for one's colleagues actually increases with exposure. Every author in this volume has worked extremely hard to produce a chapter that is both sophisticated and accessible. Professors and students alike will find much to admire and much to learn from each of the contributions.

There are many people and many institutions to thank. Let me begin by thanking the Social Sciences and Humanities Research Council of Canada (SSHRC) whose conference grant permitted us to assemble both the authors of these chapters and a bevy of superb critics. The conference that SSHRC sponsored was held at McMaster University in Hamilton, Ontario, in October 1991. Jim Johnson, Dean of the Faculty of Social Sciences, was enthusiastic in his support for the project, and I owe him a personal debt of gratitude. Graduate students David McIvor and George McLean were able assistants, and we could not have survived without the contributions of Gerald Bierling, master coffee-maker. But the success of the conference was due primarily to the efforts of one person, Mara Minini, whose dedication to the enterprise went far beyond what could reasonably be expected. Thank you, Mara, for everything.

At the end of the conference everyone was talking about the discussants. I knew that I had invited some of the very best academic analysts of policy and institutions, but I could not have hoped for a more learned, balanced, incisive, and judicious group of critics. Many authors have thanked them in their essays, but for the record I want to acknowledge the excellent help provided by Keith Banting, Stephen Brooks, Stephane Dion, Peter Hall, Les Pal, Guy Peters, Peter Russell, Grace Skogstad, and Kent Weaver.

The successful operation of the conference depended, as well, on the diplomatic skills of those who chaired the sessions. Henry Jacek,

Evert Linquist, Maureen Mancuso, and Les Pal managed all participants and observers with firmness and tact. Thanks go as well to those who attended. An audience of graduate students and professors from Ontario and beyond was not content to sit and listen. They joined in on all panels and often provided the most stimulating and lively of commentaries.

This book is brought to you by a highly professional group of editors at Harcourt Brace Jovanovich. Heather McWhinney and Daniel J. Brooks have been with this project every step of the way. They have been our conscience and our guide, helping us address the needs of students without cramping our style as academics. Dianne Horton and Celène Adams brought the same kind of professionalism to the task of preparing the book for production and then seeing it through. Our publishers are a dedicated team who have worked hard to bring students and authors together. What more could any editor ask?

On a personal note, I want to thank George Hoberg, Sharon Sutherland, Paul Thomas, and Ken Woodside, my colleagues in this project, for their very tenacious efforts to improve my work. And special thanks, as always, to William Coleman. Thank you, Bill, for your contribution, your support, and your example.

Michael Atkinson

PUBLISHER'S NOTE TO STUDENTS AND INSTRUCTORS

This textbook is a key component of your course. If you are the instructor of this course, you undoubtedly considered a number of texts carefully before choosing this as the one that would work best for your students and you. The authors and publishers spent considerable time and money to ensure its high quality, and we appreciate your recognition of this effort and accomplishment. Please note the copyright statement.

If you are a student, we are confident that this text will help you to meet the objectives of your course. It will also become a valuable addition to your personal library.

Since we want to hear what you think about this book, please be sure to send us the stamped reply card at the end of the text. Your input will help us to continue to publish high-quality books for your courses.

Contributors

Michael M. Atkinson — *McMaster University*
Herman Bakvis — *Dalhousie University*
William D. Coleman — *McMaster University*
Ian Greene — *York University*
George Hoberg — *University of British Columbia*
David Mac Donald — *Dalhousie University*
Kenneth McRoberts — *York University*
Sharon L. Sutherland — *Carleton University*
Paul G. Thomas — *University of Manitoba*
Carolyn Tuohy — *University of Toronto*
Kenneth B. Woodside — *University of Guelph*
Orest W. Zajcew — *University of Manitoba*

CONTENTS

INTRODUCTION
    Governing Canada   1
    Michael M. Atkinson

CHAPTER 1
    Public Policy and the New Institutionalism   17
    Michael M. Atkinson

CHAPTER 2
    The Canadian Cabinet: Organization,
    Decision-Rules, and Policy Impact   47
    Herman Bakvis and David Mac Donald

CHAPTER 3
    The Public Service and Policy Development   81
    Sharon L. Sutherland

CHAPTER 4
    Structural Heretics: Crown Corporations and
    Regulatory Agencies   115
    Paul G. Thomas and Orest W. Zajcew

CHAPTER 5
    Federal Structures and the Policy Process   149
    Kenneth McRoberts

CHAPTER 6
    The Courts and Public Policy   179
    Ian Greene

CHAPTER 7
    Macroeconomic Policy: Dwindling Options   207
    William D. Coleman

CHAPTER 8
    Trade and Industrial Policy: Hard Choices   241
    Kenneth B. Woodside

CHAPTER 9
    Social Policy: Two Worlds   275
    Carolyn Tuohy

CHAPTER 10
    Environmental Policy: Alternative Styles   307
    George Hoberg

BIBLIOGRAPHY   343

GLOSSARY   372

CONTRIBUTORS' PROFILE   377

INDEX   380

Introduction: Governing Canada

Michael M. Atkinson

THREE APPROACHES TO PUBLIC POLICY

Ideas, Interests, and Institutions

In December 1990, the federal government finally succeeded in enacting the legislation that authorized the Goods and Services Tax (GST). Described by some as a fiscal necessity and by others as a tax grab of unprecedented proportions, the GST is now part of the Canadian tax structure. Whatever its merits, the legislation generated deep rancour among Canadians and undoubtedly contributed to the Conservative government's free fall in popularity. The bitterness was not surprising: no one likes taxes. But in this case, the government passed the legislation over the objections of a large majority of Canadians, all of the provinces, and all of the opposition parties. Was this the politics of principle, the politics of stupidity, neither, or both?

For those interested in this specific question, and in the general issues of public policy that lie behind it, there are three typical avenues of interpretation. First, it is possible to explain the policy and the reaction to it by focusing on political ideas. In this view, contentious concepts such as equality, freedom, rights, and authority lie at the heart of our political disagreements and our policy disputes (Qualter 1986). So, debate about the GST can be boiled down to disagreements regarding the appropriate role of the state in society and alternative conceptions of fairness in taxation. Those who study political ideas believe that by examining the beliefs of Canadians on these subjects, and by tracing the actions (or inactions) of their governments back to these basic political ideas, we will be better able to understand the policy outcomes of political struggles.

To some extent the appeal of this approach is based on the assumption that Canadians have adopted a unique combination of political ideas. It is often said, for example, that while liberal ideas dominate, liberalism must share the ideological spectrum with tory and socialist interpretations of society and the relations that should prevail between the state and its citizens. This combination of ideas and interpretations distinguishes Canada from other countries and gives rise to different types of political behaviour and different patterns of public policy (Manzer 1985). In this interpretation, the GST represents an ideological victory for those liberals who maintain that a sweeping, all-inclusive tax is both efficient and fair. Others, who argued that such a tax threatens interpersonal equity, were among the losers. In defending their choice, decision-makers stuck to the efficiency and fairness arguments that their economic advisers had prepared. They seemed to believe that eventually Canadians at large would be won over.

But is public policy really the product of an intellectual dialogue? For many policy analysts, the approach to public policy down the avenue of ideas will never adequately explain outcomes. What is required is attention to a second source of policy, namely political interests. In the Canadian case this means a consideration of the character of the Canadian economy and relations among social classes. In this interpretation, the GST represents yet another victory of organized economic interests who have a disproportionate influence over the policy agenda. The removal of the manufacturer's sales tax and its replacement with the far more wide-ranging GST was intended to serve the interests of domestically located industry and provide the Conservative government with much-needed tax revenues. Poor people, women, seniors, and the retail and tourism industries were outmanoeuvred by a business-oriented government and its supporters.

Those who adopt this approach to public policy argue that Canada is ultimately governed by economic interests that take their political shape from patterns of production in the economy (Clement & Williams 1989). In academic circles this has been an enormously influential perspective on policy and politics in Canada. Of all policy initiatives it asks the simple question: who benefits? And while the answer may be framed in terms of classes or groups, there is no doubt that in this interpretation, the main source of public policy is social forces in conflict. Those who adopt this approach set themselves the task of describing economic relationships accurately and charting their influence on the conduct of politics.

The third approach is, in some respects, the most traditional. It involves an assessment of political institutions such as federalism, Parliament, cabinet, and the bureaucracy. These institutions are, of course, influenced by political ideas and economic relationships, but in Canada political institutions have also been treated as important in and of themselves. Federalism, for example, does not merely replicate the regional character of the country, it reinforces it. Parliament does not simply reflect power relationships in society, it legitimizes them. The courts do more than adjudicate, they define the limits of political action. In this view political institutions, regardless of their origins, make an independent contribution to both the conduct of politics in Canada and to policy outcomes.

From the perspective of institutions, the GST was the product of a set of rules that concentrate decision-making authority in the hands of a cohesive group of elected politicians. In Canada, a government that commands a majority in the House of Commons and is united behind a policy initiative finds its effective opposition only in the provinces, the media, and (occasionally) the Senate. In the case of the GST, provincial opposition had no legal base from which to mount a challenge, the media was divided, and the Senate was eventually converted to the government's position via the expedient of appointing additional senators. The government of the day showed remarkable political will in forcing the GST through the legislative process, but it could not have succeeded if political institutions had permitted its adversaries greater opportunities to challenge its initiatives. Where governments are divided—that is, where the legislative and executive branches are in the hands of antagonistic parties—broad-based tax initiatives such as the GST are almost impossible. In countries like the United States, there are simply too many institutional roadblocks. In Canada, the executive-centred institutions of cabinet government made the GST possible.

The Institutional Approach

In this book we adopt a modified version of this third approach to public policy, arguing that the organization and character of political institutions play a critical role in determining policy outcomes in Canada. But institutions are only a beginning point. The study of political institutions cannot take place in isolation from the study of ideas and interests.

In the first place, institutions do not suddenly appear, fully formed. They reflect conflicts among competing social forces that struggle to imbed their interests in these institutions. For example, the phenomenon known as province-building—the creation of strong provincial institutions—was not the result of some natural process. The provincial rights movement that spawned province-building in the post–World War II period was a political creation. The resource-rich provinces did not rely on the courts to discover provincial powers; Quebec did not rely on Ottawa's language legislation to protect the status of French. The governments in these and other provinces mobilized resources, fashioned arguments, and made threats. Most important, they created political institutions to defend and promote local interests, which, in turn, defended and promoted them.

By the same token, the party discipline we have come to associate with parliamentary government in Canada was also created to serve political interests. It was fashioned in the first instance by the inspired deployment of patronage. John A. Macdonald and Oliver Mowat did not wait for members of Parliament to discover the benefits of cohesiveness. They bribed, threatened, and cajoled to extend the reach of the Conservative and Liberal parties respectively. The party discipline we have come to associate with the Canadian Parliament became an instrument through which brokerage parties could make diffuse policy promises to the electorate yet remain cohesive when in government.

In these cases, and all others, institutions are human creations. But they are not the product of polite negotiation. Institutions are created and changed by those who can wield power within society and within the state. This is why the study of institutions cannot be separated from the study of political interests.

Second, institutions are shaped by political arguments in which alternative ideas about appropriate arrangements for governance contend with one another. It is one thing to know your interests, another to know what kind of political arrangement will best promote them. Besides, not all interests are antagonistic. Farmers, bankers, industrial workers, and native Canadians may have contending economic interests and still agree on the value of economic stability, policy responsiveness, and effective political leadership. The question is, what kind of institutions are best suited to deliver these political goods?

Throughout the 1980s, and well into the 1990s, Canadians debated the design of their political institutions employing arguments that often turned on the meaning and applicability of abstractions or concepts. Take the concept of equality, for instance. The constitutional debate has raised the question of whether the provinces should be treated as equals (Milne 1991). Should they all have a veto over constitutional changes; should they all be equally represented in a reformed Senate? For some, institutional equality was desirable to offset serious inequalities in population and resources. Others argued that unequals should be treated unequally and concessions should be made to recognize the distinctiveness of provinces. Naturally the different points of view reflected different interests, but to marshal support for alternative institutional designs required arguments about political goals and social values.

Institutions are shaped by these arguments and by their outcomes. Institutions are not simply discovered, they have to be invented. As Canadians reinvented theirs in the constitutional upheaval of the 1980s and 1990s, they were able to watch the same phenomenon repeated in other countries where old ideas had lost their force and political institutions their legitimacy.

So, ideas, interests, and institutions are bound up with one another. As the chapters in this volume make clear, it is not a matter of choosing one approach and rejecting the others. The choice is one of where to begin and where to lay emphasis. We lay emphasis on institutions, first, because in Canada, with some notable exceptions, the connection between institutions and public policy has not been drawn very tightly. Canadians have tended to study political institutions for their own sake or for what they can tell us about our political character. These are noble objectives, but with this volume we take matters one step further, focusing on how institutions affect the policy orientations and capacities of governments.

We also study institutions to see what might be. If, as we will argue throughout this book, institutions have a vital influence on our capacity to solve problems of collective action, we cannot be indifferent to alternative institutional designs. Institutions are means of imposing some modicum of control over our own destiny. They shape us, but we can also shape them. In Canada, the struggle to shape and reshape institutions is a familiar feature of political life. We study institutions to see what they promise and to reveal the interests and ideas that lie behind the alternatives we are offered.

WHAT ARE INSTITUTIONS?

Rules, Organization, and Human Beings

Perhaps because it is used in such a wide variety of ways, the term "institution" is seldom precisely defined. In ordinary discourse it suggests concrete objects, like buildings—mortar, brick, and glass—and their contents. When we hear the term "penal institution," for example, we think of prisons: cells, fences, and iron bars. For many of us the term "parliament" means the Parliament Buildings located on Wellington Street in Ottawa. On reflection, this usage suggests a rather naive view of institutions. After all, what would these buildings or structures be without people? But the idea of institutions as concrete structures helps to emphasize their relative permanence. People come and go, but buildings remain. They symbolize the continuity we associate with institutions even though we know that there is more to institutions than concrete images can convey.

The need to have people at the centre of institutional analysis has led some to think of institutions primarily in behavioural terms. The institution of the family, for example, refers to established patterns of human interaction based on kinship. There is a sense of permanence here as well: interaction is systematic and cumulative, not random. Each family is different, yet members are united by recognized relationships of authority and responsibility. Some of these relationships are based on trust and social norms; others are enshrined in law. The key here is human agency. Institutions are patterns of interaction established by human beings. They do not simply happen. Moreover, they are human creations in which people must justify their behaviour and accept responsibility for their actions. The permanence and structure associated with institutions is supplied not simply by regular interaction, but by a belief that the practices and procedures employed by institutions have the quality of moral rightness.

These practices and procedures are central to the study of institutions. In political science it is traditional to associate institutions with rules. For example, when political theorists talk about liberal institutions, they often mean nothing more than the rules that permit, among other things, freedom of speech and freedom of religion. Recently, the connection between rules and institutions has been drawn tighter. Specifically, it has become increasingly common to think of institutions as systems of rules. If political life is about the making of choices and the resolution of conflicts (as many scholars believe it is), then institutions are mechanisms, bundles of rules, through which choices are made and conflicts resolved. Institutions establish who is permitted to participate, how decision-making is to be accomplished, and what limits (if any) are to be placed on the range of possible outcomes. So, while human beings are central to institutions, institutions represent deliberate attempts to channel and constrain human behaviour.

The result is organization. As rules are systematized, legitimized and enforced, institutions become collective entities. The rules are the infrastructure, the main columns and beams. They establish offices, divide responsibilities, and create hierarchies of authority. Around these rules, concrete social relations are constructed. These concrete social relations consist of sets of expectations associated with institutional roles. In fulfilling their institutionally assigned roles, human beings create organizational capacity, that is, the ability to achieve collective goals. It is organization that produces capacity. Institutions will always be composed of individuals, but organization makes institutions into separate, corporate bodies often with legal identities, rights, and responsibilities.

Thus a definition of political institutions must recognize first, the central role of human beings; second, the foundation supplied by rules; and third, the capacity created by organization. The following definition, adapted from the work of Fritz Scharpf, does that. Institutions can be thought of as configurations or networks of organizational capabilities (assemblies of personal, material, symbolic, and informational resources available for collective action) that are deployed according to rules and norms that structure individual participation, govern appropriate behaviour, and limit the range of acceptable outcomes (Scharpf 1989, 152).

State Institutions

The state consists of those political institutions that together comprise a system of order that claims a monopoly on the exercise of coercive power and the authority to issue determinations that are binding on all of those living within a prescribed territory (Weber 1922, 2: 56). The state is a single organization in the sense that it is "a set of purposefully contrived arrangements" that unify the rules, roles, and resources contained in all state institutions (Poggi 1990, 19). This unity is most evident during periods of national emergency—when war breaks out, when natural disasters strike, when there are insurrections that threaten political order, or in periods of economic crisis.

Normally, however, the state is a unified entity only in the abstract. In most states, separate institutions create, consolidate, divide, exercise, and adjudicate public authority. Included among state institutions are electoral systems, bureaucracies, executives, legislatures, and judiciaries. These institutions can be harmonized—that is, they can be made to complement one another—but it is very rare that they can all be harnessed up to the same objective. Indeed, they are often deliberately pitted against one another in an attempt to create a balance of institutional forces. Only totalitarian states that are marked by exceptional levels of organizational sophistication can aspire to overall coordination and only then by destroying the autonomy of individual institutions.

It is constitutions that preserve the internal diversification of the modern state. Constitutions impose limits on the exercise of state power, in the first instance by demarcating the authority of state institutions. The division of labour within the state is intended to ensure that the state's monopoly on coercive power is subject to internal checks. Total power cannot be exercised by one institution. To ensure that the division is respected, the actions of individuals and institutions in the state are all subject to the law. Thus crown attorneys, who are agents of the state, and judges, who are also agents of the state, are each given separate bases for their authority, that is, separate roles in different institutions. Neither, however, can exercise their authority beyond what is prescribed by law.

Constitutions can also limit state power by establishing a set of political rights that give citizens, among other things, freedom of speech, freedom of association, and freedom of the press. These are negative rights in that they stipulate areas of personal freedom into which the state cannot intrude. In democracies these rights limit the exercise of state power by placing constraints on majority rule. In place of the unfettered exercise of state power by temporary majorities, constitutions substitute overarching rules about political choice to which citizens and leaders are expected to be committed. Among these rules are those that protect permanent minorities, either by granting rights to individuals or, in federal systems, by allowing sectional minorities the opportunity to make local decisions without interference by a national majority.

Since the establishment of the modern constitutional state in the eighteenth century, other political institutions have emerged to mobilize social forces and to engage in the competition to exercise formal power or to influence its exercise. In Canada, and other western-style democracies, the most prominent of these institutions are political parties and interest associations. Parties and associations are political institutions but not state institutions. Formally at least, they are not part of the apparatus engaged in the actual exercise of public authority (Skocpol 1985, 7–8). They are, instead, institutions designed for the articulation of interests and the pursuit of power. Although political parties in Canada sometimes spend long periods in government (so long that they become identified with the state itself), no party in Canada has ever become a state institution. Similarly, while interest groups often permit themselves to become the instruments of the state—setting public standards, for example, or administering government programs—the constitution prevents groups from usurping state authority.

In this volume we concentrate on the role of state institutions in public policy. However, it is vitally important to recognize that policy is affected by the political struggle to control state institutions. So important is this struggle that in most democracies, political parties have become necessary elements in the establishment of constitutional order. Many constitutions acknowledge the existence of parties and enshrine the rules of political competition. Power, after all, must be legitimized: people must believe that the outcome of political battles in some manner reflects the popular will. In constitutional democracies legitimization requires, among other things, a framework for political competition in which parties are free to mobilize societal interests and groups are able to express the claims of their members.

Thus victorious political parties and effective interest groups become part of the state apparatus to the extent that they link the state to its citizenry and supply state institutions with political leadership and policy ideas. Theoretically, parties and groups are never absorbed completely into the state. Nonetheless, victories and defeats in the realm of normal politics, where all attention is on the pursuit of power, can be expected to have an effect on policy outcomes. The institutional framework within which parties and groups operate helps determine just how much of an effect.

THE CANADIAN STATE

In the case of the Canadian state the institutional framework does not inspire much admiration or loyalty. For many Canadians, the architecture of the state is shapeless and confusing. It is almost as if the Canadian state, as such, does not exist. The institutions are there all right, but the party political battle is often so intense that the institutions seem to be nothing more than arenas for the push and pull of normal politics. And if it is not the parties, it is provincial and federal politicians bickering about powers and prerogatives, or interest groups vying for favour. The state as a coherent entity does not seem to possess much weight.

A Weak State Tradition

Canada has what has been described as a weak state tradition. The idea of the state as a unified, comprehensive organization does not have much purchase on the mindset of Canadians (Atkinson & Coleman 1989a, ch. 3). That does not mean that the state necessarily lacks the capacity for heroic policy interventions. In recent years there have been many occasions—from the National Energy Program to the GST—in which the executive-bureaucratic institutions of the state have been marshalled behind a single project, one that did not possess the support of all, or even a majority, of society's strongest actors. A weak state tradition does not mean a paralysed state. A weak state tradition means that major policy initiatives are interpreted as the priorities of particular governments. They are not linked to the state as a separate, unified, rational entity. For most Canadians, the GST was not conceived by the state, but by the Tories.

Part of the reason for this weak state tradition lies in the origins of Canadian institutions. The Canadian state was deliberately patterned on the structures of British parliamentarism. The Confederation settlement determined that Canada was to have a constitution "similar in principle to that of the United Kingdom." The additions made to this formula, chiefly a federal structure and specific religious guarantees, were prudential in nature, intended to address local problems. The creators of this institutional framework believed that they were founding a just and effective form of government. The Canadian Constitution descended from the ancient mixed and balanced constitution that had supplied the British people with liberty while curbing the excesses of democracy. In this view, Canadian political institutions may have been marked by pragmatic compromise, but they also had noble precursors.

While political elites, particularly those of British ancestry, have generally found these institutions inspiring, many others now conclude that they are confusing, undemocratic, wasteful, and unresponsive. In French Canada these institutions, while widely admired among members of the intelligentsia, were never considered a critical part of French-Canadian identity. Until the Quiet Revolution transformed political institutions in the province, the idea of the nation was much stronger than that of the state. For its part, English-Canadian nationalism has not drawn on Canadian political institutions to strengthen feelings of distinctiveness. Typically weak and shapeless, nationalism in English Canada is often associated with the products of the institutional framework—a universal medical care system, the CBC—but not with those institutions themselves. In short, the Canadian state has not engendered a national consciousness (Resnick 1990, 210). Hence, there is no deep reservoir of diffuse support for the institutions of the state. Instead, Canadians are inclined to hold their institutions up to the cold light of day and make some harsh instrumental evaluations: What have they done for me (or to me) lately?

The Ambiguous State

Part of the reason for the lack of close attachments to political institutions is their ambiguous character. The three major pillars of the Constitution—Westminster parliamentarism, federalism, and the Charter of Rights and Freedoms—send mixed signals about the nature of the Canadian state. The Westminster model of parliamentary government is supposed to concentrate effective decision-making authority in the hands of a popularly elected executive that, in turn, controls the legislative branch. In this kind of institution leaders are rewarded not just for their ability to respond to specific demands, but also for their capacity to plot the collective future of the nation. As Herman Bakvis and David Mac Donald explain in their chapter on the cabinet, the latter of these two expectations is not always as prominent as might be expected. In Canada there are strong pressures, channelled through both the electoral system and the party system, to use cabinet decision-making structures to divert resources to particular regions and favourite projects. The policy-making process at the centre lacks discipline just where the Westminster model believed it could be found. Strong politicians, backed by firm control of the parliamentary party, do enact far-reaching (and sometimes unpopular measures), but they also engage in distributive politics. Policy outputs reflect this ambiguity.

There are other sources of diffusion within the central policy-making institutions of the Canadian state. In Chapter 3, Sharon Sutherland shows how the federal bureaucracy has developed a policy capacity on which elected politicians can, and do, capitalize. Situating her discussion of bureaucracy squarely within the Westminster parliamentary model, she argues that this system permits politicians and bureaucrats to develop a healthy relationship with one another. In Canada the bureaucrat's expertise can be matched to the politician's grasp of political needs and realities. But things can go awry. Politicians do not always listen to their advisers and bureaucrats can make public policy almost autonomously in areas that are not on the contemporary political agenda. Sutherland shows how the quality of public policy is affected by politico-bureaucratic relationships, and also how adherence to the logic of Westminster parliamentary government can both address and avoid accountability problems.

Developed in the eighteenth and nineteenth centuries, the Westminster model of parliamentary government did not contemplate a large, permanent public service or the development of organizational entities lying outside of the departmental structure. In their chapter on agencies and crown corporations, Paul Thomas and Orest Zajcew explain the attractiveness of these administrative vehicles for particular policy initiatives and responsibilities. Of course, agencies and corporations can pose significant problems. Greater reliance on nondepartmental bodies has, for example, fragmented the policy-making capabilities of the state. But the introduction of these organizational forms does not necessarily produce weakness or the loss of political control. Moving beyond the formalities of accountability, the authors suggest that there is greater potential for political direction and control of these entities than is usually assumed. Crown corporations and regulatory agencies can be sources of policy change as well as policy inertia, depending on their organizational cultures, their leadership, and their environments.

Perhaps no institutional arrangement contributes more to policy diffusion and structural incoherence than federalism. Celebrated by its admirers as a means of preserving local preferences while pursuing national objectives, federalism has played havoc with the conventional ideas of political sovereignty that animate Westminster-style parliamentarism. The British parliamentary tradition does not contemplate divided sovereignty, let alone the de facto sharing of powers that has come to characterize contemporary federal institutions. In Chapter 5, Kenneth McRoberts shows how the elaborate structure of intergovernmental relations, which has grown up to mediate shared responsibilities, has made its own contribution to the evolution of public policy in Canada. For many observers, that contribution has been largely a negative one. Federal institutions have thwarted or delayed coherent and comprehensive policies in areas that would appear to need them. But McRoberts reminds us that federalism has provided significant scope for policy experimentation and flexibility. In a diverse political community these are prized qualities of the policy process. The question is whether or not the scope for distinctive policies is employed appropriately.

To a certain extent, the question of appropriate policies is a constitutional one. Which order of government is permitted to do what has been the subject of continuous constitutional debate and judicial interpretation. In recent years Canadians have added to the constitution the Charter of Rights and Freedoms, which restricts the actions of all state institutions. The courts have always had an impact on the evolution of policy, but the Charter has significantly expanded the scope for judicial policy-making. Ian Greene's chapter on judicial institutions evaluates the capacity of the court system to shoulder this responsibility given the rules it employs, its organizational attributes, and its personnel. He points out that at present the impact of the courts on any particular policy issue is very difficult to predict. The courts do not always act in a timely manner, so judicial decision-making is often not synchronized with the rest of the policy process. Moreover, there is growing evidence that the personalities and backgrounds of judges have a strong influence on the eventual determination of cases. For those who admire the Westminster model's capacity for clear political action, and who appreciate the need for strong lines of accountability to the electorate, all of this may seem rather distressing. However, judicial activism is not preordained, and legislatures do have override clauses at their disposal.

In the last few years an already ambiguous state has become even more so. The original institutional design has evolved to the point that its originators would recognize only a few of its prominent features. Yet it might be argued that for all of its ambiguity, the Canadian state does possess an inner logic. In the Canadian Constitution there is an elaborate division of labour, but that is to be expected in a modern polity where there are heavy demands placed on political authorities. Protecting ordinary citizens from both zealous and indolent policy-makers requires a host of institutions with different responsibilities. But do these institutions really permit those who direct the Canadian state to govern effectively?

THE CHALLENGES OF GOVERNING

Governing effectively entails the ability to set appropriate and attainable policy goals, to marshal resources for the achievement of those goals, and to pursue them in a manner that enhances the legitimacy of the institutions of government. Of course what is appropriate and attainable will always be the subject of political dispute. And at least some of this dispute will turn on the capacity of political institutions to realize the good society. In the eyes of some observers, that capacity is not very high.

The Left and The Right

The changing relationship between state and society in liberal democratic regimes has raised questions about the capacity of the state to develop and implement public policy. From both the political left and the political right arguments have been mounted to the effect that the role of the state in society has become fundamentally problematic.

On the political left it is argued that the crisis-prone character of capitalism puts the state in an untenable position. Responsible for maintaining high levels of both consumption and production, the modern state must provide for the welfare of its citizens and at the same time create the conditions necessary for a functioning capitalist economy. These dual requirements oblige the state to simultaneously ameliorate and reproduce inequalities. Worse, the state must perform this juggling act at a time when its scope for independent action is being seriously eroded by the increasing mobility of capital and growing pressure to harmonize domestic and international policies. The state finds itself caught in a series of structural contradictions. The most obvious manifestation of the problem is the high level of public-sector debt that many countries have acquired. But beneath the surface lies the larger problem of how to reconcile capitalism with the personal development of citizens. From the political left comes profound scepticism that the present array of state institutions is capable of performing this task.

The political right offers a similarly dismal assessment of the capacity of the state. Here, however, the argument rests not on the emerging character of capitalism, but on the idea that the state has always been an inherently flawed mechanism for the resolution of society's problems. In the absence of an adequate theory of distributive justice, any intervention by the state in the lives of ordinary citizens is seen as a challenge to their liberty. Such interventions, ostensibly made to provide public goods, are usually executed in an inefficient manner. Inefficiencies occur, it is argued, because the services provided by the state do not have to pass a market test. Instead, they are provided to suit the providers, namely politicians and bureaucrats. These so-called rent-seekers or rentiers are inclined to give in to special pleading because it profits them personally to serve the clients of the state. Critics on the right believe that while a minimalist state may be a necessity, it should confront societal problems by subjecting them to market-based solutions, not by launching self-serving interventions.

These arguments from the left and right may be incorrect, but they have been advanced in an era in which much of the policy response of individual governments appears to be inadequate to meet the scope of the problems they face. The modern state has materially improved the living conditions of the mass public in all western industrialized nations, but in spite of this progress, faith in the public sector has generally receded. While it seems unlikely that improvements in health care, sanitation, education, and the conditions of work will be forfeited, the citizens of democratic countries have been obliged to reduce their expectations, while political elites struggle with policy problems that defy easy solution.

Policy Challenges

In chapters 7 through 10 we examine four major policy areas in which the challenge seems capable of overwhelming the capacity of the state to respond. In each case the authors take pains to compare the Canadian situation with that of other nations and to focus on the role that state institutions have played in fashioning policy responses.

In his chapter on macroeconomic policy William Coleman outlines the narrow range of options available to governments that want to provide simultaneously for price stability, economic growth, employment opportunities, and balanced trade. In the post–World War II period most countries pursued, with varying degree of enthusiasm, some form of Keynesian policy. But the original coalitions that supported this option dissolved during the 1970s in the face of increased inflation, reduced productivity, and high levels of unemployment. Institutional conditions, including an autonomous central bank and a strong and orthodox Department of Finance, allowed Canada to make the transition to monetarism more easily than many other countries. However, as Coleman shows, monetarism is no panacea for Canada's macroeconomic problems, and it remains unclear whether the institutions of the Canadian state are well suited to engineer the next transition.

If, as Coleman suggests, the division between macroeconomic and microeconomic polities will become increasingly blurred, there will be a growing onus on governments to provide innovative industrial policies. These will have to take us well beyond the standard subsidy programs of the 1970s and 1980s. Kenneth Woodside argues that the negotiation and signing of the Canada–U.S. Free Trade Agreement marks an important shift away from industrial policy by the federal government. In its place, the government has been placing an increasing emphasis on trade-policy solutions to economic problems. The failure of successive Canadian governments since the 1960s to develop a viable industrial policy and the confluence of a number of domestic and international institutional developments—including a new Conservative government with a constituency that was more favourably disposed to trade liberalization—were important determinants of this shift in policy emphasis. While efforts to develop new industrial policy initiatives will continue, they are more likely to be implemented at the provincial level—such as the 1991 measures proposed by the Quebec government—and they will be constrained by trade policy commitments.

While Canada has been a reluctant follower in most areas of industrial policy, the Canadian state has led the way in certain areas of social policy. In a chapter that compares Canada's record in the health and income maintenance areas with that of other industrialized countries, Carolyn Tuohy shows that Canada is both a leader and a laggard. Indeed, she identifies certain puzzles in the development of the Canadian welfare state, such as why the country should have developed a universal health-care program, ordinarily associated with social democratic regimes, and at the same time a series of rather restrictive programs in areas such as social assistance and pensions. The social-policy area in Canada is strewn with these sorts of paradoxes. Tuohy believes that Canada's federal institutions are partly responsible; however, social policies require supportive constituencies and, as Tuohy points out, support has been much more effective in the health-care arena than in that of income maintenance. As a corollary, further decentralization of social policy through constitutional change would have different implications in the two arenas of health care and income maintenance.

Nowhere does the present arrangement of state institutions seem less able to respond to challenges of governing than in the realm of environmental policy. As George Hoberg points out, environmental policy involves enormous governing problems. There are very long time horizons associated with most environmental initiatives, considerable scientific uncertainty, and intense value conflicts. Moreover, environmental problems do not respect conventional political boundaries. All levels of government are drawn in and state-to-state negotiation is increasingly common. In Canada the institutional response has been twofold: an opening up of the pluralist bargaining process that characterizes so much policy-making in Canada, and an increasing resort to judicial remedies. As Hoberg points out, neither of these institutional changes provides much scope for strong political leadership. However, the Westminster model of parliamentarism retains considerable potential at the executive–bureaucratic centre, partly because executive actions in our system are still relatively unfettered by constitutional requirements. The question is whether state institutions are capable of fashioning policy responses that can win support among the increasingly diverse community of stakeholders in this policy area.

CONCLUSION

Will the institutions of the Canadian state be able to organize creative responses to contemporary policy challenges, or do their origins in the eighteenth and nineteenth centuries render them incapable of adapting to the circumstances of the twentieth and twenty-first? The chapters in this volume can offer only a partial answer. In the first place, not all state institutions are examined in detail, and not all policy areas are included. Faced with the inevitability of choosing, we have made an attempt to focus on key institutions and key policies, but an overall evaluation of political institutions and public policy will require an even broader picture than the one offered here.

There is another reason that partial answers are all that can be expected at this point. For the most part we remain uncertain about the way in which institutions contribute to the evolution of public policy. This Introduction began by noting that institutions, ideas, and interests are bound up together. Selecting any one of them for intense analysis leaves open the question of how the others should be factored in.

The first chapter of this volume discusses the connection between institutions and public policy at a theoretical level. It reviews alternative approaches to the study of institutions and it speculates on the way in which institutions and public policy interact. An important issue in this discussion is the degree to which institutions constrain public policy and the degree to which they create policy opportunities. Chapter 1 does not propose one right way of thinking about policy and institutions, but it endeavours to provide some guidance in considering the alternatives.

CHAPTER 1

Public Policy and the New Institutionalism

Michael M. Atkinson

INTRODUCTION

The study of public policy has become something of a growth industry in the last twenty years. Public policy has always been important, but the expanding division of labour in political science has meant that public policy can now claim a separate spot on the research agenda. Of course, the separate study of policy does not (or at least should not) entail its divorce from politics. We now study policy to better understand and to better criticize our politics. Nothing is quite as revealing about the character of political life in a society as the manner in which public resources are generated and then used up in the pursuit of public goals.

As they examine public policy, analysts find themselves torn between two rather different perspectives. In the first place they are bound to be impressed by the generality of policy problems. There is hardly any country in the world with a policy problem that is entirely unique. Every state, for example, must raise revenues in order to conduct public business. How much to raise, from whom, and in what manner are among the most general of policy challenges. Every state must also distribute these resources. How to do so in a way that both meets demands for distributive justice and ensures continued economic growth is a fundamental problem in all countries. Add to these the common problems that flow from growing interdependence among countries in terms of their trade, financial flows, scientific exchanges, and environmental responsibilities. The impact of recessions, productivity declines, rampant inflation, and debt crises cannot be contained within a single country. Our world has become increasingly small, our problems increasingly shared, and the need for co-operation increasingly pressing.

But there is another perspective on public policy. This perspective stresses the equally undeniable fact that states manage their common problems in different ways. In fact, some states seem to be much better than others at handling particular challenges. Japan has enjoyed remarkable success in managing the challenge of international competition in consumer goods; Canada has had success in fashioning a universal health-care program, Sweden in launching programs of labour adjustment, Germany at achieving macroeconomic stability. And, of course, these countries, like all others, have had their share of policy failures.

Policy analysts are naturally curious about what accounts for success and failure. Their curiosity has led them to consider everything from education systems to industrial relations. And of course they have considered institutions. The design of the state, both its basic architecture and its detailed human patterns, seems so inextricably connected to public policy that to ignore it would seem foolhardy. Yet how are we supposed to think about the relationship between state institutions and public policy? How important are institutions, and what features of public policy are they important for? This chapter explores these questions, first by discussing what we mean by public policy, then by considering how institutions and policy are connected.

DEFINITIONS AND BACKGROUND

Public Policy

In this chapter the term public policy will be used to refer to a course of action adopted by public authorities in relation to a problem on the public agenda (Pal 1987, 4). This definition implies that to engage in public policy requires a measure of consciousness and intent. No action means no policy, even though the absence of action is often as revealing and important as policy itself. This definition of policy also implies that policies are relatively broadly based patterns of action. A single decision may reflect a policy, but policy typically involves a number of decisions, each conceptually linked to the others. And policy, in the final analysis, will always be more than a collection of decisions, or even a series of programs. Programs are the manifestations of policy—the legal, financial, and administrative vehicles through which policy goals are pursued.

Consider Canada's approach to the "problem" of research and development. In the late 1960s research and development became a public issue, in the sense that it arrived on the political agenda. Politicians were seized by the idea that low levels of research and development might have devastating long-term implications for Canadian industry and hence for Canadian economic performance.

From that point until the mid-1980s the federal government's policy was to encourage public and private investment in research and development. A number of programs were introduced to give expression to this policy, including programs of selective subsidy to business, and technology transfer programs intended to encourage better liaison between public laboratories and commercial enterprises. These programs helped to clarify what investment in research and development meant, and what policy-makers expected to achieve with these measures. In this sense, programs influenced, even shaped, the policy. But they did not exhaust the policy. When politicians and bureaucrats grew dissatisfied with the performance of these programs, others were introduced to take their place.

Policy and Theory

Decisions and programs give concrete expression to policy, but policy itself is more abstract. It manifests itself in expenditures and organizations, but it also exists in the realm of ideas and public discourse. Put another way, policy is a theoretical construct. It is a course of action, yes, but action that is anchored in both a set of values regarding appropriate public goals and a set of beliefs about the best way of achieving those goals. In this sense public policy is a branch of political theory. Policies require a theory of the right and the good and a theory of how the world works. They are nourished by the belief that their goals are worthwhile and their means are effective. Doubt on either of these matters signals the beginning of policy change.

Of course, policies may linger because of indifference or because politically astute beneficiaries have devised a means of shielding them from criticism. The pace and direction of policy change is not mechanical. And ambiguity helps. Policies are often served by a loose collection of programs that support a diverse set of activities. In the process of implementing and then adjusting these programs, the problem that originally gave rise to the policy is often reconceptualized. On the surface the policy remains unchanged, but it is subtly undermined or transformed by alternative interpretations regarding its real purpose. Policy detached from theory becomes vulnerable.

The Canadian government's policy of encouraging research and development provides a case in point. This policy has never been officially abandoned, but the decisions taken and the programs adopted have become detached from the original policy goals. It was once believed that industry would devote more resources to research and development if government provided sufficient financial incentives. Nothing of the sort happened. Not only did industry prove indifferent to these schemes, but in the case of the Scientific Research Tax Credit, massive tax loopholes cost the government billions of dollars. In the 1990s research and development policy is adrift. It is still a safe rhetorical theme, because it is still on the public agenda, but it is a policy that is virtually devoid of action. The promotion of research and development is no longer considered a sure-fire way of ensuring long-term economic growth, and even if it were, successive governments have been unable to devise programs that will achieve this goal. Decisions and programs now chase other public objectives including the elusive goal of international competitiveness.

Why should we care? For some, interest in public policy is prompted by a larger concern for the problems it is intended to address. If we want to know more about economic growth, we are typically curious about policies—such as support for research and development—that are intended to promote it. If we care about the homeless, we naturally want to know what public measures have been taken to address the problem of homelessness. But the study of a particular policy area also gives us a chance to see the political system from a new perspective. Knowledge of public policy provides a sharpened appreciation of who benefits from public action and who pays, why some problems reach the political agenda but others do not, and why certain policies are consistently preferred in spite of their poor record of success. Policy is a window on politics.

When we study policy to understand politics we are led straight to an examination of political institutions. Why? First, because the study of policy forces us to ask where the theories that undergird policy come from. Are these theories fashioned in the free-floating realm of ideas, or are they connected to a larger theory of government and the broad structure of our political institutions? And if they are connected—that is, if the structure of our politics biases the content of our policy—then how strong and in which direction is the bias? Second, it is in political institutions that theory meets practice. No one studies public policy for long before wondering whether a policy that is justifiable and appropriate has any chance of being implemented. We soon detect built-in obstacles to certain policy options. And there often seem to be incentives for individuals to act on their own priorities at the expense of the larger public interest. Once we begin to wonder if perverse results can be avoided by changing the rules of behaviour, then the joint study of political institutions and public policy has begun.

INSTITUTIONS AND POLICY: CAUSALITY, CONSTRAINT, AND CREATIVITY

The Appeal of Cause and Effect

Try as we may, in the social sciences we cannot banish the language of causality. It is true that social, political, and economic phenomena are often so deeply enmeshed within one another that speaking of cause and effect seems to produce only awkward simplifications. Yet, whenever we try to explain discrete occurrences or ongoing processes, it is the language of cause and effect that we reach for, consciously or not. The idea that social phenomena simply occur, without having been caused, is just too radical a proposition for most social scientists. So when we examine the relationship between public policy and political institutions, we do so in causal terms. And more often than not we are inclined to say that differences in public policy are caused by differences in political institutions. Or at least that is how it appears. Institutions organize politics and they bias processes. As E.E. Schattschneider (1960) observed many years ago, some conflicts, issues, and groups are organized in, others are organized out. If you are interested, therefore, in why some public policies are pursued rather than others, why some are successful and others fail, you must pay attention to the manner in which the political system is organized to produce policy outcomes.

In recent years more and more researchers have been heeding this advice. The organization of the state has become a critical variable in most models of the policy process, regardless of the country. State organization has implications for the concentration and diffusion of power, for the manner in which societal actors organize and participate in policy-making, and for the process whereby some ideas are nurtured and others discarded or ignored. In one form or another, theorists have sought to bring the state back in, either to bemoan the absence of effective organization for policy goals or to celebrate the possibility that a new institutional design might liberate us from some of our nagging collective-action problems. In all of this, institutions are assumed to have a kind of causal capacity. If you change institutions, something will happen.

The Reality of Causality

Without meaning to slight in the least the efforts of social scientists to study the impact of institutions on public policy, it is useful, if not necessary, to sound some cautionary notes. First, it is unlikely that there ever exists a simple causal connection between institutional change and policy change. Jon Elster reminds us that when we examine the consequences of changes in institutions, we should avoid focusing on a single causal chain because there are often several paths from the cause to the effect (Elster & Slagstad 1989). In this case, a multiplicity of paths exists because both institutions and policies are complex entities. While it is conceivable that institutions may be entirely transformed or created from scratch, much of the change in institutions will be partial and uncoordinated. Policies are similarly complicated. Fundamental change occurs, but it is often the product of a number of discrete changes in certain aspects of policy. Only in the long term can we detect a shift in direction. Institutional effects may even cancel one another out, making it hard to estimate their net impact on policy. And if the policy consequences of institutional change show up only in the long term, it will always be difficult to estimate the significance of institutions compared with other variables.

Second, it is important to consider the effect of policy on institutions: the causal arrow can point in both directions. Policies make intellectual and technical demands on institutions. Rules and procedures typically have to change to meet these demands. For example, the introduction of rehabilitation as a goal of penal policy has had serious institutional consequences in the form of changes in the organization and staffing of penitentiaries. Once such a policy change occurs, institutional evolution and policy evolution may become so closely intertwined that the language of causality becomes awkward and even irrelevant. Are changes in inmate classification procedures policy changes or institutional changes? In the first instance, policy decisions have institutional consequences, but beyond that the boundary between the policy and the institution melts away until eventually institutional changes and policy changes become almost indistinguishable.

Third, many of the changes that occur in institutions have nothing to do with policy. Put another way, not all institutional change has policy consequences. In fact, many changes to institutions are essentially symbolic in character. They affect internal practices and they change the way people feel about institutions, but they are inconsequential in terms of defining and realizing policy goals. In Canada, the Department of Indian Affairs and Northern Development has been reorganized endless times, with power delegated and redelegated, but little has changed in terms of overall aboriginal policy. This is not to say that organizational changes of this type are worthless. If they produce improvements in efficiency, communication, and accountability, these reforms should presumably be welcomed. But it is important not to confuse these institutional changes with policy change. It is common to think of institutions as instruments, and to a certain degree that is a reasonable position, but institutions are also ends in themselves, and we must be mindful not to judge them solely on their capacity to achieve some precise policy goal.

Fourth, the effect of institutions on policy is almost always contingent. That is, institutional changes produce policy changes under some circumstances, but not under others. Thus the same formal structure may give rise to different effects. This is another way of saying that the underlying causal structure connecting institutions to policy is complicated. In this case it is not the number of causal paths that complicates the picture, but the fact that many of these paths are closed unless other conditions are met.

Take, for example, the spectacular success of Japanese industry during the 1970s and 1980s. This success was originally attributed to the presence of a powerful, centralized industrial bureaucracy in the form of the Ministry of International Trade and Industry (MITI). Agitation in other countries for a similar kind of ministry eventually died down when it was realized that the circumstances that permitted MITI to exercise such influence in the Japanese business community simply did not exist in most other systems. A host of social and political practices undergird the operation of the Japanese industrial system. Importing one institution was unlikely to produce anything but disappointment. Propositions that link institutional change to policy change are not of the universal, lawlike variety. Most of the effects of institutions on policy will be conditional effects; that is, they will exist only in the presence of other factors.

The final reason that causal language creates dissonance is that most institutions change very little. Indeed, the very idea of an institution suggests some measure of permanence. As a result, institutional change and policy change do not track one another very closely. Institutions are simply not as malleable, or as variable, as policy. We can think of something relatively constant (institutions) "causing" something relatively variable (policy) only if we understand that institutions supply decision processes, which, in turn, have persistent effects on policy. For example, in parliamentary systems the practice of recruiting ministers almost exclusively from the legislative body generally has the effect of creating a politically experienced executive. Experienced politicians are more likely to be policy generalists than specialists, and are more likely to be concerned with the political ramifications of policy than its technical qualities (Weaver & Rockman 1992). If this feature of the decision process affects policy (and there is every reason to think it will), then knowledge of institutions should help us explain long-term trends in the content and quality of political decisions. We may be unable to predict a single precise outcome, but institutions will enhance the probabilities of some types of outcomes and reduce the probabilities of others.

The Constraining Side of Institutions

What do these observations on causality tell us about the connection between policy and institutions? They suggest that if institutions influence policy, one way they do so is by constraining the range of possible policy outcomes. Institutions "rule out" options, or at least render them less likely. They do so in a variety of ways. For example, institutions create decision processes with a limited number of access points. Generally speaking, the fewer the access points, the narrower the range of interests that will be accommodated and the fewer the options that will be entertained. Those in charge of institutional agendas can further structure outcomes either by refusing to countenance certain options or by determining the sequence in which decisions are taken.

When new openings are created, new options begin to intrude and the process is not so easily controlled. Since the passage of the Charter of Rights and Freedoms in Canada, cabinet ministers have had to contend with a system that contains a broader set of access points over which they have less control. Thus, while Parliament voted almost unanimously to restrict tobacco advertising, a single judge in the province of Quebec determined that these restrictions infringed upon freedom of speech as protected in the Charter. The opportunity afforded by the Charter to challenge legislation has modified some of the constraints inherent in parliamentary institutions.

Institutions also affect the number and type of coalitions that can be formed. Where the authority over a particular policy area is diffused among a host of agencies and officials, co-operation is often difficult to achieve. Policy advocates may not recognize, let alone act upon, their common interest. Where authority is concentrated, opponents often experience difficulty mounting effective challenges to policy innovations. Potential coalition partners may never organize because they lack the capacity to meet institutionally imposed requirements of participation. In addition, institutional norms often discourage certain types of coalitions. In Canada's parliamentary model, the norms of ministerial responsibility rule out an open alliance between bureaucrats and interest groups against the cabinet. Alliances within cabinet or among bureaucrats are permitted, but some of these will be discouraged by deliberately antagonistic roles. Officials in Treasury Board are much more likely to line up with their "guardian" colleagues in the Department of Finance than with the "spenders" in the line departments.

Institutional resources are another source of constraint on policy. When budgetary systems contain no capacity to identify weak programs, control-minded politicians eventually adopt second-best tactics, including across-the-board budget cuts (Savoie 1990). They may prefer to pick and choose among the programs demanding support, but they do not have the institutional resources to do so. Similarly, where recruitment processes produce senior bureaucrats with no specialized knowledge in technical areas, they may be unable to gauge accurately the risks of alternative technologies. In fact, they may not care much about risks at all. On the other hand, as the capacity to generate a knowledge base and recruit well-trained staff increases, so does the range of options that the state can employ (Skocpol & Finegold 1982, 261; Atkinson & Coleman 1989a). Where state agencies possess their own resources, other institutions, professional associations, and interest groups are at a relative disadvantage. Instead of being policy-providers, they must accustom themselves to being policy-takers.

The rules that institutions employ to make decisions also have implications for outcomes. Most bureaucracies employ hierarchical rules, most legislatures and judiciaries use some form of majoritarianism, while intergovernmental interaction is often mediated by rules of unanimity. The rules chosen have significant implications for the chances of policy change. Take unanimity rules, for example. Unanimity rules are the most supportive of the status quo because participants can refuse to accept a policy change that disadvantages them. In Canada, federal–provincial negotiation has sometimes taken this form. Outcomes are usually very stable under these circumstances, but they may also be very unfair (Scharpf 1989, 151). Where a single province can refuse a policy change that everyone else wants, the majority begin searching for new processes and new rules. In Canada this has led to a host of special relationships between Ottawa and one or more of the provinces. What cannot be accomplished in multilateral forums is achieved on a bilateral basis.

These are just some of the ways in which decision processes, organizational capacity, and behavioural norms can constrain policy by limiting the range of possible outcomes. The list of these sorts of constraints could go on, but it is important to recognize that institutions also create opportunities. It is to the creative side of institutions that we now turn.

The Creative Side of Institutions

Our misgivings about cause and effect lead us naturally to the idea that institutions constrain outcomes rather than cause them. But what about the idea that institutions make policy outcomes possible? Is there not a sense in which institutions create possibilities that would otherwise lie beyond our reach?

Anyone who has advocated the reform of political institutions implicitly endorses the idea that institutions create opportunities. There is little point in institutional change that is not aimed at somehow improving the capabilities of government. The idea that institutions can be liberating may seem a bit paradoxical given that rules and routines would seem to limit human possibilities rather than multiply them. But paradoxical as it may seem, we know that in constraining options institutions create capacity. The most vivid example is bureaucracy: often limiting and confining to the point of suffocation, bureaucracies exist in both the public and private sectors, and they have made possible the provision of services associated with the modern state.

We can appreciate the creative side of institutions if we recognize that institutions play a critical role in the social construction of reality. The beliefs and values of most political actors are shaped within some kind of institutional context. Institutions supply the legal and perceptual boundaries that give participants and observers a sense of identity. Among other things, institutions adopt their own discourse to guide the way in which problems are defined and suggest the criteria by which solutions should be evaluated. Central banks, for example, have developed a language of monetary policy that not only channels discussion but also contains implicit understandings about what does, and what does not, make sense. If you do not speak this language, and most people do not, you become a dumbfounded observer. As this discourse becomes standardized and as interactions multiply, institutions develop a measure of autonomy. It is no longer simply a matter of humans creating institutions; institutions also create humans.

This creative process is full of implications for public policy. For one thing, many political struggles can be understood as efforts to embed systems of meaning and political discourse within institutions (Jenson 1989). If you seek to influence the course of public policy, nothing is more effective than to have problems defined and solutions proposed according to your criteria. Of course, the relationship is reciprocal. Institutions act upon society by exporting particular visions of the world and limiting policy options to those that are institutionally acceptable. In either case, the resultant public policy reflects a socially constructed reality. Institutions are no longer simply instruments created to achieve some agreed upon purpose; they help determine what that purpose should be (Atkinson & Nigol 1989, 114; Krasner 1988, 73). Constraint and creativity are joined.

In the sections that follow, the ideas of creativity and constraint are considered in separate intellectual traditions where emphasis is placed on different features of institutions. In the final section we look for some indication of how these alternative traditions enhance our ideas of creativity and constraint in the context of key policy issues.

THE NEW INSTITUTIONALISM

The last decade has seen a renewed interest in the study of political institutions. In 1984 James March and Johan Olsen wrote that "a new institutionalism has appeared in political science" (1984, 734) and proceeded to outline in tentative fashion its salient features. Since then, various groups of scholars have sought to claim the mantle of this "new institutionalism," arguing that their particular approach to institutions yields exciting prospects for the study of politics and policy.

At the moment, the new institutionalism consists, broadly speaking, of two independent, but increasingly interconnected, intellectual movements. This section of the paper reviews these movements and draws on each of them to obtain a more complete understanding of constraint and creativity. In the rational choice version, institutions are treated as negotiated rules that channel the behaviour of individuals whose preferences and beliefs are relatively stable. In the structural version of the new institutionalism emphasis is placed on the capacity of institutions as organizations to transform preferences and beliefs and in that manner shape public policy. In the rational choice tradition institutions are essentially contractual; in the structural tradition they are potentially transformative.

Rational Choice

The rational choice tradition begins its consideration of institutions at the level of individual political actors. It builds heavily on the idea that individuals will seek to maximize preferences, or at least optimize behaviour, within a rule-governed order. Where structural theorists see organizational capacity as the defining characteristic of institutions, rational choice theorists define institutions in terms of procedural rules that are capable of creating a predictable and stable set of policy outcomes (Shepsle, 1986). In this tradition, institutions are bundles of rules that make collective action possible.

Obstacles to Collective Action

Perhaps the most important obstacle to collective action is simply the fact that those whose interests are likely to be affected by action or inaction will often fail to co-operate voluntarily to secure collective benefits. Instead, they will free ride, taking advantage of the sacrifices of others, or they will defect from collective endeavours if defection secures their own short-term interests. In the rational choice model, political actors are constantly searching for opportunities to shirk their responsibilities or avoid following the rules. They may be behaving rationally as individuals, but the outcome of their rational behaviour is collective irrationality.

This paradox has significant implications for public policy. As long as people behave as rational egoists, then without institutions there will either be a chronic undersupply of public goods or severe distributional distortions. The logic is illustrated most brutally in the so-called "tragedy of the commons." Here numerous individuals, obliged to use a common resource like grazing land or the fishery, have every incentive to overgraze or overfish: they gain the direct benefit of every additional cow that is grazed or fish that is caught while personally absorbing only a small portion of the cost. Of course, once everyone uses the identical logic, the eventual result is drastically reduced grazing land and drastically fewer fish.

Solutions to these types of problems involve the establishment of institutions that set rules for collective-action games. These rules typically have one or more of the following properties: they confer disproportionate agenda and decision-making power on specific actors who then dictate the co-operative solution; they distribute property rights that participants can use to counteract the strategies of others; or they set the terms for binding contracts so that those who choose to cooperate can rely on monitoring and enforcement mechanisms to ensure that they are not taken advantage of. In the case of common property resources, there is some scope for resolving collective-action problems by creating institutions that employ a combination of these strategies. Elinor Ostrom (1990) has shown how those who face the tragedy of the commons can create binding contracts that they themselves enforce and that commit them to co-operative outcomes.

Just how participants come to agree on these rules is somewhat problematic. In this contractarian version of institutions, it is not clear why, or how, people will co-operate to create the institutions they need. The act of creation is itself a collective-action problem (Bates 1988). But the purpose of institutions is clear. In this tradition the normative goal is the design of institutions that provide incentives for co-operation, reduce the rewards for opportunistic behaviour, and improve the prospects for efficient exchanges. Of course, arriving at an institutional design with these qualities is a tall order. Rational choice theorists never tire of reminding us that the realm of politics is the realm of uncertainty. Property rights are seldom guaranteed, voting procedures produce unstable outcomes, and contracts are hard to enforce.

The object, therefore, is not the creation of a single best institutional solution, or even an institutional setup that is somehow efficient. Institutions will never be perfect; the rules will always bias the outcomes. The practical question is: Can a set of institutions (rules) be devised that will produce equilibrium (stable) policy outcomes? If so, will these institutions allow us to overcome collective-action problems without subjecting ourselves to arbitrary authority? Most rational choice theorists answer these questions in the affirmative: they believe it is possible to "get the institutions right" (Ostrom 1990). To do so requires the creative use of institutional constraint. Institutions must be designed so that incentives exist for co-operative behaviour and penalties are provided for opportunistic behaviour. Political actors will still behave rationally, but rational behaviour need not result in irrational or suboptimal outcomes.

The Principal–Agent Problem

There are as many ideas for institutional design as there are would-be designers. Much of the attention has focused on the problem of how to control those who are entrusted with public authority. Known as the principal–agent problem, it asks how those whose interests the policy process is intended to serve (citizens) can control their leaders (politicians) and how leaders can control their agents (bureaucrats).

To some extent the problem is informational: citizens and leaders do not always have the information required to judge whether or not they are being taken advantage of (e.g., Moe 1984; Niskanen 1971).

And as long as leaders and agents have their own agendas, policy outcomes will reflect an amalgam of preferences. Decentralization, privatization, and political competition are attempts to counteract this problem. So are rules designed to restrict bureaucratic and political discretion. In theory at least, detailed legislation for regulatory agencies and rules that require automatic budget cuts reduce the ability of politicians and bureaucrats to substitute their own agendas for those of citizens. Rational choice theorists are inclined to assume that unless some effort is made to restrict the strategies of leaders and agents or to compel the sharing of information, serious opportunities for exploitation will be built into the institutional design.

The principal–agent problem illustrates how rational choice theory connects institutional analysis with public policy. The institutions that confer decision-making power, establish property rights, and determine contractual obligations also constrain policy outcomes. But how tightly? For some rational choice theorists, very tightly indeed. In fact, it is not too much to say that in the rational choice tradition, the distinction between institutions and policy often melts away. Once the rules have been made and the structures are in place, most of the important policy outcomes have already been determined. As Terry Moe argues, "there is no meaningful disjunction between policy and structure. Structural choices have all sorts of important consequences for the content and direction of policy, and, because this is so, choices about structure are implicitly choices about policy" (1990, 127). William Riker suggests the same equation when he writes that "rules or institutions are just more alternatives in the policy space" (1980, 445). If you are dissatisfied with the policy, you can always change the rules that produced it. In this reading, policies and institutions join one another in constant flux. Dissatisfaction with one institutional arrangement induces a coalition to form behind a more attractive alternative (Shepsle 1989, 142). The result is policy tailored to the new coalition.

The Limits of Contractarianism

What is disconcerting about this version of the new institutionalism is its unwillingness to acknowledge the weight of the past. We have already argued that institutions do not change very rapidly, and certainly not as rapidly as policy. It does not make intuitive sense to think that participants in the policy process are constantly contracting for new institutions to produce the policy outcomes they want. Some institutional arrangements can be negotiated between interested parties, but the solution to most collective action problems must be worked out within the existing constitutional order. This order includes not just the formal rules of procedure, but also the norms and roles that constitute the informal structure of organizations (Searing 1991). Informal structures can be changed, but change is not accomplished by negotiation, or at least not by negotiation alone. Indeed, institutional change often requires coercion as much as consent. Rather than treat institutions as if they were contractual creations, it seems more reasonable to assume, as Stephen Krasner puts it, that our institutions are "path dependent." Once launched on a particular institutional path we are typically restricted to making marginal changes (1988, 85). Not only is the informal structure a powerful force on its own, but state officials are often prepared to use their positions to thwart reform-minded coalitions.

This line of thought returns us to an original observation regarding institutional constraint. Institutions may constrain public policy, but they do not determine it. A given institutional arrangement may lead to a number of stable policy outcomes. Acknowledging that to be the case, rational choice theorists have begun to wonder what effect uncertainty has on the strategies of players (Shepsle 1986). If it is not clear what outcome will emerge under a given set of rules, what is the rational response for those who have particular policy objectives? One possibility is to invest in a given institution, that is, to settle on a stable set of rules that you are familiar with or that provide some flexibility in responding to outcomes. For example, if first ministers are unsure of the outcomes of their negotiations, they may develop strategies of co-operation that are mutually beneficial, including ensuring that everyone has the opportunity to back away from agreements that are not acceptable to constituents. Rather than change institutions, they adapt to them, and the status quo is preserved. Of course, if adaptation strategies prove unworkable, that is, if no basis for co-operation develops, institutions may indeed be changed. When the Meech Lake process proved unable to generate a co-operative solution, constitutional negotiation was conducted according to a different set of rules.

The strength and weakness of rational choice is its preoccupation with rules. It is a strength because it shows that institutions are congealed power relationships. The fate of policies, and hence of political interests, is closely tied to the rules that determine agenda control, accountability relationships, access to resources, and opportunities for intervention. But a preoccupation with rules avoids the question of where political interests come from in the first place. Are policy outcomes simply a function of the rules that provide access to power, or do they depend on conflicting ideas about what is just and appropriate? Are compromises based exclusively on the best deal that can be cut, or are participants moved by considerations of what Poggi (1990) calls normative power, the ideological underpinnings of society?

Rational choice theorists are persuaded that they have said all that needs to be said about policy when they have described the rules for its creation and specified the preferences of the players. In the rational choice model, institutions constrain outcomes by imposing limits on the strategies of self-conscious actors facing uncertain futures. Opportunistic behaviour, including the private appropriation of political power, is construed as a universal tendency that can only be mitigated by negotiated rules (Perrow 1986, ch. 7). The idea that institutions can be creative by teaching participants different values, and alternative strategies for achieving them, is virtually absent in rational choice interpretations. Individuals come tailor-made as rational egoists, their preferences and desires entirely intact. The unanswered question is: Do institutions have a role in shaping and even transforming these preferences?

Structural Theory

The term "structural theory" is used here to cover a disparate array of intellectual currents that are united in the view that organizations have the capacity to transform the values and preferences of those who work within them and those who are subject to them. Whether organizational forms are studied at the macro level of the state, or at the meso level of organizations within the state, it is structure that matters. As Charles Perrow puts it, "the formal structure of the organization is the single most important key to its functioning, no matter how much it may be violated in practice; the violations themselves reflect the constraints of the formal structure" (1986, 260). But it is not just the formal structure that matters. Informal rules and norms structure the lives of political actors just as surely as formal requirements. It is in the reciprocal relationship between the two that structural theorists hope to build the new institutionalism (Searing 1991). In this section we examine how structure constrains outcomes, first at the state level, then at the level of organizations within the state.

State Structure and Public Policy

State theorists, such as Peter Hall (1986), Theda Skocpol (1985), and Gianfranco Poggi (1990), are among a host of scholars who have resuscitated the concept of the state and used it in the analysis of governance in liberal democracies. Much of their concern has focused on the capacity of the state, especially its ability to manage social power, and recast social relations. This sociological tradition has been joined in recent years by a renewed interest in constitutions. The modern state is, above all, a constitutional creation, and recent work by Jon Elster and his colleagues (Elster & Slagstad 1989) reminds us that the constitutionalism theme is central to the comparative study of institutions. For writers in this tradition, the assessment of political institutions revolves around their (often limited) capacity to marshal resources for public purposes without violating the norms of constitutionalism.

State theorists have sought to link state structure directly with policy development. Employing a deliberately historical approach and focusing on relations among institutions, interests, and ideas, authors in this tradition have endeavoured to explain the role that institutional design plays in influencing the choice and success of policy options. From this perspective one of the key features of institutional design is the constitutional fragmentation of public authority. Where the separation-of-powers doctrine is firmly entrenched and public authority is dispersed among a host of institutions, the state's capacity for concerted action is seriously diminished.

There are a number of illustrations of this line of argument. Comparing tax policy in Britain, the United States, and Sweden, Sven Steinmo (1989) maintains that different constitutional arrangements, including electoral systems, have encouraged different decision-making models in these countries, with significant results for the pattern of taxation. In the United States, for example, the fragmentation of tax authority is responsible, he argues, for the absence of a national consumption tax like the GST. Pluralist decision-making, with its roots in an institutional process (Congress) that permits a series of revenue vetoes, has provided politicians with a host of opportunities to block taxes that are common in other industrialized countries. In Britain, on the other hand, the concentration of authority in the cabinet provides governments with the wherewithal to make significant changes to the tax system. New governments write new tax laws with the result that observers complain about policy instability. Interestingly, concentration of authority is inversely related to policy continuity. In the United States, where electoral politics has entrenched a Democratic coalition in Congress, there is greater policy continuity than in Britain where power has (until recently) shifted between parties whose electoral dominance has been temporary.

What can be said about the United States is that policy change of any kind is difficult to achieve if it requires co-operation among different arms of government or reliance on a strong administrative apparatus. Writing of the American response to the Great Depression, Weir and Skocpol observed that the United States possesses "a distinctive complex of weak national administration, divided and fragmentary public authority and non-programmatic political parties" (1985, 142). The absence (or presence) of state capacity is a theme that runs through much of the work of state theorists (e.g., Skocpol & Finegold 1982). Also important, however, is the potential that dispersion of power holds for policy innovation. Weir argues that Keynesian ideas enjoyed a more receptive hearing in the United States than Britain because of the "fluid, disorderly quality" that marks policy-making in the United States. In the United States multiple sources of policy advice ensured that Keynesian views would find a hearing and that proto-Keynesians would be recruited to individual departments; in

Britain the dominance of the Treasury (at least prior to World War II) ensured that nothing of the sort would happen (Weir 1989, 60-65).

In Canada the effect of institutional configurations on policy has been studied largely within the context of basic constitutional arrangements. The role of federalism has had a special place in this analysis. In a series of important monographs, Canadian researchers have focused on federalism's ambiguous impact on the timing of policy initiatives, the redistributive impact of policies, the importance of regional considerations in policy formulation, and the overall capacity of governments to manage economic development (see, among others, Leslie 1987; Skogstad 1987; Pal 1988; Banting 1987). There can be no doubt that the dispersion of power in the federal system has played havoc with the coherence of policy, but there is no consensus on whether the advantages of dispersion—innovation and sensitivity to local preferences—have outweighed the negative impact of incoherent and even divisive policy initiatives.

The Limits of State Theory

State theorists have paid close attention to the relationship between state and society, and have never suggested that institutions affect policy in a deterministic fashion. Here, as in the rational choice model, there is considerable room for variation in the policy effects of institutions. But in this case institutions constrain not so much by providing rules as by supplying a limited amount of capacity to realize policy goals. Capacity includes the ability to define and pursue state objectives without heavy reliance on external sources of expertise or direction. For some analysts the state enjoys considerable autonomy—variations in the structure of authority are relatively unimportant given the multiple strategies available to all state officials (Nordlinger 1981). For others, state autonomy is always variable—states are strong or weak depending on their ability to realize their preferences in the face of societal opposition. In this reading, the normative goal of state theory is one of properly matching policy goals and institutional capacity (Atkinson & Coleman 1989b). Where the state does not possess the capacity to realize ambitious goals, other, more appropriate objectives should be pursued. Failure to do so results in the squandering of public authority.

If there is a problem in this kind of analysis it lies in the frequent failure of state theorists to explain just how state capacity is used and why some ends are chosen but not others. Without some appreciation of how institutions fashion ideas, facilitate coalitions, and nurture policy communities, state theory runs the risk of removing the politics from policy-making (Block 1987, ch. 1). The question of individual behaviour illustrates the problem. Whereas rational choice theorists have a clear, albeit exceedingly narrow, view of human agency, state theorists have almost nothing to say on the subject. They imply that individuals within institutions generate and use the capacity that organization provides, but state theorists rarely explain how this is accomplished, what motivates state actors, or how societal actors can be mobilized. Naturally enough, state theorists have preferred to develop their theory of institutions at the macro rather than the micro level. But by virtually abandoning the study of informal norms and political roles within institutions, they have left structural theory vulnerable to the charge that it more closely resembles the "old institutionalism"—with its stress on formal, constitutional requirements—rather than anything new.

Part of the problem here is the idea of "the state" itself. The state as a unitary, solitary reality does not lend itself to many conceptual distinctions. Yet we know that the "strength" or "weakness" of a state is a multidimensional question, one that is hard to probe at the macro level even using case studies of policy development. For state theorists the problem is how to preserve the idea of the state as a coherent whole whose overall design has implications for policy, while at the same time acknowledging that a great deal of policy is actually made in subsystems below the macro level.

Organizations within the State

The contribution of organization theory to the new institutionalism lies in its ability to breathe some life into structure. The structure of the state may be the key to its functioning, but the role of structure must be understood at the level of organizations and individual behaviour within organizations.

Perhaps the most important observation of organization theory on the matter of structure concerns the issue of rationality. Whatever the capacity of individuals to select the most appropriate institutions for governance, rationality within these institutions is another affair altogether. Institutional rationality and individual rationality are two quite different notions. A rational structure, one that employs, for example, a sophisticated division of labour and standard operating procedures—does not necessarily produce individual rationality. The requirements for rationality within organizations are more difficult to meet than the instrumental, means-ends, rationality of rational choice models. Since Herbert Simon (1956) introduced the idea in its generic form, we have come to recognize that the rationality that is exhibited within organizations is bounded rationality—rationality that is limited by structure.

Like rational choice theorists, those who are interested in organizations agree that individuals make decisions under conditions of uncertainty. But organization theorists press the point further. Not only are decision-makers typically without information adequate to evaluate alternative courses of action, but they are also often uncertain about their own preferences. They cope with uncertainty, not by changing institutions, but by changing their behaviour. Given human constraints—limits on memory and computational capacity—and the absence of knowledge about future states or future preferences, decisions in organizations are normally the product of search procedures premised on the process Herbert Simon calls "satisficing." Instead of searching for the single best solution, alternatives are canvassed sequentially until the discovery of one that is "good enough" (March & Simon 1958). This is why James March concludes that "actions are determined less by choices among alternatives than by decisions with respect to search" (March 1988, 3). Organizations contribute stability to this process by providing the routines and the rules—the structure—that establish search procedures and that make rationality, albeit bounded rationality, possible.

Implications of the Behavioural Perspective

This behavioural perspective on institutions has far-reaching implications for the study of public policy. If policies are seldom the product of a careful assessment of all the alternatives, if the organizations charged with either making or implementing policy have unstable goals, and if the ultimate consequences of policies are indeterminate given uncertainty about the future, it is hard to have high expectations about the policy-making process in any political system, regardless of its macro structure. Calls for clear, unambiguous policies are likely to be cries in the wilderness. Moreover, in their attempt to mobilize support for policies within organizations, supporters often resort to making the policies even more ambiguous than they might otherwise be. Little wonder that policies are often vague and contradictory, interpreted in different ways by different people.

The result is frequent disappointment and occasional disaster (Pressman & Wildavsky 1973). Of course, neither of these unhappy outcomes is preordained. The rules and routines that supply structure to institutions may also encapsulate wisdom. Then again, most organization theorists are sceptical about optimal institutional evolution: "The fact that institutions encode experience into standard operating procedures, professional rules, practical rules of thumb and identities, does not imply that the rules necessarily reflect intelligence" (March & Olsen 1989, 54).

In the open processes that organization theorists describe, structure supplies only a loose constraint on policy. While rules and routines exist, they do not permit tight connections to be drawn between institutions and outcomes. On the other hand, rules and routines do help define values and beliefs. With increasing boldness, organization theorists are stressing the creative side of institutions, arguing that they are capable of shaping preferences and interpreting the political world. There are a host of mechanisms at work here, beginning with the most obvious, namely socialization—the inculcation of professional standards and behavioural expectations. Beyond that lies what has already been described as the social construction of reality in which explanation is organizational explanation and truth is an organizationally established frame of reference (Perrow 1986, 126).

If institutions are genuinely transformative, that is, if they are capable of organizing reality and inculcating values, over time they will develop a distinctive character and become prized in and of themselves. The most important implication of the transformative position is the scope it provides for the internal development of group norms, what Scharpf calls "we-identities" (1989, 153). We-identities emerge from the organizational division of labour in which organizations, and groups within organizations, share a common history and experience. Out of this shared experience come rules of appropriateness for specific institutional domains. These rules are not negotiated as much as they are learned. They constrain and modify organizational behaviour, and as they are followed they create a culture of trust and feelings of solidarity among participants (March & Olsen 1989, ch. 2). In institutions that have developed a culture of trust, action is premised less on deliberate willful orders than on expectations of appropriate behaviour. Individual actors trust one another to respect the rules not because of sanctions or norms of reciprocity, but out of a sense of duty and obligation.

INSTITUTIONS AND KEY POLICY ISSUES

Each of the intellectual movements sketched above presumes that institutions are closely connected to public policy. But can they help to answer any of the key questions that policy analysts pose? Two of these questions are particularly pressing. First, whose interests are taken into account in fashioning policy? In recent years this issue has forced researchers deep inside particular policy domains where evaluations of the policy process often turn on the issue of institutional access. The second question concerns policy dynamics, that is, how policies change. Do institutions simply constrain policies by weeding out unwanted alternatives, or do they also contain some capacity for policy learning?

Access to the Policy Process

The institutional design of political systems is understood to be a key variable in the degree to which citizens are able to participate in the policy process. But participation can take many forms, and so comparison across systems is perilous. Does Canada have a less open, less participatory policy-making process than, say, the United States? If we focus only on representative institutions like Congress and Parliament, we might be inclined to answer in the affirmative, but if we turn our attention to electoral, and more recently judicial, institutions the answer is much less clear. In all probability, the most appropriate response is that it depends. In fact, the original question is not a very good one. As we have already indicated, the relationship between policy and institutions is contingent on other factors. Making global judgements is not especially helpful.

Policy Domains

One of the most important contingencies is the policy domain, that is, the type of policy under consideration. One lesson has emerged very clearly from the numerous policy studies completed in the last twenty years: there is not one, but a number of policy processes. Different policy domains—health, the environment, natural resources, and so on—have different actors, different coalitions, and different patterns of interaction (Laumann & Knoke 1987). Leon Lindberg (1977) has suggested that this segmentation of the policy process is a natural outcome of bureaucratic decision-making inasmuch as bureaucracies have a propensity to break problems into manageable parts. But even in states that have a capacity to reintegrate policy, there will always be some segmentation because of the particular nature of each policy domain. Fortunately, segmentation need not mean confusion. While there may be a host of different domains, they differ along recognizable dimensions.

One of the most important distinctions that can be made among policy domains concerns their exclusivity. Some policy domains seem to be relatively insulated from external political forces. In these domains public officials are not under heavy obligations to consult or to compromise with other political actors. Policy choices seem to be a function of the distribution of power within state organizations rather than the organizational capacity of societal forces. Foreign policy is perhaps the classic case in this regard, but monetary and fiscal policy also qualify as relatively exclusive policy areas. Of course, exclusivity is a matter of degree. As we indicated at the outset, public policy involves public discourse. The issue is whether or not this discourse is controlled and managed so that only a narrow range of interests are taken into account. One of the most important features of the policy process is the struggle to define a policy domain as more or less open.

Institutions are central to the outcomes of this struggle, but it must first be acknowledged that the nature of the policy domain itself has a strong impact on just how inclusive (or exclusive) the process can be. Some policy domains are relatively exclusive because of the nature of the goods being produced. Certain goods are very public in nature in the sense that it is difficult to restrict access to them. The logic of collective action suggests that there will be few incentives to provide these goods. One of the most compelling insights of rational choice theory is the observation that most people will be reluctant to create a service or product if those who have not contributed can nonetheless have unrestricted access to it. Public goods are subject to this free-rider problem. Where it is possible to free ride—to enjoy the good produced without having to contribute to its provision—public goods will often be supplied at suboptimal levels.

One response to this problem is for a central authority, such as the state, to supply the good. The free-rider problem reappears, however, in the process of formulating and implementing policy. Individuals will not organize to influence the policy process if they cannot, in some measure, privately appropriate the public good (Gowa 1988). That is why in some policy domains, such as agriculture, there is a rich array of groups struggling to influence outcomes, whereas in others, such as monetary policy, public authorities exercise power without serious challenge, even from society's most capable organizations. Agricultural policy can be disaggregated (to a degree) so that those who organize to influence it have some prospect of reaping the rewards of their efforts. Dairy farmers who petitioned successfully for the creation of a system of milk marketing boards obtained direct benefits in the form of quotas for the supply of milk. These were benefits that no one else could receive. Monetary policy, on the other hand, cannot be so easily disaggregated. Interest rates, for example, apply equally to virtually everyone and hence there is little incentive to organize to influence interest rate policy, notwithstanding the fact that interest rates may be a critically important aspect of economic policy, even for dairy farmers.

This distinction suggests that the significance of policy domains lies in the costs and benefits of collective action within them (Wilson 1973). Where these costs are high, the policy process becomes relatively exclusive, dominated by state actors; where they are low, there is greater potential for organized input and for broad coalitions. Thus the size and strength of policy coalitions will differ depending on the nature of the goods being produced.

Of course, it is not just the public nature of the goods that affects participation in particular policy domains. The question of who participates and under what conditions is also a function of the intellectual demands imposed by the policy. It is not too difficult to calculate gains and losses from alternative policies in cases where the effects are highly localized and the technical demands on participants are reasonably modest. Thus occupational health is a relatively accessible policy area for many groups and individuals. Not only are they directly affected, but even when there are disagreements among participants, such as those that have emerged regarding the hazardous effects of asbestos, they are not so challenging as to disable participants. But where intellectual barriers to entry are high, policy domains become much more exclusive. Certain areas of trade policy, for example, require a sophisticated understanding of the legal status of subsidies, quotas, and taxes in a variety of countries. Local coalitions, whose knowledge is limited to their own product and their own jurisdiction, are effectively marginalized by the technical demands imposed by the policy domain.

Barriers and Boundary Rules

Institutions affect the level of exclusivity in policy domains by defining the participants and raising or lowering the barriers to their participation. Some institutional arrangements seem better able than others to overcome the obstacles to participation that public goods present (Gowa 1988, 29). Rational choice theorists, for example, have stressed the role that boundary rules play in structuring participation. Institutions establish boundaries in the sense that they determine the units of collective action. Which issues are to be decided by what bodies is a crucial initial question, as is the question of who is bound by the decisions of these bodies. In federal systems the answers to these questions can have a profound impact on the development of policy. Where language policy, for example, is the sole prerogative of provincial or state governments, local linguistic minorities will be disadvantaged in their attempts to create broad coalitions to protect their interests. Indeed, the incentives for participation in any collective endeavour are bound to be influenced by the availability of potential partners, the benefits that can be privately appropriated, and the probabilities attached to different outcomes. Boundary rules have a tremendous impact on all of these questions.

Boundary rules are also important because they create and maintain political identities. Where institutional boundaries reinforce communities that have strong affective ties, the capacity for internal mobilization increases. Similarly, institutions that nurture technical discourse and allow policy knowledge to be concentrated, effectively close doors to outsiders and provide uncontested terrain for those within the policy community. The result may be an impressive attention to agreed-upon policy goals, but a lack of responsiveness to external pressures.

Structural theorists trace the development of we-identities in institutions such as government agencies and bureaucracies where redrawing boundaries can break down loyalties and create new ones, increase organizational capacity or destroy it. In Canada, for example, institutional boundary rules have provided the Department of Finance with a virtual monopoly over the making of fiscal policy. Provincial governments and interest associations clamour for attention, but the Department draws on a strong agency ideology—most officials are economists steeped in the verities of neoclassical economics—and the norms of accountability embedded in the Westminster model, to discourage the participation of institutional outsiders. In other government departments, whose interest in economic policy is premised on the service provided to an economic constituency, the barriers to outside participation are lower. These units can claim strong links with individual companies and interest associations. What they cannot claim, however, is a large measure of policy effectiveness. Departments such as Consumer and Corporate Affairs; Agriculture; Industry, Science and Technology; and Fisheries and Oceans have been organized and reorganized over the last twenty years without enhancing their capacity to contribute to strategic economic decision-making.

There are ways of lowering barriers to participation and changing the distribution of power in policy domains. It is possible, for example, to require the participation of individuals, organizations, and other institutions in the policy process. Thus, in some jurisdictions, environmental assessment processes now place significant burdens on public authorities to consult with affected groups and citizens. Similarly, the creation of an accessible knowledge base also lowers barriers to participation, as does provision for the public funding of consumer groups.

Less obviously perhaps, institutions can change the discourse in policy domains. The language of political rights, which was highly circumscribed and vaguely illegitimate before World War II, has been given enormous impetus by the Charter of Rights and Freedoms. Quite apart from the instrumental uses of particular provisions, the Charter has established a sense of citizenship among Canadians that was never encouraged by the institutions of parliamentary government and federalism. Women's groups, peace activists, and cultural and linguistic minorities have all used the Charter to achieve the kind of access to the policy process that parliamentary institutions denied them. And new rules can nurture new identities. Although the Charter provided aboriginal peoples with virtually no concrete concessions, it did open up the policy domain of native affairs, encouraging Canadians at large to consider the status of native peoples in terms of their rights and not just their interests.

Policy Learning

In all policy domains there are cycles of policy change, beginning with the identification of a public problem and ending with the termination or succession of the policy. In between are the stages of knowledge generation, policy formulation, instrument choice, organizational expression, legitimation, implementation, and evaluation. Although policy-makers are sometimes exhorted to consider all of these stages at the point of policy creation, it is rarely so simple. For one thing, while it is possible to separate these stages analytically, in reality they are normally merged with one another to the point that sometimes they seem almost indistinguishable. For example, many policies are still being formulated at the implementation stage, although not all participants will recognize the phenomenon. In addition, very few policies are actually terminated; policies typically succeed one another (Hogwood & Peters 1983).

Feedback and Knowledge

Given the tendency for the various stages of the policy process to collapse in on one another, it comes as no surprise then that the policy process is not always nicely synchronized. Allocations, technologies, and strategies that have proven successful in the past (or are simply familiar) are often retained, sometimes at the expense of new policy objectives. When research and development policies were merged with regional adjustment policies in the 1980s, the values embodied in the previous programs were preserved, even though they clashed with the new policy goals. Thus, while the new subsidy programs called for sensitivity toward regional needs regardless of the content of projects, administrators were still favouring applications that had a strong component of innovation (Atkinson & Powers 1987). The preservation of practices that are familiar is one means of coping with uncertainty. It does not mean, however, that policy learning is somehow random or irrational. On the contrary, policy learning models emphasize continuous, if disjointed, adjustment and hence a large measure of continuity.

Learning takes place via experiential feedback loops, which permit organizations to adjust their strategies, modify their competences, and reconsider their goals based on the success or failure of their policies (March & Olsen 1984, 746). Success with a strategy increases the likelihood it will be tried again, next time with increased competence. Failure, or at least perceived failure, demands either a rationalization or a readjustment of aspirations. This perspective on policy dynamics is quite compatible with the views of structural theorists who emphasize that institutions are not forward-looking but history-dependent in the sense that they embody experience with other policies and preserve practices associated with previous choices.

Knowledge plays a key role in policy learning. The ability to draw on information, analysis, and policy expertise is as important as raw political power in influencing the direction of policy. Evidence for one or another policy position may never challenge deeply entrenched beliefs, but it can force adjustment of the secondary aspects of belief systems (Sabatier 1987). In the case of social policy, for example, Hugh Heclo argues that the beginnings of the modern social welfare system lay in well-publicized empirical studies on internal social conditions in Europe (Heclo 1974, 309). Whatever people thought about the sources of poverty, they could not ignore the gravity of the problem once the evidence had been assembled.

Of course knowledge does not always have the desired forensic effect. Policy analysis has often been disparaged because it can be used to serve so many masters. And technical knowledge can seldom tell policy-makers what to do. Although they shared the same scientific knowledge base, policy-makers in Canada and the United States came to different conclusions about the need for regulation in the case of radon gas (Harrison & Hoberg 1991). The point about knowledge in the context of policy learning is not that it somehow determines outcomes, but rather that without knowledge it is increasingly difficult to achieve a hearing, at least in some policy areas. And knowledge must take a particular form. For policy learning to occur, it is necessary that participants be conversant with the language of discourse in policy communities and with the criteria used to evaluate arguments. It is in this language and with these criteria that policy-makers justify their judgements.

The Role of Institutional Design

Institutions can facilitate or impede policy learning. Patterns of recruitment and levels of turnover within organizations have an immediate impact on the capacity of institutions to teach the language of policy and to absorb policy lessons. Where barriers to personnel movement are low and turnover is rapid, the learning process is likely to be partial and unstable. On the other hand, policy learning will take place more readily where institutions have adopted professional norms that facilitate the generation, assessment, and distribution of knowledge. If structural theorists are correct in emphasizing the development of we-identities in institutions, then much depends on exactly who associates with whom over long periods of time. As Hugh Heclo describes the process, "political institutions have served as social assemblers, bunching activists into cohorts whose common exposure to outside stimuli evolves into rough bodies of shared interpretation" (1974, 313). Sometimes this process is deliberately encouraged, as when policy units are created, think tanks are established, or apolitical forums are provided for the exchange of data and interpretations; most of the time, however, policy learning (or the lack of it) is the by-product of a larger institutional design.

Structural theorists have been inclined to emphasize the cumulative impact of this larger institutional design. In a series of essays devoted to the evolution of the welfare state in the United States, Theda Skocpol and her colleagues have sketched out the role of institutions in channelling the development of social welfare policy. They argue that the party system had an unusually significant effect on the development of welfare programs. As a result, early welfare programs, which were relatively generous, were marked by a pattern of divisible, discretionary benefits directed toward well-defined constituencies. This pattern was reinforced by territorial representation in Congress where strong legislative institutions resisted the development of the broad collective programs that are often seen as the hallmark of modern welfare-state legislation (Amenta & Skocpol 1989, 314–17). In Canada, by contrast, the pattern of welfare-state development was influenced more heavily by executive–bureaucratic institutions. They facilitated the development of broad-based programs of unemployment insurance and old-age pensions in which eligibility for benefits depended on meeting national, not local, standards.

The point of this example is that policy learning is constrained by institutional design. There may be lessons for Americans in the Canadian experience with health care, but these lessons will be filtered through a set of institutions that are hostile to programs of universal entitlement. Given different institutional designs and different policy paths, it seems unlikely that any one set of rules and routines, or any single division of labour, will be always superior for facilitating policy learning. Learning can occur, but it will take place within an institutionally constrained environment.

Learning the Right Lessons

That still leaves open the question of whether institutions encourage the teaching and learning of lessons that are appropriate to a country's policy experience. Are policy-makers made aware of the available options? Do they know the experience of other jurisdictions? Can they recognize the solutions that have some chance of surviving and distinguish those from the nonstarters? We are only beginning to appreciate how institutionally constrained learning takes place, but the early research suggests that it is a rather inchoate process. For example, one rather influential model of the policy process posits that opportunities to learn and to choose arise when problems, solutions, and decision-makers are combined in a manner that opens "policy windows." For the most part, problems, solutions, and decision-makers develop independently of one another. The dismal truth is that often they never combine. Solutions may seek problems, decision-makers seek solutions, and problems seek decision-makers, all without success. Under these circumstances, problems are recognized but ignored, solutions are shelved for want of the right problem, and decision-makers grow tired of sifting through the existing agenda. This indeterminacy is the essence of what Michael Cohen and his colleagues have dubbed the "garbage can model of decision-making" (Cohen, March & Olsen 1972).

In John Kingdon's view, the ability to couple solutions, problems, and decision-makers is the special gift of policy entrepreneurs. They connect "solutions to problems, problems to political momentum, and political events to policy problems" (Kingdon 1984, 191; Heclo 1974). When John Chapman, a scientist in the Department of Communications, suggested that Canada embark on a vigorous space program centred around satellite manufacturing, he combined the technical capacity of the Canadian aerospace community (the solution) with the weakness of Canadian manufacturing (the problem) and linked these to a set of decision-makers searching for a way in which Canadians could make a distinctive contribution to research and development. The result: space was on the policy agenda.

Policy entrepreneurs like John Chapman operate within an institutional framework that dictates the supply of solutions, decision-makers, and to some degree, problems. From an institutional point of view, the key questions include the following: Is the supply of solutions and decision-makers sufficient to meet the stream of problems clamouring for attention? Do our institutions allow for the regular opening of policy windows? Are problems, solutions, and decision-makers kept apart, or are they drawn together, by institutional rules? These questions do not presume that anyone in particular controls the policy process, but the arrival of issues on the agenda is not entirely fortuitous either. Some policy windows open regularly. The budgetary process in Canada, for example, provides a host of opportunities for policy entrepreneurs to make connections. Other times, perhaps often, policy windows remain firmly closed because connections cannot be made. Under these circumstances institutions have no opportunity to make choices and eventually lose the capacity to recognize problems or learn from the past.

CONCLUSION

Institutions both constrain policy and create policy opportunities. Alternative interpretations of the "new institutionalism" illustrate just how constraint and creativity work. The strength of rational choice lies in its close association of institutions with rules and its relatively clear interpretation of human agency. Rational choice has much less to say on the subject of organizations or on the question of the relationship between institutions and society. Structural theorists are more attuned to the capacity side of institutions, the ways in which institutional resources can be employed to achieve policy goals. Here institutions are firmly rooted in society even though it is not always clear just how relations between the two are mediated. This tradition has little to say about how variations in rules might affect outcomes, but it offers an expansive version of how individuals shape, and are shaped by, institutions.

What both traditions agree upon is that institutions do not determine policy outcomes in any mechanical sense. The language of cause and effect is difficult to adapt to the study of policy and institutions. Instead, there is a strong element of indeterminacy in both interpretations of institutional effects. This indeterminacy shows up clearly in our consideration of access to policy and policy learning. Even a brief survey indicates that there are serious obstacles to designing political institutions for the purpose of realizing specific policy goals. There are simply too many other constraints on policy and too many ways in which institutions matter differently in different settings. At the same time, it is clear that institutions do constrain outcomes and create opportunities in the manner that both rational choice and structural theorists suggest. Rules are crucial to outcomes, and so is organizational capacity. It would be hard to imagine a description of the policy process that neglected either.

CHAPTER 2

The Canadian Cabinet: Organization, Decision-Rules, and Policy Impact

Herman Bakvis and David Mac Donald

INTRODUCTION

Under the Canadian parliamentary system the cabinet constitutes the single most important instrument of governance. It represents the institutional embodiment of executive authority—granted by the Constitution and sustained by majority support in the House of Commons—to develop and implement policies on behalf of Canadians. In performing its decision-making role the cabinet relies on a set of rules and norms based on both past traditions and contemporary concerns, a matrix of decision-rules if you like, that govern and constrain the selection and pursuit of particular policies.

In following the British Westminster model, the Canadian cabinet should, at least in theory, be in a much stronger position than cabinets of other types to develop coherent policies and to impose losses on significant organized groups (Weaver & Rockman 1991). Multiparty parliamentary systems, as found in many European countries, typically give rise to coalition cabinets, often fragile, which have limited capacity to act quickly and decisively. In the American system, where power is widely dispersed among the different branches of government, the cabinet itself remains relatively weak. In contrast, under Westminster-style parliamentary government, with a single government party enjoying a majority of legislative seats, the cabinet effectively controls the legislative agenda in the House of Commons and has direct formal control over the bureaucratic apparatus of the state. Furthermore, the Canadian cabinet is headed by a single dominant figure, the prime

We would like to thank Michael Atkinson, Leslie Pal, and Sharon Sutherland for their detailed and most helpful comments on an earlier draft of this chapter.

minister, who can pick and choose cabinet representatives, thereby reinforcing an already high level of centralization of political authority and policy-making capability. The norms of cabinet secrecy and solidarity further contribute to this state of affairs.

It is easy then to conjure up an image of the Canadian cabinet as an all-powerful institution, an entity able to impose its policies at will. It is also an image that fits well with commonly held perceptions of the federal government riding roughshod over the expressed interests of many citizens and groups, imposing unpopular or controversial legislation such as the free trade agreement with the United States or the Goods and Services Tax (GST).

This image of an all-powerful cabinet, however, conflicts with another impression that Canadians frequently have of it. The Canadian cabinet is also often depicted as a body that is unduly responsive to a wide range of particular interests and special pleadings, that is spendthrift, and that is unable to make hard decisions. Whether it is special subsidies for grain farmers in western Canada, the protection of aircraft manufacturers in Ontario and Quebec, or a financial bailout of fish-packing plants on the East Coast, to many observers it seems that the cabinet is incapable of saying no to special pleadings. The notion that cabinet is incapable of resisting such pleadings is strongly reflected in the business pages of the nation's leading newspapers. At the same time, it is a conclusion widely shared and it fits well with an academic literature that has described Canada as a "weak" state, one easily permeated by interest groups and lacking the capacity for concerted action (Chandler & Bakvis 1989).

It is this paradox—the Canadian cabinet acting authoritatively yet at the same time frequently engaging in distributive, disaggregative politics—that is the subject of this chapter. An effort will be made to describe the "decision-rules" operative within cabinet and its committees, the origin of those rules, and the consequences for public policy. The notion of "decision-rules" as used in this paper is based loosely on the definition developed by Fritz Scharpf (1989). For our purposes they include both the "boundary rules," defining the range of interests included in policy choices, and specific "decision-rules" (e.g., hierarchical, majoritarian, or unanimous procedures) for transforming preferences into binding decisions.

To begin unravelling our paradox, it is worth bearing in mind that the cabinet is not only the primary instrument of governance—acting as the engine driving the creation, implementation, and administration of policies and programs—but it also constitutes a representative body. It is in this latter capacity—the need to ensure that significant groups and regions are actively represented—that the Canadian cabinet's potential for strong and decisive executive action is constrained. Thus the organization of cabinet and the operative rules affecting decision-making are influenced, on the one hand, by the striving for centralization and effectiveness in cabinet decision-making under the Westminster model and, on the other, by the historical accretion of norms, reinforced through daily experience, relating to cabinet's representative function.

These contradictory forces can be illustrated by two features characteristic of the Canadian cabinet, distinguishing it from cabinets in other nations. On the one hand the Canadian cabinet is blessed (some would say cursed) with the most fully developed cabinet support system anywhere in the form of an array of central agencies. As Colin Campbell notes, Canada is the nation where government has gone furthest in "fulfilling the canons for institutionalized executive leadership" (1983, 351). At the same time, Canada also has the largest executive body anywhere that carries the label "cabinet." In the second term of the Mulroney government, the cabinet grew to 39 members, larger than such executive bodies in virtually all other Western democracies. There is no distinction made, as in Britain, between those ministers who are actually members of cabinet and those who are simply members of the ministry. In Canada even junior ministers of state are considered members of cabinet. In many respects the Canadian cabinet might better be described as a "mini-caucus" in which a host of regional, ethnic, and linguistic considerations are represented. It also makes for an unwieldy body, so that the real work of cabinet and most of its decision-making necessarily takes place in cabinet committees.

The major constraints on cabinet, and the factors shaping its form and behaviour, include the following:

- distinct norms and conventions regarding appointments to cabinet and role of ministers in representing regional interests;
- the presence of parliamentary caucuses, which are in turn broken down into regional caucuses, such as the Atlantic caucus and the Quebec caucus, and which constitute an important source of pressure on regional ministers and cabinet as a whole;
- an electoral system characterized by very high levels of competition as measured by turnover rates;
- a well-developed system of central agencies that have been designed to support the work of cabinet and its committees but that have also shown limitations as instruments for co-ordination;
- an underdeveloped party system that is weak in policy capacity and in which local constituency associations play a predominant role in the recruitment of candidates for public office;
- public opinion, which especially in recent years has shown itself to be highly suspicious of politicians, political parties, and those

bodies, such as cabinet, populated by them; and the role of the prime minister, who determines the structure and responsibilities of cabinet committees and the nature of the machinery of government serving the needs of cabinet.

What follows is a critical examination of the Canadian cabinet, of the operative decision-rules and their impact on policy, and the origins of those rules and the factors sustaining them. The concluding section addresses the issue of the overall effectiveness of the cabinet as a political institution. It is worth considering how such institutional and constitutional changes as senate reform or the devolution of federal powers to the provinces may affect the performance of the cabinet and whether changes in the institution of cabinet itself are desirable or feasible.

BACKGROUND AND DEFINITIONS

The modern cabinet originates in the executive councils found in the British North American colonies prior to the advent of responsible government in 1848. The executive councils were small exclusive cliques advising the British-appointed governor and lacked popular legitimacy. Given the scale of administrative operations in the colonies and the concern of council members with expenditures of any and all kinds, and the benefits to be derived from them, most decisions were reached collectively and issued as "orders-in-council." These orders-in-council usefully provided a patina of collective authority and disguised individual preferences and the logrolling that had taken place. Reformers in the different Canadian colonies sought both to bring the governor and the executive councils under the control of the popularly elected legislatures and to gain access to government coffers for patronage purposes (Stewart 1986). It is to the pre-Confederation period that one can trace many of the present-day cabinet decision-rules relating to collegiality and local and regional concerns.

After Confederation, the new cabinet simply took over many of the practices that emphasized local claims on central decision-making. Patronage, in fact, became even more critical as an instrument of both party organization and the appeasement of regional interests. The first prime minister, Sir John A. Macdonald, became past master in using positions in the civil service to reward "cold-water men," those hardy souls who had put in long hours on behalf of the Conservative party, in the process helping to build a national party that thoroughly penetrated Canadian society. At the same time, much of the authority over patronage needed to be delegated to regional lieutenants in his cabinet, and particularly to his Quebec lieutenant, George-Étienne Cartier, individuals who were the major sources of political clout in the provinces.

Cabinet as Chamber of Political Compensation

The Canadian cabinet of the nineteenth century has been described as a "chamber of political compensation" (Smiley 1983). Government operations remained on a modest scale and virtually all appointments to the civil service were made on the basis of "political appointments," usually controlled by the regional minister on the advice of local MPs or local party notables. The regional figures were often former premiers—Cartier, J.A. Chapleau, Joseph Howe, and Charles Tupper in Macdonald's cabinets; William Fielding and Oliver Mowat in Wilfrid Laurier's cabinet—and they had strong linkages with their provincial party systems. In fact, Macdonald's first cabinet was regarded as a coalition, in part because of the entry of moderate Liberals as well as Conservatives, but also because each premier of the four provinces had the right to membership in the new cabinet. In subsequent years the offer of a cabinet appointment was held out as inducement to bring into the fold those opposed to Confederation. The most notable example was Macdonald successfully recruiting Joseph Howe of Nova Scotia, inducing Howe to reject his implacable opposition to Confederation and to accept the position, first, as president of the Privy Council and later secretary of state for the provinces, where he played an important role in bringing the provinces of British Columbia and Manitoba into Confederation. Later, in 1896 Liberal prime minister Laurier recruited as minister of finance William Fielding, premier of Nova Scotia, who had been elected to the latter position on an anti-Confederation platform. These figures were not simply "bought off" but over time came to identify strongly with, and to support, the welfare of the nation as a whole. The cabinet of that period was also capable of acting authoritatively, as evidenced by the construction of the transcontinental railway and the adoption of the national policy under Macdonald and the opening up of the west through large-scale immigration under Laurier.

In brief, cabinet in the early formative period played a broad integrative role, allowing important provincial figures to have a direct say in national matters and considerable control over federal government operations in their province, and overall fostering a national identity within cabinet. It was in the control of federal operations in the provinces, however, that the impact was most direct in terms of specific rules and conventions. By the turn of the century the main outlines of these rules were clearly evident, and one of the more striking features was the extent to which individual ministerial authority was limited, not by the prime minister or by officials but by the prerogative of other ministers. As J.R. Mallory has described it, "ministers (do not) have untrammelled authority over the policy of their departments. Each minister tends to have a sort of veto of executive actions affecting the part of the country which he is known to 'represent' in the

Cabinet, and Ministers in the exercise of their powers thus prefer to have the authority of the Governor in council for almost any power which they exercise" (1957, 236). This norm was actually codified in 1904 by the Laurier cabinet, in the form of an order-in-council: "In the case of members of the Cabinet, while all have an equal degree of responsibility in a constitutional sense, yet in the practical working out of responsible government in a country of such vast extent as Canada, it is found necessary to attach a special responsibility to each minister for the public affairs of the province or district with which he has close political connections" (quoted in Matheson 1977, 264–65).

The practical effect of regional responsibility was that ministers, in cabinet discussions, were largely preoccupied with the minutiae of minor contracts and patronage positions. A telling 1912 report on reform of the civil service by Sir George Murray, former permanent secretary of the treasury in Britain, commented on the unusual nature of decision-making in the Canadian cabinet: almost every ministerial decision had to be brought before cabinet as a whole for its collective approval. Thus the range of subject matter of orders-in-council, Murray found, encompassed issues of high politics on the one hand "down to the acceptance of a tender for the erection of a pump, the promotion of a clerk from one grade to another, and the appointment of a lighthouse keeper or an exciseman" (Canada 1912, 7) on the other. Perhaps the most revealing observation by Murray was that ministers, in being preoccupied by the petty details of local patronage, were at the same time insufficiently preoccupied by major matters of policy, matters that by implication were often left to permanent civil servants.

This pattern of ministerial behaviour, and the norms governing that behaviour, were rooted in part in the practices of the early executive councils. They were reinforced by regional considerations. But it was perhaps purely local considerations that were most important. In a certain sense Canadian politics has always been, and remains, intensely localistic (Whitaker 1987). Even now the constituency associations of the main political parties are very resistant to interference by the national party in the nomination process, to the parachuting of outside candidates for example (Carty & Erickson 1991). Among other things, the local party shapes the process of recruitment of those elected as MPs and, ultimately, those who become ministers. Furthermore, Canadian electoral politics at the constituency level has always been very competitive, in the sense that there are relatively few safe seats (Lovink 1973; Blake 1991). In the nineteenth century the effects of this competition were literally doubled insofar as ministers, after being elected to the House, had to resign their seats and run once more in the same constituency in order to accept the invitation to join the cabinet (this double-election provision was abolished in 1931). Given the overwhelming importance of local patronage, this meant that ministers were constantly inundated with solicitations from constituents, requests that had to be met, at least in part, in order to maintain adequate electoral support in the next election. John Thompson, minister of justice in Macdonald's cabinet and later prime minister, at one point hopelessly frustrated by the imperious entreaties from his constituents in Nova Scotia, blurted to his wife: "I revolt against Antigonish the more I think of it" (quoted in Waite 1986, 162).

The Departmentalized Cabinet

Industrialization and urbanization, the opening up of the west, and the reforms of the civil service after 1918 altered the character of the cabinet. In the words of Stefan Dupré (1987), cabinet as chamber of political compensation came to be superseded by the "departmentalized" cabinet. During the era of Liberal prime minister Mackenzie King the number of civil-service positions available for patronage purposes shrank considerably; a small but highly effective cadre of civil servants was recruited from the universities, which in turn improved considerably the policy advice received by ministers and cabinet. This group of senior civil servants, which met regularly for lunch in the cafeteria of the Château Laurier hotel, came to constitute a distinct political class in its own right with its own separate views and sources of influence (Granatstein 1982). The department and the individual ministers began to play a more critical role, and departmental operations were no longer as amenable to being influenced by other ministers, providing of course that the minister in charge had a firm grip on his portfolio.[1]

The regional dimension was certainly not absent and in important respects became more important. Particularly the era from 1935 onward saw the rise of regional figures who combined broad regional influence with power that was often national in scope. J.G. (Jimmy) Gardiner, minister of agriculture for 22 years in the Mackenzie King and Louis St. Laurent cabinets, represented Saskatchewan; but he dominated the Prairies as a whole and his influence extended anywhere agricultural issues were of consequence. C.D. Howe, who entered cabinet in 1935 at the same time as Gardiner, became known as "minister of everything" for his capacity to handle the difficult economic portfolios. He was also an astute defender and promoter of his own particular region, in this case northwestern Ontario. The third major figure of that era, at King's side from 1921 until his death in 1941, was Ernest Lapointe, who came to epitomize the role of Quebec lieutenant, both promoting Quebec's interests in cabinet and acting as chief supporter of Mackenzie King in that province.

There was an absence of any meaningful presence of central agencies; there was the clerk of the Privy Council and very little else. Co-ordination was provided directly by the prime minister, through the frequent informal meetings of the senior civil-service mandarinate, and through discussion in cabinet itself, which remained relatively small (fourteen members in the 1930s). Power was essentially lodged in the hands of the prime minister and a few key departments and their ministers.

Party organization was professionalized, specifically that of the dominant Liberal party—the government party as it became known (Whitaker 1977). In the postwar period under Louis St. Laurent, the emphasis of government policy was much more national in scope; many of the policies aimed at postwar reconstruction and avoiding recurrence of the economic calamities of the 1930s were designed by a second generation of the "Ottawa men," the senior civil-service mandarinate. Yet the professionalization of the party, the increasing importance of the mandarinate, and the presence of a few dominant ministers in charge of hefty portfolios simultaneously made the government more remote. While the regional presence was still there in the form of Howe and Gardiner, now abetted by others such as Jack Pickersgill representing the new province of Newfoundland, local party organization atrophied. Particularly during the House of Commons debates in 1956, the new leader of the Progressive Conservatives, John Diefenbaker, easily exploited the obvious high-handedness of Liberal ministers such as Howe.

Diefenbaker's narrow election victory in 1957, reinforced by his landslide election triumph in 1958, spelled the beginning of the end of the departmentalized cabinet. Among other developments, the mandarin class, identified in Diefenbaker's eyes with Liberal Party interests, came under attack both by Diefenbaker and a number of his ministerial colleagues. A good part of the Conservatives' newly found support was rooted in populist sentiment in western Canada. Diefenbaker's minister of agriculture, Alvin Hamilton, had an active interest in rural redevelopment and began tackling these issues through less conventional means, resorting to outside advisers and the creation of new agencies not part of the normal hierarchical structures of the department (Careless 1977).

Diefenbaker's cabinet, however, was run in highly chaotic fashion. Diefenbaker was reluctant to delegate and at the same time wanted virtually all issues discussed in cabinet as a whole, a body that also expanded considerably in size, to close to 30, twice the size of King's last cabinet. As well, the prime minister's commitment to unhyphenated Canadianism made it very difficult for him to accept the need for a Quebec lieutenant. His unwillingness to recognize the unique position of Quebec in cabinet and within Parliament,[2] contributed to the loss of most Quebec seats and the defeat of his government in 1963.

The Institutionalized Cabinet

The arrival of the Liberal cabinet under Lester Pearson encouraged the transition to the third phase in cabinet organization, the "institutionalized" cabinet, in which the emphasis is on collegiality and extensive regional demands but also because they could no longer use their department and portfolio to serve regional purposes in the way that Gardiner and Howe had been able to do fifteen years earlier. In part to compensate and in part to rationalize the process, the PMO established a series of regional desks to provide the prime minister and cabinet with regional intelligence.

Yet, in an interesting way, the new stress on collegiality and the collective assessment of departmental proposals dovetailed with the earlier traditions of individual ministerial authority being circumscribed to allow other ministers to protect their regional turf. This reversion, if you like, was reinforced after the government's near defeat in the 1972 election. Trudeau was persuaded to eliminate the regional desks within the PMO and instead to designate a "political" minister for each province, a figure who would be responsible for all patronage and party matters in that province. As well, ministers found ways of mastering the intricacies of their portfolios and circumventing the central-agency maze in order to steer desired goals, more often than not regional in scope, through the system. Thus the discussions and playing out of interests within cabinet tended to revert back to a more traditional pattern: ministers poked into the affairs of other departments and logrolled with fellow ministers to ensure the protection of their interests or the promotion of a pet project.

The propensity for central-agency solutions to deal with the management of political issues, budgeting problems, and the co-ordination of government programs continued unabated, however. The mid-1970s saw the creation of the Federal-Provincial Relations Office and the Office of the Comptroller-General. And in the late 1970s the Board of Economic Development ministers (shortly thereafter to become the Ministry of State for Economic Development, or MSED) and the Ministry of State for Social Development (MSSD) were struck to support the work of what became the Cabinet Committee on Economic Development and the Cabinet Committee on Social Development respectively. In 1979 the Progressive Conservative government under Joe Clark implemented a new budgeting system, the Program Expenditure Management System (PEMS), which forced cabinet committees to tie program decisions directly to expenditure decisions. In other words, committees, in deciding to proceed with a new program, were at the same time responsible for funding the program out of the budgetary envelope allocated to the committee. This could be done, for example, by cutting existing programs. Paralleling the dozen or so cabinet committees were the "mirror" committees of deputy ministers who attempted to co-ordinate and anticipate developments beforehand to allow discussion within the cabinet committees to flow more smoothly.[4]

The central-agency solution reached its apotheosis with the government reorganization of 1982, when a number of departments and agencies in the economic development sector were dissected and reassembled into new entities. The Department of Regional Economic Expansion (DREE) was abolished and its regional development programs were turned over to other line departments and to a reorganized Department of Regional Industrial Expansion (DRIE) based on the old Department of Industry, Trade and Commerce. MSED was made responsible for regional policy, as distinct from regional programs. It also became an interesting organizational experiment—a decentralized central agency whose senior officials were based in the provinces (Aucoin & Bakvis 1984). Relabelled the Ministry of State for Economic and Regional Development (MSERD), its responsibility was to support the work of the Cabinet Committee on Economic and Regional Development (CCERD).

Ministers in the Trudeau cabinet at the time were far from enthralled with an additional expansion of the central-agency system, seeing it simply as a yet further complication in their lives. The introduction of senior federal officials into the hinterlands as an extension of MSERD was seen as more than an echo of the earlier PMO regional desk experiment and as a direct threat to the prerogatives of the regional ministers. Officials in line departments shared the distaste of yet more central-agency hurdles, and even other central agencies were discomfited in that the responsibilities of the newer agencies could conflict with their own. MSERD, for example, in reviewing proposed expenditures in the economic development field, was essentially performing some of the same functions as the Treasury Board Secretariat.

In brief, these organizational innovations were treated by many ministers and civil servants as additional obstacles to be overcome rather than as welcome support for their activities. Ironically, however, a number of the MSERD senior field agents—called federal economic development co-ordinators—proved to be quite supportive of the work of ministers acting in their regional capacity, much to the chagrin of the MSERD staff in Ottawa.

The Hierarchical Cabinet

The arrival of John Turner as prime minister in June 1984 spelled the end of MSERD, MSSD, as well as the mirror committees. Cabinet became more streamlined and hierarchical in structure. Prime Minister Brian Mulroney initially made few formal changes in the structure of cabinet and supporting agencies he inherited from Turner later that year. P & P and CCERD, for example, remained as the two premier cabinet committees. The changes that were evident were in a sense extensions of developments that had begun during the Liberal era. The position of chief-of-staff (a political appointment) in ministers' offices was formalized and the use of exempt staff (partisan political appointees) expanded; the PMO was strengthened relative to the PCO;

the minister and the Department of Finance received clear-cut recognition of its authority and standing as the dominant department (a trend begun under Liberal Finance minister Marc Lalonde); and the prime minister began paying less and less heed to the formalities of PEMS, a system that was already under considerable strain. Mulroney also made an initial effort to restrain the regional proclivities of ministers by centralizing the distribution of patronage and by having Conservative party stalwarts, as opposed to the ministers, controlling the committees responsible for patronage recommendations in each of the provinces.

Two considerations—the transactional, brokerage style of Mulroney and the resurgence of the regional dimension—forced major changes to internal cabinet operations. PEMS was officially abandoned near the close of Mulroney's first term in office. The prime minister's penchant for one-on-one deals with ministers and the wish of Finance minister Michael Wilson to retain much more direct authority over the expenditure process, combined with the unwieldiness and unrealistic expectations generated by PEMS, contributed to the demise of the "envelope" system of budgeting.

Earlier, in the summer of 1986, Mulroney had announced the appointment of "political" ministers for each province; in 1988 these ministers also obtained direct authority over the patronage process. By 1987 three new regional development agencies—the Atlantic Canada Opportunities Agency (ACOA), the Western Diversification Office (WDO), and the Northern Ontario Development Board—had been created. To each was assigned a senior minister from the region, and in addition the minister in charge of ACOA was assisted by a special advisory committee consisting of all six Atlantic ministers (Bakvis 1989).

The cabinet committee system itself also experienced a transformation. The Operations Committee, chaired by the deputy prime minister and officially a subcommittee of P & P, became chiefly responsible for managing the work plan of government with respect to emerging issues. Effectively it replaced P & P in performing the gate-keeping function and as the prime arena in which the issues of allocating budgetary resources are tackled and trade-offs between key ministers are made (Aucoin 1988). The P & P committee retains its status as the chief committee for the discussion of major issues and comes closest to constituting the equivalent of an inner cabinet; but with respect to agenda-setting it no longer plays a key role.

The Operations Committee gained formal status in January 1989; at the same time, the Mulroney government created the Expenditure Review Committee of cabinet, which initially was to be chaired by the prime minister (Koerner 1989). Charged with reviewing all significant expenditures, membership on the committee became crucial for ministers wishing to protect their favourite projects, departmental or regional. Like the Operations Committee, it also reports to P & P. In April 1991, at the time of a general cabinet shuffle, further changes were made. The cabinet committees on economic and regional development and on international trade were collapsed into a single economic and trade policy committee. More critically, the prime minister also announced the creation of a special cabinet committee concerned with Canadian unity and constitutional negotiations. Chaired by Joe Clark, newly responsible for constitutional affairs, the committee was made responsible for developing a set of proposals to chart the country's constitutional future in the aftermath of the failed Meech Lake Accord.[5] Figure 2.1 describes the organization of cabinet as a whole as of 1991, including the reporting relationships between the different cabinet committees.

The striking of the unity committee highlighted a role of the federal cabinet that has waxed and waned over the years, that of a forum for regional representation and national conciliation. For example, the outlines of the government's 1991 constitutional proposals were first developed in this committee. The committee's proposals were then extensively discussed in P & P where, under the direction of the prime minister, a number of the more contentious issues relating to the distinct-society clause, for example, were resolved before the package was officially released in the form of the document entitled *Shaping Canada's Future Together*.

The Operations Committee was first chaired, significantly, not by the prime minister but by the deputy prime minister, Donald Mazankowski. Equally significant, the office of the deputy prime minister (DPM) expanded considerably both in size and responsibilities and moved to the Langevin Block, which also houses the PMO and PCO. Largely responsible for managing the government's political agenda, the deputy prime minister in the Mulroney government can be seen as the equivalent of a chief executive officer with the prime minister playing the role of chairman of the board. The DPM office is also responsible for liaising with the regional caucuses, ensuring that government proposals receive a good sounding in the privacy of the caucus room, where conflicts can be resolved, before they are released.

CABINET ORGANIZATION: THREE FACTORS

Corporate Organization

The organization and operation of cabinet depends on three main factors. First, the Westminster model and the fact that membership in cabinet and responsibilities of ministers are based on functional portfolios, lead naturally to a corporate form of cabinet

FIGURE 2.1
THE MULRONEY CABINET STRUCTURE

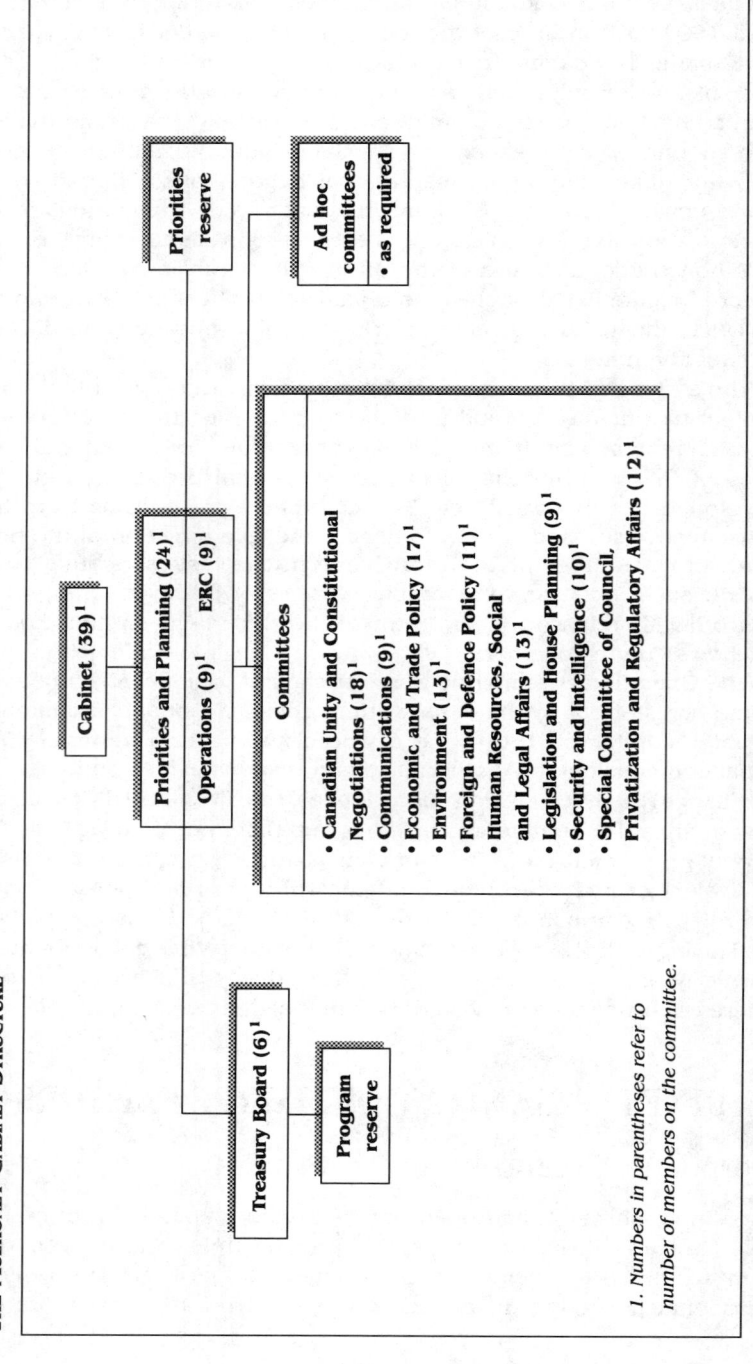

- Cabinet (39)[1]
  - Priorities and Planning (24)[1]
    - Priorities reserve
    - ERC (9)[1]
      - Ad hoc committees
        - as required
    - Operations (9)[1]
    - Committees
      - Canadian Unity and Constitutional Negotiations (18)[1]
      - Communications (9)[1]
      - Economic and Trade Policy (17)[1]
      - Environment (13)[1]
      - Foreign and Defence Policy (11)[1]
      - Human Resources, Social and Legal Affairs (13)[1]
      - Legislation and House Planning (9)[1]
      - Security and Intelligence (10)[1]
      - Special Committee of Council,
      - Privatization and Regulatory Affairs (12)[1]
  - Treasury Board (6)[1]
    - Program reserve

1. Numbers in parentheses refer to number of members on the committee.

Source: Privy Council Office, Machinery of Government Division.

organization (Aucoin 1991). Given the interdependence of many government functions, and the need for collective solidarity to ensure the integrity of the government's program as presented in the House, many, if not most, government decisions are cabinet decisions rather than individual ministerial decisions. A major responsibility of the supporting agencies, such as the PCO, lies in co-ordinating the flow of business and initiatives emanating from line departments and other sources.

Regional Representation

The second factor relates to cabinet's role as a representative body; in Canada representational need has been largely regional in character. This representation is far from passive; ministers are expected to be visibly involved in bringing valued projects to the provinces or specific ridings or to protect the interests of the province when they appear to be threatened. Much as in the nineteenth century, there exists in cabinet a set of norms governing the conduct of cabinet business concerning the right of ministers to be heard, if not necessarily enjoying a right of veto, when matters affecting their provinces come before cabinet. These norms have never fitted comfortably with the ethos of a professional civil service and government organization on the basis of function. It is noteworthy that these cabinet norms have survived significant transformations in the Canadian party system during the course of this century.[6] It is also noteworthy that in a large body, such as a 39-member cabinet, the collegiality and mutual interaction these norms require may be difficult to achieve. As a result, the exercise of mutual veto is more likely to take place within specific committees or between individual ministers outside the confines of committee meetings.

The Prime Minister

The third factor is the role played by the prime minister. At the simplest level, questions regarding the machinery of government remain the prerogative of the prime minister. This individual decides on the size of cabinet, number and type of committees, budgetary systems, and supporting agencies. Furthermore, given the dominance of the prime minister as leader of the governing party and the constant focus of media attention, the contemporary prime minister is more than first among equals. And while a prime minister may not have an explicit philosophy on machinery of government and cabinet organization, the structures and processes of cabinet must over time adapt to the needs and foibles of the prime minister. Trudeau had an unreserved "rationalist" philosophy that led to the adoption of a specific organizational regime. With experience, this regime was altered to take into account the political needs of ministers and of the Liberal Party. In the case of

Mulroney, initially he had little conception of the kind of organizational system required to implement his wish for enhanced political control of the bureaucracy, other than expanded use of political staff in ministers' offices networked directly to the PMO. It took approximately two years to make the changes and adjustments in structures, procedures, and personnel appropriate to the prime minister's transactional, brokerage style of decision-making. These changes included the recruitment of an experienced civil servant as Mulroney's own chief-of-staff.

Peter Aucoin (1986, 1988) and Colin Campbell (1988) make clear that the change from Trudeau to Mulroney involved significant shifts in terms of decision-making style and government organization. Under Trudeau, efforts were made to delegate most business to cabinet committees; PEMS was established and committees were obliged to assume direct responsibility for financing new programs. As a result, much of the discussion was contained within committees and a premium was placed on the ability of the chairs of the committees to play the role of honest broker. It also resulted in a particular dynamic in the interplay between structure and the behaviour of individual ministers. Typically, a committee would agree on a package of proposals that more often than not exceeded the limits of the budgetary envelope. As a result, the committee would then also collectively agree to lobby the Finance minister to increase the size of the envelope, often with some success, particularly when Allan MacEachen was Finance minister. Later, Marc Lalonde, as Finance minister, ran a much tighter ship. At the same time, he was more willing to make side deals with individual ministers, which provided a powerful incentive for ministers to circumvent PEMS and the committee system.

Under Mulroney it was mainly the prime minister himself who encouraged one-on-one dealing between ministers and the by-passing of the committee system. Committees began meeting less frequently and it became clear that a higher premium was placed on connections with key ministers and on the ability to use personal influence behind the scenes. As a result, a clear hierarchy of ministers developed and ministers had less in the way of a formal right to be heard on regional issues in cabinet and committee meetings than they did under Trudeau. The negotiating, lobbying, and logrolling between and among ministers was now more likely to take place outside rather than within committee rooms. Behind-the-scenes manoeuvring has always been important, as ministers working directly or through exempt staff attempt to prepare or "pre-sell" a committee on a particular issue. But in the Mulroney cabinet many decisions were no longer made within the standard committees. Several issues were either decided between ministers or handled through the Operations Committee, a body much more restricted in size than the P & P committee.

DECISION-RULES

Among political scientists there is debate over the importance of the functional bases of cabinet organization versus the regional proclivities of ministers. Much of the literature of the previous decade has stressed the increasing functional orientation of the "institutionalized" cabinet. Supposedly, ministers were principally concerned with general social and economic problems that transcended regions and specific locales, despite the existence of a federal form of government and the fact that the electoral system is territorially based. Thus Paul Pross in his classic article on "space versus function" wrote that the continuing rise of the special-interest state, in which special interests and bureaucratic agencies form functionally defined "policy communities," would mean a profound transformation. "The sea change that politicians undergo as they become ministers must surely mean that they become less and less capable of appreciating the local needs and aspirations that have been the well-spring of party influence. Increasingly they are oriented to the demands of the special interests of their policy fields" (Pross 1982, 122).

In the early 1980s all indications were that political norms related to "space" or territory would indeed come to be seriously challenged by norms related to function. By virtue of their portfolio responsibilities, cabinet ministers would become increasingly sensitized to important sectoral issues relating to communication, transportation, the environment, culture, and international trade. Within the bureaucracy the arrival of "managerialism,"[7] involving the creation of "stand-alone" agencies and the endowment of departments and individual civil servants with greater authority to "get the job done," all in the name of improving the efficiency and performance of the federal bureaucracy, has generated new strains that could undermine the capacity of ministers to use the traditional spatial dimension as the criterion for allocating benefits.

Such changes within cabinet and the bureaucracy would also be consistent with, and be reinforced by, changes in the basic mores and values of society itself. Certainly the "new politics," fostered in part by the 1982 Charter of Rights and Freedoms, has taken hold of a good part of the politically active portion of the population. The "new politics" is characterized by the rise of numerous public-interest groups organized to protect the environment and advance the rights of women, aboriginals, and the disabled (Nevitte et al. 1989). These activities, often carried out through the media, have exposed ministers, and all politicians for that matter, to pressures and demands that were much less common a decade earlier and are much more sectoral in their implications.

All these changes would lead one to expect a major shift in the matrix of decision-making norms within cabinet itself, with ministers becoming more sensitive, and responsive, to these newer, sectoral issues. This has not necessarily been the case, however, as evidence from the most recent decade demonstrates. While the cabinet has been able to respond to a number of issues that are functional in nature and national in scope, it is surprising that, first, the number of such issues is decidedly limited and, second, the preoccupation of cabinet continues to be with regional and local issues.

Functional and Strategic Issues

The Mulroney cabinet settled on three issues as the key focuses of its political agenda: a strong anti-inflation policy as pursued by the Department of Finance and the Bank of Canada through a restricted money supply and support for a strong dollar; a revamping of taxation policy as illustrated by the introduction of a broad-based, value-added tax, the GST, which replaced a manufacturers sales tax; and national unity, as demonstrated first by the failed Meech Lake initiative and subsequently by the Clark committee and other proposals. The free trade initiative, changes in the income taxation system, and again Meech Lake can be seen as the major strategic issues pursued during the first Mulroney government from 1984 to 1988.

In the case of the Liberal government under Trudeau from 1980–84, one can also discern three main items on its agenda: national unity, as demonstrated by the controversial patriation of the Constitution; energy policy, as manifested through the ill-fated National Energy Program (NEP); and transportation policy, specifically grain transportation with respect to changes in the Crow's Nest Pass rate. One is also tempted to add Trudeau's peace mission in the latter part of the government's term, although this issue never did achieve much momentum or a high public profile. With respect to the first three issues, there was full agreement by cabinet that these would constitute the primary focuses of the government. It also represented a conscious strategy—what Tom Axworthy, the prime minister's principal secretary, called "the strategic prime ministership."[8] The constitutional issue unfolded largely under Trudeau's direction. The NEP was placed squarely in the hands of Energy minister Marc Lalonde, who was able to recruit a high-powered team of civil servants to draft and implement the policy (Doern & Toner 1985). The Cabinet Committee on Economic Development had authority over neither the energy policy nor the budgetary envelope for that sector. Enjoying the backing of the prime minister, Lalonde retained full control over energy policy. Transportation was placed in the hands of a minister, Jean-Luc Pepin, who was committed to altering the way grain transportation was subsidized and who had few obligations to the affected groups, such as wheat producers (Skogstad 1987).

In brief, in recent Liberal and Conservative governments the key leadership (the prime minister and three or four key ministers) have been able to stake out an explicit agenda (though not necessarily an agenda that was fully or publicly acknowledged), focusing on two or three issues. They were then able to obtain the support of both cabinet and caucus for the government's stance on these issues and to see the relevant policies implemented. With respect to these strategic issues, then, cabinet is able to show its authoritative side, to use the capabilities of the Westminster system to introduce major policies in the face of opposition from significant interests or even the electorate as a whole. Within cabinet and the government caucus, there is an understanding that these policies are sacrosanct, that dissent (certainly dissent publicly voiced) will not be tolerated. Decisions on these issues are essentially rendered in hierarchical fashion. Here, then, the boundary rules are quite explicit and clearly articulated.

The Spatial Dimension

Beyond these strategic issues, however, quite a different set of rules and expectations holds sway. Here the boundary rules tend to favour spatial or regional rather than functional interests. Furthermore many of these issues are settled through a process that approximates in part the "garbage can model of decision-making" (Atkinson & Powers 1987) whereby the participants often do not always realize their interests, or act upon them, until well into the decision-making process. In brief, the boundary rules tend to be informal, not always readily identifiable, and highly fluid.

Where cabinet decision-making involves the spatial distribution of projects and services the process is also characterized by mutual logrolling. Over the course of a number of expenditure programs discussed within cabinet (that is, programs that lend themselves to a degree of disaggregation or where there are opportunities on the margin), ministers will expect to gain at least something for their particular region or for their own constituency. A loss on one issue, particularly where the minister felt she or he had a very strong claim, can be compensated by promises of future projects. For example, when Manitoba lost the CF-18 maintenance contract in 1986, the regional minister was able to announce in the ensuing months the winning of a smaller maintenance contract for the CF-5 fighter aircraft and the arrival of the new Disease Control Laboratory of the Department of Health and Welfare that was originally slated for the Ottawa area. When policies of a regulatory nature arise that bear on the interests of a province represented by a minister, that minister can expect to have, if not an actual veto, at least a special claim to being heard on the issue. Examples of such policies include fishery licence regulations on the east coast, the environmental review of a dam in Saskatchewan, and the proposed banning of cigarette smoking on international flights (which stood to affect in particular the economic welfare of Canadian Airlines International based in Calgary, Alberta). In all three cases, representations were made by ministers from the provinces that stood to be affected by proposed or actual changes in those areas. In all three cases the ultimate outcome was consistent with the ministers' preferences.

The importance of norms favouring project-oriented programs, mutual logrolling, and mutual veto can be further illustrated with reference to Donald Savoie's book (1990) on the budgetary process in Canada. In it he draws on a typology of ministerial behaviour in which ministers are classified as one of the following: status participants, mission participants, policy participants, process participants, and departmental participants. Status participants are preoccupied primarily with public visibility; mission participants with the pursuit of strongly held views, whether political, religious, or otherwise; policy participants with attempting to influence the actual policy direction of their department; process participants with the striking of deals and the delivery of specific projects; and departmental participants with espousing the views held by their departmental officials. According to Savoie, process participants are by far the most numerous: "Policy content, political ideology, government organization, management issues—and even government programs themselves—are all of limited interest to the process participants. ... Projects are what matters, and the more the better. They will look to their own departments to come up with specific projects for their own ridings or for the regions for which they are responsible" (Savoie 1990, 193–94).[9]

In contrast, departmental participants are far fewer in number and considered much less effective: "Ministers suffering from departmentalitis are quickly spotted by their colleagues and they will find it more difficult to be heard in cabinet" (Savoie 1990, 195). The least numerous are policy participants, those with a genuine interest and often specialized expertise in public-policy issues. They are also the ones most unhappy, frustrated by not being able to effect changes in those policies they feel important and dismayed with what appears to them as an unruly scramble for pork-barrel-type projects. Sectorally oriented ministers, such as Jean-Luc Pepin in the Liberal cabinet, complained vociferously that more than half their time was spent fending off the imprecations of ministers championing regional projects (Bakvis 1991, 293). As described by Savoie, "anyone who has attended a cabinet or cabinet committee meeting—particularly the economic development committee—knows full well that the clash of regional interests dominates the discussion" (1990, 196–97).

Because the process tends to be fluid and often chaotic, and because deals are often consummated outside the formal confines of committees, it is difficult to describe the actual rules involved in support of cabinet decision-making through specialized central agencies (Dupré 1987). These agencies, such as the Privy Council Office (PCO), the Prime Minister's Office (PMO), and the Treasury Board Secretariat, were concerned, on the one hand, with helping cabinet and the prime minister deal with major issues such as the demands being put to the federal government by Quebec, and on the other with co-ordinating and monitoring the activities of the different departments. New techniques such as the Planning-Programming-Budgeting System (PPBS), developed in the United States, were implemented with the expectation that cabinet would be able to make more rational and informed decisions. Cabinet committees, which had functioned only sporadically under Diefenbaker, were revitalized, new ones created and generally made important arenas in their own right for the discussion of cabinet business (Campbell 1985).

The transition to the institutionalized cabinet became complete with the arrival of Pierre Elliott Trudeau in 1968. Like Diefenbaker, Trudeau was wedded to a philosophy of pan-Canadianism, but quite unlike Diefenbaker he was committed to a professional civil service and technocratic means for resolving issues. As well, Trudeau was in principle willing to delegate important issues to cabinet committees for final decisions in order to optimize use of cabinet time and resources. The single most important committee of cabinet became the Priorities and Planning (P & P) committee, chaired by the prime minister and responsible for setting the government's agenda and making decisions on trade-offs between major goals. It came closest to constituting an inner cabinet, although it was never labelled as such.[3] With the rise of P & P, positional politics became paramount—being in cabinet was no longer adequate; ministers needed to be on P & P in order to exercise real influence. Decisions by committees could still be appealed to cabinet as a whole by the minister signalling his or her formal dissent to the PCO, but this was not a practice the prime minister wished to encourage.

Trudeau placed a premium on rational, informed debate by ministers, and while he valued a professional bureaucracy, at the same time he did not wish to see ministers beholden to a set of views developed by civil servants within departments. Ministers were expected to deliberate and debate policy packages coming from other ministers. Hence the central agencies, in Trudeau's vision of things, played a principal role in providing ministers with countervailing advice in the form of critical briefings and assessments of departmental proposals. The immediate consequence, however, was an enormous paper burden and a rapidly escalating schedule of cabinet committee meetings. Ministers discovered they were spending less time looking after departmental matters and more time in meetings and reviewing cabinet documents. The handling of regional issues also underwent a transformation, in part because ministers had less time to cope with the rendering of final decisions. Not only are these rules unstable, but the term "final decision" is a misnomer. If a minister is not careful, a decision can be easily reversed at a meeting of a given committee two weeks or a year later.[10] Finally, the personalities and the skills of individual ministers can make a considerable difference in influencing both how the game is played and the outcomes. The essential setting for the game, however, continues to be a preoccupation with regional and local concerns.

The Sources of Parochialism

The sources of this preoccupation, and the norms that help sustain them, are numerous. Savoie (1990) accounts for it in part by the fact that many ministers are relatively unschooled in the areas of their portfolios. They are, in the best possible sense, ordinary people—teachers, automobile dealers, small-town lawyers—who suddenly find themselves formally responsible for a major portfolio, the contents and responsibilities of which are likely to be unfamiliar to them. The localistic bias of party recruitment practices are evident here. Furthermore, many MPs and ministers have an inherent distrust of civil servants, something that is part of their political upbringing, including direct experiences in the House (e.g., difficulties in extracting information or favours from a civil servant). Hence MPs, upon becoming ministers, may be leery of relying too much on their deputy ministers. They prefer, instead, the advice of their cabinet colleagues and their own political assistants. And most MPs, regardless of their ministerial portfolio, remain well attuned to the prevailing political winds, particularly those emanating from the regional caucus and from their own riding.

As well, ministers can be quite receptive to the political agenda in their province—even if the provincial government is of a different political stripe—especially that part of the agenda that is dependent on federal aid. Examples include: a natural gas pipeline to Vancouver Island in British Columbia, wheat production in the Prairie provinces, the cod fishery in Newfoundland, and transportation generally.

One political fact of life of which most ministers are acutely aware and that influences much of their behaviour is their electoral vulnerability. As one minister has put it, "the constituency is where the rubber meets the road" (quoted in Savoie 1990, 291). In Canada incumbency as a factor in re-election is much weaker and turnover is much higher than in either the United States or Great Britain (Blake 1991; Ferejohn & Gaines 1991). In the 1988 federal election approximately 60 percent of incumbents were re-elected. In the United States in the same year the incumbency rate for the House of Representatives was close to 99 percent. Electoral margins are much narrower in Canada, again a reflection of the high level of competition in the Canadian electoral system. For all MPs this acts as an inducement to pour more money into the constituency in the form of pork-barrel projects to capture those few hundred votes to help put them over the top. Cabinet ministers, however, are really the only ones in a position to help steer desired projects to their ridings; other government MPs are in turn dependent upon their regional minister for a share of the pork barrel. For most ministers the clamour for specific projects, either from their own constituents or other MPs, forms a major part of their daily routine.

Additional or excessive expenditure by a minister in his or her constituency does not guarantee re-election. Nonetheless, most ministers cleave strongly to the belief that such expenditures will improve the odds. Both ministers and constituents realize there is an extra cachet associated with being a minister in terms of doing good things for the riding, whether it is help to save a faltering enterprise or funding for a new park or office building. Patronage in the traditional sense, such as appointments and inducements proffered to specific individuals, is no longer available on a sufficiently large scale to be effective as an electoral tool in the constituency.[11] The modern-day substitute is pork-barrel projects—make-work projects through Employment and Immigration, a military contract for a local firm, or reconstruction of the local wharf. Ministers, therefore, in part out of a sense of obligation but more critically as a way of increasing chances for re-election, will do all they can to ensure substantial projects for their riding and secondarily for their fellow MPs in the province. In turn, various groups within the constituency will be aware of the minister's vulnerability to proposals for expenditures around election time and will step up pressure on behalf of their projects accordingly.

The result is often intricate logrolling not only among federal ministers but involving provincial governments and ministers as well. For example, the cabinet minister for Nova Scotia, Elmer MacKay, in 1986 helped transform a $200-million federal government loan to the province for offshore oil development into an outright grant. The province obligingly spent approximately $18 million of it directly in MacKay's riding, mainly on roads (Bakvis 1991). Lloyd Axworthy, minister from Manitoba in the last Liberal cabinet (and the only elected minister from western Canada), developed a very close relationship with the provincial New Democratic government on matters relating to regional economic development agreements for northern Manitoba and urban development in Winnipeg. A good part of the spending on the latter took place in Axworthy's riding in Winnipeg. In the 1984 election Axworthy was the only Liberal MP to survive the Tory sweep of western Canada.

Thus there is an underlying rationality underpinning much of the seeming parochial behaviour of ministers in cabinet. They strongly feel the need to protect their voting support in the constituency from the vicissitudes of the electoral tides. They are constantly pressured by MPs from their regional caucus on matters of general policy (e.g., the criminal justice system or taxation), about which they can do relatively little, and on specific projects in MPs' ridings, about which they may be able to help. They are also pressured by fellow ministers from other regions to do things concerning projects or activities in their departments. Furthermore, while in the present system it is almost impossible to effect large-scale policy changes by oneself, it is still possible to succeed in prying loose small- to medium-sized projects. In short, all existing incentives drive ministers to becoming what Savoie (1990) refers to as "process participants." The norms dating from the nineteenth century concerning the prerogative of ministers to be consulted on matters relating to their province are still very much in place.

POLICY IMPACT

The Canadian cabinet, then, is schizophrenic in character. On the one hand, it appears capable of engaging in strategic behaviour in two or three policy areas of its choosing.[12] On the other hand, in most other areas it appears trapped by a host of particularistic demands, more frequently than not articulated through regional representatives in cabinet.

These distinctive, and to some degree opposing, qualities of cabinet decision-making have implications for public policy. In the areas of broad policy, the capacity of cabinet to act in an authoritative fashion, often in the face of considerable opposition, should not be discounted, even if this capacity is limited to the two or three major issues during the life of any government. Free trade and the NEP are a few recent examples of controversial or unpopular policies that the incumbent government, wisely or unwisely, felt were worth having in the best interests of the country. Medicare, the Canada Pension Plan, and the federal–provincial equalization system can be seen as major policy initiatives of earlier times. They are also policies that, many would argue, could never have been adopted in the United States given the diffusion of power inherent in the congressional system and the many opportunities special interests have for impeding unwanted measures.

This feature of Canadian cabinet government can be seen as a positive benefit. Most would agree that governments at various times should have the capacity to act decisively and authoritatively. Yet there are costs involved, if only because it is no easy matter to find a broad consensus as to when such actions are indeed appropriate. In other words, government actions in announcing and implementing major policy changes such as the NEP or the free trade agreement typically take place in the absence of a broad consensus within or among political leaders and/or the public. The legitimacy of both the specific government in question and the basic institutions of parliamentary government is thereby undermined.

It could be argued that over the long haul, when the benefits of the policy become evident, rifts are healed and the political community as a whole accepts the policy as legitimate. Medicare, adopted in 1966 amidst much acrimonious debate but now generally accepted, might be one such example. But it is also worth noting that the legislation was introduced during a period of minority government, when support from the New Democratic Party within parliament was crucial for its passage. Arguably the consensus was already broader than it would have been under a majority government. It should be noted that these sorts of costs—the delegitimizing effects of strong executive actions in the absence of a broad consensus—are common to all Westminster-type systems, including Britain, and are not unique to Canada. In addition, there are the costs entailed by the lack of stability in government policy, as a newly elected government seeks to overturn the major policy decisions of the previous government (see Chapter 1). In Britain in the early postwar period this resulted in a pattern of nationalization of certain key industries under Labour, which were then returned to the private sector when the Conservatives came back to power. In Canada, uncertainties emerge with the approach of each election. In contentious areas, such as monetary policy, the prospect of a new government and a reversal in direction can produce money-market instability.

What distinguishes Canada from other Westminster systems, and what makes the problem of delegitimation in this country more acute, is the fact that Canadian society is less homogeneous and its economy more complex. The presence of highly salient and politicized cleavages linked to language and territory and the increasing importance of the so-called "charter" groups in Canadian political life (Cairns 1991) makes it difficult to create a consensus upon which to base new government initiatives. These difficulties are compounded by the simultaneous presence of economic sectors highly dependent on ready access to foreign (mainly U.S.) markets.

Of course, not all government initiatives require a broad-based social consensus. As we stressed already, there are many policy areas not considered strategic to the government's main agenda. It is here, in an apparent trade-off, or a series of trade-offs, where the prime minister and the collective cabinet often permit national programs to be diluted or disaggregated to fit particularistic needs. It also gives rise to the seeming inability of cabinet to bring discipline to the expenditure claims of ministers, many of them being presented on behalf of regional or provincial interests or representing a project directly in a minister's own riding. Many of these trade-offs are linked to the national unity issue. For example, over the past two decades considerable effort has been made to demonstrate the economic benefits of Canadian federalism to Quebec by ensuring that a significant number of federal undertakings of a high-technology nature are placed in Quebec. The new Canadian space agency and a portion of the Canadian navy's frigate program are two such instances. It is also the case that the Quebec caucus and Quebec ministers in both the Liberal and Conservative governments tend to be well-organized in tracking down prospective projects and making a compelling case as to why they should be in Quebec.

Quebec is not the sole or even primary supplicant for, or recipient of, such projects. One of the more substantial recent expenditure commitments, a $236-million contribution toward the construction of a Kaon subatomic particle accelerator, went to British Columbia, a decision received with considerable consternation by the scientific community outside of that province and inconsistent with current science policy as established through various federal advisory committees.[13] In general, the federal government has delivered, through a variety of programs and government agencies, numerous projects and rescue packages across the country.

One contemporary sectoral but nonstrategic policy area that runs a particular risk of being transformed to fit the distributional norms within cabinet is the environment. The environment is an area that lends itself all too easily to the creation of highly flexible criteria for the assessment of alternative projects. A number of regional or industrial development projects, as well as strictly environmental ones, may qualify for support. There is already some evidence that funds from the Department of the Environment have been used in rescue packages to salvage faltering firms, allowing them to upgrade their facilities to meet environmental standards.

Nonetheless, assessing the overall magnitude of pork-barrel-type expenditures, and the extent to which they can be specifically attributed to the regional predilections of ministers, is no easy task. A simple recitation of examples may be misleading or fail to indicate nuances. For example, with Canada caught in the crossfire of a subsidies war between the European Community and the United States, the Mulroney government had little choice but to make financial support available to agricultural producers. Of course, the manner and timing of the support likely had a lot to do with the links between the federal minister of Agriculture, William McKnight, who was also minister for Saskatchewan, and the provincial Conservative government.

For these reasons it is important to review the different categories of expenditures, noting which ones are more and which ones less susceptible to regional political influence. For the sake of convenience, we have taken the 1988–89 budget year, mainly because expenditure commitments add up to a round $100 billion, after discounting debt payments. The eight basic expenditure categories, with more detailed breakdowns, are presented in Table 2.1.

Note that more than half the budget allocated to programs goes to transfer payments to individuals and governments under programs such as child-care allowances and the Canada Assistance Plan. While ministers from the less well-off provinces no doubt have an interest in maintaining the overall level of support, there is relatively little

TABLE 2.1
BUDGETARY EXPENDITURES, 1988–1989

Category	($ billions)	Susceptibility
Transfers to persons		
Old age security benefits	15.4	low
Unemployment insurance	10.8	medium
Family allowance	2.6	low
Veterans	1.2	low
Subtotal	**30.0**	
Transfers to other levels of government		
Equalization	7.0	
Established Program Financing	7.0	
Canada Assistance Plan	10.3	
Subtotal	**24.3**[1]	**low**
Major subsidies and transfers		
Agriculture	2.6	medium
Industrial and regional development	1.6	high
Job creation and training	1.8	medium
Indian and Inuit	2.0	medium
Other (energy, student loans, transportation)	3.2	medium
Subtotal	**11.2**	
Major payments to Crown corporations	4.4	medium
Defence	11.1	medium
Official development assistance	2.8	medium
Operations/other programs	16.2	medium
Total program spending	**100.0**	
Public debt charges	33.0	
Total spending	**133.0**	

1. Does not include tax transfers.

Source: Adapted from M.H. Wilson (1989), Budget papers,The fiscal plan: Controlling the public debt (Table 3.4, p.26, and Table 4.4, p.42). Ottawa: Department of Finance. Reproduced with the permission of the Minister of Supply and Services Canada, 1992.

opportunity to steer expenditures away from some regions toward others. Certainly it would be well-nigh impossible for ministers to redirect such monies to their ridings or to insulate particular groups from program changes. The exception may be payments made under the unemployment insurance program (UI), where eligibility criteria are tailored on a regional and subregional basis to fit the needs of particular regions and socioeconomic groups (for example, fishermen benefit from special rules making them eligible for UI even though many of them are self-employed).

It is in the remaining categories where expenditures are more susceptible to the machinations of regional ministers, particularly when expenditures can be broken down into discrete chunks and allocated on a regional basis. Regional development expenditures are particularly vulnerable given the lack of clear-cut criteria and the direct involvement of ministers from the affected regions in agencies such as ACOA and the WDO. National defence expenditures, including both the acquisition of military hardware and the maintenance or closure of military bases, are of major concern to ministers and subject to considerable cabinet jockeying. Technical complexity and limited options available in the case of high-technology items such as fighter aircraft can limit the impact of purely political criteria on the final outcome (Atkinson & Nossal 1981). Nevertheless, the requirement for industrial offsets and special treatment for high-unemployment areas as part of any major acquisition program provides ministers with significant opportunities for obtaining subcontract work or industrial "offsets" for their region even if the main bulk of the project goes elsewhere.

It should be noted that the only category with a "high" susceptibility rating—regional and industrial development—and the one most likely to generate negative publicity regarding alleged profligate spending by government, is also the category representing one of the most modest expenditure items in the budget. In contrast, spending through UI, though rather less susceptible to political influence, may be more significant in terms of influence exercised by regional ministers simply because the amount of money involved is so much greater. Particularly, for the Atlantic region, UI transfers are far more important than regional development expenditures and rival those under equalization, Established Programs Financing, and the Canada Assistance Plan.

Overall it should be emphasized that many of these regional expenditures are ones that, while not absolutely required for the general welfare of Canadians, are in most instances highly desirable. Mainly at issue are the location, timing, and particular shape of the program. It is here, arguably, that many of these programs are rendered suboptimal because of pork-barrel considerations or carry a distinct premium for being placed in a particular location. There is little doubt, for example, that splitting the Canadian navy frigate construction program between

Quebec and New Brunswick contributed to both the considerable cost overruns and time delays experienced by this program. Placing the new disease control laboratory of the Department of Health and Welfare in Winnipeg rather than in Ottawa exacted a premium of approximately ten percent in both construction and operational costs. And the rendering of several hundred decisions involving commitment of more than half of ACOA's five-year budget in a period of approximately twelve weeks just before the 1988 election likely did not contribute either to the quality of the projects being funded or to the overall credibility of ACOA's "Action Program."

Mention should also be made of programs that did not receive funding because of the nature of cabinet decision-rules. In 1988, then Transport minister John Crosbie cancelled the purchase of 130 new double-decker rail cars by Via Rail because of escalating costs (from $286 million to $500 million). These costs arose mainly because of cabinet's decision to split production of the cars between UTDC in Ontario and Bombardier in Quebec. Ministers from neither Quebec nor Ontario were willing to tolerate the entire project going to one province or the other (Bakvis 1991). This example illustrates the combined effect of two decision-rules. On the one hand, it indicates that there are limits to what cabinet or specific ministers are willing to accept or pay for a politically advantageous but inefficient project. On the other hand, it underscores the fact that such projects need to be divisible and distributional in character in order to obtain support: a project that is cost-effective but neither easily divisible nor deemed essential has a much reduced chance of being approved by cabinet. In short, the realization that a program may become too costly because of regional considerations may lead cabinet to terminate a suggested project. Yet failure to make a project distributional in character may also lead to its rejection.

In light of the foregoing budgetary analysis, it can be argued that regional logrolling and the like are mainly to be found, and funded, on the margins, and do not represent the main body of expenditures. But there is still the issue of time spent on these activities and time *not* spent on matters of broader policy or merely the general interests of the minister's department. A recent description of Benoît Bouchard, minister of Industry, Science and Technology until April 1991, is instructive. His main preoccupations, according to news reports, were, on the one hand, the hearings of the Bélanger-Campeau Commission in Quebec City (as Mulroney's Quebec lieutenant) and, on the other, finding money for projects in Quebec:

> But Bouchard is no champion of the system that furnishes the money he loves to spend. And his department is positively floundering in frustration. The problem: an acute absence of political leadership. There is simply no evidence that Bouchard has any interest in using the resources at his disposal to develop the national policies needed to strengthen Canada's economic performance (Gherson 1990, 7).

Thus the concentration on the national unity issue on the one hand and small-scale regional projects on the other has more than direct expenditure costs; there are also distinct opportunity costs. It could be argued, of course, that the direction of the department is simply left in the capable hands of civil servants. It may not be that simple, however, for as Andrew Johnson (1981) has shown, the relationship between ministers and departmental officials is essentially a symbiotic one. Officials need an astute and capable minister to argue their case in cabinet and to protect their interests; ministers in turn need capable staff to manage the department properly, to provide them with information, and, ultimately, to deliver on at least some of the projects, both regional and sectoral, that the ministers favour. Officials in most departments are fully aware that it is better to have a strong regional minister of the likes of John Crosbie or Donald Mazankowski than a minister well disposed to the department but essentially weak in cabinet. With one or two exceptions, in the Canadian system, ministers weak in cabinet typically lack a strong regional base.

CONCLUSION

The paradox of a focus on a limited number of strategic issues combined with a penchant for project-oriented logrolling on other issues can be said to have the following implications. Aside from the two or three issues deemed strategic for the government's agenda, broader issues of national scope will generally not receive the attention that such issues may warrant. Most programs, in turn, are subject to being shaped by regional- or project-oriented concerns. A program that provides little opportunity for being divided into discrete, concrete entities suitable for distribution into different locales is not likely to fare very well in cabinet discussion or, alternatively, stands to become radically transformed to make it more acceptable to the regional proclivities of ministers. Overall, this type of distributional politics is not all that dissimilar to what is found in the U.S. congressional system. The Canadian version of the Westminster model has some pronounced American characteristics.

There is also the issue of accountability. One of the alleged strengths of party government under the Westminster system is that cabinet can be held responsible to the legislature, the members of which are elected directly by the people, for the government's overall program. Individual ministers in turn can be held responsible for specific items of policy and behaviour related to their department. Particularly where individual ministerial responsibility is concerned, the overlay of the regional licence in cabinet clearly weakens the link insofar as actions of a department may have been initiated not by the minister nominally in charge of the department but by another minister exercising his or her regional prerogative. The extensive use of the order-in-council instrument by the Canadian cabinet has been noted, a use that stands in contrast to British practice where orders are typically issued in the name of the minister (Mallory 1957). Ministerial resignations on the basis of policy disagreements with the cabinet or the prime minister are much more rare in Canada than in Britain (according to Sutherland (1991c), in Canada, about one-fifth of all ministerial resignations are policy-based, while in Britain, four-fifths are). It can be argued, therefore, that cabinet as a key link in the accountability process is badly flawed.

Perhaps the most important consequences of accountability problems concern the overall legitimacy of cabinet government. The cabinet's essential characteristic of secrecy does not help matters in light of the present clamouring for greater openness and direct democracy. As noted, the exercise of the cabinet's inherently strong executive powers with regard to the government's key items on its agenda is frequently done in the absence of a broadly based political consensus. One of the strengths of European-style coalition cabinets is that when the government does act on major issues, its action is much more likely to be based on a wide-ranging consensus (Weaver & Rockman 1991). In Canada, however, a number of the actions of recent Liberal and Conservative governments on issues such as the NEP, free trade, and the GST, in the absence of a clear-cut consensus, have likely contributed to an undermining of political authority and political institutions.

Compounding the problem of legitimacy are the results of the other side of the paradox: logrolling and "garbage can decision-making" in which a premium is placed on regional/local criteria. The propensity for this type of decision-making is exacerbated by the electoral cycle; particularly in the lead-up to an election there is an unseemly rush to secure projects for key ridings. The inclination of governments to fund inappropriate schemes for regional development, or the rescue of enterprises that have fallen on hard times, contributes to the other image of government—its inability to make hard decisions, its misuse of public funds, and its propensity to use politically expedient criteria. The presence of an underdeveloped party system, featuring parties that are primarily electoral machines and that lack the capacity to sustain activities in the realm of education and policy-making between elections, helps intensify the pressures associated with achieving short-term electoral gains.

From the foregoing it is clear that as an institutional body, constituting executive authority at the highest level, the Canadian cabinet could, and should, be far more effective. On the one hand, major decisions rendered by this body should be premised on a broader consensus both within Parliament and within Canadian society; on the other, operative decision-rules should be more attuned to the needs of newer, nonterritorial political constituencies and a more results-oriented federal bureaucracy and less attuned to the parochial needs of the electoral districts of specific ministers.

The question then arises as to what reforms might be undertaken to bring about a better balance between the two, a question that is far from academic insofar as constitutional changes, such as an elected senate, may have considerable impact on the performance of the cabinet. These changes may well alter or constrain the role of cabinet; they may also provide opportunities for making specific modifications in the institution of cabinet itself. Yet, with or without these exogenous forces, it is not at all clear that specific organizational reforms would yield significantly different results. For the origins of many of the problems within cabinet—the limited horizons of ministers and the like—lie elsewhere, with the national political parties (their lack of policy capacity, the localistic bias in candidate selection, etc.) and the electoral system among other factors. Without changes in the larger institutional framework, tampering with cabinet itself in the hope of altering ministerial behaviour would be akin to pulling against gravity.[14]

Changes in the context of cabinet that could lead to changes in the internal structure of cabinet decision-rules might include some of the following:

- The acceptance of coalition government by the political parties and the general public, where the governing coalition had not just majority support in the House but also a majority in terms of electoral support, would help ensure there was greater consensus underpinning major initiatives undertaken by cabinet.

- The presence of an elected Senate, where senators would be permitted to accept cabinet positions and where proportional representation was the basis of election, might encourage the articulation of broader regional considerations, concerns that are less parochial and not constrained by the narrow interests typically generated in the Canadian single-member-plurality electoral system.[15]

- The removal from the political arena to high-level advisory bodies or commissions, certain areas of decision-making such as defence-base closures and the allocation of scientific projects, would help overcome the tendency to employ narrow political considerations in evaluating alternatives. Decisions by such bodies could still be overturned by cabinet, but only in very limited or unusual circumstances. Cabinet would not have the final say as a matter of routine.

Ultimately, however, in contemplating reform of cabinet, one would want to keep in mind overall objectives and unintended consequences. It is one thing to ensure that strong executive action is based on a broader consensus; it is quite another matter to eliminate the present cabinet's capacity for action altogether. Furthermore, while one would want to insulate cabinet from narrow parochial pressures, this concern should not lead to the restriction of the expression of regional sentiments within cabinet (regionalism and parochialism are not necessarily one and the same thing). Cabinet has historically carried part of the burden of national unity, of reconciling the interests of different regions of the country. The issue here is one of effectiveness, and it can be argued that in recent decades the performance of cabinet has been less than stellar, even negative in this regard. That this role of cabinet is still important and relevant is illustrated by the process that led to the federal government's 1991 proposals for constitutional change. It was the cabinet, not a first ministers' conference, that provided a forum for the reconciliation of at least some of the differences separating Quebec from the rest of Canada.

In conclusion, the cabinet is one of our most important political institutions. For this reason, and in light of the several problems detailed in this chapter, it warrants a searching examination with respect to its effectiveness both as an instrument of governance and as a representative body. At the same time, there are hazards in making changes in the present cabinet system. These hazards lie essentially in the failure both to realize the extent to which cabinet reflects the more fundamental problems inherent in our polity and to appreciate the strengths and benefits that the present system of cabinet government does already possess.

NOTES

1. This was not always the case. For example, Mackenzie King at one point wrote in his diary: "It is perfectly appalling how little many ministers will exercise authority themselves and how completely they get into the hands of members of the permanent service" (quoted in Whitaker 1977, 89).

2. It was not until 1960 that Diefenbaker appointed a French Canadian to a major portfolio (Léon Balcer to Transport). He also refused to let the Quebec caucus meet on its own.

3. The brief exception came during the short-lived Progressive Conservative government (1979–80) under Joe Clark, who transformed Priorities and Planning into an inner cabinet. This caused consternation, however, when it was discovered that no ministers from the Atlantic region served on the committee.

4. For details concerning these organizational developments, see Aucoin & Bakvis (1988). On the Program Expenditure Management System, see Van Loon (1983).

5. This committee at the same time replaced the cabinet committees on federal–provincial negotiations and cultural affairs and national identity.

6. See Carty (1991) and Smith (1985) for the three distinct phases of the Canadian party system since 1867. These phases have been labelled by Carty as "patronage politics" (1867–1917), "brokerage politics" (1921–57), and "electronic politics" (1963 onward) and coincide with the shifts to a multiparty system (with the Liberal Party dominant) in 1921 and the arrival of television and the focus on the national party leader as the single most important tool for electioneering in the 1960s.

7. The main initiatives here have been the Increased Managerial Authority and Accountability (IMAA) program of 1986 and the Public Service 2000 (PS2000) program launched in late 1989. On the former, see Aucoin and Bakvis (1988); on the latter see Canada (1990c).

8. It meant, in Axworthy's words, that "we cut his [the Prime Minister's] meetings and memos on secondary subjects to nil, we spun off patronage and party affairs to the ministers, we pushed as much as possible out and kept as little as possible in" (quoted in Graham 1987, 64). See also Axworthy (1988).

9. This penchant for projects and disaggregative policy-making is not unique to ministers in the Mulroney cabinet. Tom Kent, at one time a key policy adviser to Lester Pearson, related to J.J. Deutsch (a major figure in the Ottawa mandarinate in the 1950s) the difficulties he had in communicating with C.D. Howe. Deutsch responded: "You are concerned with policies. What's a policy? You can't construct it, you can't see it. For C.D. it doesn't exist. The only reality for him are projects. And you don't disagree very much with his projects. So he can't understand you at all" (Kent 1988).

10. One of the better-known instances of this occurred in the 1970s and involved an aircraft overhaul contract that Defence minister James Richardson from Manitoba had obtained for the CAE plant located in Winnipeg. Shortly afterward he left the cabinet, and Jean-Pierre Goyer, minister of Supply and Services, succeeded in redirecting the contract to a Montreal firm. CAE successfully sued the federal government, effectively arguing that it had been caught between two feuding ministers (Bakvis 1991).

11. For an elaboration on the distinction between patronage and the pork barrel and on the dangers courted by politicians in mixing the two, see Noel (1987). Patronage is still important, but in a much different way. It is now much more of an elite commodity, targeted

toward reinforcing support from critical election campaign experts such as pollsters and advertising executives or those involved in successful leadership campaigns. See Smith (1985) and Noel (1987). On the relationship between pork-barrel politics and the nature of the electoral system, and why the single-member-plurality system provides such a powerful inducement to this kind of politics, see Lancaster and Patterson (1990).

12. It can also be argued that many of these putative national, strategic programs have a distinct regional dimension to them. The National Energy Program, for example, was targeted mainly toward meeting the needs of the energy-consuming central and eastern provinces. The free trade agreement appeared to favour mainly western Canada and Quebec. In both cases, however, the federal cabinet was convinced that it was acting in the national interest and, more crucially, was able to avail itself of the instruments available under Westminster cabinet government to push the issue through in spite of considerable opposition.

13. The announcement was made by Justice minister Kim Campbell, from British Columbia. The contribution represented one-third of the anticipated construction costs. The federal commitment also extended to paying one-third of the costs of the project's $100 million operating budget. Opposition to the project was led by the federally appointed chairperson of the Science Council of Canada (Howard 1991).

14. A number of these recommended cabinet reforms, particularly in relation to budgetary practices (including those put forward by Savoie 1990), are reviewed by Lindquist (1990), who points out that these proposals, in not dealing with the underlying problem, are unlikely to have much impact in altering the behaviour of ministers.

15. The issues regarding the responsibilities of, and electoral system used for, an elected Senate in relation to cabinet government and the nature of regional representation are explored at greater length in Bakvis (1991, ch. 12).

CHAPTER 3

The Public Service and Policy Development

Sharon L. Sutherland

INTRODUCTION

Many modern countries govern without democracy, but none govern without bureaucracy. Regardless of whether generals or politicians are at the helm of the state and of which political party forms the government, the work of the state will be done by salaried bureaucrats, working closely together in large-scale organizations.

In addition to who does the work, the state's approach to management of its activities will be and *ought* to be fully "bureaucratic" in the sense described by Max Weber (1922) and his successors. At the least, administrative business ought to be organized on the principle of hierarchy of authority, and should be expert and rule-oriented, fair or even-handed in its decisions on individual cases, and formal in that records are kept and work is verified on the same principles as it was performed. In both senses, then—first, of the state's own workforce and second, of the principles of organization of its work—good bureaucracy is the first necessary condition for good government, and therefore, for democracy.

There are only two broad independent ideals that can substitute for bureaucratic principles or bureaucrats. These are democracy and decentralization (Smith 1988). The so-called solution of keeping government on "a human scale" is not much help, for it leaves the most important questions hanging. These concern the ideal size (in population and territory) of the democratic unit and the kinds of decisions that each unit should be assigned.

I would very much like to thank Michael Atkinson for his comments at every stage, and also Paul Thomas, University of Manitoba; Peter Aucoin, Dalhousie University; Stéphane Dion, who commented on the paper at the conference; and my colleague at Carleton University, Vince Wilson.

As for democracy, there is no way in which all the necessary functions of the modern state could be accomplished by people doing voluntary work for the common good. The question of making bureaucracy democratic thus resolves to the question of how the will of the people or of its representatives can be imposed over or threaded through the ubiquitous bureaucracy. In an important sense, this is the problem of this chapter. How can the description of democracy as a form of self-government of citizens by citizens be squared with the reality of a state that is dependent upon professional bureaucrats for developing public policy options as well as for doing routine business?

It is important to keep in mind that *each* of the major forms of democratic government provides a unique answer to the above question. The work of politicians is integrated with that of officials in one way in the American political system, for example, and in another manner in the Westminster parliamentary governments of Britain and some of its former dominions, including Canada (Tupper 1985). These approaches to the dilemma of bureaucracy are not, however, captured in a sentence or so, but are embedded in a state's political institutions, in its constitution. That is, the design of the state's institutional framework and the rules for conducting political business—how executive, legislative, and judicial functions relate to one another; who starts business and who can stop it, delay it, or provide a final interpretation of what has been decided—create a particular kind of relationship between democratically elected politicians and the state's bureaucrats. This constitutional effect is more general and abstract than the laws that establish agencies and departments of government and that set out the boundaries of bureaucratic activity within them.

To concentrate for the moment on work done by officials, one might say that the way in which individual institutions fit together at the political level sets up pressures for administrative work and policy ideas to flow in certain ways through particular channels. The institutional plumbing is rationalized by a set of values and norms that describe the obligations individuals have to one another and to the system itself. Thus bureaucrats will anticipate and react to the political level in ways that help the state's business to move along and that they believe are legitimate within the framework.

The goal of the chapter, then, is to set the Canadian federal bureaucracy into the context of the political institutions of the Canadian state: to assist in the assessment of how the workings of the Canadian bureaucracy are actually, ought ideally, and can in reality be subjected to the political will. The various aspects of this relation are often expressed in words like control, accountability, responsibility, answerability, responsiveness, disclosure, and transparency. Singly and together, these words are inadequate: they have meaning only in the context of the political system.

The theoretical approach of this chapter is based in the structural version of the new institutionalism set out in Chapter 1, which describes the ways in which organizational factors can make a difference in political life (March & Olsen 1984). The chapter's thesis is that the Canadian form of parliamentary government is, in principle, beautifully suited to direct and control bureaucracy so that public policy will maximally reflect the wishes of the elected government and the electorate.[1] In the first section of the chapter, the bureaucratic and organizational structures of the federal government are reviewed. In the second part, the framework of political and bureaucratic control as provided by the Canadian system of government is examined in both theoretical and practical terms. The object is to identify the points of contact that gear the political institutions into the institutions of bureaucracy. Of course, parliamentary government is not the only feature of the Canadian Constitution that profoundly affects policy results and democratic practice. Others include federalism and the character of political parties, both of which are discussed in this chapter.

DEFINITIONS AND BACKGROUND

Ministerial Responsibility

Canada is often described as a "parliamentary system of government on the Westminster model," or, more briefly, a "Westminster system".[2] In fact, the British North America Act of 1867 (now often called the Constitution Act) established our political institutions and then simply stated that they would operate along the lines of the British model.

Crown and Executive Power

In constitutional terms, the chief executive or head of state in Canada is the "Crown": the King or Queen of Canada, acting through a representative, the governor general. But the real or "efficient" executive, to use the term employed in Walter Bagehot's 1882 work, *The English Constitution*, is the cabinet of ministers, whose advice the Crown must accept. This cabinet is, as we know, led and even dominated by the prime minister. In constitutional terms, legitimacy to undertake executive acts is traditionally thought to flow from the Crown, rather than from the consent of the governed as in republics.[3]

The political executive "executes" in the sense that it is the active, initiating part of government. To execute a plan, command, law, or judicial sentence, or even a person's last testament, means to carry it into effect. No major new state policy can be breathed into life, whether by the uniformed or civil services, without an explicit order of the executive, either a ministerial or a cabinet directive.

Collective Responsibility

The central convention in a Westminster system of government is ministerial responsibility, both collective and individual. Collective responsibility is foundational: "The substance of the Government's collective responsibility could be defined as its duty to submit its policy to and defend its policy before the House of Commons, and to resign if defeated on an issue of confidence" (Marshall & Moodie 1971, 55). In Canada, Peter Hogg has noted that confidence has come to mean a test on a substantial bill, most commonly to do with supply (1985, 204). The idea of collective ministerial responsibility in the modern state is closely allied with the idea of party government, discussed in a later section.

Individual Responsibility

The convention of individual ministerial responsibility assigns exclusive legal and political responsibility for the actions of the state in any given policy area to one member of the House of Commons, and one alone. Since the monarch is not legally answerable in person for acts of the Crown, legal responsibility for acts of state must be assumed by the Crown's ministers (advisers) and servants. The principle of legal responsibility extends to all acts of the Crown within the administrative jurisdiction of the department. Thus the idea of a division between politics and administration is not natural to this form of government. The current minister must answer also for the acts and omissions of all former ministers (and by extension their officials) unless those acts were solely private and criminal (in which case the offending minister will be responsible under the law like any other individual).

The Crown's Ministers in the Commons

Ministerial responsibility in the House of Commons is the way in which political accountability is both allocated and rationed under the Constitution. For the cabinet is not so much responsible to the membership of the House of Commons as it is responsible within the House of Commons: the executive is embedded in the legislature rather than being more separate in the American fashion. For this reason, some writers, John Stewart among them, do not like to use the word "executive" in describing the Canadian system, preferring the term "the government." Stewart says that the House has five specific functions:

> first, to support a government; second, to prevent clandestine governing; third, to test the government's administrative policies and legislative proposals; fourth, to constrain the ministers; and fifth, to educate the electorate (1977, 30).

Civil-Service Roles: Administration and Policy

No country refers to its state bureaucracy by that word, for it hovers between neutrality and negativity. The first meaning of "bureaucracy" in the *Shorter Oxford Dictionary* is government by bureaus, by officialdom. In the Anglo-American democracies, the friendlier generic term "civil service" designates officials serving in the core functions of the state, distinguishing this group from the army and other uniformed services, and from employees of state industries or enterprises. In the Canadian federal government, the term was changed to public service in the Public Service Employment Act of 1967. The rationale was that the words public servant would mean more to the public. (Most provincial governments, however, have retained the term civil servant.) In this paper, the term civil service will be used in the traditional sense to identify the core functions of the Canadian federal government, where departmental organizations are headed by ministers.

The Civil Servant: Tinker, THINKER, Soldier, Sailor

The first civil-service role is to administer the state as the state was yesterday, providing the accretion of goods and services that has come to define the state over time.

The state has had a monopoly on the use of force through its police, army and judicial systems. It also has a monopoly on the right to collect the taxes to pay these mercenaries of law, order, and external force. The state alone conducts relations with foreign states, and controls the supply of money. Beginning with the state's guarantee of shipping and overland routes to support commerce, it has developed a rich array of laws and services that support business and, more generally, the economy. In the last 60 years, all modern western governments have developed quite similar large programs for public education, health care (with the partial exception of the United States), and income support for workers.

Because of its responsibility for state operations, the bureaucracy has unrivalled knowledge of the detailed organizational framework and capacities of the polity, as well as a unique perspective on the characteristics of various clienteles and policy communities. This knowledge of the administrative setting—and in fact of the society wherever it is administered—makes officials indispensable players in a second role.

This second role can be described as continuous policy formulation, or even bureaucratic policy design. On many issues that the public has never heard of, and that may be noticed by a minister only very rarely, the "backwater" of departmental or civil-service preferences will congeal into public policy. But if a matter should find its way onto the political agenda, the bureaucracy's habitual preferences will be challenged and often overturned. Yet only a tiny fraction of the total political settlement, which includes established public policy, is ever under active consideration in normal times. Thus the fact remains that in the many areas of traditional state activity, bureaucrats will make policy as naturally as we all speak in prose.

A third function of officials is to provide explicit policy advice to elected leaders on clearly defined topics. Officials will think about how a particular option compares with other possibilities for meeting substantial partisan goals within the democratic process. They will consult widely with their networks of stakeholders and experts, including interest groups, and then write policy papers for politicians about the risks and benefits of using particular tactics and methods to reach particular goals. Some of this work will be initiated by politicians at one time or another, but some will be started up by bureaucrats, when they think that the timing might be right for an idea.

Still another function of officials is to provide counsel of direct political significance to the executive—advice that will have an impact on re-election prospects. Working from the context of how a new policy might benefit some important groups of voters and hurt others, high-level bureaucrats will provide the information that partisans need to think clearly about what a particular policy action might mean for their own future in office. In short, modern democracy is built upon the institution of bureaucracy. The relation between bureaucracy and public policy is such that if an issue is important from a policy perspective the bureaucracy studies it. The bureaucracy administers established policy, implements policies devised by politicians (and retouched by bureaucrats), and even *develops* both minor and major policies. Of the major policies developed internally by officials, departments implement those that will be approved or "signed off" by the executive. Many incremental or minor policy decisions are within the scope of bureaucrats to implement.

THE STRUCTURE OF THE FEDERAL PUBLIC SECTOR

As of September 1991, there were in the Canadian federal government some 33 major departments and agencies, reporting to and being co-ordinated by a cabinet of 39. (This is a large cabinet in comparative terms; see Kingdom 1990a, 1990b.) Statistics Canada reported in 1990 some 529 000 public-sector employees at the federal level, of whom about 218 000 are members of the core departmental civil service as such, working under the discipline of ministers in these departments, and employed under the conditions of the Public Service Employment Act of 1967 (Canada 1990d, 5.8) (see Table 3.1). The other officials are employed in organizations that are run by nonpolitical heads appointed by the prime minister (through orders-in-council)

TABLE 3.1
FEDERAL GOVERNMENT EMPLOYMENT, DECEMBER 1990: VARIOUS EMPLOYMENT TYPES AS A PROPORTION OF STATISTICS CANADA UNIVERSE

Employment Type	Personnel	% of Whole
Core Civil service[1]	217 735	41.1
Personnel whose employer is Treasury Board but who are not covered by the Public Service Employment Act [2]	13 486	2.6
National defence military personnel	88 873	16.8
Corporations and agencies	32 749	6.2
Royal Canadian Mounted Police uniformed personnel	19 409	3.7
Government enterprise personnel	156 299	29.5
Others	593	0.1
Total	**529 144**	**100.0**

1. Includes employees in both Public Service Commission and Treasury Board universes.
2. Includes 13 051 persons appointed for less than six months and 1 160 order-in-council appointments.

Source: Adapted from Public Service Commission (1991), Annual report 1990 (Cat. no. SC 1-1990 p. 58). Ottawa: Minister of Supply and Services Canada. Reproduced with the permission of the Minister of Supply and Services Canada.

These bodies are the so-called "crowns": regulatory bodies, military and policing bodies, audit and rights organizations, research or granting councils, royal commissions, boards of inquiry, special task forces, and so on.

The "meta" organizational map of any government is largely the product of historical accretion and accident. This is true even in a relatively new political entity like Canada where, unlike Britain, the spheres of action of government departments are defined in the statutes that confer precise powers and responsibilities on ministers.

Ministerial Departments versus Other Organizational Forms

The way in which government business is organized across departments and nondepartmental organizations represents the combined historical judgements of politicians about how direct a control or leverage they need over particular areas.

An important feature of nondepartmental employment is the considerable ease with which it can be shifted out of or drawn into the core civil service. The status of organizations as "departments" or as other kinds of bodies is specified by legislation, and is thus in the control of the government of the day. The Post Office, for example, was long managed as a core department of government because its communications service was essential to both business and government. Then, in 1981, a statute transformed it at a stroke into a corporation to be run on a business footing. Even without legislation, large numbers of employees can be shifted quite readily from the centre. In the Estimates year 1985-86, for example, some 16 000 Royal Canadian Mounted Police noncivilian employees were simply "decontrolled" by Treasury Board (Sutherland 1987, 60), and shifted out of the core civil service. This means that it is easy to shrink the civil service without cutting the bureaucracy (or at least total public employment).

In comparative terms, total federal and provincial public-sector employment in Canada is not large. Of the modern welfare states, Canada has fewer public employees per capita than any country excepting the United States, whose reported public-sector employment is only slightly lower than Canada's. But in the United States, some forms of public employment are simply kept off the books, including employment provided through defence industries and in transportation enterprises such as Amtrak (Savas 1982). As well, the Canadian taxpayer gets a qualitatively different mix of services for his or her tax dollar, health care and low-cost postsecondary education being two major examples.

Federal Jurisdictions and Populations

The federal jurisdictions with the largest numbers of civil servants are the following: national defence; employment and immigration; taxation; transport; corrections; agriculture; environment; customs and excise; health and welfare; energy, mines and resources; and fisheries and oceans, respectively. The bulk of federal employment is thus largely in the traditional or core functions of the state: law and order, revenue generation, and resource and infrastructure development. For most citizens the federal government is an abstract, even unpleasant entity; only federal cultural institutions such as the Canadian Broadcasting Corporation are regarded with fondness. The functions that dominate provincial employment are health services and education, as well as protection of the person and provincial enterprises.

Over the past twenty years, provincial employment has grown more rapidly than federal so that total federal employment is now roughly about one-quarter of that of all provinces combined (Sutherland & Doern 1985, ch. 3). Thus, of any four bureaucrats who receive a salary provided by a public purse in Canada, only one will be an employee of the federal government. Provinces have taken the lead in spending and taxing, with about 20 percent of all final expenditure on goods and services at the federal level, and more than 60 percent of the access to tax revenues being at provincial and municipal levels (Stewart 1991). And employment in the federal bureaucracy has been cut, particularly since 1985. In fact, the only major federal employer with more work than ever is Revenue Canada partly because of the Goods and Services Tax but also because the federal government collects taxes for most provinces. (Services to Parliament and to the political level in general have also grown.) For another kind of measure, the federal budget documents since 1985 show that the rate of growth of program expenses has been held at 3.7 percent per year, well below the inflation rate of 4.4 percent and about half the rate of growth of the economy.

Once the distinction is made between departments and other organizational forms, how does one think systematically about the departmental core? Useful distinctions to help one understand the mixed body of departmental organizations include the following: policy departments versus operational departments and central or horizontal organizations versus the body of "managed" departments.

Policy Departments versus Operational Departments

There are numerous ways of describing the operations of government departments. Their principles of organization are said to be according to a function that they serve, or a process, clientele, or industry, and even occasionally an explicit regional or geographic principle. Transport, for example, is said to serve a function, Agriculture an industry, and Veterans Affairs a clientele. Revenue Canada arguably serves a process, and the Atlantic Canada Opportunities Agency clearly serves a region.

The policy-operational distinction is of a higher order. Policy departments are those whose work is intellectual and advisory, including the organizations that manage government itself, and/or whose field of action is expert problem-solving. Such departments have a greater need than operational departments for highly educated analytical and creative staff.[4] Departments that preside over shared federal-provincial jurisdictions, or that "poach" in the provincial areas are also of necessity analytically engaged. Policy advice forms a great proportion of the activity of departments like External Affairs, Justice, Communications, Consumer and Corporate Affairs, Environment, the Ministry of the Solicitor General, and Health and Welfare, as well as being virtually the whole work of a number of "central agencies," discussed below.

Operational departments are, roughly, those that deliver relatively stable or at least polished major services or "programs." Statistics

Canada, Corrections (prisons), National Defence, Revenue Canada, the Royal Canadian Mounted Police, Canada Post (although now formally a crown corporation), and Customs and Excise come readily to mind. There is also within this category a number of departments that provide services to government without having a policy role or direct contact with the public: Supply and Services, and Public Works. The legal-services function of Justice is likewise a common service.

Other departments have their own mixes of program delivery and policy and even knowledge development. Agriculture has a significant number of economists, scientists, and policy and program analysts who work on difficult and specialized subjects such as the linkages between techniques of agriculture and the quality of the environment. Employment and Immigration delivers two enormous programs, but also maintains a large intellectual capacity on the employment side to monitor the effects of government policy on employment. More will be said below about the different categories of research or general intellectual activity undertaken in departments to assist ministers.

Central Agencies and the Harmonization Function

Central, or "horizontal," organizations are those whose job it is to advise their political masters on policies that harmonize or co-ordinate the actions of the collectivity of departments. They include both the classical central agencies—discussed below—and the relevant ministries of state. (All others are the so-called "vertical" bodies that reach down to a clientele, industry, or function—that is, the so-called program or spending departments that make up the body of activities to be managed.) Central agencies present a strong challenge to the theory of responsible government because their co-ordinating role in effect transcends the powers of individual ministers of departments. In most cases their actions and decisions, those that have a policy importance of whatever kind, are brought back under the Constitution because their work is the political responsibility of either the prime minister (Privy Council Office), a single minister (Finance), or a committee of ministers (Treasury Board): a departmental minister can always insist on political review of central-agency decisions.

The most important central agencies, even though their establishments are comparatively small, are the Privy Council Office, the Department of Finance, and the Treasury Board Secretariat. These three organizations strongly affect policy because they regulate the resource-seeking behaviour and indeed the "policy imaginations" of departments and even of ministers. They are responsible for setting the conditions that the spending departments have to meet in order to obtain resources, and in a more general way they set the tone of government by their style and civility (or lack of it).

The Privy Council Office

The Privy Council Office (PCO) is the centre of the centre: the prime minister's department and the gatekeeper and secretariat to cabinet. It was established in 1940 when the incoming clerk of the Privy Council (whose job was to assist the prime minister) was given an additional title: the secretary to the cabinet. A secretary implies a secretariat or supporting organization, and thus was founded the modern PCO (Canada Communications Group 1990, 317). In fact, the PCO is one of the very rare organizations lacking a formal founding statute. It must be distinguished from the Prime Minister's Office, the political bureau whose tasks include managing the partisan supporters of the government and ensuring that important policy bears the stamp of the party.

PCO specifies the conditions that must be met before a minister can bring a proposal before cabinet to get the approval of his or her colleagues. Gordon Robertson, a former clerk of the Privy Council, claims that PCO tries not to "play on the field" (Robertson 1971), by which he means that PCO does not wish to impose any particular preferences on the substance of policy. PCO realizes this delicate task of rationing access to the centre, without apparently affecting the content of a proposal (a form of immaculate control), by a process of dramatized worrying about the political and administrative sacred cows that can derail a proposal. The worries that may be listed from year to year include general "political considerations" or particular matters that are high on the political agenda at the moment: federal–provincial relations; the five-year financial forecast; evidence of full consultation with other interested federal departments and agencies; a review of the proposal's probable impact on women and minorities; and a good communications plan to bring the initiative before the public as an important realization of one of the government's stated priorities. Any number of other screening principles may be operating under the surface.

Departmental officials with responsibility for drafting a cabinet paper will find themselves convoked to meetings where polite PCO officers ask them carefully nondirective questions, much like reluctant anthropologists forced for career reasons to study a lacklustre primitive tribe. The facial expressions of PCO officials which typically suggest great regret and sadness provide clues as to what must be dropped in order to get past them. The other duties of the PCO sustain and reinforce its powers in the policy area: it plays a role in machinery of government concerns, in sorting out tasks and responsibilities as between ministers, and gives advice on senior appointments. The PCO is always the central player when the mandarins' energies are called upon for major efforts such as the mission exercise of Public Service 2000 and background papers for constitutional discussions.

The Department of Finance

Finance has concentrated on policy and analysis since the 1930s when most of its operational responsibilities were conferred on other departments. Finance's job is to understand the Canadian economy and the international situation and explain them to the minister, to make proposals for revenue generation, and to set policy conditions for resource allocation. Finance officers are the most theoretical of officials. They think in terms of a small number of economic indicators whose relations to one another are set by formulas. Because of its need to monitor probable effects on the economy, Finance has a factual veto on what policy instruments other ministers and departments can use to realize their initiatives.

Although it may sometimes seem that Finance's powers have been decentralized, power rather abruptly returns to the centre when the economic environment is difficult. For example, from 1980 to 1984 the structure of PCO was elaborated and enlarged in order to better capture and rationalize (read "centralize" and thereby "screen out") the variety of departmental initiatives that the system had become habituated to producing through the years of high revenue. Two self-standing ministries of state were created, one to screen social policy proposals and one to look over economic policy proposals, essentially substituting for PCO analysis in these areas. They conducted muscular reviews, and through their committees of deputy ministers made recommendations to their respective cabinet committees as to how to dispose of departmental initiatives. Some time after these ministries were disbanded, one saw skeletal replications of them drift to the surface in the Finance Department. Finance was again the uncontested gatekeeper to revenue. Finance officials have no reluctance to play on the field: it is their field.

The Treasury Board and its Secretariat

In many other governments, the functions of the Canadian federal Department of Finance and Treasury Board Secretariat (TBS) are combined in one organization called "the treasury." In Canada, however, the Treasury Board is a group of ministers, the only committee of cabinet specified in the BNA Act. The Board and its bureau were separated from Finance under the Government Organization Act in 1966. The Secretariat advises the Board on its work as the employer of most public-sector workers, on the annual allocations to be made to spending departments, on the rules to be followed in making allocations, and on the format of the expenditure budget. Since the mid-1960s, TBS has single-mindedly attempted to achieve some control over the individual spending decisions of departments through reasoning rather than by re-centralizing authority, pinning its hopes on the fragile science of program budget theory (Sutherland 1990). In 1978 the Office of the Comptroller General was established parallel to the Secretariat to develop methods for measuring the success of spending programs.

Other Bodies That Have Central-Agency Roles

There are a small number of other organizations that are normally counted as central agencies, the most important of these for public-policy purposes being the Federal-Provincial Relations Office (FPRO) and the Public Service Commission (PSC). The FPRO is a separate agency under the shadow of PCO, differentiated from the parent organization by an Act in 1975. The core job of FPRO has been to manage federal–provincial diplomacy and to understand its implications for policy content.

The Public Service Commission, dating from 1908, has two distinct characters. It takes its "central-agency" character from the employer-type functions that are shared with TBS or that have been delegated to it by TBS. In its parliamentary agency aspect, acting independently of government, it defines "merit," reviews the staffing that has been delegated to departments for compliance with merit, hears appeals, and administers the prohibitions against partisan political activity by officials. It is headed by a triumvirate of officials, appointed under the order-in-council for fixed terms to be responsible to Parliament.

Policies and definitions developed by the PSC have importance for the way in which core civil service can conduct business and for the design of programs. Its policies, after all, regulate entry to the workforce and the way in which the workforce can be administered.

Parliament's "Watchdogs"

It has already been noted that the PSC reports to the House of Commons in its role as guardian of the merit principle in staffing. The Office of the Auditor General (OAG) of Canada is another agency of Parliament that is a now a major institution of Canadian government. Its traditional role was to audit probity in the use of financial and material resources. In 1977, after the passage of enabling legislation, it began giving opinions on nonfinancial and value-related topics. Its opinions can exert pressure on officials and ministers, creating a dilemma for the doctrine of responsible government, as the OAG has neither a responsible elected leadership, nor a scientific methodology, nor a limited sphere of action. Other organizations with a watchdog responsibility include the Office of the Commissioner of Official Languages, the Information and Privacy Commissioners, and the Canadian Human Rights Commission.

FACTORS AFFECTING THE POLICY CAPACITY OF THE CIVIL SERVICE

Senior Civil Servants as Advisers

Senior officials are quick to make a distinction between the policy advice provided to the minister by the deputy minister and assistant deputy ministers in person, and the general work done in departmental bureaus that are concerned with analysis and information gathering.

Deputy and associate deputy ministers are intended in the Westminster system to be the senior policy advisers to government as well as the senior professional managers in the department: they advise ministers on administrative matters, instruments of government in their policy fields, departmental and governmental organizational capabilities, the economic situation, and political factors. The secretary to cabinet is the prime minister's own *aide-de-camp* and has the responsibility to be watchful about the capacity of the whole government, including whether ministers or deputy ministers seem to be up to the job.

Richard Rose has said "the problem of party government can be defined as that of finding ways in which elected politicians can ensure that the signals from the electorate are stronger than the signals that civil servants derive from their own expertise" (1987, 211). One can turn this dictum on its head and say that the job of the deputy minister is to understand and master his or her department in order to be able to advise the minister about how to match up electoral signals with administrative and policy possibilities.

Deputy ministers, if they are true mandarins, are the products of their own educations and 20 to 30 years of professional experience and observation in the civil service. These top officials with policy advisory responsibilities have always been highly educated, usually in the humanities (Bourgault & Dion 1990). In this sense, their "policy minds" are about as good or bad as they have ever been.[5] What does clearly change is the willingness of politicians to listen to them. When the Conservative Party came to power in 1984, after close to twenty years in opposition, it was suspicious of officialdom. In the view of many senior civil servants, the party came to power well informed about the content of the neoconservative agenda of the contemporary American presidency, but without an understanding of Canadian institutions.

As a result, policy initiatives were on occasion simply announced by ministers without any consultation with the bureaucracy, as though a presidential theme (such as the war on drugs) were being launched to inspire co-ordination in the loose American agency framework. The departmental bureaucracy would then scramble to put together policy studies and to reach out to affected interest groups almost overnight, while the cabinet would ask the Prime Minister's Office, that is, the political bureau, for a basic policy design. All bureaucratic expertise would be shut out. The education initiative of the Prime Minister's Office of 1990–91 was perhaps the major such episode of Conservatives' second mandate. Some of these initiatives, such as proposals for day care, eventually settled into departmental homes.

Another impact of the Conservatives on the senior mandarinate is that they have emphasized the need for new management policies, mission statements, and a more businesslike management process. This insistence has brought some new people with different skills and beliefs to the fore in the middle-executive ranks.

For the deputy minister, having a political boss is a life line to decisiveness. When the party in power is not willing to think of the civil service as a partner in government, the senior departmental officials become prey to the circling sharks in the central agencies and regulating bodies whose job it is to ensure that their organization's governing values are given primacy. On the other hand, it is within the minister's discretion to give senior officials permission to pursue policy substance before bureaucratic form.

But overall it is simply not possible for a government to govern well for long without a respect for senior officials' assessment of the limiting factors in any established policy area. Anything else would be willful ignorance. There is a sense in which policy is only an abstraction from practice, and must be reconciled, by definition, with operational capacities.

Corporate Capacity for Policy Research

As for the "corporate research" type of analytical work, it is performed inside departments in many different places, for very many purposes. At any one time, any major spending department might have under way the following kinds of intellectual activities:

- financial and other monitoring of key areas of departmental activity;
- analysis to fill out current legislative proposals;
- studies broadly relevant to potential policy proposals of interest to a minister, including reviews of international experience with policy instruments and technologies in that policy area;
- pure scientific "university type" research oriented to problems in the area, such as the rate at which pesticides break down in different climatic conditions.

In the mid-1970s, after several years of expansionary budgets and in a climate of general high faith in rationalism, many policy departments and some central agencies had built up good-sized cadres of professional researchers and analysts. Some contained up to 100 persons.

The 1960s and the Fad for Analysis

That the 1960s were rationalistic in many ways is attested by the worldwide movement for "social indicators" and planning. It was assumed that data collection and analysis of statistical data would eventually yield clues for scientific laws of causation and means–end technologies, even in intractable human problem areas such as poverty, delinquency, or alcoholism. The idea was to keep track of all programs, registering degrees of success, so that the way in which things were done could be brought into line with new science even as it was being revealed. The Planning-Programming-Budgeting System (PPBS) initiated in 1970–71, was itself a creation of this kind of scientistic thinking. It set in motion the requirements for planners and specialized analysts in government departments. Formal requirements for program evaluation followed in 1977.

Reverse Trends Arising from Scarcity

Reverse trends were well under way by the late 1970s. The fad of social indicators and planning fell out of favour in the United States and Great Britain earlier because of the theoretical implausibility of comprehensive rational schemes (Lindblom 1959, 1979) and because of their complete lack of demonstrated success. By the late 1970s social scientists in these countries had come to terms with the fact that, as far as human affairs are concerned, lack of knowledge of the means–end relationships needed to guide human engineering is the rule. Thus, just about the time that federal government central-agency bureaucrats were doggedly putting the final touches on a policy to require rigorous planning and evaluative activity inside departments, it was clear to everyone else that the PPBS was based on tidy fiction. Most departments thus did the least possible to meet requirements, and began to ignore them as soon as they decently could.

In addition, the Conservatives intensified the general restraints upon the civil service begun in the late 1970s, with cuts of some 15 000 person-years between 1984 and 1992. These have hit the staff (or advisory) functions quite hard. Finally, the Conservative government has been ideologically opposed to building an in-house research capacity, preferring to buy the services from universities, the corporate sector, and think tanks.

But the trend to cut general departmental analytical capacity can go only to the bone and no further. Departments must always keep a base-line capacity necessary to manage commissioned research. Deputy heads will always do whatever they need to do in order to feel in command of a subject, from hiring an assistant deputy whose strengths complement the deputy minister's, to commissioning studies. In addition, technological "solutions" have a life of their own, driving government analysis to search for any kind of response or difficulty with which to pair them. Biotechnology in agricultural applications is one example. Private-sector pesticide producers can engineer biological organisms to attack the pests that reduce crop productivity. The state must therefore leap in and learn how to regulate their production and use. For an example in transportation, high-speed rail capacity is being developed by the private sector, and is currently being promoted for use in certain transportation corridors. It thus becomes imperative for government to know about the new technologies and their strengths and weaknesses to keep the minister informed for the inevitable lobbying. Experts, in all their unfathomableness, will always be part of the fabric of government no matter who is in power.

POLITICS AND BUREAUCRATIC FORM AS CONTROLS ON OFFICIALS

Party Ideology as a Control over Bureaucracy

The role of political parties is to voice feasible social goals and identify the way in which they can be made real. Political-party thinkers should have views about what instruments of government are available in the actual social context to realize their party goals. They should understand the probable range of consequences of the various means of executing policy. This is not so big a job as it might seem, for the tools of government are few. Governments can affect the behaviour of citizens by transferring money, launching programs (implemented by the bureaucracy), making laws and regulations, and persuading or inciting through information (Hood 1986). Choosing from among these policy instruments is a highly political act as each implies a different level of coercion (among other things).

Party platforms persuade the public that elections do make a difference to policy goals, policy instruments and policy outcomes. The responsibility of party government is to ensure that is true.

The Parties' Failure to Deal with Ideas

Many observers of the Canadian scene believe that Canadian parties fall far short of fulfilling their pivotal role in democratic government; that they must be strengthened as mechanisms, first, for registering mass preferences and, after that, for providing guidelines to the civil service and for monitoring policy. Robert Young (1991), for example, argues that Canadians must seek the structural changes to the political system that will give the parties a capacity to consolidate citizens' opinions into clear platforms that can then become policy agendas for governments. Such changes would assist these governments to become genuinely responsible.

Canadian parties are, effectively, electoral machines that fade away after leadership contests and election campaigns. Out of power, the parties are desperately short of money. Thus there is next to none for education or research and development between elections. As Young notes, the national Liberal Party actually has fewer analysts on staff than the Canadian Bankers' Association or the Canadian Pulp and Paper Association: "How can it hope to integrate policy sensibly across all fields and to control a bureaucracy when in office?" (1991, 77).

Lacking a foundation of political ideas, parties are unable to provide a sophisticated training in public policy matters to their activists while out of power. Politics reduces to partisanship. The existence of a political class reduces to the existence of partisan operators. When a party is in power, polling can become a substitute for thought, as party tacticians construct platforms from wish lists made up by canvassing voters.

In the absence of partisan policy stances, partisan life even in the House of Commons tends to resolve to blame and vituperation for all types of failures. Political life at the federal level also has a tendency to concentrate on questions of narrow probity. Worthiness to govern boils down to a relative lack of proved corruption.

In Canada, as Young's remarks indicate, political ideas play a very small role in disciplining either politicians or the public service. In Britain, 80 percent of all resignations of ministers from active cabinets are offered on the grounds that the minister cannot agree with a major policy stance of the government. This shows at least that the government has a clear set of goals and associated strategies, that they are understood by ministers, and that there are animated conversations about policy among ministers and in cabinet. In Canada, by contrast, the proportion of all ministerial resignations offered on the basis of principled disagreement with cabinet policy is less than 20 percent.

Lack of Continuity of Parliamentary Elites

As might be expected in a politics without many ideas, continuity, or emphasis on political principles, it is not really very difficult for middle-class persons (in particular, lawyers) to become MPs or even prime minister in Canada. Because of electoral volatility, the average length of a parliamentary career after World War II is said to be only six years, a figure that has been given formal recognition as the threshold for a parliamentary pension. In almost all governments some individuals are appointed to ministerial office in the course of their first parliament. The governments with fewest experienced politicians were the Liberal government of 1963, with nine ministers who had no previous experience in Parliament, and the Conservative government of 1984, which had to try to operate with fifteen novices. Turning to prime ministers, it took Pierre Elliott Trudeau two years to become minister of Justice after his first election, and then one more to become prime minister. Brian Mulroney won the Progressive Conservative leadership contest in 1983, and shortly reached Parliament through a by-election. Following a general election in 1984, he was Prime Minister of Canada.

The contrast with Britain is strong: scholars calculated in 1991 that it takes on average 23 years of service as an MP in the House of Commons to become a leader of a major political party, and 26 years to become prime minister (Jones & Kavanagh 1991, 94). In this length of time politicians can be expected to absorb a number of ideas about what their party stands for, and how policy can be pursued. John Major, who took over the prime minister's job in 1990, by means of a leadership challenge within the parliamentary Conservative party, is the least-experienced prime minister in British history. He was first elected to Parliament in 1979, learned the ropes as a whip, junior treasury minister and social security minister, until 1989 when Margaret Thatcher marked him as her successor, making him senior Foreign Office minister and then Chancellor of the Exchequer. The following year he had her job. Were Major a Canadian, his background would make him remarkably well qualified, even as prime minister and certainly as minister.

Party "Attitude"

While Canadian governments are not usually tied to ideology, they do tend to have a style or an attitude toward the bureaucracy. Perhaps because the Liberals governed for so long, they have appeared to be at home with the civil service, and with the understanding that the civil servant adheres to the ideals of public service. On several occasions from 1945 to 1975 the Liberals recruited mandarins, appointing them after their election to the portfolios they had managed as officials. In opposition, the Liberals behaved gallantly. On the other hand, John Diefenbaker, when in opposition, fulminated against officials as though he were talking about subversives. He raged against former civil-service ministers as having taken "the easy way" to highest office, the correct way being long years on the backbenches (Newman 1963, 1968).

Some theorists on the right, unlike the Diefenbaker Conservatives, are not interested in "conserving" or safeguarding the classical elements of Canadian constitutionalism. They are in favour of a radical reduction in the role of government in society (Rothbard 1982). The right sometimes argues that the centralization of political capacity in the Westminster system promotes the (unjustified) assumption that the state has a positive right to act in most if not all spheres of social and economic life (Johnson 1977). Seen from this perspective, responsible cabinet government looks to be a particularly awful kind of political regime. For this reason the right withholds loyalty to the regime, cleaving to what is seen as the higher principle of unfettered individual freedom, and would willingly deplete institutional and state capacity.

There was some of this ideological rejection of civil servants, civil-service policy advice, and state capacity in the Conservative government of the period from 1984. Prime Minister Brian Mulroney campaigned on a promise to greet his senior officials with pink unemployment slips and running shoes (Zussman 1986). His first cabinet cut itself off from career civil servants by putting a "chief of staff" in each minister's office to filter bureaucratic advice to the minister. The second government from 1988 experimented, in the Al-Mashat affair, with the idea of direct accountability of officials before Parliament, as a substitute for ministerial answerability (Sutherland 1991b). More generally, the Conservative insistence on a leaner and more businesslike civil service, combined with a view that big government must go, expresses a different vision of what is to be desired from the civil servant:[6] perhaps to be more productive, to be seen and not heard, and to be less insistent on a civil-service responsibility toward an abstract public interest.

The House of Commons: Acting Upon Ministers

How does the operation of political responsibility lock into the gears of the bureaucracy to make it accountable? The answer is brief: the play of politics and information in the House of Commons creates pressures on a minister to learn the whole job of leading a department, and to do it. These pressures should ensure that minister and departmental officials share one major goal, to make the minister look as good as possible: in cabinet, in the House, and in the media. For as long as this can be done, the political heat will not be focused on the department.

But in fact, many students of politics and administration dismiss the importance of individual ministerial responsibility as impractical for modern times. The bureaucracy, they say, became too complex, too "expert," and too large to be controlled by politicians with the expansion of the welfare state after World War II. At this point, they say, management became a qualitatively different challenge.

Yet if ministerial responsibility had ever been based on the real capacity of a minister to know and delegate all departmental work, to see every little sparrow fall, we would have to admit that it has never been a realistic theory of government. This would be a strange charge against the British who designed it, famous as they are for pragmatism over principle. But a British scholar's historical work challenges the "overload" thesis. Harry Parris counted all the documents that entered and left the Colonial Office in the calendar year 1870. This was, it may be noticed, just shortly after Walter Bagehot removed the veil from the British constitution and described its true workings. Parris found that

13 541 documents entered, and 12 136 were sent out (Parris 1969, 112). One must add administrative overhead—officers, clerks writing by hand, messengers on foot or bicycle—and the requirement to consult with political colleagues. Divide this activity by the number of days in the week, and one quickly understands that neither the minister nor his top official could have controlled such an enterprise as though it were a tobacconist's shop. The system that Bagehot described, therefore, was elaborated in full knowledge that a minister does not need to exert coverage over the whole field of business in order to provide political leadership to a department.

Reactive Accountability and Retroactive Ownership

The House of Commons exerts a reactive accountability. It thus imposes the ownership of any file or issue on the minister, retroactively if she or he were not personally involved at an earlier stage. Ministerial responsibility is thus founded upon what one can call "living agendas." Ministers manage all important contemporary contentious files, with no distinction being made between policy tasks and administrative tasks, or between ministerial actions as opposed to those of officials. In the House, the current minister is alone the "constitutional mouthpiece through which departmental actions will be defended or repudiated and from whom information is to be sought" (Marshall & Moodie 1971, 65). To emphasize, if a decision was not the minister's in the first place, it becomes the minister's in the process of explanation and/or redress.

Any MP can ask questions on the floor of the House and in committees about any aspect of work in the departmental civil service. Potentially, every constituent is a source of information for the MP about the state's actions and how they affect lives. MPs pursue the minister: if a constituent's land has been expropriated under unjust terms, it is more interesting to know what the minister proposes to do than to ask for the identity of some long-departed official. MPs also enjoy the protection of parliamentary immunity. Any subject can be pursued, with any degree of verbal inflation, without danger of being charged with libel or slander. The only rules are that ministers must not knowingly lie in answering questions, and that they have a duty to provide a plausible explanation. Because of this pressure, civil servants will do their utmost to brief the minister on business that has a potential to be troublesome.

A minister who is not pleased with departmental performance can discipline or even fire senior officials appointed under the order-in-council if the prime minister is compliant. As to whether civil servants could be held to account personally in the forum of Parliament or one of its committees, the suggestion exists in a theoretical no-man's-land. The idea contradicts the centralizing logic of the system.

Accountability as a Process Value

Political accountability for departmental activity at all levels is thus a process, like education or policing, and not an end result, like wisdom or justice. Whether a minister's performance in any one case is satisfying depends on several factors: the skill of the civil service in explaining the problem and providing an attractive rationale; decisions about what ought to be secret, resulting in suppression of facts and thus sketchy presentations; the energy of the opposition in the House of Commons; interest of voters; and strategic decisions in cabinet on whether to support a colleague under fire, after counting backbenchers to be sure.

A minister might thrive in some situations of active accountability, be weakened in others, and even, much more rarely, be forced to resign. In Canada, there is not one example since Confederation of a ministerial resignation brought about by an official's administrative error. Ministers in both Britain and Canada resign only under rather special circumstances: if they cannot accept the government's policy line on any given matter, whether or not it falls under their own portfolio, and insist on speaking out; if the minister commits a criminal action or grave moral error; or if the minister is seen to be in a situation of conflict of interest. Punishment is also generally less dramatic than a forced resignation, usually taking the form of warnings or a demotion in the next shuffle.[7] Interestingly, ministers often escape resigning even when they have personally imposed policies that are revealed to have been wrong. This is because major policies usually flow from governments as a whole.

In summary, ministerial responsibility provides two democratic mechanisms with importance for the shape of policy and the quality of administration: one, the amateur minister at the head of the department conveys the electorate's signals to the bureaucracy; and second, the House of Commons publicly explores the character of whole governments by challenging them in the heat of events. The voters watching the interplay ought to learn how best to use their franchise. That they may not is a major tragedy of Canadian political life.

House of Commons: "Independent" of Ministers

A.H. Birch (1964) has explored the two languages that are used to talk about the Westminster-style constitution: the language of the holders of power and that of outsiders. Only about 70 of the MPs on the winning side will be importantly involved in government, from a House of 295 in 1992. The legislature's backbenchers, whether on the government or opposition benches, thus tend to talk the language of decentralization of power, vigorously damning the executive dictatorship they see in the Westminster system. They often long to change the nature of their legislature from being largely reactive to being much more active, along American lines (McKown 1985; Page 1989; Peters 1989b). They want to initiate legislation on the floor of the legislature, to amend government bills, and to cut or raise the budgets of government bodies—to do things that U.S. legislators can do.

Further, they also long for "free votes" (ones not disciplined by the parties) as permission to think. Many MPs experience party discipline as arbitrary, which points again to the lack of success of parties in developing ideas.

Parliamentary Reform

In 1986, the Conservative government implemented a number of parliamentary reforms that had been recommended by the McGrath Committee the year before (House of Commons 1985). The vision of the McGrath Committee was to work for enhanced accountability of departmental officials to ordinary members of Parliament. Underoccupied backbenchers would be given something important to do. The key reform, under Standing Order 96, was to give standing committees the right to initiate their own inquiries into departmental policy and administration (Gunther & Winn 1991; House of Commons 1985). Another important reform established a deadline for the government's obligatory response to their recommendations.

In operation, the Canadian reform has been considerably less radical than might have been expected. Scrutiny of financial administration and estimates fell to one side while the committees followed diverse research agendas and made themselves feared in a number of attacks on particular civil servants (Sutherland & Baltacioglu 1988; Sutherland 1991a). With the qualified exception of the Standing Committee on Finance, it is fair to say that no House standing committee 1986–90 had a serious impact on public policy. Even the Blenkarn Finance committee, while it did manage to do technically proficient policy analysis of particular subjects, did not take on broad fiscal policy.

Thus the same backbenchers who had raged against their own meaningless exclusion from policy topics learned that they could exhaust themselves and terrorize civil servants without influencing policy. To the extent that politicians made a difference to public policy content, those politicians were still ministers. The ministers, furthermore, continued to be more influenced by any number of sources other than the policy ideas of backbench MPs.

Evaluation of Backbench Nostalgia for U.S. System

Perhaps not surprisingly it appears to many Canadian backbenchers that American government is better, in that ordinary legislators have more of a voice in what will become public policy in the United States. There, entry of ideas to the legislative arena is pluralistic; any members can, in principle, get floor time in either House to introduce their bills. Officials who have ideas must entrepreneurially capture the ear of a politician, because the civil service does not necessarily have the ear of power. Interest groups have to keep a presence in many places at once.

But the need for agreement is also "pluralistic" in the U.S. system. To become law, a bill must be agreed in the same form by the two independent houses of the legislature, each only loosely organized on party lines, and then must be signed by the president, three assents representing three different majorities (McKown 1985). Thus interest groups have many opportunities to scupper policies, or to insist that the legislation be amended to suit them. The bureaucracy comes into its own to translate the policy idea into reality, making the judgements that will affect citizens' lives on the street. While political appointees hold top agency jobs, they are not collectively the public captives of a legislature that has the right to regularly ask them questions about how their decisions have affected policy results. The observer raised on a Westminster system might say that Americans have government, but not *a* government.

In some contrast, the backbencher in the Westminster system is almost in the same position as a lobbyist with good contacts. She or he is not in fact a lawmaker in the American sense. Neither is the backbencher a privileged spectator to the conversation between cabinet ministers and officials as they explore the political and administrative realities, seeking a maximally achievable policy. Indeed, the organization of political support is normally internal to the executive, or "private," before caucus is even consulted. But this does not mean that the Westminister system cannot countenance a plurality of sources of policy, including direct relationships between departmental bureaucrats and interest groups. What is most different between the two systems is the manner of legitimation of a policy idea. However an idea may have arisen and gained popularity, in the Westminster system its legitimation is centralized: a cabinet minister must adopt it as his or her own, and then sponsor it in cabinet. The battlefield of contending ideas is thus largely inside the heads of ministers and not on the floor of a legislative chamber.[8]

To bring the argument back to control, the departmental minister must always think about implementation, because her or his next sight may be an opposition MP theatrically waving constituents' letters or tabling a petition. Thus political management is encouraged by the threat of concentrated political answerability.

Bureaucracy as a Mechanism Assisting Accountability

Bureaucratic procedure itself is another factor that assures responsible administration and controls the bureaucratic contribution to the shape of policy by concentrating it in a few identified individuals. Established procedure stands between bureaucracy and arbitrary responsiveness to the pressures and opportunities of the day.

A Vertical System

First, there is the rigidity of a bureaucratic structure, bureaucracy being the most differentiated form of human organization for decision-making and for task performance. In a traditional departmental bureaucracy, each individual is supervised by a superior who, in turn, is responsible to her or his own supervisor for the quality and quantity of the work of every person in the unit, all the way up to the deputy head and the minister. Since Max Weber (1922), this principle is conveyed by the words, "hierarchy of authority," which also assumes that decision-making ability and power are directly related in a purely logical way to the hierarchical position of the occupant. Decision-making and administration in a bureaucracy is therefore predictable and verifiable: nothing is simpler than to find the author of a legitimate action and therefore to control quality in the sense of uniformity and predictability.

The Classification System

Second, there is the control represented by the job classification system. Every position in every unit is reviewed and classified to cross-service standards. No job can be classified as, for example, a Program Manager Five (PM5) unless it is composed in fixed proportions of certain types of work and supervisory responsibilities.

The employees of the federal departmental civil service are currently classified into six broad occupational categories: management; scientific and professional; administrative and foreign service; technical; administrative support; and operational (see Table 3.2). The first four are thought of as "officer level" appointments, while the last two are the pink- and blue-collar ghettos respectively. Each except management is elaborately subdivided into families of occupational titles or "groups." (Legislation tabled in the fall of 1991 under the rubric of the PS 2000 mission exercise changed this structure.)

Merit as a Control of Quality

Perhaps most importantly, there is the probity control of merit hiring, which draws the line against patronage and corruption. R. MacGregor Dawson (1922) spoke of merit as the principle underlying the justified professional independence of the official. No person below executive levels can be staffed into any job unless she or he meets the requirements of merit as stated by the Public Service Commission. In the departmental civil service, only the permanent or deputy heads

TABLE 3.2
Employment under the Public Service Employment Act, by Occupational Category

Category	1980	1990
Management	1 309	4 775+
Scientific and professional	21 460	23 682
Administrative and foreign service	51 539	65 189
Technical	25 918	26 232
Administrative support	68 169	62 689
Operational	99 555	35 205[1]
Total	**269 139**	**218 328**

1. In 1982, other grades performing management tasks were reclassified as "senior managers" (or SMs), this group being the feeder to the executive group. The 1990 figure reflects the consolidation of SMs with the executive cadre to form a unified management category. The drop in operational employees largely reflects the change in status of the Post Office.

Source: Adapted from Public Service Commission (1980, 1990), *Annual report 1980* (Cat. no. SC 1–1980), and *Annual report 1991* (Cat. no. SC 1–1990), Ottawa: Minister of Supply and Services, 1981, 1991. Reproduced with the permission of the Minister of Supply and Services Canada, 1992.

and a small number of associate deputy heads are political or order-in-council appointments. The very great majority of such jobs are awarded to people who have made their careers in the merit system. To date, there has never been a major turnover of senior officials following a federal election.

Merit is the principle of minimal competence—that is, the principle that blocks the use of government jobs as patronage. Under the rule of merit, the federal civil service has proved to be a great consumer of qualifications. Personnel in the scientific and professional category have specialist university training, and many as well have membership in professional groups that are independent of government: lawyers, doctors, nurses, veterinarians, architects. Most of the groups in the administrative and foreign service category have postsecondary education as a selection requirement, and in some cases candidates must have postgraduate education.

Because of the great emphasis on qualifications, government work has been an avenue for the upward mobility of educated white males of working-class origins (Porter 1958). But the merit system has disappointed both women and francophones regardless of their social class: it has not promoted equally qualified women or francophones at the same rate as anglophone males. It has therefore been necessary for the political level to engage in "affirmative action" using its order-in-council appointments at the very highest levels of the bureaucratic hierarchy to improve the representation of these two groups (Bourgault & Dion 1990)

The Law as a Control on Discretion

The law constitutes still another set of rules that bureaucrats must observe. As Peter Hogg notes, any government action that infringes on the liberty of the subject requires the authority of a statute. This is the principle of validity—that every official act must be justified by law. Nor do civil servants have discretion about whether or not to apply a law in a particular case. The courts have acted to limit the discretion of individual officers by holding that power vested in civil servants may not be exercised for an improper purpose or on irrelevant considerations, and have sometimes insisted that the principles of natural justice be respected in the exercise of statutory powers (Hogg 1985, 631–32). Crown officials can be sued in ordinary action, or lawyers can sometimes make use of the common-law prerogative writs to challenge state action or lack of action.

Bureaucrats holding particular administrative positions also have some precise legal responsibilities invested in them to ensure probity and prudence in the use of financial and human resources. These stewardship responsibilities are specified principally under the Financial Administration Act and the Public Service Employment Act, as well as under other statutes or directives dealing with human rights, official languages, and conflict of interest. They are reviewed for compliance by the array of watchdog agencies mentioned above.

The Internalized Beliefs of Participants

Officials are socialized to understand their own broad duties and obligations by their comprehension of the conventions of the Westminster system, and more particularly by the culture of their organization. A department or agency is a collection of structures and of standard operating procedures: it encompasses a scope of action, rules for action, as well as values and even a style for participants (as suggested in regard to PCO and Finance). We must certainly hope that our individual civil servants are normatively bound by the expectations established by the institutional framework. Were they adherents of rational choice theory, they might individualistically approach their duty to serve the public much as some corporations are said to approach their tax burden: willing to exploit every loophole to contribute the least and get the most. It is the author's suspicion that rational-choice theories of individual motivation and the predictions deduced from them are ideological statements about human nature (in this connection, see Pennock & Chapman 1977). They seem to overlook the socializing "glue" between persons that is constituted by expectations of reciprocity and the desire to master the environment and win approval for one's own performance. They fit very well with the Conservative liking for a small state. As is also true of other theories of motivation, evidence is scarce.

Threatening Doctrine by Innovation

A 1989–91 exercise in "renewal" of the federal bureaucracy, called Public Service 2000 (Canada 1990c), challenges many of these assumptions about bureaucratic systems and structures, as well as the ideas of political responsibility that were described in the earlier part of this chapter. Legislation was tabled in June 1991 by the president of the Treasury Board that would make departmental managers more autonomous. At the same time, more personal risk and challenge will be introduced into the bureaucratic environment by removing old barriers to flexibility in both human and material resource use. Another exercise is also under way to relocate work traditionally done under ministerial supervision to independent agencies, called "special operating agencies" (Roth 1990; Kemp 1990).

One reason one should not be too sanguine about the retreat from ministerial responsibility is that administrative law is underdeveloped in this country. While there is some possibility for judicial review of administrative decisions in Canada, the fact is still that Canada does not have a comprehensive system of administrative law operating through its own system of courts, as in some European countries. There are grave doubts about the independence of some of Canada's administrative tribunals, and about the quality of justice that they dispense. Thus, if ministers will not answer for actions of civil servants, it will become more important to ensure easy and affordable access for the aggrieved citizen to the ordinary court system.

Practice in the United States, which also lacks a system of administrative law and courts, does not provide a complete guide in this matter. While the discretion delegated in law to American federal agencies is subject to challenge in the federal courts and the Supreme Court, with perhaps a third of all cases heard by the Supreme Court involving the activities of the bureaucracy, access to legal forums depends on having the money to pursue claims and absorb the penalty if the case is lost. Generally only very wealthy individuals and corporate interests will take the risk (Chandler 1990).

Federalism as a Spoiler for Parliamentary Control

The British constitution was elaborated within a unitary government in an island-state. Canada is a federation of far-flung entities with great cultural and ethnic differences. Some scholars, such as Douglas Verney, feel that the fusing of federalism with parliamentarianism puts in doubt Canada's capacity to mature as a political society, because these two are in fundamental contradiction (Verney 1986). Perhaps March and Olsen might say that federalism and parliamentarianism mutually impede each other's accumulation of means–end knowledge over time by introducing noise into the other's feedback. Each institution makes the other inefficient (March & Olsen 1984).

The genius of Westminster government is that it consolidates and centralizes political power and then ensures that power is held responsible in a popular assembly. But federalism is a legal device for decentralizing power: the use of power by contending governments requires negotiation, compromise, and time. Thus, under federalism, the exercise of power is pluralistic, in the sense that there are several governing elites (Verney 1986).

Federalized Electorates

In an earlier section of this chapter, the lack of ideology in Canadian federal parties was deplored. Yet in talking about federalism we must admit that whenever federal parties do succeed in being really clear—while in power to be sure—they offend at least some of the provinces. It is one of the chestnuts of Canadian political science that the same group of electors elects provincial governments to oppose the federal government and vice versa.

In this sense, federalism encourages irresponsibility in the electorate. For one example, the electorate can apparently have an affordable welfare state by electing a socially interventionist provincial government at the same time as electing a tax-cutting, free-enterprise federal government. Or Quebeckers can hedge their bets by voting for a sovereignist provincial government along with a centralist federal party, thereby expressing a preference for an independent Quebec within a united Canada.

Total governmental activity levels are outcomes of adjustments and bargaining on the spot. As in Damon Runyon's rolling crap game, there are always players, but no one public plan, forum, or accounting for the total kitty of money and effort. Thus there is a "float" of accountability. Seen in this light, the institution of federalism with its elections at two levels and at irregular intervals seems to be in exact opposition to the goal of responsible party government.

Federalized Competition

As the provincial government identities have matured and become less like large municipal governments, and more like states, competition between them has tended to sharpen. The share of federal government employment, for one example, is a public "good" that has long been argued over in the context of the distribution of military bases, prisons, post offices, airports, and major federal contracts for aircraft or installations such as the space agency. Federal government statistics track jobs provided to provinces by the federal level, and thus one sees that post offices and military bases are distributed across the country with a surprising exactness. Sometimes politicians even seem to think in terms of hostile provincial "nationalities" and quarrel over their province's share of employment in the national capital, rather as though they were watching over coveted jobs in the United Nations headquarters and mobility were not an issue. (See, for example, a speech by Alberta MP David Kilgour, House of Commons *Minutes of Proceedings and Evidence*, May 23, 1991, 447.)

In such a competitive climate, routine actions by the federal government, such as a contract or aid decision, can put a chill on files anywhere else in the system. During the years of the National Energy Program, relations between federal and Alberta officials were tense even in unrelated areas such as culture and health. It is not surprising then that there are civil-servant "fixers" in both federal and provincial governments, officials whose specialty is federal–provincial diplomacy and intergovernmental machinery. Even outside the areas of heaviest diplomacy, many federal officials must possess exceptionally good interpersonal skills, and must have the capacity to think strategically and tactically. These are characteristics one thinks of as necessary to politicians.

CONCLUSION

Given the space, one could list other problems of accountability in Westminster systems. The secrecy that appears to be endemic to them, and which is exacerbated by executive federalism, is perhaps the most important. But enough has been said to defend the central contention that, *grosso modo*, public policy in an idealized Westminster system can conveniently be developed by officials who understand the system, and still be properly laid at the door of government, which can then be motivated to change it if the electorate so wills.

One can list the elements of civil service that are important in the realization of responsible government:

- constitutional ethics and respect for democracy and the law;
- impartiality between political parties;
- procedural correctness and substantive competence;
- loyalty to the service, including a respect for the files and a strong corporate memory.

The other side of the bargain, that is what the political regime offers the civil service, should be as follows:

- the potential for a career (no spoils system saving the top civil-service jobs for partisans);
- fair and balanced treatment from departmental ministers who have the ability to understand the politics of administration and the administrative implications of policy;
- energetic and principled monitoring of policy effects and of administrative transparency; disclosure by MPs making fair comment on what their constituents tell them;
- co-operation in political forums to ensure that the minister's political responsibility is not diffused, and thus the civil service is not politicized.

If these conditions are met, Westminster-style government will be effective in making sensible public policy and in learning about and redressing problems and thus changing policies that rub the wrong way. One might be somewhat mischievous and say that, even when least energetic, Westminster parliamentary systems can provide for responsible bureaucracy.

On the other hand, responsibility within separate governments can do little to legitimate the policy result of interactions between governments. And political reforms that weaken the minister's ownership of the department's field of action will inevitably insulate the bureaucracy from the signals sent by the electorate. We may well then have a less responsible, and hence less responsive, bureaucracy and, as a direct result, less democracy.

NOTES

1. Of course the system also respects, and is informed by, certain cultural understandings, such as the high public value given to honesty and even to expertise, which would seem to legitimate the independent action of bureaucrats in defined areas. See Dawson 1922; Smith 1988; and Mosher (1968) 1982.

2. The system is named for the Palaces of Westminster, the buildings that house the British Parliament. Occasionally one also sees "Whitehall system," for buildings occupied by the civil service. Sometimes the latter is meant to mock the claims of Westminster, by suggesting that most power resides with officials.

3. But Professors David J. Bercuson and Barry Cooper, in an unpublished paper, have argued that Canada has now evolved into what they call a quasi-republic, where the people are sovereign rather than subjects of a Crown. Nevil Johnson (1977) long ago proposed that the notion of the Crown has created confusion for the British in coming to terms with the idea of the modern state. Graham Wilson has in turn argued that such confusion in both Britain and the United States has created for these countries quite unusual problems in coming to terms with bureaucracy, such as the responsibility of officials toward an abstraction like the public interest (1991, 23). In connection with the Canadian Crown, it should be recalled that the Statute of Westminster in 1931 provided, among other things, that the Canadian governor general was a representative of the monarch (in right of Canada) rather than of the British government: some scholars thus choose December 11, 1931, as Canada's independence day. Hogg (1985) can be consulted on the royal prerogative.

4. More than 60 percent of employees in the Finance department, for example, are highly educated officer-level officials, while civilian employees of National Defence are mainly blue- and pink-collar workers, with fewer than 20 percent of officers. The Department of the Solicitor General, set up as a policy department, operates with about 60 percent officers, as does the Privy Council Office and the largely scientific Department of Fisheries and Oceans.

5. Some authors, however, allude to a trend toward social scientists and management specialists for top jobs (Carroll 1990).

6. I owe the idea to Paul Thomas, personal communication, December 1991.

7. In contrast, there have been a number of civil-service resignations to give political comfort. In 1982 the deputy minister of finance resigned, accepting full responsibility for the content of policy advice to the minister of Finance. In 1985, after the Progressive Conservative government victory, an official was forced out of his job as associate secretary of TBS because of his identification with the unpopular National Energy Policy of the previous Liberal government. Another senior official was forced out of a job at the Secretary of State, largely because of earlier visibility in the central agencies. In 1988, the deputy minister of Employment and Immigration was hounded by the Parliamentary Standing Committee, resigning to work in the private sector, and in 1989 the assistant deputy minister of Transport was forced to resign because he had given explanations that could not be squared with the minister's version of his own behaviour.

8. Seen in this light, the Canadian backbencher's insistence that policies must be seen to have originated with politicians, and that support must be organized afresh on the floor of the House of Commons for each issue, boils down to a radical challenge to the Westminster system and its definition of a government. To insist that "the House" must decide on substance, and that civil servants must then account to the House along with ministers for the way policies are implemented, implies quite a different political settlement, perhaps by coalition or one-party government.

CHAPTER 4

Structural Heretics: Crown Corporations and Regulatory Agencies

Paul G. Thomas and Orest W. Zajcew

INTRODUCTION

In May 1984, the Trudeau government introduced a new airline policy that was intended to achieve its objectives through greater reliance on competition and less emphasis on regulatory protection for the industry. The policy was the outcome of a long and arduous process that involved overcoming resistance, not only from the private sector, but also from within government itself. Reflecting upon his experience as minister of Transport at that time, Lloyd Axworthy observed that the traditional view—that ministers direct and control a responsive public service, that regulatory agencies simply administer policy, and that crown corporations operate at arm's length from the government of the day—was in need of serious revision (Axworthy 1985). According to Axworthy, when bureaucratic interests were aligned with those of powerful outside elites, the forces of policy inertia were very strong indeed.

Many past and present ministers would identify with Lloyd Axworthy's complaint about the difficulty of introducing large-scale policy changes into a system of existing policies, departments, crown corporations, and regulatory agencies such as that found in the air transportation field. This chapter focuses on the role played by semi-independent crown corporations and regulatory agencies. As institutions within the policy process, such bodies can be both a constraint on policy innovation and a source and means for policy innovation. At times, they may frustrate, either deliberately or inadvertently, the policy intentions of cabinet, but we wish to suggest that there are means available for ministers to bring them under greater political control.

The Administrative State in Canada

To begin our analysis of the policy roles of crown corporations and regulatory agencies, it is necessary to say a brief introductory word about the nature of the modern administrative state in Canada. Simply put, the state is characterized by tremendous organizational variety. The popular image of the bureaucracy as a monolithic, homogeneous enterprise is inaccurate. Rather, the administrative arm of government represents a diverse agglomeration of organizations performing widely varying functions.

While departments represent the main part of the public sector, there is also extensive reliance by both federal and provincial governments upon crown agencies for policy formulation and implementation in a wide range of policy fields. Use of independent or semi-independent crown agencies fits uncomfortably within our constitutional framework. Organizations that lie outside of the structure of regular departments have been described by J.E. Hodgetts (1973) as "structural heretics," a term intended to highlight the fact that they represent a compromise of the principles of ministerial responsibility. In the case of the structural heretics, the extent to which ministers are able and willing to answer for organizational performance is problematic given that, in theory, there is not the same degree of ministerial involvement in their operations as exists with regular departments.

Crown corporations and regulatory agencies comprise the bulk of the crown agency population. It is difficult to think of a field of social or economic policy where there is not a crown corporation or regulatory presence, and often there is both. The massive presence of structural heretics is usually seen as a product of pragmatic necessity combined with political expediency. Canadians have shown distinctly ambivalent attitudes toward the proliferation of nondepartmental bodies that appear to lie beyond the boundaries of textbook theories of accountability. While nominally under the scrutiny and control of ministers and legislatures, crown corporations and regulatory agencies represent institutions of enormous complexity. They are repositories of deep technical expertise for which existing mechanisms of ministerial responsibility and legislative surveillance seem grossly inadequate. Growing concern about the potential loss of accountability, compounded by revelations of policy mistakes and mismanagement, has led to numerous official inquiries into crown corporations and regulatory agencies at both the federal and the provincial level during the past two decades.

This chapter seeks to examine how the substance of policy, the institutional framework for the governance of nondepartmental bodies, the procedures for decision-making, and the dynamic environments in which such organizations operate all shape their policy roles. A richer understanding of the policy behaviour of crown corporations and regulatory agencies can be generated by taking a broader, less static view of their development as organizations. The complicated, variegated, and dynamic nature of such organizations makes any interpretation organized around one, or even several, defining characteristics too simplistic to fit with reality. The application of several analytical frameworks is likely to yield a richer understanding of the behaviour of crown corporations and regulatory agencies than a single model would provide. The neo-institutional perspective offers a valuable, complementary approach to the available literature. Within this approach, which has become quite broad, it is the emphases on state autonomy and organizational theory that offer the greatest potential for broadening our understanding of structural heretics.

A Neo-Institutional Perspective

In Chapter 1, Michael Atkinson identified two major streams of theorizing under the heading of "The New Institutionalism": rational choice and structural theory. In this chapter we will draw on the latter stream, emphasizing, in particular, the role of crown corporations and regulatory agencies in defining policy problems, establishing appropriate procedures for their resolution, and transforming those who participate in organizational decision-making.

Although the crown corporations have certain superficial similarities, they differ in their governance structures and their internal cultures. The same can be said for regulatory agencies. The term "governance structure" refers to informal understandings about the core purpose of the organization, who should make particular kinds of decisions, the rules for decision-making, and the most appropriate responses to environmental change and policy uncertainty (Hult & Walcott 1990). Obviously, formal administrative arrangements—physical structure, legal authority, and assigned resources—are important in defining the governance structure, but they are not synonymous with it. The governing structure also includes the often-submerged administrative cultures that make each crown corporation and regulatory agency a distinctive entity.

The rules and routines that constitute a governing structure are driven by the ideas, values, and norms embedded in the organization. These, in turn, are derived for society at large from the principles of state structure and from the ethos of administration that pervades it (Peters 1989a). But each organization selects and interprets these cultural signals, thus moulding its own distinctive culture within a community of organizations engaged in the same process. Organizational leaders have a significant role to play in the formation, maintenance, and transformation of internal cultures (Schein 1985). Leaders interpret, express, dramatize, and change cultural values through their statements and their actions. Skilful leaders, we will suggest, are crucial to the performance of crown corporations and regulatory agencies.

In order to gain some perspective on the importance of structural heretics to the policy process, we begin with a brief description of the crown corporation and regulatory agency system in Canada. The chapter seeks to characterize the predominant approaches to the study of structural heretics and then suggests how the neo-institutional perspective can add to our theoretical understanding of such bodies. The recent academic literature treats regulation and public ownership as two distinctive types of policy instruments available to government. Although crown corporations and regulatory agencies share some institutional characteristics that set them apart from regular departments, there are also important differences between them that make it appropriate to discuss them separately.

The main sections of the paper seek to "get inside" the institutional world of these two types of institutions to see how distinctive governance structures emerge within each. The causal connections between policy consequences and the use of these two types of institutions cannot be drawn precisely, but some possible linkages are suggested. A final section reinforces the main findings, and identifies some areas for further research. Through this chapter, readers will gain a fuller appreciation of the complexities of policy-making in the realm of crown corporations and regulatory agencies.

DEFINITIONS AND BACKGROUND

Crown Corporations

Crown corporations can be described simply as government-owned enterprises that are engaged in the provision of goods and services mainly, but not exclusively, to the private sector. Other terms used to describe such organizations are public corporations, public enterprises, state enterprises, and public firms. By the late 1980s the government of Canada had a direct or indirect interest in over 450 corporations, only a portion of which were crown corporations strictly defined.

In 1989 there were 53 parent corporations and 114 wholly owned subsidiaries covered by the Financial Administration Act (1984), which sets forth the accountability requirements for crown corporations at the national level. These corporations controlled assets approaching $60 billion and employed 180 000 persons, making them a rival in terms of size to the 25 regular federal departments that now employ just over 200 000 people. In addition to the main group of crown corporations covered by the FAA, there were 16 crown corporations that so closely resembled regular departments that they were listed separately for purposes of the legislation. These departmental corporations are under stricter political and administrative controls than the more familiar commercial crown corporations. There are also approximately 100 mixed and joint enterprises in which the government of Canada is a partial owner with private-sector partners or other levels of government.

The justification for the creation of crown corporations has been more developed and consistent than that advanced to support regulatory bodies. Choosing the corporate form has been seen as a way to combine public ownership with public accountability and business expertise. The objective has been to permit crown corporations a measure of political direction and control over the policies and performance of crown corporations while still allowing sufficient freedom for their managers to operate the firms in a businesslike fashion. Freedom from continuous political involvement has been seen as necessary to attract top management talent, to promote the use of business criteria in decision-making, to facilitate expeditious decision-making, and to encourage longer-term planning horizons. Boards of directors for crown corporations are seen as both a buffer to prevent short-term political meddling and a conduit to transmit the broad policy wishes of government.

Regulatory Agencies

Regulation has been described as "the hidden half of government" (Doern 1978, 1) even though it "has come to rival, and to some respects eclipse spending and taxing as instruments to modify social and economic behaviour" (Schultz 1982b, 91). In 1978, it was calculated that 29 percent of Canada's gross domestic product (GDP) was subject to some form of direct economic regulation (Stanbury & Thompson 1980). Even though no comprehensive inventory of provincial regulatory agencies is available, a 1989 report for the Ontario government identified a total of 580 administrative agencies, of which 91 had regulatory responsibilities as their main function. The report also noted that 600 different statutes were supported by about 1 500 regulations occupying over 25 000 pages of paper.

Various definitions of regulation have been offered. For our purposes, we will describe regulation as governmental legislation or agency rules, having the force of law, that proscribe certain activities or behaviour on the part of individuals or institutions, mostly private but sometimes public; this is done through a continuing administrative process. Regulation takes place through both regular departments of government and through statutory regulatory agencies (SRAs). It is the latter organizations that concern us here because such agencies are intended to enjoy some degree of institutional autonomy from the cabinet and individual ministers.

Available definitions of regulation stress the imposition of constraints as the essence of regulation. However, Schultz and Alexandroff (1985) have argued persuasively that in the Canadian context not all regulation is proscriptive and negative in purpose. Regulation also serves the purposes of promotion and planning. Promotion entails the enhancement or the protection of the economic well-being of the entity under regulatory control. Planning involves adjustments among competing economic interests in different fields and the co-ordination of different types of economic and social activity.

Generally, SRAs have been established "to take regulation out of politics" (Economic Council of Canada 1979, 54–55). More specifically, two related arguments have been advanced to justify the departure from orthodox constitutional principles involved with the use of SRAs. First, because of their politically sensitive nature, it is desirable to separate from political interference certain activities such as the award of licences to engage in certain kinds of economic ventures. An example would be the awarding of radio and television broadcasting licences. A second and related argument was that SRAs should be used in emerging policy fields where the technical requirements of policy-making were so high that they could not be met by normal legislative enactments and within the constraints of normal departmental structures. A virtue of the SRA format was its apparent capacity to attract "experts" (scientists, businesspeople, and other specialists) to work in government. The influence of politics was less pervasive and there was less bureaucratic red tape in terms of hiring, classifications, and salaries. In institutional terms, regulatory agencies are supposed to represent expertise, flexibility, adaptability, and freedom from partisanship.

A desire not to add to the burden of ministerial supervision of administration appears to have been a secondary consideration involved in the creation of some agencies. On a more retrospective basis, the argument has been made that the diffusion of power represented by the delegation of policy-making to SRAs and their reliance upon open hearings and guarantees for participation by outside groups, represents a healthy antidote within a political system that otherwise concentrates power in a limited number of actors in cabinet, central agencies, and the upper echelons of the public service (Mullan 1985).

PREVAILING IMAGES AND NOTIONS OF STRUCTURAL HERETICS

The governmental and the academic literature dealing with structural heretics has expanded greatly over the past two decades. Attempting to characterize its main normative and practical concerns is made easier by the relatively limited range of issues investigated by the available studies. Three main questions have dominated discussions:

1. Why does Canada have such a huge crown corporation sector combined with an extensive range of regulatory activity?

2. What are the costs, if any, in terms of economic efficiency, either at the level of the individual firm or within sectors of the economy, arising from the use of crown corporations and regulation?

3. How could the performance of crown corporations and regulatory agencies be improved, especially through greater political accountability?

The search for enhanced accountability has been the overriding preoccupation of government studies over the past two decades, and this concern has greatly influenced academic studies.

The accountability issue has been framed as a debate over independence versus political control. The debate has been mainly a normative rather than a positive one; that is, it has emphasized what relationships ought to exist between structural heretics and political authorities (legislatures, cabinets, and central agencies serving cabinets) not what actually takes place. Reliance upon independent bodies needs to be justified because it compromises the principles of ministerial responsibility and the administrative norm of relying upon regular departments to deliver government policies and programs. During earlier decades, the main concern with respect to crown corporations was to preserve the autonomy of corporations in order to promote sound business practices. Recently the emphasis has shifted to ways of bringing crown corporations more into line with government policy and of enhancing their financial and managerial accountability. The general reassessment of the role of governments, their financial difficulties and recent examples of mismanagement in the crown corporation sector, have all contributed to a shift toward greater government power over crown corporations. Most of the recent literature has involved debates over the merits of different political and administrative controls, either existing or proposed, over crown corporations, such as:

▶ the need to provide corporations with more precise mandates that differentiate more clearly their policy roles from their commercial purposes;

▶ the provision of authority to cabinets to issue binding policy directives to crown corporations as a means to update and refine their mandates;

▶ the development of more comprehensive and substantive classification schemes for crown corporations to support the adoption of different accountability regimes for different types of corporations;

- improved governmental and parliamentary controls over the creation of subsidiaries;
- the strengthening of the approval processes within government for the approval of corporate plans and budgets;
- the clarification and strengthening of the roles of boards of directors as crucial links in the accountability process;
- the strengthening of the internal and external audit processes, along with more complete disclosure of financial and other information through the annual reports of corporations.

In a similar manner, the literature on regulation has dealt with the merits of existing and proposed political controls over SRAs. The focus has been mainly on cabinet, rather than legislative controls. Legislative scrutiny of regulatory activity is either nonexistent or weak at both the provincial and the federal level. This contrasts sharply with the situation in the American Congress, which has created an elaborate set of procedures for overseeing regulatory agencies, at the cost of some impairment of their ability to accomplish the policy tasks assigned to them (Bryner 1987a).

Canadian cabinets have a variety of controls available to render SRAs accountable: the power of appointment, approval of decisions before they take effect, appeals to the cabinet from decisions, the establishment of regulatory mandates (usually through approval by the legislature), the issuance of binding policy directives, and the approval of budgets. The availability of these controls can differ from one agency to the next, so there has been no one formula followed to achieve accountability. These controls appear to give the cabinet a tight grip on their independent agencies, but only limited attention has been paid to the political and administrative circumstances that might condition the use of such devices.

In summary, available studies of structural heretics have not offered much escape from the rhetorical debates over independence versus control and have reflected an underlying normative ambivalence to the use of such bodies. The result has been to present simplified caricatures of crown corporations and regulatory agencies rather than to portray them in all their organizational complexity. It is not just the relationships with the central political and administrative structures that must be more thoroughly investigated; attention must also be paid to the wider environment of policy-making, including the changing economic conditions and industry structures, evolving technology, and shifting public opinion in which crown corporations and regulatory agencies find themselves. Adoption of this wider interpretive perspective is encouraged by streams of inquiry found within the neo-institutional literature.

Organization Theory

Following March and Olsen (1984, 1989), it is possible to suggest that people within institutions are more than physicists calculating the strength of external forces and formulating policies accordingly. Political meaning and political preferences are moulded by experiences and/or institutions. Institutions are neither "neutral reflections of exogenous environmental forces nor neutral arenas for the performances of individuals driven by exogenous preferences and expectations" (March & Olsen 1984, 742). Instead, institutions structure policy agendas and transform participants. They help to define what is treated as a policy problem and what sort of responses are deemed to be appropriate. The structure of institutions affects how issues reach decision-makers and how they are handled once there.

Governance Structures

Adopting this perspective, we wish to use the concept of governance structures to analyze the informal and usually submerged process by which political executives and the representatives of crown agencies interact to develop and implement policy. Hult and Walcott suggest that governance structures emerge as people in organizations strive to develop patterned ways in which to discover and articulate goals, select among means, cope with uncertainty and controversy, and foster legitimacy and commitment inside and outside of the organization (1990, 36). Such structures reflect more than the day-to-day activities of actors; they also reflect past policy choices. Informal understandings arise among the relevant policy actors about the core purposes of the organization, who should make particular kinds of decisions, the rules for making decisions, and the ways in which the organization should react to environmental change and policy uncertainty.

The formal administrative arrangements for organizations, consisting of their physical structure, legal authority, and assigned resources, obviously influence behaviour. At least as important, however, are the shared political and administrative cultures that also serve to define the governance structures for crown corporations and regulatory boards.

Definitions of Culture

Within each institution there is a set of rules, written and unwritten, about what constitutes appropriate behaviour. The applicability of such rules to a particular situation may be ambiguous, or different actors may perceive their relevance differently, giving rise to controversy over what constitutes appropriate behaviour. The ideas, values, and norms embodied in institutions, including their procedural norms, are collectively referred to as the culture of a policy sector or the culture of an organization. These cultures set parameters, subject to periodic redefinition, within which actors seek to define policy problems and apply policy solutions. Most of the literature on crown corporations deals with the actions and reactions, either real or hypothesized, of different actors and institutions, but more attention must be paid to the pervasive pre-decisional influence of the various levels of culture that provide the wider context in which policy choices are formulated and implemented.

Analysts offer many definitions of culture and cultures can exist on several levels: within the general society, within the political system, within particular policy sectors, and within particular organizations. B. Guy Peters (1989a) suggests the existence of three types of culture at the macro level: societal, political, and administrative. All three will influence the conduct of public administration. Very general value orientations in the society will influence the behaviour of individuals in formal organizations, as well as the manner in which these organizations are formed. The political culture will structure the relationship between political and bureaucratic elites, and between the population and the bureaucracy. By defining what in government is good or bad, the culture may virtually mandate some actions and prohibit others.

Peters adds that one component of this set of prescriptions is the conduct of policy; governments must do certain things in order to be a proper government. Moreover, the general orientation of society toward management and impersonal authority in formal organizations will also affect the behaviour of public officials (Peters 1989a). Finally, individual organizations in government will also develop their own culture.

The literature on policy communities suggests that there exist among the relevant actors and institutions cultures of policy-making (which may be mainly conflictual or co-operative) within particular substantive fields of government activity. Kaplan (1989) suggests, for example, that there is an identifiable and basically stable culture within the transportation field. The culture consists of widely accepted premises about what the transportation problem is and what policies would best deal with the problem.

At the level of the individual organization, Schein (1985) states that the term "culture" refers to basic values, norms of behaviour, symbols, structural features, and other elements of organizational life. However, he argues that available definitions frequently ignore a fundamental dimension that comprises the basic assumptions on which the organization operates. Often unspoken and invisible, these assumptions concern the fundamental purpose of the organization, the relationship between the organization and its environment, the potential for different kinds of actions, and the nature of the relationships with and among the so-called stakeholders of the organization.

Schein attaches great importance to the role of leaders in the formation, maintenance, and transformation of cultural orientations within organizations. Leaders interpret, express, dramatize, and change cultural values through their statements and actions. More successful leaders set directions, provide meaning amidst ambiguity, manage attention, enlist followers, and utilize opportunities to move organizations ahead despite the constraints of the environment in which they work. Skilful leaders, we suggest, are often crucial to how well crown corporations and regulatory agencies cope with the policy challenges they face.

THE INSTITUTIONAL PERSPECTIVE ON CROWN CORPORATIONS

Crown corporations can be described as hybrids. They are not just like regular departments of government, nor are they just like private firms; rather, they are meant to combine attributes of both. Both the public administration and the business administration literature is relevant to the study of crown corporations. In this section, we wish to use concepts more popular in business literature such as culture, leadership, organizational development, and environmental change. The leadership of crown corporations must not only manage their relationships with the political system, but also must deal with external forces that can affect the performance of their companies.

State Involvement in Crown Corporations

Policy Mandate

The policy mandates of crown corporations are typically vague. For example, until the most recent revisions to the Broadcasting Act, the CBC was given no more direction from Parliament than the instruction to provide a "national broadcasting service." More than a poverty of imagination or uncertainty on the part of policy-makers accounts for the vagueness of corporate mandates. Sometimes there is a desire not to handcuff the corporation by placing it within a policy strait-jacket, and other times ambiguity reflects the political requirements of gaining approval for the creation of a new crown corporation. Accountability critics, like auditors general, tend to ignore these political facts of life when criticizing the lack of operational precision in corporate mandates. They concentrate on the fact that ambiguous goals make it difficult to measure progress.

Informal Objectives

In addition to the formal, statutory definition of a corporation's purpose, there typically exist informal government objectives that are of equal importance. These include the desire to create employment, to develop the economy by creating infrastructure, to alleviate regional disparities, and so forth. Most of these informal objectives cannot be easily reconciled with the degree of independence that the corporate form of organization implies. Reconciliation of the full set of government objectives with the authorized purposes of the corporation occurs by means of various formal and informal processes. These include ministers or government officials (political staff and/or public servants) signalling the government's full intent to the corporation, or boards of directors and management anticipating what is wanted in the areas mentioned above. These processes are part of the governance structures of crown corporations.

The preference of ministers for informal, unpublicized direction to crown corporations is understandable. It allows for discretionary accountability: when praise for accomplishments is being bestowed, ministers can claim part of the credit, and when blame for mistakes is being laid, they can point to the independence of the corporation. Of course, in the adversarial world of legislative politics, opposition parties will do their best to pin the blame on government when mistakes occur.

Only in Quebec and Ottawa do governments currently possess the authority to issue binding policy directives to their crown corporations. In practice the power has been used sparingly. The reliance upon private informal communication with corporate officials allows governments to minimize the opportunities for opposition challenges. For their part, corporate officials tend to be ambivalent about the creation of a directive power. There is a tendency to resist the idea initially as an infringement on their autonomy, but, once in place, the directive power may be seen as a protective device, as a way to signal to the legislature and the interested public that they are being forced to do something against their wishes. In 1979, for example, Petro-Canada was asked by Energy, Mines and Resources to experiment with a new hydrogen-cracking process. Even though the corporation felt the project was uneconomic, an order-in-council forced it to comply with the department's wishes (Halpern, Plourde & Waverman 1988).

Strategic Plans

Several jurisdictions now require their corporations to prepare strategic plans (usually five years in length), but the political attention paid to such documents has apparently been limited. The requirement may serve more as a symbolic accountability gesture than a real accountability device. Under the federal legislation, there is an effort to prescribe the contents of corporate plans, but the quality of plans has been uneven. Federal ministers rarely interfere in broad corporate strategies; instead they have been mainly interested in the location of the economic activity generated by corporations (Savoie 1990). All of Quebec's 40 crown corporations are expected to prepare plans, but again little political interest has been shown. An exception has been Hydro-Québec where successive governments have pressured corporate officials to modify supply–demand forecasts of electricity requirements to fit with the government's own development priorities (Latouche 1984).

The Memorandum of Understanding

The Ontario government has followed a more individualized approach to defining relations with its crown corporations through a device called a Memorandum of Understanding (MOU). For most corporations these are mandatory. Once approved by the responsible minister and by the cabinet, MOUs are tabled in the legislature. Their purpose is to set out the objectives and performance expectations for each corporation and to communicate the government's policy priorities. However, according to Kirsch (1985), the process of signing MOUs has done little to clarify the policy mandates of crown corporations.

Ministerial Involvement

Unofficially, shifting government objectives are communicated to crown corporations through several channels. By far the most prevalent is through the responsible minister who occasionally sits on the board (as vice chairman of all boards in Saskatchewan), meets with the board periodically, or otherwise maintains close contact, usually through the chairperson of the board and corporate management. In some provinces, ministers receive copies of agendas and documents for board meetings. For their part, corporate officials pay close attention to the comments of ministers in question period, in speeches, and to the legislature. They prepare briefing books for ministerial use and try to anticipate which issues could become politically sensitive. At the heart of the relationship between the minister and corporate officials is an implicit bargain. From the corporation, the minister expects no surprises that might prove politically embarrassing. In return, boards and management expect ministers to respect their freedom to manage the corporation on a daily basis, while recognizing the need for continuing ministerial support.

The Board of Directors

Boards of directors of crown corporations might be described (somewhat unflatteringly) as the "meat in the sandwich." They are caught between the government, which has a legitimate policy and political interest in corporate affairs, and the management of the corporation, who represent an enormous reservoir of expert knowledge that they cannot hope to match. Directors are appointed by the cabinet on the recommendation of the prime minister, who may receive advice from the responsible minister. It is difficult to describe the typical board, because the composition and functioning varies widely among provinces and even among corporations within the same province. In British Columbia and Saskatchewan, ministers serve on the boards of corporations for which they are responsible. In many provinces, civil servants are also appointed to boards. For many years Manitoba has followed the practice of placing government members of the legislative assembly on boards. In contrast to the private sector, the presidents of the corporations are seldom board members.

Political patronage figures prominently in filling board positions. As friends of the governing party, directors are naturally somewhat sensitive to the short-term political concerns of the government and to the policy wishes of the ministers. In some jurisdictions, directors are actually made legally responsible to the minister. At the same time, several provinces and Ottawa have recently decided that the legal duties that apply to directors of private corporations should also apply to directors of crown corporations. Thus, directors are now legally liable to act "in the best interests of the corporation" and "to exercise the care, diligence and skill" of a reasonably prudent person. The result is a potential role conflict for directors: are they primarily agents of the government or trustees of the longer-term interests of the corporation? While they may initially identify with the wishes of the government, one suspects that over time they are socialized through their work on the board to adopt more of the corporate perspective. Actual conflicts with governments are infrequent because of the tendency, mentioned earlier, to anticipate the government's reaction to corporate decisions and because of the continuous communication between the parties.

The trend is toward wholesale turnover of boards when governments change, and this means that there is a lack of continuity and experience in their memberships. In selecting directors, governments pay attention to the representation of regions, special-interest groups and gender, with more women increasingly being appointed to boards. Few directors bring a background in the industry to the job. The pay for crown corporation directors is on average low compared with private-sector directors, and there are no financial incentives like stock options to motivate directors to do the hard work involved with monitoring management's behaviour. Appraisals of the work of boards seldom occur and directors are rarely dismissed for nonperformance. These are all examples of formal and informal rules that can create unique cultures within crown corporations and contribute to the types of policies developed by these institutions.

Leadership in Crown Corporations

The Chief Executive Officer

Boards rely heavily upon the senior management, especially the CEO, to develop policies and corporate strategies. Only rarely are boards capable of taking the initiative. It is also management that controls most of the information needed for informed decision-making. The dependence of boards on management is not unique to public corporations; it is also the prevailing pattern in the private sector.

The CEOs of crown corporations usually face greater leadership challenges than their private-sector counterparts both by reason of the unique nature of the organizations they lead and the way in which they obtain their positions. Cabinets appoint CEOs; in a minority of situations this is done on the recommendation of the board of directors. More governments are undertaking national searches for the executive talent to lead major crown corporations, but the prevalent pattern remains appointment from within the corporations or from the ranks of the senior civil service. Treating the CEO position as part of the overall management lineup has led to the extension of some administrative policies (such as compensation packages) from the public service to the corporations. As order-in-council appointees, most CEOs can be removed by the cabinet at any time. In practice, formal performance appraisals do not take place on a regular basis and, in any case, the removal of a CEO would entail political controversy. These arrangements for appointment, compensation, and removal may create among CEOs a degree of responsiveness to the government of the day. By extending the civil-service system into the corporate world, they may contribute to the bureaucratization of the corporate culture.

The success of CEOs depends at least as much on their small "p" political skills as on their business skills. How well they can navigate the rocks and shoals of the political and bureaucratic world will determine their success in pursuing corporate strategies. The institutional constraints they face are numerous. With the recent shift to stricter controls, the number of accountability requirements to be met has proliferated in most jurisdictions. Writing in 1985, Elaine Kirsch identified no fewer than eight governmental entities (in addition to the legislature) involved in monitoring corporation performance in Ontario: the responsible minister, the cabinet, Management Board, the Ministry of Treasury and Economics, the Public Accounts Committee and the Provincial Auditor, the various policy fields committees in the legislature, and, in many cases, outside regulatory bodies. In 1991 in Manitoba, the CEO of the Manitoba Telephone System was accountable to no fewer than ten governmental sources. In addition, as one of the four monopoly crowns in the province, MTS was required by law to hold annual accountability meetings with its customers and to maintain a log of customer complaints to be filed quarterly with a Crown Corporations Review Council. While CEOs of all crown corporations face an array of accountability relationships, the maintenance of the confidence of the minister and of the government is obviously the most vital one.

Successful leaders in the private sector are exalted in the business press and studied extensively in the management literature. In contrast, very little has been written about successful leadership in the crown corporation sector. Without a series of detailed case studies, our comments on the importance of leadership to successful policymaking in crown corporations must be rather general and tentative. A distinction between leadership and management is now widely accepted in the literature. "By leadership, most people mean the capacity to direct and energize the willingness of people in social units to take actions to achieve goals" (Rainey 1991, 157).

Recently, theories about transactional versus transformative leadership have gained popularity. Transactional leaders motivate their followers by recognizing their needs and rewarding them for their efforts. Transformational leaders motivate and give meaning to the work of their followers by achieving identification with a set of higher values, rather than relying mainly on directions and rewards. They work their influence through the creation, maintenance, and transformation of an organizational culture. When an organization has a culture that is widely shared and embraced by the executives and employees alike, it is said to have a sense of mission. As James Q. Wilson (1989) notes, the mission of an organization must match its jurisdiction. Debates over the mission of public organizations tend to be never ending and require continuous negotiation with numerous stakeholders (i.e., individuals and institutions who have an interest in and can affect the success of organizations).

Constraints from the wider environment can impede the creation of a culture appropriate to the achievement of a corporation's goals. The CEO must be in touch with political, economic, social, and technological changes taking place outside of the organization that will affect its performance. In the real world, the notion of a boundary line between the organization and its environment is artificial. For the CEOs of a major crown corporation, the environment is not just a context in which they operate and to which they need to adjust; rather, it is an integral part of the endeavour itself. Wilson (1989) suggests that constraints more than tasks tend to drive managers of public agencies. CEOs must identify, within the vague policy mandates granted to crown corporations, particular tasks that are feasible and politically supportable. They must have a vision and strategic sense of direction that they can communicate effectively to people both inside and outside of the organization.

Leaders as Public Entrepreneurs

There is evidence that strong intuitive leaders can overcome institutional constraints to reshape organizations—both their structures and cultures—in dramatic ways. These individuals have been called public entrepreneurs. They combine vision, ambition, energy, technical knowledge, political skills, and communication skills. Their emergence is associated with a contradictory mix of values within organizations combined with a turbulent environment.

Daniel Latouche (1984) could not identify any public entrepreneurs within the eight Quebec crown corporations he studied, despite the prevalence of conditions that might encourage the appearance of such individuals. Their absence may be related to the selection of corporations studied. In the case of the Manitoba Telephone System, bold and decisive leadership produced a dramatic turnaround in the fortunes of the corporation. The new CEO inherited a company devastated by a scandal involving an overseas subsidiary that had lost $27.4 million. Morale within MTS had been destroyed, the debt load was well above the industry norm, the company faced stiff competition, and the prospect existed that there would be a shift from provincial to federal regulation. The RCMP and management consultants had investigated the operations of the subsidiary. Five senior officials, including the CEO, were released, reflecting the fact that the government had lost confidence in them.

The story of how the new CEO, Reg Bird, his executive team, and the board of directors worked together to turn things around is very complex. In essence, the corporation adopted a strategy that included a multi-year Service for the Future plan to bring modern telecommunications services to rural Manitobans. Corresponding rate increases and a larger share of long distance revenues promised to restore MTS's profits and to lower the crippling debt-equity ratio. Recognizing greater competition as inevitable, the corporation prepared for this eventuality in the business premises equipment and the interprovincial long-distance markets. Strategic business units with revenue targets were established. To provide employees with a sense of direction in a highly turbulent environment a mission statement was adopted and an extensive two-way communication program was begun. The training and development function received large budgetary increases. Changes to organizational culture take years to accomplish, but by 1990, when Bird left, MTS was embarked on important changes to prepare itself for the future.

Leadership Requirements for Crown Corporations

More studies of crown corporation leadership are required to support generalizations. We have not advanced to the point in the study of public-sector leadership where we know exactly why some individuals adopt one leadership style and not another and exactly what consequences different styles have for organizational effectiveness (Wilson 1989). The leadership requirements for different corporations will likely differ. Weaver (1984) suggests on the basis of a study of the Canadian National Railways that corporate officials choose from among three objectives and pursue three corresponding political strategies in their dealing with government. Two types of constraints are likely to determine a corporation's choice of strategy: the nature of the firm's financial dependence on government and the character of the government's command structure for controlling the corporation. Corporations choose between maximizing autonomy or maximizing political support.

As an attempt to model government–corporate relations on a more systematic basis, Weaver's scheme deserves testing and refinement based on more case studies. The model tends to see governments and corporations as unitary actors, which may not be the case in the real world. Corporations deal not only with the responsible minister, but also with political staff, central agencies, and officials from several departments. Leverage for the corporation can sometimes be obtained by playing one group of political–administrative actors off against another. Corporate officials recognize that complete autonomy is not achievable. Instead what is sought is a domain of freedom that protects central management processes from political interference.

Crown corporations are dynamic entities, and the leadership requirements may vary within a particular corporation over time. Boothman is one of the few to pay attention to the organizational dynamics of crown corporations. Based on an investigation of the organizational histories of five national commercial crown corporations, he identifies five sequential phases of development (with a couple of subphases). Each phase of a crown corporation's existence will require different strategies and different types of leadership. During the initial period, aggressive leadership is required to solidify its mandate, whereas during later phases a more defensive posture is followed.

Boothman's typology is based upon the study of five commercial crown corporations out of the hundreds that exist. Many crown corporations begin their organizational life as public-service bodies without a commercial rationale, which suggests that the evolutionary path he describes for crown corporations will not fit all circumstances. On the other hand, there has recently been a trend toward the commercialization of all crown corporations as governments have sought to substitute market discipline for political direction as the guiding force.

Summary

In summary, the level of ministerial interest and involvement with particular crown corporations will vary depending upon such factors as the scope of their operations, the extent to which there is change in their policy environments, the degree of their financial dependence on the government, and their recent performance record. As suggested above, for each crown corporation there develops a distinctive, shared policy and administrative culture. This culture is a product of past policy choices and the ongoing processes of interaction between political and corporate actors. These cultures include both the formal and informal expectations of both parties and the governance structures that represent established ways of formulating and implementing policy. The distinctive institutional setting that emerges for each crown corporation can represent, at times, a source of policy freedom and, at other times, a source of policy constraint. Coping with the constraints is one of the key roles of the leaders of crown corporations, particularly the chief executive officer. Successful leadership involves not just mobilizing political support for corporate actions when required, it also involves developing a strong corporate culture and adapting to changing circumstances outside of the organization.

THE INSTITUTIONAL PERSPECTIVE ON REGULATORY AGENCIES

Regulatory agencies exist outside of any government department, and they are granted important rule-making and adjudicatory powers; however, most of these agencies are connected to government departments, to varying degrees. Some measure of independence is desired to ensure objective, nonpartisan decision-making in the adjudication of individual cases. It is also intended to create a professional regulatory climate in which experts develop and refine policies, and apply them to different factual situations, often through a process of open public hearings. Such hearings are intended to allow for the presentation of all viewpoints and provide for a fair hearing.

State Involvement in Regulatory Agencies

Ministerial Involvement

While Canadian regulatory agencies are placed at some distance from direct political control, ministers retain important powers in relation to them in order to fulfil the principles of ministerial responsibility. Ministerial powers include: the setting of mandates, the appointment of members, the issuance of policy directives, the authority to approve decisions before they take effect, the authority to vary or rescind decisions based on appeals to the cabinet, and some administrative authority in relation to agencies, such as the approval of budgets.

Role of Regulatory Agencies

There are two conflicting perspectives on the current role of SRAs. Richard Schultz expresses the majority view when he argues that "existing political controls over some regulatory agencies suggest that such agencies in fact do have a degree of independence that is inconsistent with the principles of democratic government" (1982b, 79). While Schultz recognizes that cabinets possess powers to control SRAs, he claims that these powers rarely serve to direct the policy-making activity of agencies.

The minority view, popular among legal reformers, sees the alleged independence of SRAs as an elaborate hoax that allows ministers to wield influence in their decision-making without accepting political responsibility (Law Reform Commission of Canada 1985, ch. 2).

These conflicting assessments reflect in part a difference in importance attached to the policy-making function as opposed to the adjudicative function of SRAs. Without a clear theory of SRAs, two competing bases of legitimacy for their action emerge. First, SRAs are said to behave in a legitimate and responsible fashion when they adhere to the policy intentions of elected representatives in cabinets and legislatures. Second, legitimacy for regulatory decision-making can have a procedural basis. It arises from the process of independent, nonpartisan decision-making, open hearings, fairness to all sides, a reliance upon professional analyses, and the application of clear criteria on a consistent basis. These conflicting perspectives reflect the fact that the concept of an independent commission was borrowed from the United States without regard for the political implications of using it in a very different institutional setting.

We wish to suggest in this section that there is greater political responsiveness and accountability found in the Canadian regulatory system than is usually acknowledged. Adoption of a less legalistic and mechanistic interpretation of how existing control structures operate reveals that accountability is a complex, dynamic process involving diverse claimants on the attention of the regulators. Shared cultures of policy, institutional and procedural values emerge out of the ongoing social networks that develop within different regulatory settings. Participants come to value certain cultural norms as the way to structure and stabilize their interactions, not just as a means to pursue their individual goals. These informal rules of the game define the roles of different participants, provide predictability as one group of actors anticipates the reactions of others, and defines what constitutes successful performance. The shared cultures surrounding individual regulatory agencies will differ, but in all cases they represent both institutional constraints as well as institutional opportunities.

Policy Mandates of Statutory Regulatory Agencies

The policy mandates granted to most SRAs are vague. The need for policy flexibility in new policy fields and the desire to grant policy discretion to experts who possess the technical knowledge and time that legislators lack are the official reasons for the use of semi-independent agencies. It would be antithetical to the purpose of such agencies if governments sought to spell out all the policy choices in advance. Regardless of the reasons, regulators are usually expected to fill a policy vacuum. They are expected to develop general rules that give specific meaning to broad legislative standards, and subsequently they must apply these rules on a case-by-case basis in complicated and often contentious factual circumstances where the exercise of professional judgement is required. For example, a provincial trucking authority will be instructed to issue licences for commercial trucking operations where "public necessity and convenience" justify it in doing so. Other regulatory bodies are entrusted to regulate in the "public interest" or are required to ensure that "just and reasonable" rates are charged to consumers.

Regulatory Agencies as Policy-makers

Ambiguous statutory mandates mean that many regulatory agencies are a source of both primary and secondary policy-making. Legal reformers acknowledge that some vagueness is inevitable, but they suggest that obscure mandates lead to public confusion about the goals and priorities of agencies, to problems of regulatory enforcement when agencies are challenged by interest groups to justify their policies and decisions, and to difficulties in evaluating how effectively agencies are performing in terms of the policy framework set by the legislature (Law Reform Commission of Canada 1985).

Setting the policy parameters for regulatory agencies through their enabling legislation has been seen as a blunt instrument of political control. Governments are said to lack the time and inclination to review and update regulatory mandates periodically because of the political controversy such re-examinations involve. This pessimism respecting the willingness and capacity of governments to reorient the policy directions of their agencies is overdone according to a recent study of several Ontario regulatory agencies (Johnson 1988). With respect to the Labour Relations Board, the Workers' Compensation Board, the Human Rights Commission, the Liquor Licence Board, the Film Review Board, and the Residential Tenancy Commission, Ontario governments used their control over the enabling legislation to redirect the policy orientation and administrative operation of the agencies in response to controversies about their existing approaches. While provinces like Ontario and Quebec have the civil-service capability to conduct agency reviews, smaller provinces may be compelled to leave agency mandates unexamined for decades. This is just one way in which differences in scale may have an impact on government–agency relationships.

Cabinet Directives

There is a continuing debate about the wisdom of providing cabinets with the authority to issue binding policy directives to their regulatory agencies as a means of refining and updating their mandates. Only a few of the constituent acts of national regulatory agencies now provide for directives, and the power has been used sparingly. As legally binding orders that flow from statutes, directives must be distinguished from ministers' informal policy statements, which are taken into account by agencies in making decisions (but are not legally binding), and from administrative directives, which are meant to apply system-wide administrative standards to the internal operations of agencies. Resistance to the suggestion of policy directives has come from the agencies themselves, but more independent commentators have also doubted their potential for the swift and effective transmittal of government policy.

The availability of a general power of direction, it has been argued, would have several advantages. It would focus accountability where it belongs, that is, with responsible ministers in cabinets. It would allow for government influence at the front end of the regulatory process and would therefore be less disruptive of that process than appeals to cabinet after regulatory decisions have been reached. If properly structured, the process of policy direction could be open to public input and would be less time-consuming than amending the statutes that created the agencies.

Against these arguments, several disadvantages are cited. A directive power would compromise the adjudicatory role of regulatory agencies by permitting political interference in individual cases. The line between policy-making and adjudication is often blurred in practice. A directive power would also lead to increased lobbying of ministers and cabinet by the regulated industries, thereby undermining the public-hearing processes conducted by SRAs. Under the guise of policy directives, governments may, in effect, amend the enabling legislation for regulatory programs without appropriate parliamentary authorization. To the heads of regulatory agencies, the insistence of governments on the need for a directive power is seen as a vote of nonconfidence, reflecting a lack of trust in their willingness to stay within the policy parameters set by the legislature. Finally, it has been suggested that a directive power would lead to game-playing and abuses by regulatory bodies (Roman 1985). Agencies might, for example, request political direction to avoid criticism for unpopular decisions or to forestall successful appeals to cabinet.

The Debate over the Directive Power

The debate over the directive power reflects differing starting assumptions about the appropriate role of SRAs. Even with the advance publication and public consultation requirements proposed by some advocates, critics argue that the directive power would lead to inappropriate political interference with the interpretation and implementation of policy by independent regulators. The main justification for the proposed directive power is to resolve policy conflicts between independent agencies and their home departments. Such conflicts appear to be a relatively rare occurrence, although the confidentiality surrounding department-agency relations makes it difficult to draw conclusions on this point.

Disputes between SRAs and departments can arise out of an unclear and perhaps unworkable division of responsibility between the department and the agency with respect to policy formulation and implementation. This was the situation in the transportation policy field at the national level after the 1967 Transportation Act left virtually no policy role to the Department of Transport and granted the Canadian Transport Commission (CTC) a broad regulatory mandate. Failure by the Commission to pursue its policy role vigorously led the department to fill the vacuum and this in turn led to several high-profile policy clashes (Janisch 1978). In the case of the Canadian Radio-television and Telecommunications Commission (CRTC) there were sharp policy disagreements with the Department of Communications over CRTC policies on commercial deletion, cable hardware ownership, and pay-TV during the 1970s because of the conflict the policies generated in federal-provincial and Canada-U.S. relations (Johnston 1980). The potential for the abuse of the directive power is seen in the 1982 cabinet order to the CRTC respecting cross-ownership in the media, which arose in response to a royal commission report on the future of newspapers. According to Bartley (1988), the cabinet order served purely political rather than policy purposes since it did nothing more than symbolically confirm existing CRTC policies on the question.

Appeals of SRA Decisions

The debate over policy directives has often been linked to the question of appeals to ministers or full cabinet from the decisions rendered by regulatory agencies. Such appeals are restricted to questions of policy and not to matters of law, which must be appealed to the courts. The extent to which executive review of agency decisions by means of appeals to cabinet is allowed and actually occurs is far from clear, especially with respect to provincial regulatory agencies. The 1989 report on agencies in Ontario simply noted that "some agency decisions are subject to *petitions* to the cabinet, which has the authority to substitute its own decision" (Ontario 1989, 2-22) and "a few statutes permit an *appeal* to a minister from a decision of an agency" (Ontario 1989, 8-106). The wording of most Ontario statutes grants only parties to the original agency proceedings the right to petition, unlike the situation at the federal level where parties other than those involved in the original proceedings can request a review. Earlier surveys suggested that appeals at the federal level occurred infrequently, were usually launched by organized interests and were mostly unsuccessful; their frequency and success at the provincial level is unknown.

To some, appeals represent the ultimate assumption of political responsibility, whereas to others they represent a threat to the integrity of the regulatory process. The ministers who must decide appeals will necessarily work with a broader range of public-policy considerations than narrowly focused regulatory agencies, which hear mainly from interested parties. On the other hand, appeals may cause delay and contribute to politicization of the regulatory process, demoralize regulatory officials, and contribute to discretionary accountability when ministers choose to override only unpopular decisions. In the debate over cabinet appeals, there are several complaints about the procedures for dealing with them, most notably the absence of any obligation on the cabinet to provide reasons for its decision. Without meaningful reasons, cabinet appeals settle little in public policy terms. The majority view among commentators on the issue of cabinet appeals tends to favour their abolition and replacement with wider use of directive power (Economic Council of Canada 1979, 62-67).

The Power of Appointment

Another control device available to governments is the power to appoint individuals to serve on regulatory bodies. It is conceivable that through the selection of particular individuals a government could direct the policy orientation of an agency. Appointments at both the federal and the provincial level are made by the cabinet, usually on the recommendation of the responsible minister. At the federal level, terms run from five to ten years, with the average being seven years. When governments change at the provincial level there is usually a complete turnover of membership as terms expire. At the federal level, renewal of full-time members occurs quite regularly, partly because of the pattern of appointing people with public-service backgrounds. The combination of political appointment with fixed terms, rather than "at pleasure," was intended to achieve a balance between political responsiveness and independence on the part of agency members. Ministers seldom attempt to dictate regulatory policies or decisions because regulatory agencies are composed of people sympathetic to their policy concerns.

A 1985 report suggested that the way in which members of federal agencies were appointed contributed to underachievement when governments showed too little respect for the importance of such bodies (Law Reform Commission of Canada 1985, 77–79). The report was referring politely to the well-established habit of appointing friends of the governing party who lacked appropriate background experience. With the multitude of regulatory positions available, there are obviously some jobs that are much more challenging than others. For the full-time positions on major agencies, governments usually pay more attention to the question of competence. For the remainder of the agency memberships, a balancing of representation criteria such as region, sex, ethnicity, and ideology, together with competence and willingness to serve, takes place. Not all regulatory jobs attract interest. There is a world of difference between a position that pays $14 per hour for part-time work and one that pays $114 000 a year full-time, which was the range of salaries paid to agency members and chairs in Ontario in 1990.

Canadian regulatory memberships differ from those in the United States in typically providing for longer terms and the renewal of appointments for the senior jobs. In the United States, regulatory memberships change when presidents change, and presidents typically recruit regulatory talent from the relevant industries. A recent profile of the backgrounds of Canadian agency members is not available, but earlier analysis of national regulatory bodies suggested that individuals with political and public-service backgrounds were the largest group of members. If this remains the pattern, it has a couple of potential implications. First, the tradition of placing at least some of the top regulatory jobs in the hands of former public servants rather than industry representatives may reduce the susceptibility of agencies to *capture* by the industry perspective, an issue that is discussed more fully below. Second, the use of former politicians and public servants who possess general knowledge of the governmental process but lack extensive background in the industry involved, may mean that the depth of policy expertise represented by regulatory agencies is less than is usually assumed. This problem is aggravated by the limited number of staff experts in Canadian agencies compared with their U.S. counterparts.

Budgetary and Staffing Processes

The budgetary and staffing process for regulatory agencies is largely an unexamined mystery of regulatory life. The potential for governments to use budgetary controls to compromise the independence of regulatory agencies excites the passions of legal reformers. Political scientists see the budget approval process as providing few, if any, opportunities to control the policy directions of agencies. Part of the problem is to interpret the significance of financial constraints when all government organizations face a climate of restraint cutbacks. However, Johnson (1988) suggests, based on his study of Ontario agencies, that selective financial restraints were used as means to curb the activist orientation of the Human Rights Commission and to take over the inspectorate activities of the Liquor Licence Board. There is little evidence that economic analysis has been used as part of the budget process to challenge agencies on their current policy directions.

Although questions of organizational design have long been central to the study of public administration, it is surprising how little has been written in the Canadian context about the feature of regulatory agencies that most distinguishes them from departments, that is, the collegial nature of their decision-making. In the absence of careful studies, we can only offer some general, speculative comments and call for more research. Most of the important regulatory agencies in Canada have both full-time and part-time members, with a full-time chairperson who serves, in effect, as the general manager to oversee the administration of the agency. The inclusion of part-time members is intended to keep agencies in touch with the regional and local impacts of their decisions. In complicated fields like telecommunications it is difficult to see how part-time members can cope with the economic, technological, and financial issues involved. To promote the development of more specialized knowledge, most national regulatory agencies have adopted the practice of using separate panels to process applications and to conduct public hearings on policy proposals. Specialization among regulatory members may be necessary, but the use of panels can lead to problems of co-ordination, as revealed in an earlier study of the Canadian Transport Commission (Janisch 1978).

The Role of Leadership in Regulatory Agencies

The role of the chairperson of a regulatory agency can be crucial to its success. The importance of leadership in a regulatory agency has been documented in several recent studies of the deregulation programs implemented by the Reagan administration (Bryner 1987b; Harris & Milkis 1989), but similar studies for Canada are unavailable. The chairperson of an agency is responsible for developing strategic policies and directions; working with full- and part-time members to ensure their full contribution; selecting senior staff and ensuring the efficient management of the agency's operations; conducting hearings and giving final approval to written decisions; reviewing annual budgets and presenting them to the minister; and, more generally, reporting and responding to the minister, the cabinet, and the legislature. It is the chairperson who deals with the home department on a regular basis and develops an understanding of the policy direction and procedures that the minister wishes to see followed.

Decision-making Procedures

One dimension of agency performance that the chairperson may influence are the procedures followed for decision-making. Procedures can have important implications for the actual decisions made by determining to some degree which assumptions, interests, and values will have influence in administrative decisions. Two broad approaches to the refinement and implementation of the regulatory mandate are potentially available. The most prevalent approach is to build policy incrementally through the adjudication of individual cases. Since applications for licences and the adjudication of cases form the bulk of the workload of most regulatory agencies, the development of policy on a case-by-case basis is to some extent inevitable. There is a strong institutional bias in favour of the incremental approach because of the flexibility it offers to regulators. The alternative approach is to issue tentative policy statements on emerging concerns. Policy statements are said to facilitate the elaboration of agency mandates, encourage greater consistency in decision-making, and promote voluntary compliance with regulatory requirements. For a brief period at its outset, the CRTC adopted an open and consumer-oriented approach to its regulatory tasks, which included the regular use of discussion papers on broadcasting issues. By way of contrast, the Canadian Transport Commission (CTC) dealt with its broad regulatory mandate in a piecemeal fashion and seldom made use of policy statements to guide the handling of cases.

The chairperson of a regulatory agency serves as the manager of its administration, which includes the selection of senior staff. Very little is known about how the staff of agencies interact with commissioners to render decisions and to develop policy. Staff analyses are prepared to weigh the pros and cons of applications. Staff members participate actively in the pre-hearing conferences that are held with intervenors before regulatory hearings. Questions to be posed to applicants are often developed by staff. Usually the legal counsel to a commission will play the leading role in the cross-examination of witnesses. The responsibility for the writing of decisions usually falls on staff members. Staff members are also responsible for direct dealings with the regulated sector in terms of securing compliance with rulings. In fields like environmental regulation, officials are often left with wide discretion in selecting enforcement targets and imposing sanctions. The reliance on informal consultations with interested parties has led to concerns about unfairness and regulatory capture.

Clearly, commissioners depend heavily upon staff for policy and technical advice. If the staff do not challenge industry submissions, no one else may do so because countervailing perspectives are often not adequately represented in the hearing process. There has been a continuing debate over whether internal studies prepared by agency staff should be made available to all participants in the hearing process. Most agencies have been reluctant to allow access to materials and arguments presented by staff, which reflects the general tradition of administrative secrecy. The passage of freedom-of-information laws in some jurisdictions and some court rulings in support of access on the grounds of procedural fairness have improved access somewhat. As Mullan has observed, "the more competent and more trusted the staff, the greater is the danger that the hearings themselves will become a charade because the real forum for the exchange of information and debate becomes the communication that takes place between staff and tribunal members" (1985, 172).

It is the task of the chairperson to ensure the continuing support and contribution of various actors: the minister, senior departmental officials, central agency staff, other commissioners, the permanent staff, and the outside parties affected by the regulatory agency. Balancing these different interests and values is important, but serving the minister and the government usually takes priority. As seen, ministers have important powers over agencies. As a last resort they can utilize such authority to bring agencies into line. But the more important exercise of ministerial power is largely invisible. It consists of defining the shape of the regulatory system: what premises are assumed, what regulatory issues are open or settled, what kinds of demands should be seriously considered, and how the various demands should be processed and accommodated.

Political Environment of Statutory Regulatory Agencies

How regulatory agencies interpret and apply their regulatory powers is influenced not only by their relations with government, but also by the wider political environments in which they operate. Earlier works on regulation in the United States took a deterministic view of environmental influences, arguing that regulatory agencies passed through a predictable organizational life cycle and eventually ended up being captured by the industry they were intended to regulate.

The capture theory was never held to apply to all U.S. regulatory agencies and probably has even less validity in the Canadian context for several reasons. First, many agencies have had the promotion and development of the industries they regulate as an explicit or implicit part of their mandates from the outset. This promotional purpose is seen in the fact that some agencies, like the CTC, dispensed subsidies as well as monitored corporate behaviour. A second difficulty in applying capture theory to Canada is the degree to which Canadian regulatory agencies, more than their American counterparts, impose rules on public enterprises which themselves embody public policy objectives. The privileged status of crown corporations before regulatory agencies is discussed further below. Third, the capture theory presumes a degree of freedom from political control that does not exist to the same degree in Canada as in the United States, as was seen in our earlier discussion of the various modes of ministerial intervention. Finally, part of the capture theory was based on the revolving-door phenomenon that was said to operate between regulatory commissions and the regulated sector in the United States. The same pattern has not been found in Canada. Instead, individuals with political and bureaucratic backgrounds predominate in agency memberships and this may produce not an industry-oriented culture but instead a public-management culture that has at its core the need to accommodate conflicting interests and values.

If there are reasons to doubt the general applicability of the capture theory, there are still situations in which outside interests exert powerful influence on agency behaviour. Wilson (1989) suggests that the influence of outside groups will depend on the pattern of representation within an agency's political environment. He goes further to describe four types of political environments:

- client politics: a situation in which an agency confronts a dominant interest group favourably disposed to its goals, and in which the benefits of regulation are narrowly distributed and the costs are diffused;
- entrepreneurial politics: a situation in which an agency confronts a dominant interest group hostile to its goals, and in which costs are concentrated on a particular industry or locality and benefits are widely spread;
- interest-group politics: a situation in which two or more interest groups compete over agency goals and there are recognizable winners and losers as a result of regulatory action;
- majoritarian politics: a situation in which no important interest group is continuously active because the stakes of the regulatory game are not big enough to induce involvement.

This is an oversimplification of Wilson's typology, which itself simplifies the regulatory realities found in the United States at the national level. Transposing the scheme to the Canadian context suggests, on an impressionistic basis at least, that it could have interpretive value.

There are several examples of client politics including the case of Bell Canada and its relationship with successive regulatory bodies at the national level. In his excellent study of telecommunications policy, Babe (1990) suggests that Bell Canada has been successful in using regulation to achieve its expansion into a corporate empire spanning the globe. Predatory pricing, protective restrictions on entry into the industry, and the manipulation of its corporate structure were used by Bell to avoid the possible negative impacts of regulation. All along, regulation seemed more designed to serve corporate development goals than to be a policing operation. An example of interest-group politics might be the various trucking regulatory bodies at the provincial level that must reconcile the competing demands of shippers versus truckers and be concerned about the competition arising from other modes of transportation. These examples notwithstanding, there is still much empirical work to be done in Canada charting the relationships between agencies and industry.

Can the Government Regulate Itself?

In an earlier article, Wilson and Rachal have suggested that "large-scale public enterprise and widespread public regulation may be incompatible" (1977, 14). The authors based their conclusion mainly on the United States and did not look closely at the experience of other countries. Paehlke (1991) has recently suggested that the question posed by Wilson and Rachal—"Can the government regulate itself?"—needs to be refined to ask more precisely: Which sort of corporation, public or private, is more likely to be a better target for effective regulation and under what circumstances? Utilizing a comparative framework, Paehlke assesses government self-regulation in the case of Canadian and U.S. public corporations, including the Tennessee Valley Authority, Atomic Energy of Canada Limited, Ontario Hydro, and the Ontario Waste Management Corporation. He concludes that public corporations are not necessarily more difficult to regulate as regards environmental concerns. Public corporations do not automatically show more respect for environmental protection, and ownership is not the crucial variable in determining whether a corporation is amenable to effective environmental regulation.

The widespread presence of crown corporations in many regulated sectors creates other complications in terms of governance. With the exception of Alberta, all provinces operate hydro companies and regulate them through public utility commissions. However, the importance of hydro-electric developments to many provincial economies means that governments pay close attention to hydro plans. Manitoba Hydro presents its strategic plans to cabinet, and previews its proposed rate increases with the energy minister before presenting them to the Public Utilities Board for approval. At times cabinets will be required to mediate disputes between a regulator and a crown corporation. This happened when the CRTC ordered the CBC to drop commercials from all children's programming and the corporation complained to cabinet that it could not comply unless it was given a larger grant to make up for the revenue shortfall. When crown corporations operate in a competitive market setting, they are often seen by their competitors to have a preferred status before the regulatory body. As the policy instrument of the government of Canada, Air Canada was said to have priority on all the preferred routes.

Further analysis of the political environments of regulatory agencies should be linked to the distinction that is often made in the literature between traditional economic regulation and so-called new social regulation. Social regulation differs from the more familiar economic regulation in several ways (Reagan 1987). It seeks the removal or alleviation of social harms rather than the correction of market failures. It involves issues of risk assessment and risk management that call upon scientific and technical analysis more than economic analysis. In social regulation the focus is not on particular industries, but on the treatment of problems that transcend industry boundaries, such as environmental protection and occupational health and safety. These characteristics of social regulation are said to give rise to political environments that are more diverse, complex, and conflictual than those faced by traditional business regulatory agencies. Because regulation is not industry specific and because more public-interest groups are active, social regulation may not involve the same danger of regulatory capture and agencies may have greater freedom to exercise policy discretion because of the conflicting demands they must regulate.

Summary

In summary, the institutional setting in which most Canadian regulatory agencies operate presents both broad policy opportunities and some significant policy constraints. While often provided with sweeping policy mandates, agencies are also potentially subject to significant political controls that emanate almost exclusively from the political executive, not the legislature as is the case in the United States. The powers of cabinet in relation to agencies and the pattern of appointing political friends or former public servants tend to foster a regulatory culture of elite accommodation of competing interests and values more than the application of pure policy expertise and strict procedural norms. The governance structures of regulatory agencies are not well understood, but the available evidence suggests that there is greater responsiveness to the shifting policy concerns of governments than the conventional wisdom implies.

CONCLUSION

Almost without exception, recent works on crown corporations and regulation have been produced in the form of reports of governments or through the sponsorship of quasi-governmental bodies like the Economic Council of Canada and various royal commissions. Research has been shaped by the political debates of the day and by the desire to have an influence on decisions. The emphasis on control and accountability reflects these practical concerns. The research takes as its starting point a hypothesized model of how the Canadian political system is supposed to work and seeks to explain (and justify) how structural heretics have been grafted on to the orderly accountability relationship involved with ministers leading departments. However, to continue to treat crown corporations and regulatory agencies as structural heretics is probably inappropriate given their long tenure and significance within the modern administrative state. Moreover, as we have argued, neither crown corporations nor regulatory agencies are exceptional organizational arrangements. As suggested above, there are reasons to question whether crown corporations and regulatory agencies are less subject to ministerial control and less accountable than regular departments. An independent status cannot be assumed just from the title of a crown corporation or SRA: it must be determined by an analysis of the actual working relationships. Furthermore, the extent to which ministers have knowledge of and therefore can answer for departmental operations will continually lessen if current trends toward devolution of authority and contracting out continue. Finally, in terms of the overriding preoccupation with accountability, several authorities have argued that the high visibility, openness, and public participation involved with most regulatory hearings stands in sharp contrast with the more closed and secretive deliberations of cabinet, central agencies, and line departments (Mullan 1985; Schultz 1982c).

A significant consequence of the preoccupation with accountability has been to draw attention away from the dynamics of organizational life as crown corporations and regulatory agencies adapt to changing external environments. The forces that cause crown corporations and regulatory agencies to come into being, to fulfil some or little of their mandates, or to give them power at different periods of time, escape attention when we are debating the merits of different control devices. How governments combine crown corporations and regulatory agencies as instruments to pursue policy objectives can only be understood within the context of shifting ideologies, technological changes, economic developments, and shifting power relations among government, industry, and the public. The structural heretic population represents an important dimension of the modern state, and we must map its shifting configurations more closely if we are to understand the grey areas within the state–society dichotomy.

The historical backgrounds and institutional frameworks of crown corporations and regulatory agencies vary widely. This fact is a powerful argument in favour of more case studies to develop, refine, and test theories regarding both types of structural heretics.

For policy-makers the lesson of the above discussion is that they should not place their faith in simplistic gimmicks to control the policy behaviour of officials within structural heretics. Rather, they should strive for clearer policy direction as the basis for measuring the performance of crown corporations and regulatory agencies. In making appointments they must pay more attention to the leadership skills required for different types of organizations. They must be aware of the way in which institutional incentives condition the behaviour of officials. Finally, they must appreciate the impacts of external environments on the performance of such institutions. For officials, the message may be that there is no universally accepted definition of the appropriate relationship of their organizations to governments. They are likely to operate in a swirl of controversy for the foreseeable future as society debates the continuing role of governments. Pursuit of success will require political sensitivity, attention to their internal cultures, and an awareness of the changing environmental conditions that will have an impact on their organizations.

CHAPTER 5

Federal Structures and the Policy Process

Kenneth McRoberts

INTRODUCTION

As countless observers have noted, discussion of politics in Canada is pervaded by the issue of federalism. It seems to be impossible to discuss matters of public policy without first addressing the perennial question: In which government's jurisdiction does it lie? Moreover, given both the ambiguities of the constitutional text and the ingenious ways in which Canadians (or their governments) can interpret it, the answer often is far from clear.

Yet, if federalism so manifestly shapes discussion of politics in Canada, does it follow that federalism actually influences the content of policy? Surprisingly, many scholars hesitate to conclude that it does. In the words of three leading scholars of Canadian federalism,

> there is no clear answer to the question "Does federalism matter?" ... It is difficult to avoid the temptation to fall into the trap of the "fallacy of the obvious" and to attribute too much weight to the influence of institutional factors (Norrie, Simeon & Krasnick 1986, 147).

Nonetheless, while bearing this injunction in mind, we will try to show how a strong case can be made that federalism does indeed "matter" to public policy in Canada. In this chapter we will argue that not only can federalism directly structure the policy-making process, it can influence policy indirectly both by shaping our understanding of

---

Careful commentaries on the first draft of this paper were kindly provided by Grace Skogstad, Herman Bakvis, Andrew Goodman, Jamie Lawson and Garth Stevenson. In addition, Michael Atkinson was a masterful editor, providing both direction and support in a highly effective manner.

politics and by redirecting the influence that social forces bring to bear on Canadian politics.

DEFINITIONS AND BACKGROUND

Defining Federalism

Our first task is to develop a working definition of federalism. There is considerable variation among the definitions offered by scholars, with some being far more inclusive than others.[1] However, if federalism is to be defined in a way that clearly differentiates it from other arrangements, then it can most usefully be identified as: a sovereign state with central and regional governments that have exclusive areas of activity in which they can directly regulate the activities of citizens. Typically, these different areas are delineated in a constitutional document that cannot be unilaterally altered by one level of government and that, in turn, is subject to interpretation by some recognized arbiter.[2] Federal systems may also feature arrangements for the representation of regions within the institutions of the federal government. A common example is an elected senate in which representation is based not on population but on some rough equivalence among regions. To this extent, regional interests are safeguarded not through control of separate governments but through representation within common institutions. Some scholars refer to the former as "interstate" federalism and to the latter as "intrastate" federalism. Nonetheless, accommodation through separate institutions remains the hallmark of federalism. There is no reason to see "intrastate" arrangements as either necessary or sufficient to qualify a system as federal.[3]

Understood in these terms, Canada's political system is clearly federal, although there have certainly been attempts to characterize it otherwise. After all, Canada's constitution-makers chose to dub their creation a "confederation." Apparently, they believed that this would make it more palatable for those, especially in French Canada, who feared incorporation in a union of British North America (Stevenson 1989, 16). Yet the term "confederation" is generally used to denote a system in which sovereignty lies with the member states. Nowadays, few scholars would contend that the Canadian provinces are sovereign. Conversely, a strict reading of the Constitution might suggest that the system is not even federal in nature. After all, the British North America Act (now known as the Constitution Act, 1867) contains a variety of ways in which the federal government can intervene in provincial affairs, even to the point of invalidating provincial legislation.[4] Yet, if the system's form may not be purely federal, its functioning is: these quasi-unitary features have fallen into disuse (Smiley 1980, 22–23). It might even be argued that by convention they are no longer part of the Canadian Constitution.

Reasons for Federalism

There are two primary rationales for adopting a federal system. Within a purely "political" line of argument (which underlay the adoption of federalism in the United States), the virtue of federalism lies in the very fact of two levels of government. With the authority of the state divided in this manner, citizens are safeguarded from the degree of oppression by the state that could occur in a unitary system, where a single state enjoys total authority. By the same token, groups of citizens who are ignored by one level of government can turn to another government to secure their objectives. To put it somewhat differently, when politicians in two different levels of government must compete for public support, there is a greater likelihood that citizens' concerns will be met. For economist Albert Breton, the rationale for a federalist state

> is to provide the political system with more (additional to those in government) competition to ensure that over the long run, political power is exercised both efficiently and legitimately in the interests of citizens (1985, 506).

Within a "sociological" approach, federalism's virtue lies in its ability to lead very diverse people (or "peoples") to share the common political system. It can bring together collectivities—whether they be differentiated by culture, language, religion, or mere physical separation—that simply lack sufficient confidence in each other to entrust fully their fates to the same government. Federalism offers the possibility of collectivities sharing the same government for certain purposes, while controlling autonomous governments in areas where their interests differ (Trudeau 1968, 182–203). In fact, Lord Acton, the nineteenth-century English thinker whose arguments in favour of federalism so influenced Pierre Elliott Trudeau's writings on the subject, even argued that such a state is a superior one:

> A great democracy must either sacrifice self-government to unity or preserve it by federalism ... The co-existence of several nations under the same State is a test, as well as the best security of its freedom. It is also one of the chief instruments of civilization (quoted in Trudeau 1968, 179).

By the same token, some scholars have argued, it is only because of these divisions that a system will remain federal. Otherwise, the states or provinces will atrophy and the system will become effectively unitary. (For his part, Breton rejects this "communitarian federalism," which wrongly views the units of federal systems as homogeneous communities.)

The "sociological" rationale certainly rings true for the Canadian case: it was primarily through the insistence of French Canadians that the unitary system favoured by most English-Canadian proponents of Confederation was not adopted. The terms of Canadian federalism clearly reflect this. Jurisdiction over matters that could directly affect the cultural distinctiveness of French Canada was reserved exclusively for the provinces: education, health, welfare, and property and civil rights (which included Quebec's distinctive Civil Code). As the leading scholar of Canadian federalism, Donald Smiley, noted, "the Dominion of Canada was established as a federation, albeit a federation of a somewhat centralized kind, primarily because of French-English duality" (1980, 214).

The Distinctive Features of Canadian Federalism

With a working definition of federalism in hand, the next step is to map out the specific features of a Canadian version of federalism.

Relative Decentralization

At first glance, the most straightforward way to characterize federal systems might be in terms of the balance of power between the federal and provincial, or state, levels. As it happens, a host of conceptual and methodological problems bedevil such an enterprise (Simeon & Robinson 1990, 152; Leslie 1987, 86–103). For instance, how can we determine the relative significance of the jurisdictions held by the two levels of government? For that matter, how do we determine whether governments actually occupy the jurisdictions that are constitutionally assigned to them? These problems might prompt us to look at government spending. Here we have estimates of government activity all expressed in terms of the same unit: the national currency. Yet how meaningful are such comparisons? Provincial or state spending may be relatively high yet heavily constrained by federal norms or guidelines.

Even with these caveats in mind, it is difficult to avoid the conclusion that the contemporary Canadian federal system is relatively decentralized (Riker 1964; Stevenson 1977, 71–73). Not only is the proportion of government spending assumed by the provinces relatively high but provincial governments have taken on a wider range of functions than are assumed by their counterparts in most federal systems. For instance, Canadian provincial governments have had state enterprises functioning in a variety of fields (including railways and airlines); many of them maintain extensive networks of government offices in foreign countries; and they have succeeded in imposing a variety of non-tariff barriers to the free movement of goods, services, and capital within Canada (Stevenson 1977, 86–90).

Weakly Developed Intrastate Federalism

A second feature of federal systems is the degree to which accommodation of regional difference through province or state autonomy is complemented by devices to afford regional representation within central institutions. Here, Canada's relative situation is indisputable (Smiley & Watts 1985). Intrastate federalism has always been far less developed than in most federal systems. The Senate clearly is not a forum for regional representation. In the House of Commons the single-member-plurality electoral system regularly produces party caucuses that are much more skewed away from some regions, and toward others, than is the actual distribution of party support. And the parliamentary system, with its emphasis upon majority rule and party solidarity, further weakens the impact of regional interests that are underrepresented in the government party caucus. As a result, the burden is all the greater on interstate federalism alone to provide an accommodation of interests.

Asymmetry

A third feature of Canadian federalism is the degree to which there is asymmetry in the relations between the federal government and the provinces. Within contemporary Canadian federalism a wide variety of functions assumed by one or a few provincial governments are taken on by Ottawa in the rest of the country. For instance, Ontario and Quebec both maintain their own provincial police forces; all the other provincial governments have this function performed by the Royal Canadian Mounted Police, under contracts with Ottawa. Ontario, Quebec, and Alberta collect their own corporate income tax; in all the other provinces, Ottawa alone collects corporate income tax and then transfers a portion to the respective provincial governments. Ottawa has entered into agreements with most, but not all, provinces regarding immigration, a concurrent (shared) jurisdiction. The agreements range widely in scope; in only one case, Quebec, has the provincial government assumed the right to select permanent immigrants. Finally, there have been a variety of instances of federal–provincial and even exclusively federal programs in which Quebec, and only Quebec, has taken advantage of the opportunity to "opt out" and operate its own program, usually with compensation (McRoberts 1986).

The formal definition of responsibilities under the Constitution Act, 1867, is virtually the same for all provincial governments. Thus, Canada does not have the asymmetry in formal constitutional terms that characterizes other systems. Yet, on the basis of federal–provincial administrative agreements as well as unilateral actions by particular provincial governments, Canadian federalism displays an asymmetry in the actual discharge of functions that apparently exceeds that found in most federal systems.

Interpenetration of Functions

Finally, Canadian federalism is characterized by a high degree of interpenetration of functions. To a very great extent, activities of the federal government impinge upon provincial activities and vice versa. Governments may claim to be operating within different jurisdictions, yet actions in one area are bound to affect actions in another. Clearly, Canadian federalism was not always like this. In the early decades of Confederation, Canada did conform to a certain degree to a classical federalism in which the activities of federal and provincial governments are quite removed. However, since at least World War II, this has no longer been the case.

Executive Federalism

Given these general features, it should not be surprising that Canadian federalism is also marked by the development of an elaborate structure of intergovernmental consultation, negotiation, and administrative agreement that exceeds most other federal systems. If both federal and provincial governments are important actors whose activities constantly affect one another, they will need to confer with one another—if only to reduce the degree of conflict and contradiction between their respective activities. As it happens, much of the federal impact on provincial activities is based upon cost-shared and other joint programs. By the same token, asymmetry has often entailed the negotiation of federal agreements not only with the participating provinces but with the nonparticipating province(s), in the latter case to spell out the conditions of nonparticipation. Finally, the weakness of regional accommodation in central institutions means that the burden on direct federal–provincial dealings is all the greater.

Scholars have dubbed this pattern of intergovernmental consultation "executive federalism," which Donald Smiley defines as "the relations between elected and appointed officials of the two orders of government in federal-provincial interactions and among the executives of the provinces in interprovincial interactions" (1980, 91).

The structure of executive federalism in Canada is indeed elaborate. The most visible institution is the first ministers' conference, composed of the prime minister and the ten provincial premiers. But it is just the proverbial tip of the iceberg. Not only do most federal ministers periodically meet with their provincial counterparts, but so do deputy ministers and a host of administrative personnel. In 1972, according to one estimate, there were already 400 federal–provincial liaison bodies (Van Loon & Whittington 1981, 533). In 1983–84, there were close to 250 federal–provincial programs in operation (McRoberts 1986, 75). In addition, structures for interprovincial consultation are in place, on both a regional and a Canadawide basis.

The potential for conflict within executive federalism clearly is greater when it entails elected officials rather than administrators (Dupré 1986). During the 1950s, when the edifice of executive federalism was first emerging, the primary actors were administrators: federal and provincial officials responsible for a given program or group of programs. Sharing professional norms and a desire for concrete programs, they had a clear interest in collaboration. In the 1960s, federal and provincial politicians sought to insert themselves more fully into these intergovernmental dealings over programs. Moreover, first ministers were increasingly drawn into discussions of constitutional revision.

As politicians, they had an electoral interest in presenting themselves as vigorous defenders of the interests of their respective jurisdictions. Thus, executive federalism among politicians increasingly became a public affair in which politicians sought to mobilize support among their constituents in order to secure the most favourable arrangements possible. In the process, executive federalism became increasingly conflictual.

While the structures of executive federalism have become central components of Canadian federalism, their rules of operation are not always clearly defined. Often, formal decision-making has been based, implicitly or explicitly, on a unanimity rule. Fortunately, for the functioning of Canadian federalism, the worst effects of such a unanimity requirement have been avoided. Fritz Scharpf (1988) has demonstrated how the requirement of unanimity in the West German federation led to a "joint-decision trap," in which the federal government was weakened by the need to placate all the Lander, and how both federal and Land budgets were driven up excessively by the fact that, with jointly financed programs, neither level of government had to assume the full cost. Martin Painter (1991) has shown that Canadian federalism contains a variety of devices through which this undesirable, if not "pathological" (Scharpf's term), state of affairs has been avoided: provincial opting out of federal–provincial programs, accommodation of individual provincial concerns through variation in the terms of federal–provincial programs, the ability of governments to avoid intergovernmental deadlock by acting unilaterally, and so on. At the same time, Painter notes that much of this flexibility would be lost if executive federalism were to become more formalized, for instance through a permanent first ministers' conference.

Adaptation of Canadian Federalism

Beyond the form and structures of Canadian federalism, we also need to consider the mechanisms through which change is secured in this institution. Here too we find part of the explanation for the prominence of executive federalism in Canada. In effect, executive federalism has filled a void created by the relative ineffectiveness of two other mechanisms of change: formal constitutional amendment and judicial interpretation.

Formal Constitutional Amendment

Historically, there have been very few alterations of the terms of Canadian federalism through constitutional amendment: a 1940 amendment gave the federal government the right to establish a scheme of unemployment insurance; a 1951 amendment authorized federal old-age pensions; a 1964 amendment authorized federal supplementary benefits to old-age pensions, as well as survivors' and disability benefits; and the 1982 constitutional revision entailed an affirmation of provincial jurisdiction over some matters involving renewable energy resources. The primary explanation of this relative infrequency of constitutional amendment appears to lie in the presumption that agreement of all first ministers was necessary. On this basis, for instance, the amendment for unemployment insurance was delayed until all nine provinces gave their consent. Quebec had been the most adamant opponent but had a change of heart thanks to the election of a Liberal government. (Of course, the 1982 patriation demonstrated that unanimity was not necessary after all.)

Judicial Interpretation

More important to the evolution of Canadian federalism has been judicial interpretation of the constitutional division of powers. During the first 82 years of Confederation the ultimate judicial body was in fact the Judicial Committee of the Privy Council, based in London. Clearly, the overall thrust of the Committee's decisions was to interpret the Constitution in a manner that enhanced the power of the provincial governments—in all likelihood beyond what most of the framers of the Constitution had intended. It can be compellingly argued, moreover, that such an enhancement of provincial power was needed for Canadian federalism to correspond to the general structure of Canadian society. As Pierre Elliott Trudeau declared in an oft-cited passage written in 1964,

> it has long been a custom in English Canada to denounce the Privy Council for its provincial bias; but it should perhaps be considered that if the law lords had not leaned in that direction, Quebec separatism might not be a threat today; it might be an accomplished fact (Trudeau 1968, 198).

Ironically, this primary instance of adaptation of Canadian federalism may well have been fortuitous. There is little evidence that the decisions of the Judicial Committee were based more upon an informed understanding of Canadian society, than upon a simple adherence to a classical notion of federalism (Cairns 1971, 327–32; Vaughan et al. 1986).

Intergovernmental Agreement

Otherwise, adaptation of the terms of Canadian federalism has been achieved on an ad hoc basis through the instrumentality of intergovernmental agreements. Through cost-shared programs, Ottawa has been able to play a major role in exclusive provincial jurisdictions, without having to secure any alteration of the constitutional division of powers. Moreover, bilateral agreements between the federal government and individual provinces have facilitated asymmetry, as a response to the differing needs of provincial governments. At times, intergovernmental agreements have served to reduce the overall levels of policy duplication or conflict. As instruments of adaptation, intergovernmental agreements have the advantage of flexibility and impermanence. But they also have costs. In particular, they have the effect of impeding popular participation in the political process.

HOW FEDERALISM STRUCTURES POLICY-MAKING IN CANADA

Having clarified our understanding of federalism as a form of government and having delineated the distinctive features of federalism in Canada, we can now turn to our primary objective: exploring the impact of federalism on public policy in Canada.

In ascribing effects to federalism we need to remember that we may be positing an alternative political order that is not at all realistic. In all likelihood, Canada could not persist without federalism. A unitary Canada would not be able to contain Quebec, and perhaps other provinces as well. Thus, the implicit comparison should be between public policy within a federal Canada and policy within a considerably smaller unitary Canada. By the same token, some of the specific features of Canadian federalism, such as asymmetry and relative decentralization, may also be necessary for the retention of Quebec, if not other provinces. In a Canada without Quebec, federalism might take a quite different form. We will return to these issues in the conclusion.

In the following pages we will review three different ways in which federalism may influence policy-making in Canada. As many scholars agree, federalism has a direct influence through the ways in which it structures the policy-making process. But, drawing upon the insights of institutionalism, we will develop a second argument that proposes that federalism can influence policy indirectly by the manner in which it shapes the general understanding of politics in Canada. Finally, we will turn to state theory to trace the ways in which federalism can indirectly affect policy by redirecting the impact of social forces upon politics in Canada.

One way of capturing the impact of federalism upon public policy in Canada is to examine the manner in which it structures the policy-making process. This is, in fact, the most common approach among students of Canadian federalism. They point to a variety of ways in which policy-making might be different if Canada were to have a single level of government rather than two. By the same token, it can be argued that many of these effects of federalism are reinforced by the specific form that federalism takes in Canada, with such features as relative decentralization and executive federalism.

Incoherence in Policies

One proposition that most scholars are prepared to support is that coherence in public policy is more difficult to achieve under federalism than in a unitary state. With two levels of government, the activities of one level may well affect the activities of the other, even if each is acting within a separate jurisdiction. For instance, in selecting a site for a new airport, a responsibility that falls squarely within the federal government's exclusive jurisdiction over interprovincial transportation, Ottawa may upset a province's own plan for economic development by attracting new industries to an area that is not favoured within the provincial scheme. This was precisely the issue in the 1960s conflict between Ottawa and Quebec City over the location of what was to become the Mirabel airport. With Canada's strong provincial governments and extensive asymmetry, this type of policy incoherence is likely to happen.

Beyond that, in the Canadian case, the two levels of government often pursue policies within precisely the *same* areas. In fact, one policy may be explicitly designed to offset the impact of the other. For instance, both government may adjust their public spending in an effort to alter the state of the economy. In the early 1970s the federal government decided that inflationary pressures, which were based primarily in Ontario, had to be curtailed. To that end, Ottawa reduced its spending. Yet, for its part, the government of Ontario, the region at which the federal government's austerity policies were primarily aimed, feared that these policies would produce an unacceptably high level of unemployment and set about to raise its spending to offset Ottawa's actions.

As we have seen, this interpenetration of the actions of the two levels of government is one of the most striking features of Canadian federalism. With the relative strength of the provincial governments it would appear to be unavoidable.

Not surprisingly, then, there is considerable evidence that Canada's brand of federalism has contributed to policy incoherence. For instance, in the case of economic policy, one observer has flatly stated:

> At the heart of our difficulties is the fact that we have developed a deadlock in federal-provincial relations that has set the pace for other relations, especially between business and government. This has prevented us from agreeing on our economic goals. ... We have allowed this sterile process to prevent us from making rational allocations of our resources, to plan for the maximization of productivity in order to succeed in the scramble that the international market has become. (Thorburn 1984, 242)

Of course, not all observers share this view (Atkinson 1984), and certainly federalism alone is not responsible for policy incoherence in Canada. Bureaucratic specialization and competing political pressures can lead the same government to pursue contradictory policies. For instance, the federal government has simultaneously launched campaigns to encourage the public to refrain from cigarette smoking and provided financial assistance to support the production of tobacco. And it might be argued that policy coherence is an overrated or unattainable ideal in any event.

Nonetheless, Canadian federalism has surely supported policy incoherence. As Donald Smiley recognized in his final monograph, "to the extent that effective government requires the rationalization of public policy, federalism stands squarely in the way of this goal" (1987, 22).

Experimentation and Innovation

It has often been argued that federalism allows for greater innovation and experimentation in public policy than would be possible under a unitary system. Particular jurisdictions may be prepared to experiment with policy ideas that do not have general support in the country as a whole. Once the experiment has succeeded, the other jurisdictions may be induced to adopt the policy as well. Thus, in his classic attack on the historical centralism of English-Canadian socialists, Pierre Trudeau wrote: "Federalism must be welcomed as a valuable tool which permits dynamic parties to plant socialist governments in certain provinces, from which the seed of radicalism can slowly spread" (Trudeau 1968, 127). By the same token, with several jurisdictions all separately addressing a common problem, novel ideas and approaches may emerge that would not appear if a single national government were to be responsible. Once again, these effects should be especially strong in Canada, with its relatively high degree of decentralization.

The best-known case of a particular province pioneering a new policy that is then adopted for the country as a whole is health insurance, which was first developed by the Co-operative Commonwealth Federation (CCF) government of Saskatchewan. Once it had been put in place and acquired a certain degree of national acceptance, the scheme was adopted by the federal Liberal government under Lester Pearson. The federal government proposed to the provincial governments that they join it in a cost-shared scheme. While all the provinces agreed, some were exceedingly reluctant to do so. In fact, in their survey of the literature on Canadian federalism, Fletcher and Wallace found a number of such instances in the health field:

> A number of programs began in one or two provinces and then were established in other provinces because the federal government, under pressure from the provinces with programs or from consumer groups, saw some electoral benefit in offering cost-shared arrangements. Other provinces then introduced the programs, sometimes reluctantly, to get a share of the funds (and political credit) (1986, 137).

Also, programs pioneered in a province may be adopted by other provinces in a simple "diffusion" process, without clear inducement for them to do so. Examples are public automobile insurance, human rights commissioners, ombudsmen, and public ownership of hydro. Nonetheless, ever mindful of their relative ability to attract investment, most provincial governments will hesitate to copy these innovations if they are likely to force up levels of taxation—unless a province shares the ideological commitments of the pioneering provincial government and/or the innovations have powerful electoral appeal. For that matter, these factors constrain any province's capacity to innovate in the first place.

Thus, in his survey of the impact of federalism on the adoption of social policies, Keith Banting notes that

> federalism is clearly a conservative force in welfare politics. ... Theories which suggest that social reform can be introduced more rapidly in a federal system than a unitary one, since innovations can be established in one province and the "seeds of radicalism" can then spread across the nation, underestimate the withering effects of regional disparity and provincial economic competition (1987, 174).

Banting demonstrates that the growth of the welfare state depended upon the post–World War II centralization of responsibility for social policy in federal hands.

Delay in the Adoption of National Policies

If federalism can open up the policy process, by allowing for experimentation and innovation at the province or state level, it can also constrain the policy process by impeding the adoption or modification of policies at the national level. If the federal government should need unanimous or close to unanimous support before proceeding, initiatives that have widespread support in the country as a whole may be blocked by one or two provincial governments. Under Canada's brand of federalism, with strong provincial governments, this situation has arisen repeatedly.

For instance, most scholars agree that the adoption of unemployment insurance was retarded by the need to secure approval of the provincial governments. In 1935, under R.B. Bennett, Ottawa sought to establish a scheme of unemployment insurance unilaterally. In light of a ruling by both the Supreme Court of Canada and the Judicial Committee of the Privy Council that the federal government did not have the necessary legislative authority, Bennett's Liberal successor, William Lyon Mackenzie King, felt obliged to secure approval of all the provincial governments to a constitutional amendment providing this authorization. Full agreement by the provinces had to await the election in 1939 of a more favourably disposed government in Quebec, under fellow Liberal Joseph-Adélard Godbout (Pal 1988, 148–52).

Rigidity in the Modification of Existing Programs

By the same token, when programs depend upon formal federal–provincial collaboration, the structures of executive federalism, with the continuing requirement of intergovernmental consensus, can hinder their growth and adaptation. For instance, the administration of the Canada Pension Plan is based upon a regime of federal–provincial vetoes, that has prevented expansion of the plan. With such a system of "multiple veto points," private-sector pension funds, opposed to expansion of the plan, have only had to secure the support of one of the three largest governments—the federal, Quebec, or Ontario governments—to prevent expansion. In the past, centred as it is in Ontario, the private pension industry has been able to count on the Ontario government to represent its interests (Banting 1987, 70).

Conversely, however, the complexities of executive federalism can serve to protect programs that might otherwise be under attack. For instance, when the Mulroney government set out to find areas where spending might be cut, it focused upon programs that were wholly under its control. In social policy, its main targets were old-age security and family allowances, both under its exclusive authority. Programs such as the Canada Pension Plan, with its multiple veto points, were changed only modestly (Tuohy, 1992).

Government Expansionism

Some scholars have argued that two levels of government, both led by politicians dependent upon electoral support, are bound to be caught up in a competition for public favour that leads to greater overall state activity than would be the case otherwise. Once again, in the case of

Canada with its strong provincial governments, this effect of federalism should be especially strong.

While intuitively compelling, this proposition is not easily confirmed. In some sectors where both levels of government are active, collaboration rather than competition seems to be the norm. For instance, in the case of agriculture, Grace Skogstad found that policy-making has not been hampered by intergovernmental conflict: "Federal-provincial relations in agriculture have been described as among the best of those in a number of areas" (Skogstad 1987, 167). She attributes this in part to internal divisions within the agricultural community and delegation of authority to regulatory agencies. But she also traces it to the fact that unlike all other areas of jurisdiction but one, immigration, agriculture is a concurrent jurisdiction—shared by the two levels of government (Skogstad 1987, 162–63). To that extent, the pattern of intergovernmental relations that she finds may be anomalous.

Evidence of intergovernmental competition leading to a greater overall level of state activity can perhaps be found in social policy, especially during the 1960s and 1970s. During this period, the federal and Quebec governments actively competed over their relative roles in the social policy field. For instance, in its effort to stake out the areas of contributory pensions for itself, the Quebec government outlined a scheme that was considerably broader in coverage and more generous in benefits than the federal proposal. After protracted negotiations, Ottawa was led to adopt a program that more fully paralleled Quebec City's model. By the same token, Quebec City's desire to establish its own family-allowance scheme apparently influenced the federal government's decision to keep its existing scheme in place (Banting 1987, 74).

At the same time, to the extent that it is valid, the proposition may need to be reformulated. Rather than the simple electoral ambitions of politicians, the explanation may lie with more profound influences within governmental institutions or with different social influences playing upon the two levels of governments. We will focus upon these broader formulations in our later discussion of institutional approaches to the impact of federalism.

Finally, even if we restrict our focus to the electoral concerns of politicians, it is not clear that these concerns should always lead to competitive expansionism. They might have precisely the opposite effect.

Avoiding Policy Initiatives

In some cases, politicians may seek to avoid state intervention. Federalism may in fact make it easier for them to do so.

For instance, Kathryn Harrison has shown how the Mulroney government's reluctance to assume a vigorous role in environmental policy was aided by the ambiguities of its jurisdictional powers to play such a role. As she shows, intergovernmental relations in a given policy area need not be competitive.

> The possibility that governments could use the federal system to avoid responsibility for environmental protection cautions against the optimism of authors who have argued that two heads of power are better than one (1991, 20)

By the same token, to refer back to the adoption of unemployment insurance, some scholars claim that federal officials, who had reservations about the very idea of unemployment insurance, were quite content to be able to claim that the constitutional division of powers denied to the federal government the necessary legislative authority. According to James Struthers,

> neither the BNA Act nor provincial rights prevented the federal government from taking positive steps to improve the care of the unemployed. ... the constitution in the 1930s, as in the 1920s, provided more of a convenient excuse for delay than a barrier to action for both Bennett and King (1983, 209).

Not all scholars share this interpretation, however.[5]

For that matter, not just politicians but private interests may use the division of powers to avoid state intervention. Confronted with the prospect of an unfavourable state action, private parties may seek a judicial interpretation of its constitutionality, hoping that the measure will be declared not to be within a government's jurisdiction (or ultra vires). For instance, the Judicial Committee of the Privy Council's first important decision bearing upon the division of powers, *Citizens' Insurance Company v. Parsons*, resulted from an insurance company's (unsuccessful) attempt to avoid obligations under an Ontario statute by having the statute declared ultra vires.[6]

In sum, we have been able to document a variety of ways in which federalism, especially in the form it takes in Canada, can influence public policy by structuring the processes through which policy is formulated. Federalism may constrain the policy process, heightening the obstacles to the creation of new national programs. But it also may broaden the range of policy options, either by providing the opportunity to pioneer programs at a local level that do not yet have national support or giving policy-makers the possibility of avoiding action by ascribing responsibility to the other level of government.

HOW FEDERALISM SHAPES OUR UNDERSTANDING OF POLITICS IN CANADA

In its attempt to capture more fully the significance of political institutions, the "institutionalist" school of political science may point the way to a fuller understanding of the effect of federalism upon public policy. This is especially so if one takes institutionalism beyond the simple notion of institutions setting the "rules of the game" for policy-makers. If one takes institutions seriously, two additional possibilities present themselves: (1) the ways in which institutions can shape general understandings of policy and politics and (2) the ways in which institutions may impose imperatives that will shape and direct policy.

In Chapter 1, Michael Atkinson suggests that institutions influence the policy process by constraining outcomes. They structure access to the process, influence the formation of coalitions, and establish decision-rules. But he notes that institutions are also creative in the sense that they mould the way in which problems are defined and solutions evaluated. In this sense, institutions influence the "atmospherics" of the policy process by encouraging particular policy styles and shaping the discourse that participants employ.

The policy impact of Canadian federalism may indeed be better appreciated if we pursue this notion of "atmospherics," and explore how federalism may have affected the very definitions of the policy process, and politics itself, not only among policy-makers but among the Canadian public.

Atkinson argues that

> where (the costs of collective action) are high, the policy process becomes relatively exclusive, dominated by state actors; where they are low, there is greater potential for organized input and for broad coalitions. (Chapter 1, page 38)

Indeed, scholars have often noted that executive federalism tends to exclude interest groups from the policy process and that policy discussion takes place in negotiations between executives of the different governments, although most scholars also have come to recognize that this effect is not universal to all policy sectors (Smiley 1980, 148–53). But the impact of executive federalism upon policy discussion may well be more diffuse and profound than conventional interpretations suggest.

In effect, executive federalism may have served to "technocratize" the policy process, rendering it opaque to most citizens. Especially in the era of executive federalism, understanding the policy process involves acquiring extensive knowledge of the niceties of constitutional jurisdiction and the infinitely complex structures of intergovernmental collaboration. Many citizens, lacking this arcane knowledge and not linked to well-equipped organized groups that do have it, can only feel excluded from policy discussions.

Second, and more fundamental, several scholars have noted how federalism has served to shape the "terms of the debate" of Canadian politics: "the language and concepts within which policy is viewed and discussed" (Norrie, Simeon & Krasnick 1986, 145).[7] Political discussion has been heavily coloured by questions of jurisdiction and the prerogatives of governments to act in a given policy area. More generally, federalism has served to magnify the extent to which policy is defined in terms of the needs of region, as represented by provincial governments, rather than class or other nonterritorial categories.

Once again, the impact of federalism on policy discussion may be much more profound. Surveys have regularly shown that the average citizen has difficulty identifying with a discourse of politics that is focused on the jurisdictions and prerogatives of governments. If at times publics are mobilized by regional interests that parallel jurisdictional divisions, in many cases they are not. To the extent that political and bureaucratic elites themselves appear to be preoccupied with these questions, publics are bound to see elites as self-regarding and unconcerned with popular needs and concerns. On this basis as well, many Canadians are bound to feel estranged from the policy process.

Yet, while recognizing how federalism has affected the timing and scope of initiatives in Canada and has even structured political debate, many scholars insist that federalism has not hindered the capacity of the Canadian political system to respond to its citizens. In the last analysis, they argue, Canadians have received the policies they desired—as long as these desires have been articulated clearly.

For instance, on the basis of the most thorough review of the literature on Canadian federalism, including over 100 case studies, Fletcher and Wallace conclude that,

> although there is considerable disagreement in the literature, the consensus seems to be that federalism does make a difference. Divided jurisdiction influences the scope, the structure, and the pace of introduction in a wide variety of fields. It effectively blocks certain kinds of policies where interregional consensus is not possible. Jurisdictional issues are given special attention in the system. Nevertheless, *the system rarely frustrates the popular will* and structural tinkering will improve its operation only if other conditions are right (1986, 151; emphasis added).[8]

Yet, if indeed governments have usually responded effectively to articulated public wishes, this may reflect less the responsiveness of governments than the extent to which publics have effectively articulated their wishes. It may be that many citizens' and citizens' groups either were unable to articulate demands, given the technical knowledge this required, or saw little purpose in doing so, given governments' preoccupations with their own interests, namely their relations with other governments. In effect, while federalism may not have *frustrated* the popular will, federalism, and especially executive federalism, may have served to *shape* the popular will.

To be sure, it is difficult to prove conclusively that federalism has had these effects. But it is striking to note how English-Canadian publics have responded to the quite different discourse of politics that was initiated through the Constitution Act, 1982. After all, the Charter of Rights and Freedoms served to establish the notion that the Constitution was concerned not just with relations among governments, and thus of little direct significance to average citizens, but with the rights of average citizens and even of governments' obligations to them.

As English Canadians have adopted this new rights-based discourse they often have become quite critical of the discourse of federalism and increasingly impatient with the sense of exclusion it implies. This was the logic of much of the public criticism of the Meech Lake Accord, and of the processes through which it was developed. First ministers' conferences have become much less legitimate not just as the arena for revising the Constitution but as the forum for making policy. The new discourse of citizens' rights has awakened a greater sense that governments should be directly accountable to citizens, and that citizens should participate directly in all manner of political discussions. In effect, executive federalism has provided a certain isolation of the policy-making process. As executive federalism loses its legitimacy, policy-making may come to involve a much wider range of participants, and policy outputs will be affected accordingly.

A second way in which one might conceptualize the impact of institutions upon public policy is in terms of requirements or imperatives that institutions impose policy. At the risk of anthropomorphizing institutions, let it be suggested that institutions have "needs" that must be met for their continued well-functioning. If the essence of the state is to regulate the behaviour of individual and corporate citizens through binding laws, it requires both revenue, if only to maintain the administrative structure through which its laws are applied, and legitimacy, as the surest way of securing citizens' compliance with its laws. On this basis, more is involved than self-aggrandizement by politicians and bureaucrats; state actors may be propelled by the "needs" of the institution to which they owe their status. Public policy can be closely shaped by these twin institutional needs of revenue and legitimacy. And where, as with federalism, two institutions are involved, policy can be seriously affected by their competition for these resources. This certainly has been the case in Canada.

Perhaps the most dramatic instance of policy being shaped by intergovernmental competition for revenue lies in energy policy. To a considerable degree, the National Energy Program can best be understood in terms of the federal government's need to secure a greater share of the windfall profits from oil extraction, especially at a time when it was concerned with the threat of the Quebec independence movement. Unable to secure a satisfactory share of revenue from oil extraction in Alberta, the federal government adopted a radical strategy: to encourage capital to shift oil and gas exploration and production to areas— the Arctic and offshore—where it would not need to share revenue with a provincial government. The federal government even dubbed these areas the "Canada Lands." Without this concern on the part of federal policy-makers to meet the revenue needs of the Canadian state, there would not have been such a dramatic policy initiative.

A struggle for legitimacy has been at the root of conflict between the federal and Quebec governments over the last 30 years. Intergovernmental conflict has been driven by more than the competing personal ambitions of politicians. With the 1960s, many Quebec francophones became focused upon the need for state intervention to promote actively the interests of the francophone collectivity. By definition, the Quebec government, responsible to an overwhelmingly francophone electorate, was better placed to assume this role than was the federal government, with its predominantly English-Canadian electorate. But in assuming this new responsibility, Quebec government leaders were implicitly or even explicitly challenging the very capacity of the federal government to meet the needs of Quebec francophones. Pushed to its logical conclusion, this claim could lead to Quebec's total withdrawal from the federal system. Not surprisingly, then, federal government leaders began, especially under the leadership of Pierre Trudeau, to stake out a counterclaim to the loyalties of Quebec francophones, arguing that the federal government could indeed respond to their needs. Thus, during the 1970s and 1980s policy-making in a wide variety of areas—culture, communications, foreign policy, immigration, social policy—was indelibly shaped by the concern of each government that Quebec francophones see it as their primary government. As a result, conflict between the federal government and the Quebec government has been far more wide-ranging and sustained than has conflict between the federal government and any other province.

HOW FEDERALISM RECONFIGURES SOCIETAL INFLUENCES ON POLITICS

An additional approach within political science that might help us to acquire a fuller appreciation of the policy impact of federalism is state theory, one of the sources of institutionalism identified in Chapter One. In particular, we need to look to that part of state theory that clearly situates the state within its societal context.

For our purposes at least, there is little additional insight to be gained from that version of state theory that seeks simply to juxtapose state and society as distinct entities and to argue for the independent significance of state as opposed to society in shaping public policy. A case in point would be the work of Eric Nordlinger (1981), concerned with demonstrating the validity of a "state-centred" theory in which political elites are able to act according to their own "preferences," which may or may not coincide with those of society.

There have been attempts to comprehend Canadian federalism in precisely these terms. In 1977 Alan Cairns delivered a celebrated address that decried "sociological reductionism" and set as its objective

> to redress the balance by arguing ... that federalism, at least the Canadian case, is a function not of societies but of the constitution, and more importantly of the governments that work the constitution (Cairns 1971, 699).

Cairns argued that the dynamic of Canadian federalism lay in the ambitions of the political and bureaucratic actors who occupied its structures. If the provincial governments remained strong and enjoyed popular support, as was manifestly the case, this was less a function of social divisions among the provinces (in some cases provincial boundaries were wholly arbitrary) than of the extent to which provincial boundaries had fragmented political life. For Cairns, the preeminent role played by federalism in Canadian political life can be traced to provincial elites—bureaucratic and political—who have fostered these structures.

Yet this "pure" institutionalism has been a difficult position to maintain in the Canadian case; the ambitions of provincial political elites can hardly explain why the contemporary federal system is less centralized than other federal systems. After all, if the primary explanation for the persistence of federalism is the normal ambition of all politicians to expand the scope of their governments or to curry the favour of their electorates, why should state or provincial elites secure so much more power in some federal systems than others? Nor can the ambitions of politicians explain the marked variations over time in the relative strength of federal and provincial governments. In any event, studies have amply demonstrated that conflict between such provinces as Alberta and Saskatchewan and the federal government does have deep social and economic roots. Quebec is not the only instance where provincial autonomism has been driven by social forces (Richards & Pratt 1979; Stevenson 1989, 224).

Even scholars who have adhered to a strong institutionalist reading of Canadian federalism have had to turn to the configuration of Canadian society to explain how federalism in Canada has developed. For instance, in the opening pages of the third edition of his classic text *Canada in Question*, Donald Smiley claimed that the book "follows the general spirit of Cairns' assertion that 'contemporary Canadian federalism is about governments'" (Smiley 1980, 7). Yet when he sought to explain what he calls "the compounded crisis of Canadian federalism," Smiley turned to sociology and political economy:

"The compounded crisis of Canadian federalism" is a result of simultaneous and in all likelihood irreversible changes in three sets of relations which have in the most elemental way determined Canadian nationhood. These relations are those between (1) the English-speaking and French-speaking elements of Canada (2) the central heartland of Ontario/Quebec and the regions to the east and west of this heartland, and (3) Canadian and American structures of political and economic power (Smiley 1980, 252).

Federalism's often intimate relationship with society commends a comprehensive approach that seeks to integrate both state and society into an explanation of public policy. In effect, this was the thrust of Skocpol's earlier work, especially her classic study of the New Deal which explored the extent to which the *structure* of the state determines the *capacity* of the state to respond to societal pressures (Skocpol 1980). But the case of federalism suggests another possibility: institutions may actually shape and redirect societal influences, weakening some and strengthening others. It is in these terms that the policy impact of federalism can be best appreciated. We can identify a variety of ways in which this has occurred in the case of Canada.

Magnifying the Influence of Regionally Concentrated Social Forces

At the most obvious level, Canadian federalism has served to project societal influences onto policy-making. A classic case is manpower policy. During the 1960s French Quebec's historical determination to control all aspects of education, coupled with a new concern to direct the province's economic development, led the Quebec government to seek to assume responsibility for training and placement. Accordingly, the Quebec government established a province-wide system of manpower centres, even though a federal network already existed in Quebec. By the early 1970s Quebec had 94 federal manpower offices and 59 provincial offices. There could not be a clearer case of duplication, and the inevitable policy contradiction and incoherence. Quebec is the only government to establish such a provincially based infrastructure. Clearly, this situation would not have arisen if Canada were to be a unitary state (which, of course, would be a highly unlikely state of affairs).

Maintaining the Influence of Past Social Configurations

Second, federalism can serve to maintain policy influence for configurations of social forces that have lost much of their strength. As with other institutions, federalism can be seen as reflecting the relative balance of social forces at the time of its creation, even after that balance has changed.

For instance, at the time of Confederation, French-speaking and English-speaking leaders agreed that education should be a provincial matter, but for profoundly different reasons. French Canadians were determined that education be free from federal intervention, since they feared the federal government might reflect the assimilationist desires of its English-Canadian electoral majority. For their part, English Canadians apparently saw education as simply a local matter that, as such, should be under provincial responsibility.

There are many indications that both national integration and the challenges of the international economy have caused contemporary English Canadians to view the matter differently. The majority of English Canadians might well support the formal transfer of postsecondary education to the federal government, or at least to the status of a concurrent power.[9] And there has been considerable support for the federal suggestion of national standards for elementary and secondary education. Yet French Quebec has remained firm in its resolve that education be an exclusively provincial matter. Thus, any assertion of federal responsibility becomes problematic, even if it had majority support within Canada as a whole. To be sure, Quebec could be excluded from any such move. Under section 40 of the Constitution Act, 1982, it could be excluded from any formal transfer to the federal government of jurisdiction over education. However, many English Canadians would be uncomfortable with such a formalization of asymmetry, just as they are uncomfortable with asymmetry in intergovernmental agreements. All this greatly strengthens the hand of those interests in English Canada that remain opposed to a greater federal role.

Heightening the Influence of Territorial Interests

By definition, federalism institutionalizes a vision of politics that groups citizens according to their place of residence rather than their class, gender, race, religion, or other attributes. As we have seen, within some understandings of federalism there is a presumption that some of these other attributes, such as language or culture, may in fact be related to place of residence. Within this "sociological" approach to federalism the various subunits are seen to be composed of people largely of the same culture. Nonetheless, the actual divisions are defined on a geographical basis; there is almost certain to be some internal heterogeneity.

One might imagine a federalism in which citizens are indeed grouped on a cultural basis. Within such a "corporate" federalism, citizens of the same culture would share the same provincial (or state) government, wherever they may reside in the country. However, Canada's federalism is a territorial one. Thus, if the Quebec government has a special responsibility to protect and promote French language and culture, this stems from the fact that the overwhelming majority of the people living in the province are francophone.

By institutionalizing a politics based on territorial divisions, federalism not only downgrades the status of nonterritorial differences but directly impedes efforts to organize political action on the basis of them. Whether they are based upon class, ethnicity, or gender, for matters falling within provincial jurisdiction, nonterritorial interests are forced to fragment their strength and energy among ten separate structures based upon territorial divisions that may have little meaning to them.

At the same time, federalism's impact on nonterritorial groups is uneven. In effect, it can modify the relative balance among them. This can be seen most clearly in terms of how federalism can alter the distribution of political power between classes, and within them.

Relative Influence of Classes

The existence of two levels of government clearly has served to strengthen certain class forces, and weaken others, with important results for public policy.

Business versus Labour

In part, this effect derives from the way in which federalism carves the economy and society into provincial jurisdictions, thus complicating the actions of nationally based economic interests. More specifically, it appears to strengthen the hand of business over labour. Labour's influence over policy is much more dependent upon organization and mobilization than is business' influence, and the fragmentation of its membership over ten jurisdictions and the need to mobilize pressure upon two levels of government impede labour's capacity to exert influence over policy (Norrie, Simeon & Krasnick 1986, 145).

Specific Segments of Classes

Federalism has an additional effect: it creates states that have a clear interest in working with specific regionally based class forces. More is involved than politicians and bureaucrats simply "imposing" their interests on society. Nor need it be a case of class interests "using" the state, as in instrumentalist versions of Marxism. Especially in the context of federalism, state officials may *share* a common interest with particular classes: class power and state power may go hand in hand.

Fred Block posits a clear division of labour between "state managers," who have an interest in expanding the state while recognizing the need to maintain "business confidence," and capitalists, who share no class consciousness but are hostile to state expansion. He describes how state officials may achieve their goals of state expansion by responding to working-class forces, at times when business' countervailing power is weak:

> Pressures from the working class have contributed to the expansion of the state's role in the regulation of the economy and in the provision of services ... the major impetus for the extension of the state's role has come from the working class and from the managers of the state's apparatus, whose own powers expand with a growing state (Block 1987, 64).

To the extent that Canadian federalism has heightened the likelihood of working-class forces being able, in alliance with state managers, to secure such extensions of the state's role, then naturally public policy is affected. However, the fact of the matter is that only at the provincial level do we find governments—CCF and NDP—that fit this general pattern: state officials responding to working-class pressures with measures that expand their own base, and are adopted by other jurisdictions, despite clear business opposition. In some instances, federalism has indeed provided "bridgeheads" through which radical policies have been established and generalized to the rest of the country, following the logic that Pierre Trudeau commended to Canadian socialists (1968, 126).

The most celebrated instance through which innovative policies were pioneered and then generalized was the Saskatchewan government of T.C. Douglas, which primarily involved not workers (in the normal sense of the term) but farmers. However, an equally important instance is the 1960s Quebec government of Jean Lesage. Infused with new middle-class administrators who had a clear interest in state expansion, the Lesage government drew upon the support of organized labour to pursue not only policies that were quite conventional in comparative terms, such as the creation of a Ministry of Education, but innovative policies that were to have major influences upon Canada as whole. Quebec pioneered the use of pension funds as an investment pool. And it was the first jurisdiction in North America to grant the right to strike in the public sector—a gesture the federal government then adopted (McRoberts 1988).

At the same time, Canadian federalism has also enabled particular segments of business to acquire a force and influence they clearly would not have secured under a unitary system. Despite Block's analysis (coloured as it is by the American experience), business interests may well perceive an interest in state expansion if it is explicitly geared to strengthening their position. Both the Alberta and Quebec governments actively supported regionally based business classes whose interests were generally opposed by the dominant business class, which had been the primary force behind Confederation and had been able to count upon the federal government to promote its interests (Richards & Pratt 1979; Niosi 1980; Coleman 1984; McRoberts 1988). Clearly, neither Alberta's resource-based business class nor Quebec's francophone business class could have emerged if Canada had been a unitary system and there had been no provincial states with an interest in promoting them. The existence of these classes has had major policy implications. For instance, Alberta's business class was a major force against the federal government's National Energy Program; Quebec's business class has forced a reorientation of Ottawa's regulation of financial institutions.

CONCLUSION

To summarize, we have put forward the case that federalism has had a major effect on public policy in Canada. In part, we have argued, this impact derives from the way in which federalism has defined "the rules of the game" for policy-makers. We have documented a variety of possible effects, ranging from expanded opportunities for innovation and experimentation to heightened rigidity in established programs. But drawing upon the new institutionalist reading of political science, especially state theory, we have also pointed to more profound influences of federalism upon public policy, such as the introduction of intergovernmental struggles for legitimacy and the modification of societal influences both in accentuating territorially based interests and in altering the balance of influence among nonterritorial ones.

At the same time, in assessing these various effects, we must bear in mind scholars' warnings about the temptation to attribute too much weight to the influence of institutional factors. First, as we have seen, the effects of federalism on public policy often are uneven across policy sectors and may be contingent upon other factors. Intergovernmental competition and a resultant incoherence in policy are the hallmark of industrial policy: typically, provincial governments become the mouthpieces for one or two industries that dominate their respective economies. But intergovernmental conflict is less evident in agricultural policy: within each province the interests of producer groups are often in conflict and provincial governments, for their part, have not wanted to assume the federal government's heavy financial responsibility for farmers (Skogstad 1987, 202, 208). In general, provincial governments have been much more reluctant to cede jurisdiction to the federal government in health policy than in social policy, apparently because the former entails a complex of organizations, such as hospitals and the medical profession, with which provincial governments have long been closely involved (Banting 1987, 51).

Second, institutions other than federalism also have important effects upon public policy. For instance, Canada's electoral system, in which each district elects a single member on the basis of a simple plurality, helps to ensure that one party obtains a majority of the seats and thus can form the government without incorporating members of other parties. By the same token, it discriminates against third parties whose support is dispersed geographically. Both effects can well influence the content and direction of government policy.

Finally, much of federalism's impact on policy occurs through its ability to reinforce or recast influences from society and economy. Federalism does not create such forces as regionalism; the fact that western Canadians are under the influence of provincial government leaders who have a certain interest in exploiting resentment against central Canada may well increase the likelihood that they will have a sense of grievance against the federal government in particular, and central Canada in general. But the roots of this grievance lie in the economics of centre–hinterland relations. Nor did provincial political leaders create nationalism in the Quebec of the 1960s; they simply reshaped a national consciousness that dates back to the 1820s. In the last analysis, Canada has a federal system because it has a "federal society."

At the same time, having noted these various effects that federalism, or executive federalism, has on policy in Canada, we need to remind ourselves that often we are presuming a purely artificial alternative. As we have already noted, it is exceedingly difficult to imagine how Canada could have persisted as a unitary system. In all likelihood, it would have lost Quebec, and perhaps other provinces as well.

By the same token, as long as Canada is constituted of all ten provinces, it is difficult to see how Canadian federalism could take a fundamentally different form. The strength of the provincial governments follows inevitably from Quebec's continuing concern to occupy fully its spheres of jurisdiction. Given the strength of the provincial governments, it would be difficult to avoid the present degree of interpenetration. Whether intentionally or not, the separate actions of two levels of active governments are bound to have an impact on each other. By the same token, the differences in the preoccupations of Quebec and the other provinces are sufficient in themselves to require an extensive degree of asymmetry in federal–provincial arrangements. Finally, these conditions virtually require the elaborate mechanisms of executive federalism.

One aspect of Canadian federalism that might be amenable to change is the relative underdevelopment of intrastate federalism. In fact, recent constitutional discussions have been heavily coloured by demands for a reform of the Canadian Senate so that regional interests might be better reflected in federal institutions. Under proposals for a "Triple E" Senate, not only would the upper body be elected and have sufficient powers to be "effective," but it would be composed of an equal number of members from each province. Western Canadians, in particular, contend that only on that basis can they be assured that their interests will receive proper attention in Ottawa.

Nonetheless, there is a tension between this western Canadian strategy, focused upon "intrastate" federalism, and Quebec's traditional strategy to protect its interests, focused upon "interstate" federalism. Over the past 30 years, demands of Quebec nationalists for constitutional reform have focused primarily upon expanding the powers and status of the Quebec provincial government. In Quebec, proposals for Senate reform are viewed with concern, not just because they entail a reduction of Quebec's representation from its present 24 percent of the Senate, but because they reflect a different vision of how to protect and promote regional interests. In the limiting case, with a massive reinforcement of intrastate federalism, interstate federalism might lose much of its raison d'être. (In fact, there has appeared considerable resistance in English Canada to formalizing the first ministers' conferences – a key element of interstate federalism – on the grounds that they are fundamentally undemocratic. Thus, the 1991 report of the Quebec Liberal Party's constitutional committee, generally known as the Allaire Report (Parti libéral du Québec 1991), called for the outright abolition of the Senate, along with a massive reinforcement of provincial jurisdiction. Yet not only are many English Canadians wedded to senate reform, they are resistant to any significant enhancement of provincial jurisdiction.

In the last analysis, English Canada and Quebec now seem to be wedded to diametrically opposed visions of "renewal" of Canadian federalism: English Canada is increasingly stressing intrastate federalism, and Quebec is more committed than ever to interstate federalism, and the expansion of Quebec's jurisdiction. These conditions might be avoided through a massively asymmetrical federalism in which the federal government assumes new functions for all of Canada but Quebec. However, this is not a viable option in political terms, given English Canada's firm attachment to the principle of equality among the provinces. For that matter, some observers contend that such a level of asymmetry would be excluded by an institutional constraint: the need to determine whether Quebec MPs would be allowed to vote on bills that do not apply to their province.[10]

One is tempted to ask what the form of federalism would be if Canada no longer had to accommodate Quebec. Clearly, intrastate federalism would be much better developed. And a Canada without Quebec might well be less decentralized. For instance, we have noted how there might be extensive support in English Canada for transferring responsibility for postsecondary education to the federal level.

However, there is every reason to believe that a Canada without Quebec would still need some form of federal system. The form of federalism would differ, as would its influences on policy. With or without Quebec, federalism will continue to be a fact of Canadian political life and, in a variety of ways, an influence on Canadian public policy.

NOTES

1. Garth Stevenson surveys the range of definitions of federalism in Stevenson (1989, 3-9).

2. This definition draws in particular upon Smiley (1987, 2) and Riker (1964, 5).

3. For his part, Smiley does include intrastate representation in his definition of federalism (Smiley 1987, 2).

4. Under the Constitution Act, 1867, the federal government has the power to disallow provincial laws during the first year of their enactment, to instruct the lieutenant governor not to sign bills passed by provincial legislatures (reservation), and to declare "works" within provincial jurisdiction to be in the national interest and thus under federal jurisdiction (declaratory power). One noted scholar of federalism, K.C. Wheare, wrote that, on this basis, Canada did not constitute a federal system (quoted in Stevenson 1982, 30).

5. Leslie Pal makes a compelling argument that the Constitution was indeed "a real barrier" to the adoption of unemployment insurance (Pal 1988, 151).

6. Richard A. Olmsted, *Decisions of the Judicial Committee of the Privy Council relating to the British North America Act, 1867 and the Canadian Constitution 1867-1954* (Ottawa: Queen's Printer 1954), 94-124, quoted in Stevenson 1989, 48.

7. See also Fletcher & Wallace 1986, 141.

8. Similarly, in their comprehensive survey, Norrie, Simeon, and Krasnick conclude:

    Divided jurisdiction *has not caused us to be denied policies or programs that were genuinely desired*, nor has it caused us to have policies thrust upon us unwillingly. However, the limits of the policies and their specific details probably do reflect the influence of federalism (1986, 148; emphasis added).

9. This would achieve several objectives that have widespread support. National standards in access to postsecondary education could be better secured if Ottawa could fund institutions, and students, directly rather than rely upon provincial governments as conduits. For that matter, Ottawa might be more inclined to fund postsecondary education if it were to receive full credit for doing so. Most important, if university curricula are to be reshaped to meet concerns about Canada's international competitiveness, as

many business groups clearly want, this can best be achieved through federal direction. Some English Canadians might even be prepared to extend the same logic to secondary and elementary education, in light of Ottawa's recent concern with national standards of literacy and work skills.

10. This particular problem may be overstated. See McRoberts (1991).

CHAPTER 6

The Courts and Public Policy

Ian Greene

INTRODUCTION

From the perspective of the policy process, the fundamental difference between courts and other institutions considered in this book is that the other institutions evolved with full recognition that they were to be part of the policy-making process, whereas the courts, as institutions for dispute resolution, were intended to be isolated from policy-making. As well, it was obviously intended that the other institutions would produce policies that functioned effectively, which often meant that these institutions were expected to be creative and innovative. Courts, on the other hand, were supposed to be predictable—to promote stability and order. An innovative judge is often regarded with suspicion by colleagues on the bench because innovation implies a tendency to tamper with the established common law.

Notwithstanding these expectations, courts have always had some impact on the policy process in Canada, whether by filling in the gaps in laws that have been carelessly drafted or by developing their own interpretation of the text of clear laws (with such interpretations, at times, at variance with the intent of legislators). It is common knowledge that the Judicial Committee of the Privy Council, which as part of the House of Lords in the United Kingdom functioned as Canada's highest court of appeal until 1949, was vital in turning Canada into one of the world's most decentralized federations in spite of a centralizing constitution (Russell, Knopff & Morton 1989). More recently, the Canadian Charter of Rights and Freedoms has undeniably broadened

---

I would like to thank Peter Russell for his very helpful comments on an earlier draft of this chapter. As well, I am indebted to Michael Atkinson for his careful reading of the chapter and his thoughtful suggestions for improvements.

the policy-making role of the courts. Judicial decisions under the Charter—such as the renunciation of the Lord's Day Act in 1985, the striking down of the abortion provisions in the Criminal Code in 1988, and the rejection of part of Quebec's French-only outdoor signs legislation in 1988—have drawn widespread public attention to the policy-making role of the courts for the first time (Supreme Court of Canada 1985c, 1988a, 1988b).

This chapter analyzes the connection between the courts as institutions in Canada and public-policy outcomes. It will argue that the way in which courts are structured as institutions makes them poorly suited for a major role in policy development, but well-suited to episodic intervention into the policy process to promote procedural fairness and equality of treatment. This intermittent intervention is important because the more policy-oriented institutions are usually evaluated in terms of their contribution to efficiency, effectiveness and political expediency, rather than the promotion of procedural fairness and equality.

Too often, debates about court involvement in the policy-making process are framed in somewhat artificial terms of whether the courts should or should not be involved. Notwithstanding that courts were designed purely as dispute-resolution devices, they have always been involved in the policy process and always will be, because judges must necessarily flesh out the bare structure of laws. It is more useful to analyze exactly how the courts are involved and then discuss means to promote what courts are good at in the policy process and minimize the harm they could do in the realms to which they are not suited.

DEFINITIONS AND BACKGROUND

Courts

For the purposes of this chapter, the term courts refers to both the judicial tribunals staffed by the nearly 2 000 officials known as superior or inferior court judges, and the hundreds of administrative tribunals established by federal, provincial, and municipal governments that perform quasi-judicial functions.

Thanks to Peter Russell's insights into the impact of courts on public policy, Canadian political scientists cannot help but appreciate the influence that judicial decisions have had on public policy. (See, for example, Russell 1985, 1988a.) To analyze the causal interrelations from a slightly different perspective, focussing on the impact of court structure on public policy, presents a challenging task. However, the job is made easier by the implicit link between judicial policy-making and court structure, which is a theme throughout Russell's classic analysis of the Canadian court system, *The Judiciary in Canada: The*

Third Branch of Government (1987). Readers who desire a more comprehensive knowledge of the nature of courts in Canada are well advised to familiarize themselves with these sources.

The chapter will begin by exploring the nexus between judicial policy-making and public-policy outcomes. It will then explore three elements of political institutions that come to mind as a result of the definition of political institutions employed by Michael Atkinson in his Introduction to this book: "configurations or networks of organizational capabilities ... that are deployed according to rules and norms that structure individual participation, govern appropriate behaviour, and limit the range of acceptable outcomes." The three elements are institutional rules, institutional capacity, and the human element in the courts.

Public Policy

This chapter will utilize the same definition of public policy as that employed by Michael Atkinson in Chapter 1: "a course of action adopted by public authorities in relation to a problem on the public agenda."

The policy-making process involves public servants, legislators, interested members of the public, interest groups, and judges. One realistic and insightful description of this process is that developed by Hogwood and Gunn (1984), except that like most policy analysts, they neglected to take into account the role of the courts. Figure 6.1 summarizes the policy process according to Hogwood and Gunn, but in addition takes into account the impact of judicial decisions.

FIGURE 6.1
STAGES IN THE CIRCULAR PUBLIC POLICY-MAKING PROCESS, ACCOUNTING FOR THE INTERVENTION OF COURTS

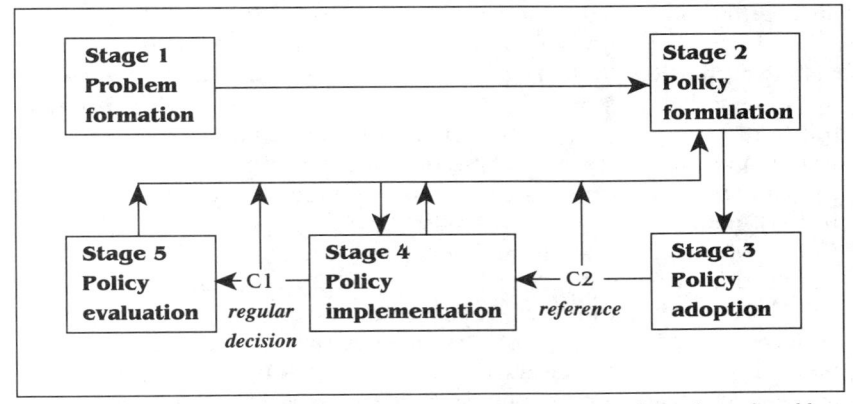

Stage 1 Problem formation	→	Stage 2 Policy formulation
Stage 5 Policy evaluation	←C1— *regular decision* — Stage 4 Policy implementation ←C2— *reference*	Stage 3 Policy adoption

Source: Adapted from B. Hogwood and L. Gunn (1984), *Policy analysis for the real world*. Oxford and New York: Oxford University Press

Stage 1 refers to the way in which legislators, government policy analysts, and interest groups conceptualize a particular problem that they perceive as requiring a public-policy solution. Stage 2 alludes to the development of various approaches for tackling the problem identified in Stage 1. At Stage 3, one of these approaches is selected and codified into law and at Stage 4 the policy is implemented. The policy as implemented is usually somewhat different from the policy formulated at Stage 2 or selected and legislated at Stage 3 because of the involvement of different personalities and the institutional structures of implementation. Stage 5—a systematic evaluation of the policy to determine the extent to which it is actually solving the problem first identified in Stage 1—does not occur often enough, although the prevalence of good program evaluations has increased at all levels of government in Canada over the past decade.

Adjudication

Courts are government-sponsored dispute-resolution centres in which officials, called judges or adjudicators, have been given the power to decide controversies. The decision-making process employed by courts is known as "adjudication." Adjudication is distinct from other dispute-resolution systems such as negotiation, mediation, and arbitration. Once a party takes a dispute to court, the opposing party must also appear or face sanctions determined by the state. Unlike negotiation or mediation, it is the judge who decides the controversy, not the disputing parties. Like mediation and arbitration, in adjudication there is a neutral third party (the judge), but unlike a mediator, the judge has the power to decide the dispute rather than simply encourage a settlement. And unlike most forms of arbitration, the judge must decide in conformity with the whole body of relevant law.

Adjudication is appropriate for disputes whose settlement is necessary for the preservation of order in a society. Adjudication is inappropriate in cases where public order is not so important and where the disputing parties could reach a satisfactory settlement themselves (here, negotiation is more appropriate) or with some help from a neutral third party (here, mediation is more appropriate). Adjudication is also inappropriate in cases where an imposed settlement is necessary, but where that settlement need not be decided according to the whole body of relevant law (here, arbitration is more appropriate).

One of the disturbing trends in modern society is the use of adjudication to settle disputes for which another form of dispute resolution would be more appropriate. The reasons for the overuse of adjudication are beyond the scope of this chapter, but they relate to a lack of public knowledge of alternative forms of dispute resolution, the private interests of some members of the legal profession, and the breakdown of community and the resulting personal isolation connected with industrial and postindustrial society. This latter trend makes it difficult for many to understand opposing points of view so that when they are involved in a dispute, there is a tendency to believe that they are "in the right" and the other person is clearly "in the wrong." Given these assumptions about right and wrong, it is easily concluded that a court of law will decide in favour of the "right" party, and therefore the most logical means to settle the dispute is to take it to a court of law.

THE COURTS IN THE POLICY-MAKING PROCESS

Courts become involved in the policy-making process when a litigant claims that a policy related to the dispute being litigated has not been implemented according to law, or that the policy itself is unconstitutional. The greatest court-related influence is likely to occur at the point labelled "C1" in Figure 6.1. At this point, an adjudicator may make a decision that changes how a policy is implemented; in 1985 the Supreme Court of Canada changed the way in which policy toward drinking drivers was implemented when it ruled that police must inform drivers suspected of drinking of their right to counsel before taking them to a police station for a breathalyzer test (Supreme Court of Canada 1985d). Occasionally, a court may completely end the implementation of a policy, as the Supreme Court of Canada did when it struck down the federal Lord's Day Act (Supreme Court of Canada 1985c).

But Canadian courts can sometimes intervene at point C2, which represents a decision in a reference case that occurs before a policy is fully implemented. A reference case results from a question put to a provincial court of appeal by the provincial cabinet, or to the Supreme Court of Canada by the federal cabinet. For example, in an attempt to stop the Trudeau government's plans to patriate the Canadian Constitution in 1981 without substantial provincial consent, the provincial cabinets of Manitoba, Quebec, and Newfoundland sent reference questions to their provincial courts of appeal to ask whether the Trudeau government's plans were legally permissible and whether they violated a constitutional convention. The three courts produced different answers, all of which were considered by the Supreme Court of Canada later in 1981. The top court's answer, which was that Trudeau's plans were legal but a violation of convention, forced the provinces and the federal government to resume their talks, and these negotiations resulted in the 1982 constitutional settlement (Russell 1982). It should be noted that reference cases do not always occur prior to the implementation of a policy; they may sometimes occur later at point C1.

On most occasions when a court intervenes in the policy process whether at point C1 or C2, it is more likely than not that the court will simply rubber stamp the policy so that its implementation proceeds as it normally would. For example, from 1982 to December 1988, the Supreme Court of Canada decided in favour of individual Charter of Rights claims—decisions that changed policy implementation—only 30 percent of the time (Russell 1988a). In the courts below the Supreme Court of Canada, individual Charter "wins" varied from 26 percent to 32 percent up to 1985 (Morton 1987).

The possible outcomes of court intervention into policy can be divided into three general categories:

- The policy may be confirmed as conforming to standards set by relevant legal tests such as the Canadian Charter of Rights and Freedoms. For example, in the 1987 Alberta Labour Reference, the Supreme Court confirmed the validity, in the face of the Charter, of Alberta's labour laws with regard to their restrictions on the right to strike of public employees (Supreme Court of Canada 1987b). As noted above, confirmation of an existing policy is the most likely potential outcome.

- The implementation of the policy may be amended to some extent, as in the Supreme Court's 1985 decision in the *Singh* case. This decision resulted in a major change to the method in which the Canada Employment and Immigration Commission implemented its refugee-determination policy. Prior to this decision unsuccessful refugee applicants might be deported without ever having had an oral hearing before an impartial tribunal. As a result of the *Singh* decision, all refugee applicants on Canadian soil are entitled to at least one oral hearing (Supreme Court of Canada 1985b).

- The policy may be completely abolished, leaving a policy vacuum. Such was the result of the Supreme Court's 1988 decision in the *Morgentaler* case, which left the federal government without an implementable abortion policy (Supreme Court of Canada 1988b). The complete negation of a policy by a court is the least likely outcome.

The examples given above all refer to the Supreme Court of Canada, and all refer to Charter of Rights cases. It should not be forgotten, however, that policy-making can occur at all levels of judicial and quasi-judicial proceedings. Although the Charter has provided new scope for the policy-modification role of courts, the courts have always had some influence on policy both in constitutional and nonconstitutional cases. For example, until 1988 Saskatoon pet-control officials had taken it for granted that a city by-law that prohibited dog-owners from allowing their dogs "to run at large" in a public park meant that the owners had to keep their canine friends on a leash. However, in

1988 a University of Saskatchewan mathematics professor, who had recently moved to Saskatoon, read the by-law and innocently concluded that it required him to have control of his dog, but not necessarily to have the dog on a leash. While walking his unleashed dog one day, the professor was charged with breach of the by-law. He pleaded not guilty and won his case: as a result, the city of Saskatoon suddenly had a new policy for preventing dogs from running at large (McCormick & Greene 1990, iv).

An example that illustrates an administrative tribunal's effect on policy through a Charter case is a decision of an immigration adjudicator in Montreal who, on October 10, 1991, ruled that "a two-year delay in hearing a refugee claim violates the Constitution and entitles the claimants to apply for admission to Canada as landed immigrants" (Oziewicz 1991). As a result of this decision, Canada's immigration policy affecting the thousands of refugee claimants whose cases have been delayed two years or more was changed, at least pending an appeal of this decision to a higher court.

A third example is the 1984 decision of an Alberta trial court judge that resulted in the abandonment of the section of the federal Elections Expenses Act that prohibited advertising for or against candidates by groups other than political parties. This section of the legislation, which regulated political advertising, was passed in 1983 with the support of all three major national parties. The rationale behind the legislation was that without such restrictions, the legislated limits on election spending would be meaningless. The provision prohibiting advertising by nonparty groups was challenged by the National Citizens' Coalition, a right-wing lobby group, as a violation of the Charter. The NCC won the case in the Alberta Court of Queen's Bench, the province's superior trial court, three months before the 1984 federal general election. The Liberal government decided not to appeal, possibly because of the unknown political fallout that would result given the approaching election. Although the decision only affected the federal election laws as they were applied in Alberta, the chief electoral officer decided not to enforce the nonparty advertising provisions in other parts of the country so that the same rules would apply Canadawide (Hiebert 1989).

It should be noted that policy decisions of courts can sometimes have an impact on the policy process in distant jurisdictions. For example, in July 1991 a Quebec Superior Court trial judge found that the legislated prohibition of tobacco advertising constituted a violation of freedom of expression as guaranteed by the Charter of Rights. More significantly, the judge found that this Charter violation could not be justified as a "reasonable limit" under Section 1 of the Charter because there was inadequate proof that banning tobacco advertising reduces tobacco consumption. Leaving aside the fact that few judges are trained in the assessment of social-science evidence, this decision had a limited impact on the Canadian policy process regarding tobacco advertising because of the possibility that the decision would be reversed on appeal. Nevertheless, thanks to the reputation of the judiciary as being impartial and incorruptible, a judicial pronouncement on a policy can carry a great deal of weight in the forum of public opinion. Recognizing this, the Tobacco Advisory Council in the United Kingdom, a lobby group for the tobacco industry, took out a full two-page advertisement in *The Times*, a leading British newspaper, on February 13, 1992, to make the following claim:

> (The European Community) wants to ban the advertising of tobacco. Their argument is that this would bring about a reduction in the consumption of tobacco. The facts, however, do not support this view. ... Well, there has now been a real and thorough judicial examination of all the evidence. For the first time ever, an impartial authority has assessed the evidence and weighed the merits of the arguments. The results were published in a Canadian court judgement in July of last year. The court found *no* proven connection between advertising and overall tobacco consumption. And *no* proof that a ban on advertising causes a decrease in overall consumption of tobacco. In fact the court also found a ban on advertising to be "a form of censorship and social engineering which is incompatible with the very essence of a free and democratic society." So there is no proof that the banning of tobacco advertising reduces overall consumption (Tobacco Advisory Council 1992).

Adjudicative policy-making itself can be defined as the process of interpreting the law in a manner that changes a public policy. In other words, if a policy changes at Stage 2, 3, or 4 in Figure 6.1 as a result of the court intervention, adjudicative policy-making has taken place. Even when a court merely confirms the legal validity of an existing policy, this endorsement can sometimes have an impact on the policy in question. For instance, with regard to the Alberta Labour Reference example referred to above, the Supreme Court's stamp of approval on Alberta's legislation limiting strikes of public employees was subsequently used by the provincial government as a justification for dealing more harshly with striking nurses than it might otherwise have done (Greene 1989, 89–90).

THE STRUCTURE OF THE COURTS AND THE POLICY PROCESS

There are three features of the hierarchical structure of courts in Canada that are important when analyzing the policy process. First, as Figure 6.2 shows, the appeals hierarchy is a centralizing one. This means that all public policies, whether federal or provincial, may eventually be called into question by federally appointed judges in the

FIGURE 6.2
CANADA'S COURT STRUCTURE

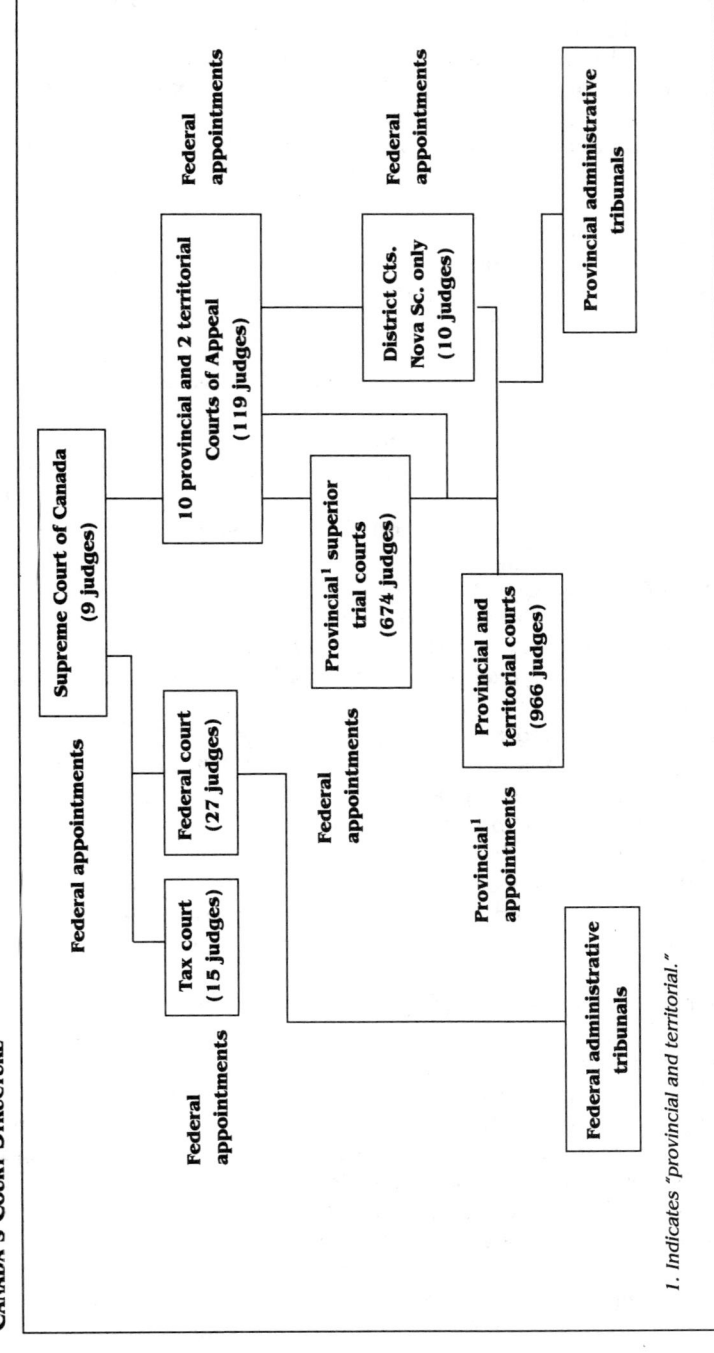

```
Federal appointments

                    Supreme Court of Canada
                          (9 judges)
                              |
        ┌─────────────────────┼──────────────────────┐
        |                                            |
   Federal court                           10 provincial and 2 territorial
   (27 judges)                              Courts of Appeal
        |                                     (119 judges)      — Federal appointments
   Tax court                                       |
   (15 judges)                            ┌────────┴────────┐
                                          |                 |
                                  Provincial¹ superior   District Cts.
                                   trial courts          Nova Sc. only
                                    (674 judges)         (10 judges)     — Federal appointments
                                          |
                                  Federal appointments
                                          |
                                  Provincial and
                                  territorial courts
                                    (966 judges)
                                          |
                                  Provincial¹
                                  appointments
                                          |
                        ┌─────────────────┴──────────────────┐
                 Federal administrative              Provincial administrative
                       tribunals                            tribunals
```

1. Indicates "provincial and territorial."

Source: Adapted from I. Green (1991), The administration of justice. In R.M. Krause and R.H. Wagenberg (Eds.), *Introductory readings in Canadian government and politics* (p.328). Mississauga: Copp Clark Pitman.

provincial superior courts or the Supreme Court of Canada. Second, a typical case in which a policy is on trial is heard first in a provincial trial court and then appealed to the provincial Court of Appeal. After this, an appeal to the Supreme Court of Canada can occur with the permission (leave) of the Supreme Court of Canada itself, and the Court grants leave only to about one-fifth of the, approximately, 400 leave applications that it receives each year. Therefore, the time it takes for a case to wend its way from a provincial trial court to the Supreme Court of Canada is almost always measured in years. Third, the 800 or so superior and district court judges (45 percent of the total number of judges) are appointed by the federal cabinet, while judges below the superior and district court level are appointed by the provincial cabinets.

Since Confederation, political patronage has played a major part in the appointment of judges at both levels, but since the early 1970s most provinces have adopted nonpartisan judicial selection procedures (McCormick & Greene 1990, 37ff.). The story is not so rosy with regard to the federally appointed judges, however. A 1990 study showed that in spite of some improvements to the procedure for appointing federal judges during the past two decades, the Mulroney government tended to appoint judges who were ideologically aligned with the Progressive Conservative Party (Russell & Zeigel 1989). Some improvements were made in the early 1970s when the federal minister of Justice established a system of nationwide contacts with prominent jurists and deans of law schools to recruit outstanding candidates; as well, the names of potential appointees began to be screened by a committee of the Canadian Bar Association. In 1988 the Justice minister established a system of provincial and territorial assessment committees to advise the Minister whether potential federal appointees are qualified for the job. These five-member committees represent the bench, the legal profession, the provincial or territorial attorney general, and the federal minister of Justice. The major weakness of these committees is that they are limited to commenting on names put forward by the minister of Justice.

One result of the system of recruitment and appointment of judges in Canada is that a disproportionate number of them are drawn from the ranks of the economically priviledged. Those of English and French ethnic backgrounds are overrepresented and so are men (only about 7 percent of Canada's judges are women). The average age of judges at all levels in Canada is 57. Judges—especially superior court judges—tend to be high-achievers, and two-thirds of the superior court judges have held executive positions in the law society or bar association. Most have been members of a political party (most frequently of the party in office when they were appointed). With the exception of a very few provincially appointed judges, all judges in Canada are lawyers, and most have many years experience in a private law practice. Very few, however, have any experience in public-policy analysis (McCormick & Greene 1990, ch. 3). Given their backgrounds, it is unlikely that judges would make many policy-related decisions that could be considered radical.

The association between court structure and the modification of public policies might be represented, in an oversimplified manner, as in Figure 6.3. It is important to keep in mind Atkinson's cautionary advice in Chapter 1 about investigating causal links. As Figure 6.3 indicates, court structure is just one factor that should be taken into account when analyzing the relation between adjudicative decisions and the modification of public policies; other influences are probably more cogent in explaining both adjudicative decisions and public policy outcomes in most situations. Even so, a full understanding of the policy process cannot come about if the impact of courts is ignored.
The way in which court structure affects adjudicative decisions that modify public policies can be diagnosed from the perspective of three subject areas: the rules of courts, the institutional capacity of courts, and the "human element" in court organization.

RULES OF COURT ORGANIZATIONS

For the purposes of this chapter, the relevant rules of the adjudicative process in Canada can be divided into three categories: impartiality, the settlement of disputes according to law, and the adversary system.

FIGURE 6.3
CAUSAL LINKS BETWEEN COURT STRUCTURE AND POLICY MODIFICATION

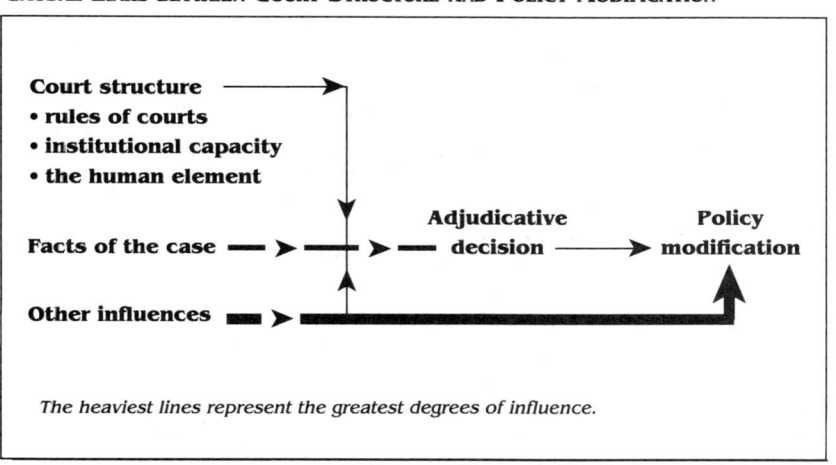

Court structure
• rules of courts
• institutional capacity
• the human element

Facts of the case → → Adjudicative decision → Policy modification

Other influences →

The heaviest lines represent the greatest degrees of influence.

Impartiality

Complete impartiality is impossible, but adjudicators are expected to be as impartial as humanly possible. One way in which impartiality is encouraged is through providing adjudicators with independence: the ability to make impartial decisions without interference from others, especially other government actors. As a result, judges are appointed until retirement age, their salaries are insulated from executive-branch tampering, and they have a right to control court procedures that have a direct bearing on adjudication (McCormick & Greene 1990, 4 ff.). Adjudicators in administrative tribunals are expected to have the degree of independence that is appropriate to their functions.

The impartiality rule means that it is not legitimate to attempt to co-opt adjudicators into taking a particular stand in the policy process. For example, in 1979 the deputy attorney general of British Columbia was of the opinion that a particular provincial court judge might make a decision that could call into question the constitutionality of the province's new Family Relations Act. He feared that such a decision would have a disastrous effect on the implementation of the policy authorized by the Act. As a result, the deputy telephoned the judge to inquire whether he might be willing to transfer himself to another court so as to avoid hearing a case in which the constitutionality issue would be raised. The judge made public the telephone call; a subsequent judicial inquiry not only confirmed a violation of judicial independence, but through the publicity surrounding the issue made such violations unlikely to happen again (Greene 1988, 202–203).

The Settlement of Disputes According to Law

An impartial adjudicative system is the cornerstone of any rule-of-law regime. The normative goal is that the country is to be ruled by laws applied equally to everyone, and not by the arbitrary decisions of public officials. The result is that when courts become involved in the policy process, the wording of the policy in the form of statutes and regulations becomes all-important, even if that wording is at variance with what was originally intended by the policy. According to conventional wisdom, judicial intervention in policy development is confined to the "interstices" of legislation—to filling in the gaps not covered by legislation while applying literally the words actually employed in legislation.

At Stage 3 of the policy-making process shown in Figure 6.1, a policy must be translated into law and approved by the appropriate legislature or regulatory body. Because of the possible intervention of courts, this step in the policy process is critical, but its importance is often underestimated by students of public policy. Frequently, the lawyers who work as legislative draftspersons do not have the policy expertise to understand fully the policy implications of their drafts, and most commonly the policy analysts in the various government departments do not have enough legal expertise to catch potential policy lapses in draft legislation.

A personal anecdote may help to illustrate the potential discrepancy between policy implementation and legislation. During my three years working in middle-management for Alberta Social Services, it was a rare experience for me to meet a social worker who had actually read the income-security or child-welfare legislation that he or she was enforcing. What was relied on instead was the policy manual. The policy manual, although an interpretation of the legislation, was sometimes at variance with the legislation in subtle ways. Occasionally an overzealous child-welfare group-home inspector might force the group-home operators to conform to standards—however important—that did not exist in legislation; sometimes applicants for income security were turned down because of departmental policies that were not reflected in legislation. As a result, I was initially surprised that the department was not involved in more lawsuits, but then I learned that the poor rarely litigate, and few lawyers have a grasp on social policy. Thanks to legal aid and an increasing number of lawyers with a background in social policy, however, this situation may be changing; if so, the result may be increased court intervention in the implementation of social policy.

The Demand for Specificity

The rule of law demands a certain amount of specificity in laws intended to put a particular policy into effect. In some fields, especially health and social services, there is a tendency for the policy-makers to give professional health and social workers a fair degree of discretion in administering government programs. But at some point, too much discretion can lead to arbitrary decisions and therefore to unwarranted discrimination. The old ideological debate between A.V. Dicey, who argued in favour of limiting the discretion of public servants as much as possible, and Sir Ivor Jennings, who advocated giving more flexibility to modern, educated public servants, especially those in the social services, will likely always be with us (Dicey 1885; Jennings 1959). What this means is that judges will not infrequently be called on to decide whether the actions of public servants as justified by their policy manuals go beyond what is permitted by legislation.

The Role of Precedent

Precedent is an integral part of the legal regime in both the civil and common-law traditions, but thanks to the doctrine of *stare decisis*, precedent is stressed a great deal more in most common-law jurisdictions. *Stare decisis* is a particularly rigid version of the doctrine of precedent that holds that the decisions of higher courts in the same jurisdiction are always binding on lower courts concerning the interpretation given to the law. As well, the decisions of courts of equal or higher status in other common-law jurisdictions are persuasive. How a particular law will be interpreted by the courts, therefore, is contingent on the whole history of interpretation of other relevant laws. Without an adequate grasp on that history, legislative draftspersons could produce legislation that, from a legal perspective, does not accurately reflect the policy outcome desired by those who originally adopted the policy at Stage 2 (Figure 6.1). For example, the "Peace, Order and Good Government" (POGG) clause contained in the preamble to Section 91 of the Constitution Act, 1867, has had a long and torturous history in the courts, which policy-makers designing an anti-inflation policy, for example, need to be aware of. The most recent precedents would allow the federal Parliament to rely on the POGG clause to enact temporary legislation to control serious inflation, although such legislation need not be worded so that it is obviously temporary (Supreme Court of Canada 1976).

Stare decisis has also resulted in a body of rules of interpretation developed by the courts that guide adjudicators when faced with applying seemingly contradictory laws. These contradictions might result from two laws enacted by the same legislature, from a federal and a provincial law, or from an ordinary law and the Constitution. The court factor in the policy process therefore makes it incumbent on legislative draftspersons to be aware of the context of the laws they are drafting, that is the larger legal regime. For example, one rule of interpretation is that in case of an incompatibility between two laws enacted by the same legislature, the more recent law takes precedence. Two related government departments, such as a provincial department of social services and a provincial department of health, have interests that overlap to some extent. It might happen, therefore, that a new law sponsored by the Department of Health regarding the health benefits available to the mentally handicapped might inadvertently amend an older Department of Social Services law regarding income-security benefits for the mentally handicapped without the policy-makers in the latter department being aware of such a development until litigation draws it to their attention.

Stare decisis produced a body of rules of evidence most of which has now been translated into statutes. These rules limit the kinds of evidence that may be considered by courts. For example, hearsay evidence, or evidence obtained about a particular event by listening to someone else's account of the event, is not acceptable in a court. Survey research is an integral part of policy development and program evaluation, but sometimes judges give some survey results little weight because of their resemblance to hearsay evidence.

Over the years, courts have developed strict rules of procedure designed to be fair to both sides in a dispute. (These rules are updated from time to time usually by a committee of judges or a joint bench-and-bar committee, and then rubber-stamped by the appropriate legislature.) The rules provide deadlines for the filing of appropriate documents, procedures for giving notice of certain facts and arguments to the other side, and rules for argument in court. Witnesses may not provide evidence on their own, but only in reply to questions from counsel or the adjudicator, and they may be cross-examined. Evidence must be introduced at the appropriate time in proceedings or not at all, and so on.

This court-developed method of uncovering the facts relevant to a dispute, and then applying the appropriate law to these facts, is quite different from the methods used at the various stages in the regular policy process. In most stages of the process, procedures are at the same time more informal and flexible, and more rigorous in terms of social-science methods. As noted by Horowitz (1977), courts are good at discovering what actually happened in a particular factual situation, but not good at the policy-development process of determining what ought to happen. As well, when policy analysts are called on to give evidence in court, they may fail miserably in getting their points across, whereas in the forum of departmental policy analysis, they are extremely skilled.

The Adversary System and the Role of Lawyers

The adversary system is part of the particular style of adjudication that has developed in the common-law world. The nine predominantly anglophone provinces in Canada are part of the common-law world, as is the federal legal system. Even in Quebec, which remains part of the civil-law world, the adversary system has developed a strong foothold. The two basic tenets of the adversary system are, first, that it is up to one or both of the parties in a dispute to take that dispute to court, and, second, once a dispute is in court, it is up to the parties themselves to present evidence and arguments. Judges may not do their own investigation of the facts of a dispute.

Courts hear whatever cases come to them according to the rules of filing cases. They cannot search out disputes to resolve, nor can they refuse cases that come to them and are within their jurisdictions. They have been compared to defective clocks: they have to be shaken to get them going. The result is that whether courts get involved in the policy process at the points shown in Figure 6.1 is very much a hit-and-miss affair. It depends on factors outside of the courts themselves: for example, the eagerness of particular counsel or interest groups to question a policy in court, whether the legal expenses can be covered, the potential use of litigation to slow down the implementation of a policy or bring publicity to it even if the case is weak, and so on.

In the common-law world, courts are heavily dependent on an independent legal profession. Members of the legal profession have privileges in the adjudicative process not open to non-barristers, and adjudicators rely almost entirely on members of the profession for evidence. Therefore, lawyers control access to the courts, and the quality of public policy evidence provided to courts is dependent on the ability of lawyers to find and understand the evidence and to present it accurately and in a fashion which is comprehensible to adjudicators.

Arguments presented by lawyers pursuant to Section 1 of the Charter of Rights illustrate this point. Section 1 is the limitations clause, which guarantees the rights and freedoms contained in the Charter "subject only to such reasonable limits prescribed by law as can be demonstrably justified in a free and democratic society." In Charter cases in which the validity of legislation implementing a public policy is the issue, there is often a prima facie limitation on a Charter right somewhere in the legislation. Therefore, the outcome often depends on the adjudicators' interpretation of Section 1 of the Charter. The Supreme Court has stipulated that, among other things, two criteria must be met in order for a limitation to a Charter right to be legally acceptable. First, the limitation on rights must be rationally connected to the policy objective of the legislation. Second, the limit must interfere with rights as little as necessary in order to achieve the policy objective of the legislation (Supreme Court of Canada 1986; Greene 1989, 220). For a Section 1 argument to be effective in court, therefore, counsel arguing in support of the legislation must have a clear understanding of the objectives of the policy that the legislation represents, must be able to explain how limiting a right is rationally connected to the policy objective, and must be able to show how the policy selected limits rights less than other feasible policy alternatives. It would appear that some judges are not overly impressed with the ability of the legal profession to present such policy-oriented evidence competently. Even at the level of the Supreme Court of Canada, in at least three decisions the judges have complained in their opinions about the poor quality of the Section 1 arguments by lawyers (Greene 1989, 220).

Another implication of the adversary system is that when courts become involved in the policy process, there is a tendency to exaggerate arguments for and against particular policies. As noted by George Hoberg in Chapter 10, when environmental policies go to court there is an "assumption of conflict, a far cry from the consensus-building efforts of multistakeholder forums." The rules of court, designed to settle sharp disputes between two parties where one is clearly in the wrong, divide policy stakeholders into two camps, one completely in favour of the policy and the other dead-set against it. Few policies are as good or as bad as counsel make them out to be. Counsel for the government usually adopt a stand that is the opposite of their opponents, whether or not that stand contradicts a larger policy agenda of the government. In Charter cases, this means that government lawyers usually argue for the most restrictive possible interpretation of the document, while at the same time their political masters may be giving speeches about the importance of a broad protection of human rights in the constitution.

Overall, the impact of the rules that courts have adopted ensure that they become involved in the public-policy process on an intermittent and unpredictable basis, and that when they become involved, public-policy evidence must be presented in ways that neither lawyers nor public policy specialists are used to. The result is that, unless the potential impact of court involvement is better understood by public policy analysts, such court involvement is likely to throw a monkey wrench into the machinery of policy development.

ORGANIZATIONAL CAPACITY

Adapting the analysis of Chapter 1, this chapter will refer to the organizational capacity of the courts as the ability to define and pursue (organizational) objectives without heavy reliance on external sources of expertise or direction. To what extent can the courts pursue their primary organizational objective as it relates to the policy process—the adjudication of disputes involving public policy issues in a fair, expeditious, and impartial manner—without heavy reliance on external sources of advice and expertise?

Independence of the Judiciary

One important feature of courts, as noted above, is their independence. The principle of judicial independence is now, to some extent, enforceable by the judiciary itself thanks to Section 11(d) of the Charter, which guarantees persons charged with offences the right to a hearing by an "independent and impartial tribunal" (Greene 1988). Judicial independence does guarantee the courts a great deal of autonomy in the sense that they cannot be subjected to external direction in decision-making. This autonomy enhances the capacity of courts to impact the policy process.

The independence of administrative tribunals is sometimes questionable, however. For example, a 1991 review by the Law Reform Commission of Canada of the procedures for determining refugee status expressed some question about the ability of members of the Immigration and Refugee Review Board to decide independently (Law Reform Commission of Canada 1991). Given the renewable nature of their appointments, concern was expressed that some board members may tend to decide cases in favour of the Department of Employment and Immigration's perceived goals in order to improve their chances of renewed appointment. The less the independence enjoyed by an administrative tribunal, the less the capacity of the tribunal to make an original contribution to the policy process.

Reliance on External Expertise

Another critical element in assessing the institutional capacity of courts is the extent to which they must rely on external expertise for information. It has already been pointed out that because of the adversary system, adjudicators must rely on the expertise of counsel for evidence. Some superior courts in Canada, particularly appeal courts, have been able to overcome this limitation to some degree by obtaining approval from the executive and legislative branches to hire law clerks to assist the judges with their research. The primary qualification of the law clerks, however, is their grade-point average in law school; expertise in public-policy analysis does not appear to figure highly in the selection criteria. The result is that courts are, and will likely always remain, highly dependent on external sources for expertise regarding public-policy issues. This situation would not necessarily be a handicap to the courts in adjudicating public-policy issues if counsel presenting public-policy evidence could be counted on to make quality presentations. But as we have already pointed out, few lawyers have much expertise regarding public-policy analysis, and the legal profession in Canada is only beginning to develop links with public-policy specialists.

One possible reaction of courts to the problem of lack of internal expertise in policy-related matters is to attempt to limit decisions to the consideration of traditional or technical legal issues, and therefore avoid having to deal with policy questions as much as possible. Such an approach is consistent with the philosophy of judicial restraint, to which most judges appear to be sympathetic (McCormick & Greene 1990, 236). Another indication of the attractiveness of the policy-avoidance solution is the extent to which the Supreme Court has cut down, in recent years, on granting intervenor status to public-interest groups (Russell 1987, 353). Interventions by public-interest groups can sometimes provide the Supreme Court with the policy information often lacking in the factums of counsel for the two primary adversaries, although Mandel (1988) has noted that even public-interest groups are limited in providing useful policy information to courts because they tend to be controlled by lawyers. However, given the time constraints under which the Supreme Court is already operating, this additional policy information may not necessarily be welcomed to the Court.

Timeliness

As every student of public policy knows, the timeliness of a policy's implementation is critical to its success. The courts, however, cannot be counted on to intervene in the policy process in a timely manner. With regard to policy-related cases, delays in case processing can be a critical variable. Some public policies become quickly outdated so that by the time a final court decision is reached on their legal validity, the program in question has terminated or the policy in question has been replaced by a new one.

For example, in 1978 Joseph Borowski began a battle in the courts of Saskatchewan in support of protecting the legal rights of the fetus. His ultimate goal was to challenge the provisions of the Criminal Code that permitted abortions under certain conditions. By the time the substantive issues that he raised finally reached the Supreme Court of Canada in October 1988, the Supreme Court had already struck down, in January 1988, the abortion provisions in the Criminal Code as violating the rights of women. The Supreme Court declared that Borowski's case was now moot, and so the legal issues he raised could not be decided. In the end, Borowski may have come to the conclusion that the courts did not constitute the most appropriate forum for the policy issue he was pursuing. In a newspaper interview after the Supreme Court announced its decision, Borowski said, "I think it would be a waste of my time to ever go back before those gutless ... judges who have wasted ten years of our time" (Greene 1989, 180).

In other cases, a party might be able to obtain an injunction to halt the implementation of a program until the legal issues are finally decided. The exhaustion of all appeals, however, may take a number of years, causing delays that are expensive and disruptive to all parties involved. The long history of court battles over injunctions to stop the construction of the Rafferty-Alameda dams in Saskatchewan, the Oldman River dam in Alberta, and the Great Whale hydro-electric project in Quebec, pending statutory environmental reviews, come to mind.

In some courts, cases are scheduled in open court on a monthly basis. In others, trials rarely occur at first appearance; rather, this first appearance is used as an opportunity to schedule a trial in the presence of counsel for both sides. In still others, an administrative official sets the hearing date after receiving direction from the appropriate judge and after checking with all counsel involved. Needless to say, regardless of the system used, the speed at which cases come to a hearing depends to a large extent how long counsel estimate it will take to prepare their cases, and the degree to which adjudicators are willing to allow counsel to determine this issue. Once a case has been decided at trial, appeals may engender additional delays. "Thus, occasionally one comes across a Supreme Court of Canada decision concerning a factual situation that occurred ten years earlier" (McCormick & Greene 1990, 32).

Although some adjudicators can and do intervene to try to force counsel to argue cases as expeditiously as possible, most do not. The result is that the involvement of courts in the policy process throws another wild card into the picture: whether court decisions relevant to the policy process are timely enough to have an impact is usually no more predictable than a throw of the dice.

What can be concluded with regard to the organizational capacity of the courts vis-à-vis the policy process is that, on the one hand, judicial tribunals (but not necessarily administrative tribunals) are independent in respect to the content of their policy-related decisions. This independence might inject an impartial voice into the policy process to ensure that rule-of-law values such as due process and equality of treatment are respected. On the other hand, courts are heavily dependent on outside sources to provide expertise and on lawyers to determine the pace of litigation. Since both of these factors can have a tremendous impact on exactly how a court decision may affect a public policy, the result is that the nature of court intervention in the public-policy process becomes highly unpredictable.

THE HUMAN ELEMENT

In his Introduction to this volume, Michael Atkinson pointed out that "institutions are patterns of interaction established by human beings. They do not simply happen. Moreover, they are human creations in which people must justify their behaviour and accept responsibility for their actions." The reason for considering the human element in relation to court structures is to determine to what extent the preferences of individual judges may impact on policy decisions in spite of the rigidity of court rules and the constraints of organizational capacity.

One of the purposes of courts in a rule-of-law country is to ensure that disputes are settled, as much as possible, so that the law is applied equally to everyone. Interview data indicate that individual judges in Canada generally do their best to apply the law equally and impartially (McCormick & Greene 1990, 245). However, when the law is unclear, individual judges can and do differ from each other about how the law should be interpreted and applied.

For example, being a constitutional document, the Charter of Rights is, by and large, phrased in vague and general language. In the early days of the Charter, with few guiding precedents from the Supreme Court of Canada, decisions in the lower courts about how the Charter should be applied varied enormously (Morton & Withey 1986). As well, there is some evidence that the backgrounds of judges might help to explain some of the differences among them regarding how they decide cases. In Alberta, judges whose fathers were farmers or labourers tended to decide against individual Charter claims significantly more frequently than judges whose fathers were professionals or businessmen (McCormick & Greene 1990, 242). And there is evidence that Supreme Court of Canada judges appointed by Liberal governments tended to decide some types of cases somewhat differently than judges appointed by Conservative governments (Tate & Sittiwong 1989).

But Charter cases are certainly not the only ones in which the predispositions of judges can have an important impact on the public-policy process. For example, refugee applicants who fail in getting their refugee claims approved in the refugee-determination process do not have a right of appeal, but may apply for leave (permission) to appeal or leave for judicial review before judges sitting alone in the Federal Court of Appeal. To a policy analyst working on refugee policy for the Canada Employment and Immigration Commission, it might be expected that the success rates of the leave applications would provide an indication of the effectiveness of the refugee-determination process: the higher the success rate of leave applicants, the greater the possibility that the refugee-determination process is not operating fairly. In fact, the acceptance rates of the individual Federal Court of Appeal judges during 1990, based on a representative sample of cases, varied from 9 percent to 49 per cent, the average being 25 percent. A number of possible intervening variables that might have explained differences in acceptance rates among the judges were tested, such as variations among the judges in the kinds of cases they were assigned, but none of these tests could account for the extreme variation among the judges (Greene & Shaffer 1992). From the point of view of the policy analyst, because the individual acceptance rates vary so much and there seems to be no reason for the variation other than the individual predispositions of the judges, it is difficult to draw any firm conclusions about the efficacy of the refugee-determination process. One explanation for the variation may be that there are no statutory criteria within the Immigration Act to guide the judges when making decisions on these leave applications, thus allowing greater scope for the influence of judicial predispositions.

In a study of the decision-making process at the trial level, McCormick and Greene asked a representative sample of 41 Alberta trial judges to describe the process they followed to reach decisions in particular cases. Most of these judges assumed that "all judges followed pretty much the same approach" (1990, 121), and so most judges found it curious that they would be asked such a question in the first place. As it turned out, a variety of different approaches was employed, and these were grouped into four categories. Of the 41 judges, eighteen were labelled "pragmatic formalists" because they followed a strict set of procedures in assessing the evidence (although few procedures among the judges were the same), but they admitted that regardless of how well judges adhered to the proper procedure, sometimes different judges might reach varying conclusions concerning the outcome of the case. Nine judges were "strict formalists"; like the pragmatic formalists, they followed a strict set of procedures, but they implied that all judges following the same procedures would necessarily reach the same conclusion. Ten of the judges were labelled "intuitivists" because they relied primarily on what we could call intuition in sorting out the truth when presented with contradictory evidence. Four judges were "improvisers" because they did feel they followed a consistent method in deciding cases (McCormick & Greene 1990, 135).

The procedure adopted by adjudicators in assessing evidence and reaching a conclusion is likely to have a major impact on the outcome of policy-related cases where the evidence is seldom cut-and-dried, as are many policy-related cases. Given the variety of decision-making methods employed by judges and the lack of standardized judicial training, we can conclude that in policy-related cases, individual differences in the decision-making approach may be another factor that militates in favour of adjudicative decisions that are difficult to predict in advance.

Moreover, judicial predispositions probably play a larger role in policy outcomes when the law is unclear; the more vague the law, the greater the scope for the human element.

CONCLUSION

It is no doubt the hope of most policy-makers that the courts will not get tangled up in their policy process—that the policy can be implemented in such a way that it will give no one reason to invest in the expense of litigation. However, as long as the possibility exists that a policy as legislated violates the Constitution, or a policy as implemented goes beyond its legislated mandate or violates the norms of fair procedure and equality, policies will be taken to court.

Nevertheless, the rules of the court organization, combined with the lack of control that courts have over the quality of policy-related evidence and the speed at which policy-related matters move through the courts, in addition to the human element in judicial decision-making, all suggest that courts are not always well-suited for intervention in the policy process. Although in the majority of policy-related court cases the courts will not accept an invitation to intervene, court intervention is always a possibility that policy analysts need to prepare for. What steps can be taken to maximize the good that might come about from court intervention and minimize potential harm?

Pal and Morton (1985), in comparing the policy-analysis undertaken by courts with that of policy-analysis units in the public service, have shown that judges tend to lack both the background knowledge and the resources to make decisions about how policies ought to be reformed. In contrast, judges tend to be good at (1) determining whether policy implementation is in conformity with the relevant legislation, (2) determining whether policy implementation is in accord with due process safeguards (such as the legal rights contained in the Charter of Rights), and (3) determining whether clearly worded legislation is in conformity with clearly worded constitutional provisions. The quality of judicial performance tends to decrease as the vagueness of either statutes or the Constitution increases, and is poorest when judges feel they must prescribe a remedy for defective legislation.

A comparison of two judicial interventions in policy discussed above — one more beneficial than the other — will help to illustrate. In the Supreme Court of Canada's decision in *Singh* (Supreme Court of Canada 1985b), three of the six judges who participated in the decision claimed that the denial of an oral hearing to a refugee applicant violates the right to fundamental justice in Section 7 of the Charter. Among other things, fundamental justice includes the right of litigants to state their case adequately. Where a serious issue of credibility is involved, as in refugee cases, an oral hearing is required so that the applicant will be able to determine what evidence the minister has contrary to the applicant's claim and have the opportunity to respond to such evidence. The other three judges came to a similar conclusion based on Section 2(e) of the Canadian Bill of Rights, which stipulates that persons whose rights and obligations are being determined have a right to a fair hearing. The remedy resulting from the *Singh* decision was that, henceforth, refugee applicants would be entitled to one oral hearing during the refugee-determination process.

If there is anything a judge ought to be thoroughly familiar with, it is the ingredients of fundamental justice and a fair hearing. The *Singh* decision detected and corrected a major flaw in the government's refugee-determination policy, a problem not obvious to departmental policy-makers because of their greater concern with administrative efficiency than with the principles of a fair hearing. From the perspective of the fundamental principles of justice of our legal and constitutional system, it is more than disconcerting that a refugee applicant on Canadian soil might have been deported, possibly to face torture and death, without ever having had the opportunity to know and respond to the evidence contrary to his or her claim. Wisely, the court did not strike down the entire refugee-determination process, but limited itself to prescribing that refugee applicants whose claims were opposed by officials had to be given the opportunity of an oral hearing.

A contrasting decision is that of an Alberta Court of Queen's Bench judge in a 1984 decision striking down the provisions of the federal Election Expenses Act prohibiting advertising for or against political parties by groups outside the umbrella of party spending limits. The reason for this provision was to facilitate the enforcement of legislated spending limits for parties and candidates, thus promoting the principle that an election should be a fair contest between candidates, parties, and ideas, rather than a contest whose outcome is determined by which candidate has the richest patrons. The legislation left interest groups outside the parties free to spend as much as they wished in advertising their views on specific issues as long as parties or candidates were not mentioned (Hiebert 1989).

There is no doubt that the nonparty advertising provisions violated the principle of freedom of expression in the Charter, as claimed by the National Citizens' Coalition (NCC), the group that brought the issue to court. The essential issue was whether the provisions could be justified as a "reasonable limit" under Section 1 of the Charter. At the time of this decision, the Supreme Court had not had the opportunity to lay down guidelines for the application of Section 1; the guidelines were later set out in the *Oakes* decision of 1986 (Supreme Court of Canada 1986). The Alberta judge decided to base his decision on whether the Crown was able to show that the absence of non-party advertising provisions would result in actual harm to the conduct of a fair election. Lawyers for the Crown had presented evidence showing how some candidates had benefited, prior to the legislation in question, from nonparty groups advertising on their behalf, but the judge decided that these examples did not demonstrate that the electoral process had been harmed. (Of course, lawyers for the Crown did not know in advance that the judge would decide to base his Section 1 decision on the question of harm to the electoral process; if they had, their presentation might have been stronger. This case demonstrates how the rules of procedure in court were not designed for putting public policies on trial.)

In this case, the judge was not applying a set of standards for traditional legal safeguards of fair procedure, but rather was second-guessing the policy-makers of Canada's electoral laws and prescribing a remedy for a perceived defect in the policy. The electoral policy-makers had the benefit of having studied royal commission inquiries and social-science research, and had the background skill to analyze that research; the judge had whatever evidence the counsel for both sides happened to produce, and no background in the social-science study of elections. If the judge was not able to adopt a restrained approach concerning the alleged Charter violation, then he could at least have adopted a restrained approach concerning a remedy. It would have been possible, for example, for the judge to have given Parliament a year or two to find an acceptable policy remedy for the Charter violation.[1]

In this case, the victory of the National Citizens' Coalition did not seem to have much effect on election spending in 1984. However, the 1988 election campaign was a different story. As it turned out, the Conservative Party, which was supported by businesses in both Canada and the United States that were in favour of free trade, was the primary beneficiary of the ability of nonparty groups to spend as much as they wished on party advertising. It is impossible to say whether the outcome of the 1988 election would have been different had the NCC lost its election advertising case in 1984 or if the judge had imposed a less intrusive remedy, but the decision illustrates the potentially far-reaching impact of judicial intervention into the policy arena.

Concern has often been expressed that judicial intervention in the policy process is antidemocratic or at least nondemocratic. When nonelected judges second-guess the policy decisions of elected legislatures, as in the *National Citizens' Coalition* decision, this criticism has some validity. On the other hand, when judges intervene to ensure that the essential democratic values of fair procedure and equality are respected, as in the *Singh* decision, judicial intervention could be seen as supportive of democracy. Democratic institutions do not always function perfectly, and they can sometimes operate so as to undermine the values they were established to promote. If they are conscious of their roles as adjudicators in a democratic society, judges can frame their decisions so as to enhance democratic values (Monahan 1987).

Returning to the question of what can be done to promote the positive aspects of judicial intervention in the policy process, it would be a mistake to point the finger only at judges. Certainly, given their broader policy role under the Charter, judges need to improve their knowledge of policy analysis. To some extent, this is already happening through courses being offered by the National Centre for the Judiciary (formerly the Canadian Judicial Centre), which is a continuing-education centre for Canadian judges established in Ottawa in 1987. As judges gain a better understanding of the policy process, it is possible that they will also become more aware of their own limitations in prescribing policy remedies. As well, the judiciary and the bar might give some consideration to recommending improvements to the rules of court procedure as they affect presenting evidence regarding public policies.

As well, there is much that ought to be done by government policymakers, private lawyers, lawyers for the Crown, schools of public administration, and legislatures. Given the importance of the Charter of Rights in expanding the intervention of courts, one measure that could be taken by government policy-makers is to expend more energy in considering the relation between the Supreme Court's test for Section 1 of the Charter, and the content of their policies. Both the quality of argument in policy-related Charter cases, and the quality of public policies themselves might be improved if the following questions were considered and the answers documented at every stage in the policy process:

- Does the policy impinge on any Charter rights? (And most do in some way.)
- If yes, is there a real need for rights to be limited in order to achieve the objective of the policy?
- If yes, have rights been limited as little as necessary to achieve the objective of the policy?

Lawyers for the Crown would benefit from the establishment of in-house expertise in policy analysis, and closer links with the policy-development units of government departments so that they can obtain a better understanding of the rationale for particular policies. As well, government law departments might consider attempting to align their defence strategies more closely with overall government policy so as to avoid simply taking the opposite policy stand from their opponents — a stand that might blatantly contradict government policy.

More opportunities could be made available for lawyers to specialize in public-policy litigation not only by learning the relevant law, but by gaining expertise in public-policy analysis. Such opportunities could be created through greater co-operation between public-policy programs and law schools in our universities. If and when this happens, the quality of argument on policy-related issues will improve, and the quality of court-related intervention in the policy process may also increase.

The human element in adjudication will always be there, but its more objectionable results can be reduced through more carefully drafted legislation that provides judges with clearer guidelines for decision-making. Legislation such as the refugee-determination procedures in the Immigration Act, which provide judges with no guidelines regarding the acceptance of leave applications, is inexcusable in a rule-of-law country. As well, legislatures could develop more routinized procedures for scrutinizing judicial decisions that impact legislative policies, such as creating standing committees to review judicial decisions affecting legislation. Members of legislatures could learn much about fair procedure by reading decisions like the *Singh* decision of 1985, and would be in a position to recommend quicker legislative remedies to the less successful forms of judicial intervention, such as the *National Citizens' Coalition* decision of 1984.

NOTE

1. A similar remedy was imposed by the Supreme Court of Canada on the province of Manitoba in 1985 when the Court found that all Manitoba statutes passed since 1890 were invalid because they were passed only in English. The Court declared Manitoba's laws temporarily valid, and gave the legislature three years to re-enact its laws in French and English (Supreme Court of Canada 1985a). Similarly, in 1986 a Manitoba judge found that the province's Election Expenses Act violated the Charter of Rights by denying all prisoners the right to vote regardless of their offence. The judge, however, gave the legislature the opportunity to amend its Elections Act; he resisted the temptation to amend the act himself, for example, by ordering that the names of certain classes of prisoners be added to the voters' list (Manitoba Court of Queen's Bench 1986).

CHAPTER 7

Macroeconomic Policy: Dwindling Options

William D. Coleman

INTRODUCTION

Following its surprising victory in September 1990, Ontario's New Democratic Party government brought down its first budget in the spring of 1991 and boldly proposed a deficit of nine billion dollars. Floyd Laughren, the provincial Finance minister, argued that the gravity of the economic recession required the government to spend more in order to give the economy a boost and to preserve as many jobs as possible. During the same period, the federal government's budget took a different tack; the minister of Finance announced a series of steps to bring inflation down to zero over a period of years. In its constitutional proposals released shortly after, the Mulroney government suggested revising the mandate of the Bank of Canada to require it to concentrate only on price stability, that is, keeping inflation close to zero.

If these events had taken place 30 years ago, scarcely anyone would have taken issue with the Ontario government and just about everyone would have criticized the federal proposals. Yet, in 1991, the Ontario budget was attacked viciously by the business community, was castigated by the federal government, and was used by the Social Credit Party in British Columbia as an example of "socialist irresponsibility" in its unsuccessful election campaign against the B.C. NDP in the fall of 1991. In contrast, the federal proposals for fighting inflation first, and not unemployment, elicited less comment. Most people knew

---

I would like to thank Michael Atkinson, Robert M. Campbell, Peter A. Hall, and Henry Jacek for their comments on this chapter.

nothing about the mandate of the Bank of Canada and saw little of importance to the changes proposed. These different reactions over a short period of three decades reflect profound changes in how Canadian governments conceive their role in the economy, particularly as it bears upon employment. This chapter examines these changes, and notes the important role institutions have played in defining what kind of macroeconomic policies were most likely to emerge.

DEFINITIONS AND BACKGROUND

What do we mean then by macroeconomic policies? Macroeconomic policies are government strategies and programs designed to influence aggregate characteristics of the economy such as employment and growth. In contrast, microeconomic policies, discussed by Kenneth Woodside in Chapter 8, include those programs that take as their target the individual properties of sectors and firms or the economic structure of a particular region.

In reviewing the contemporary histories of developed capitalist economies in the postwar period, most scholars suggest that the early 1970s mark a crucial watershed. Before 1970, these economies experienced a long run of rather sustained economic growth and prosperity. To varying degrees, national macroeconomic policies in support of this expansion took their inspiration from the work of John Maynard Keynes, an English economist, whose writings have had a considerable influence on contemporary economics. Anchoring these national policies was an international monetary system dominated by the United States, with the U.S. dollar serving as the world's reserve currency. Exchange rates of the world's major currencies tended to be relatively fixed in relation to the dollar, contributing further to stable economic conditions.

Beginning in 1970, this combination of sustained growth, Keynesian-oriented policy, and a stable international monetary system began to unravel. U.S. spending on the Vietnam War sparked a sharp rise in world-wide inflation, putting intense strain on the international monetary system. Canada floated its currency in 1970, and, by 1973, the whole fabric of the fixed-exchange-rate international monetary system negotiated at Bretton Woods, New Hampshire, at the end of the war was in shreds. Major international currencies floated in relation to one another, with exchange rates being determined by markets. This crisis intensified in 1973 when the first oil price shock pushed inflation to new heights, contributed to a lowering of industrial production, and gave rise to higher unemployment and mounting trade deficits.

The economic crisis that began in the early 1970s generated a multidimensional political crisis in most nation-states.[1] The inability to achieve simultaneously all principal macroeconomic objectives forced governments to choose among continued growth, high employment, and price stability. The direction taken by governments in making these choices depended significantly on institutional arrangements (Campbell 1991). The relationship between the central bank and the treasury ministry, the centralization of fiscal capacity, the governing opportunities available to social democratic parties, and the organizational development of encompassing organizations representing business and labour all played a crucial role. Moreover, making a choice had profound implications for how politcans put together support in the electorate, in particular, their ability to maintain a "coalition" of support from labour and business (Gourevitch 1989). The forging of new coalitions involved considerable debate over economic ideas with monetarism, in particular, rising to challenge Keynesianism.

Canada's institutional arrangements favoured a conservative monetarist outcome. Its central bank, the Bank of Canada, enjoyed considerable autonomy from the government. Fiscal policy became gradually disabled over the 1980s as the current accounts deficit rose steadily. Neither business nor labour as social classes possessed sufficient organizational capacity for engaging in a long-term dialogue with government on economic policy options. Finally, social democractic parties, which are normally strong supporters of a full employment policy, had neither regular nor strong influence on government.

This chapter develops the argument that institutional arrangements favoured monetarism, and makes this argument in three steps. We begin with an overview of macroeconomic policy approaches in Western countries in the period between 1945 and 1970. The second section examines the crisis period that began in the mid-1970s by noting the new policy options and by describing the institutional conditions for their successful pursuit. The third part of the chapter analyzes policy and political developments in Canada in light of these options. This section describes the institutional factors favouring a monetarist policy path, whereby price stability is elevated to first choice among macroeconomic policy objectives.

MACROECONOMIC POLICY, 1945–1970

Objectives and Policy Instruments

Governments normally consider one or more of four objectives when thinking about macroeconomic policy: economic growth, full employment, price stability, and balanced trade relations with other countries. Depending on the economic environment, the economic theories with most influence in government circles, and political and electoral calculations, governments may give primacy to one or two of these objectives over the others. Such a choice depends on which of the problems associated with these objectives—weak economic growth, unemployment, inflation, unbalanced trade—is identified as the most pressing and is seen to have the most troubling electoral consequences.

Decision-makers normally have access to four sets of policy instruments—monetary policy, fiscal policy, exchange rate policy, and union wage policy—that they use for influencing the economic environment. These instruments can be targeted toward one or more of the objectives just noted (Scharpf 1991, 28–30).

Monetary Policy

Monetary policy refers to the regulation of the stock of money (Boreham 1988). Central banks around the world attempt to influence the money supply by intervening in short-term money markets.[2] By buying or selling in these markets or by varying the interest rate they set for very short-term borrowing by credit institutions such as banks or trust companies, central banks, in turn, seek to influence other longer-term interest rates and, ultimately, the exchange value of their currency. Monetary policy becomes *expansionary* when central banks intervene to promote lower interest rates, thereby permitting banks to offer credit at more favourable terms, and thus facilitating an increase in aggregate demand in the economy as a whole. Monetary policy becomes *restrictive* when central banks act to increase the cost of borrowing money.

Before 1970, when domestic economies were less open to international markets and national banking systems were protected against foreign intrusion, central banks had various options available to them for restricting the supply of money. They could restrict the flow of credit by allocating quotas to credit institutions. Or they could act more informally and attempt to influence the availability of credit through informal advice to, and special arrangements with, credit institutions. This use of "moral suasion" was most effective in banking systems in which a few large banks dominated a protected national financial system. The Bank of Canada used this approach occasionally in the postwar period, with the last known attempt occurring in 1981.[3] With the fall of barriers to entry for foreign banks and the liberalization of capital controls in Western Europe, controls on credit and moral suasion have lost their efficacy as instruments. Central banks now rely exclusively on one instrument to limit money growth: raising short-term interest rates.

Fiscal Policy

Fiscal policy refers to the government's decisions on taxing and spending. An *expansionary* policy on the spending or demand side involves the use of budget measures that increase public investment or public consumption. On the supply or taxation side, the government seeks to encourage aggregate demand by reducing taxes in ways that increase business profits (Scharpf 1991, 29). Policy-makers practise *fiscal restraint* by reducing the public-sector deficit or, more classically, by realizing a budgetary surplus (government revenues exceed government expenditures).

Exchange Rate Policy

This instrument may be used in both expansionary and restrictive ways. If a government acts to *devalue* its currency, it raises the costs of imports and reduces the prices of exports. Other things being equal, then, demand for domestically produced goods should rise as they become more price competitive with imported goods. The prices of exported goods will fall abroad, leading to some expansion in their sales. *Revaluing* the currency has the reverse effects and thus has a restrictive impact. The cost of imports falls, putting price pressure on domestic producers, and the prices of exported goods go up. Overall demand in the domestic economy thus falls. Successful use of this instrument is particularly difficult in an international system with flexible exchange rates. Exchange markets tend to be driven by the peculiar psychology of market participants that often emphasizes short-term political questions at the expense of longer-term economic performance.

Union Wage Policy

Depending on factors such as the density of unionization and the degree of organizational development of labour and business associations, the wage policy of trade unions may be open to influence by government. Governments may ask unions to restrain wage demands in exchange for other policy outputs. When available, this instrument is particularly effective for restraining demand as a means to curb inflation (Scharpf 1991, 30).

The Keynesian Perspective

Governments devise macroeconomic policy by working with a set of political ideas that match objectives with instruments. The match becomes workable when a coalition of social forces including, at a minimum, significant representation of the business community, supports the choice of objectives and instruments. In the immediate postwar period, a cognitive framework highly influenced by the writings of John Maynard Keynes achieved considerable prominence in the governing circles of most Western nations. The approach to macroeconomic policy that was developed on the basis of this framework came to enjoy the support of parties of the left and the right.

Keynesian Ideas

The classical marginalist analysis of the economy had argued that markets were fundamentally stable and tended to move toward equilibrium at the highest practicable levels of employment. Upon reviewing the performance of the more advanced Western economies particularly that of Britain in the aftermath of World War I, Keynes found this assumption unrealistic. He countered that rigidities introduced by producer organizations, by variations in business confidence, and by other factors left markets fundamentally unstable (Hall 1989, 6). Left to their own devices, markets would often stagnate and operate at unnecessarily high levels of unemployment. Consequently, he concluded, governments had to take some action to limit these effects.

In considering what form this action should take, Keynes reflected further upon conventional theories of the relationship between savings and investment. The conventional view held that savings would be channelled into investment in response to variations in interest rates. Thus, when the price of capital fell because of a decline in interest rates, investment would rise. Governments, the classical position added, could best assist this process by limiting the amounts they themselves borrowed in capital markets.

Keynes replied that this view was too simplistic because investment responded to many factors. He argued that governments should not restrain their economic activity to the extent prescribed in classical economics. In the face of economic recessions and depressions, they need not stand helpless, but should act to stimulate the aggregate demand for goods. By carefully managing aggregate demand over time, governments could influence overall levels of growth and employment and thereby prevent wholesale collapses of the economy.

Of the four sets of macroeconomic policy instruments outlined above, it follows that the Keynesian approach favours the fiscal tools. As Scharpf (1991, 30) indicates, Keynesians fear most of all a situation in which households, uncertain about the future and worried about recessionary trends, increase their savings at the expense of consumption. Even though interest rates might be low, savers avoid productive investments because they fear losses. Governments can best halt this downward spiral of mutually reinforcing fears by increasing effective demand through an expansionary, deficit-financed fiscal policy. Keynesians believe that such intervention will reassure savers, encouraging increased investment and consumption, and thus will pull the economy out of stagnation.

If the problem is reversed, with the economy overheating and inflation on the rise, Keynesians suggest again that the first recourse be fiscal policy. By reducing public investment, increasing taxes, and budgeting for a surplus, governments should be able to cool off demand. Keynesians are reluctant to rely on a restrictive monetary policy in these circumstances. They believe this approach leads to unacceptable levels of unemployment. If other policy instruments are required to lower price levels, Keynesians prefer to moderate union wages, re-value the currency, or liberalize foreign trade.

Institutional Requirements for Keynesian Policy

The institutional prerequisites for the conduct of Keynesian demand management in the immediate postwar period were not particularly difficult to attain for most Western countries. Three institutional attributes were especially necessary. First, policy-makers needed rather complex and detailed information about the state of the economy and a capacity to trace the effects of given fiscal stimuli (Gourevitch 1989). Most countries developed this expertise and analytical capacity in the first twenty years after World War II. Certainly, statistics bureaus expanded their economic data gathering and policy-makers gained access to rather sophisticated models of the economy during this time.

Second, demand management works best when fiscal and monetary policy are closely co-ordinated. Since responsibility for the former normally lies with the treasury or finance ministry while the latter is housed with the central bank, co-ordination requires that the finance ministry and the central bank work closely together. In practice, when exchange rates are fixed most of the time, as they were under the Bretton Woods system for the majority of Western countries, the degrees of freedom available in monetary policy are fewer and thus opportunities for mis-coordination are relatively scarce.

Third, successful use of fiscal policy depends on the central government of a country having sufficient fiscal weight. Earlier in the century when state budgets accounted for a very small proportion of GNP, demand management by way of fiscal policy would have been close to impossible. By the postwar period, state intervention into social life had grown sufficiently to make fiscal policy a viable instrument. Still, in federal states, the question remained open whether the central government had enough fiscal capacity to manage demand and, if necessary, to countermand wayward territorial governments.

It is also important to note that Keynesians assumed that state intervention would be restricted to the demand side of the economy. They believed that the processes of structural and technological adjustment on the supply side were market driven (Matzner & Streeck 1991). Labour markets, the training of workers, investment decisions—all needed rather little tending by the state. Hence the kinds of questions raised in Chapter 8 about microeconomic policy were simply not attended to in Keynesian thinking. It follows that the institutional requirements for implementing Keynesian macroeconomic policy were not high. States, it was believed, would not be intervening deeply into economic affairs.

The Keynesian approach to macroeconomic policy, with its focus on economic growth and full employment and its preference for fiscal policy, had considerable potential for winning the support of a broad political coalition of supporters in civil society. As Gourevitch has noted, demand management offered the possibility of a "collective game" (1989, 93). If governments, savers including workers, and business worked together, the economy would grow, everyone would be employed, and all should be wealthier over time. The promise of full employment went a long way in drawing support from labour. The focus on economic growth, indirect demand-oriented state intervention, and productive investment struck a chord with business. "Progressive" elements in the business community concluded further that support for better wages and working conditions, institutionalized industrial-relations systems, and social-welfare insurance not only assisted in achieving the Keynesian agenda, but also helped persuade labour to support more liberalized international trade and the fixed-exchange-rate international monetary system. When an institutionalized system of subsidies to encourage the modernization of agriculture was added to the package, the Keynesian approach ended up with the support of an impressive coalition of business, labour, and agriculture in most countries including Canada (Gourevitch 1989, ch. 6).

Canada and Keynesianism

The degree to which Keynesian demand management enjoyed support in ruling circles and was actually practised varied considerably among Western democracies. In Canada, Keynesian ideas garnered considerable support among professional economists and senior federal government officials. Yet after an initial burst of enthusiasm in the immediate postwar period, demand management did not remain a prominent feature of Canadian macroeconomic policy. Two factors, one economic and the other political, help explain this outcome.

First, Keynesian demand management was better suited for large, relatively closed economies than for small, open ones. The latter face particular challenges when they seek to use Keynesian-oriented fiscal policy instruments (Scharpf 1991, 211). If fiscal policy is relaxed in an economy with a high proportion of imports, for example, then many of the benefits of the new demand may flow abroad unless other supply-side policies are added. Or, when fiscal policy is tightened in an economy with a strong export sector, the impact may be small as exporters compensate for restraint by expanding in foreign markets. These problems soon began to confound Canadian politicians when they attempted to put Keynesianism into practice. When problems arose, the political commitment to full employment proved to be weak because of the absence of labour in the governing coalition.

Hence, the second factor explaining the weak commitment to full employment was that neither the labour movement nor a social democratic party, both normally keen supporters of demand management because of its promise of full employment, enjoyed much influence in national politics in Canada. Planning the Canadian war effort and the postwar reconstruction had never included significant representation of labour, the class most supportive of full employment. Unlike the business–labour concertation found in many European countries, businesspeople and their profits-centred philosophy had monopolized societal participation in government during the war (Coleman & Nossal 1991). The single-member-plurality electoral system helped prevent the socialist Co-operative Commonwealth Federation (CCF) from entering into the national government even though it enjoyed considerable public support. The labour movement remained fractious and highly divided. Hence Canada did not possess the support in government or the intermediary organizations that would provide a sustained commitment to full employment in the postwar period.

Rather, government's adoption of full employment as an objective in 1945 was the result of a commitment to Keynesian thinking by senior public officials. Many of the related macroeconomic questions associated with wage policy and collective bargaining policy were not dealt with in the party system as they had been in Europe, but in decentralized private collective bargaining (Jenson 1990). Hence, when full employment came into conflict with the continentalist approach to economic growth, it was gradually and quietly set aside without promoting a crisis in the governing parties.

In the immediate postwar period, a consensus existed in the two major political parties, the Liberals and the Conservatives, that full employment should be the overriding goal of macroeconomic policy (Campbell 1987, 38). Therefore, policy centred on maintaining low levels of unemployment by keeping aggregate demand high. Yet it did not take long before these commitments were softened. The rise in unemployment in 1949–50 did not spark concerted government intervention. Rather, the government responded that the periodic development of unemployment was inevitable because of the fluctuations in international markets and thus a layer of unemployment would always exist in Canada (Campbell 1987, 94). The government was to repeat this message often during the 1950s. Its economic strategy had shifted quickly to the promotion of economic growth through natural resource exports and the encouragement of U.S. foreign direct investment in manufacturing. Such a strategy accentuated the openness of the Canadian economy and thus hobbled any resort to Keynesian demand management (Jenson 1989a, 80).

In the mid-1960s, when they formed a minority government, the Liberals did express a renewed, albeit weak, commitment to full employment (Doern 1985, 34). But in practice Canadian budgetary policy never respected Keynesian precepts particularly well. The majority of budgets prior to 1970 were rather passive in the face of economic cycles; they neither created nor reacted to cyclical swings (Purvis & Smith 1986, 31; Campbell 1987, 191). Among the factors cited for this reluctance to practise demand management, Campbell notes a certain sense of powerlessness in the face of international variables. Governments feared that an increase in public investment would be wasteful if unemployment was largely the consequence of international economic changes rather than a domestically-induced slump in demand (Campbell 1987, 191).

Governments' emphasis on economic growth rather than full employment enjoyed broad support within the business community. When they coupled this objective to the development of income support policies in the most vulnerable agricultural sectors, the business–farm juggernaut afforded labour few opportunities to forge coalitions that might have promoted full employment. Political identities were not formed around the notions of class. Instead, national and regional foci became more important and the Liberal Party was particularly successful in integrating ethnic working-class communities into a coalition centred on a redefined Canadian identity (Smith 1986). Hence the Canadian labour movement entered the crisis of the 1970s as one pressure group among many (Yates 1990), with its social democratic ally, the New Democratic Party, playing a minor role in the national party system.

CRISES AND POLICY OPTIONS, 1970–1990

The advanced capitalist economies entered the 1970s in an increasingly difficult economic situation. High U.S. spending on the Vietnam War had raised inflation in the United States, an inflation that gradually spread beyond U.S. borders. The international monetary system came under increasing stress and finally foundered in 1973. The Bretton Woods regime of fixed exchange rates gave way to a flexible-rates regime with attendant instability in foreign-exchange markets and in interest rates. This difficult economic situation took a sharp turn for the worse when the first oil shock sent oil prices sharply higher in 1973 and 1974. Demand sagged and unemployment began to rise to levels unprecedented in the postwar period. When inflation continued in the face of the worsening employment situation, Keynesian theory itself came into question. The 1970s and 1980s were to become years of crisis in economic theory as well as in the economy itself.

The crisis affected all the capitalist countries including Canada. But not all countries responded to it in the same way. Understanding the differences in responses requires again some attention to institutions.

The Economic Context

The macroeconomic policy problem took the following form in the 1970s.[4] Two sources of inflation may be distinguished. "Demand–pull" inflation arises when an increase in aggregate demand takes place at the same time that capacity is fully utilized or profits are too low. The demand then translates into rising prices. In contrast, "cost–push" inflation occurs in a situation of relatively fixed wage and price rates. Increases in costs induce increases in prices, which, in turn, spark wage increases and ultimately a wage–price spiral. The decade began with demand–pull inflation initiated by spending on the Vietnam War, but the problem shifted in the middle of the decade to the cost–push variety when the first oil price shock occurred.

Similarly, there are two sources of unemployment. Demand-gap unemployment arises when demand is insufficient to require the full utilization of productive capacity. In contrast, investment-gap unemployment refers to a situation in which "firms fail to hire all job-seekers despite sufficient demand... because increased production would be unprofitable given existing factor costs and goods prices" (Scharpf 1991, 26). By 1974, the oil price shock presented the advanced capitalist economies with increasingly significant demand-gap unemployment. The combination of demand-gap unemployment and cost–push inflation came to be known as *stagflation*.

The Keynesian cure for demand-gap unemployment was straightforward: fiscal and monetary policy should be eased in order to raise aggregate demand and ultimately to reduce unemployment. The solution to cost–push inflation was less obvious and the debate led to a clash in economic theories. Keynesians viewed the source of the problem to be inflexibility in wages and prices, and thus argued that factor costs had to be lowered and more competition introduced into markets. Neoclassical economists saw matters differently and argued that the inflation arose from a too rapid expansion of the money supply. They thus argued for a restrictive monetary policy supported by fiscal policy as the solution. Keynesians were reluctant to rely on restrictive monetary policy arguing that it would push unemployment even higher. Even so, Keynesians, by agreeing that at least part of the problem could be traced to factor costs, had to argue for some limits on fiscal and monetary policy.

The Keynesian Policy Dilemma

Thus the policy dilemma emerges for Keynesians. If demand-gap unemployment is to be reduced, fiscal and monetary policy must be eased. But an easing of policy would confound attempts to control factor costs and, in the process, feed cost–push inflation. In contrast, if fiscal and monetary policy were tightened in order to counter cost–push inflation, demand-gap unemployment would worsen even further. Policy-makers were thus faced with difficult choices: the familiar principles of Keynesian economics no longer offered a clear direction, but the monetarism of the neoclassicists would lead to high unemployment, at least for the medium term. The decisions taken in different countries depended heavily on the composition of political coalitions and, in particular, on the presence or absence of the labour movement in those coalitions.

Compounding the Crisis

Whatever the decision taken, it was quickly confounded by a second oil shock in 1979. Again the rise in oil prices lowered aggregate demand, creating demand-gap unemployment. But this time, the oil crisis and the more unstable international monetary system led to a Third World debt crisis. After heavy borrowing in the 1970s and faced with rising oil prices, developing countries were forced to reduce capital goods imports from the developed economies. International banks increased the interest rates on their loans in order to cover better the newly perceived risks resulting from exchange rate and interest rate volatility in the post–Bretton Woods system. Thus, Third World countries could import less and less from abroad because they needed to save money in order to pay the rising interest costs on their debts. The resulting drop in Third World demand for Western goods added to unemployment.

Yet the oil shock sparked a new round of cost–push inflation as well, forcing governments to reconsider their overall macroeconomic policy. The U.S. government chose to fight strenuously against inflation, adopting a monetarist approach in targeting the money supply. Interest rates rose dramatically as a consequence.

Countries outside the U.S. had little choice but to follow these interest rate increases. The internationalization of money and capital markets had intensified following the collapse of Bretton Woods, making it very difficult to insulate national capital markets. Financial markets were linked ever more closely together. Thus, if a country lowered its rates, capital would flow outward to the U.S. markets, where demand remained high as the Reagan tax cuts and defence spending increases took hold. Consequently, the given country would not be able to meet its own capital needs. In fact, as long as U.S. interest rates remained high, countries outside the U.S. were more or less forced to follow a highly restrictive monetary policy (Scharpf 1991, 245).

To the extent then that they were concerned with unemployment in the early 1980s, and it was a problem that was extremely difficult to ignore, governments only had fiscal policy available. But an expansionary fiscal policy in this economic environment promised to bring its own special problems. First, in the absence of a supportive monetary policy, the fiscal stimulus would have to be even stronger than normal to have an effect. Yet a highly expansionary fiscal policy promised to be very expensive: high interest rates made government borrowing very costly. Extensive government borrowing might lead to a spiralling deficit fuelled by the cost of servicing the debt. Such a deficit might, in the end, greatly restrict governments' ability to apply a discretionary fiscal policy. In short, by the mid-1980s, Keynesians reflecting on policy strategy were left with a blinding headache.

Devising Policy Solutions

Preliminary to a consideration of two broad policy solutions to stagflation, some discussion of the role of wages is necessary. As Scharpf (1991, 33) emphasizes, wages play a peculiar double role. On the one side, they figure prominently in economic problems because they normally are the largest contributors to aggregate demand and to factor costs. On the other side, as we have noted, they are potentially an instrument of macroeconomic policy. Nominal wages are not set through the operation of faceless labour markets, but through collective bargaining between trade unions and employers under rules set out by public policy. Depending on these rules and the views of the actors involved, wages are more or less sensitive to economic policies. In some circumstances, it is at least conceivable that wages might be set above or below inflation rates in response to policy stimuli. As a policy instrument, wages are particularly attractive because, unlike fiscal and monetary policy, they have an inverse rather than a reinforcing impact on demand and supply. Thus, if wage policy is aggressive, aggregate demand rises while productivity and the profitability of investment fall. In contrast, if wages are restrained, aggregate demand falls while business profits rise.

The Corporatist Full-Employment Solution

For Keynesians, the idea of coupling wage policy to the traditional fiscal and monetary instruments offered one avenue for attacking the unfortunate combination of unemployment and inflation. But travelling along this avenue, which promised to lead to the traditional goal of full employment, required concertation and agreement between the government and trade unions. The trade-off took the following form. In countries such as Austria and Sweden, trade unions would pursue collective agreements that would restrain the growth of wages. This curbing of wage demands would serve as a powerful counter to cost–push inflation. With the need to attack inflation considerably diminished, governments thus became free to practise an expansive fiscal and monetary policy that would, in the classic Keynesian way, stimulate aggregate demand. This demand stimulus would, in turn, reduce the levels of demand-gap unemployment.

All parties should thus be satisfied. Labour would see progress toward full employment. Business would appreciate lower inflation and improved profits. Governments could claim before their electorates that they had had some success in fighting both inflation and unemployment. It should also be added that some countries, especially Sweden, saw microeconomic policy as an essential complement to this macroeconomic strategy. In responding to the crisis, they also concentrated considerable effort on improving labour markets and training and retraining workers.

The Seesaw Solution

Suppose, however, that governments could not reach agreements with trade unions or that philosophically they were loath to incorporate labour into the macroeconomic decision-making process. What then were the options available? Two possibilities might be considered. First, governments might seek to remain committed to the Keynesian ideal of full employment under stable prices and attempt to combat inflation and unemployment alternatively. That is, they might begin with an expansive fiscal and monetary policy in order to drive down unemployment. After a period of time, with unemployment down, they might then reverse policy and set their sights on inflation. This approach proved to be an economic failure. When tried in Britain and, as we shall see, in Canada, it solved nothing. Unemployment proved to be remarkably stubborn and inflation levels soared to unprecedented heights in the postwar period.

The Monetarist Solution

An alternative approach was to abandon the Keynesian concern for full employment and to target inflation as the primary problem. Monetarist theories in economics, which argued that price instability was the most serious of economic problems, offered theoretical support for this approach. Until prices became stable, they suggested, other economic problems such as employment or low economic growth could not be effectively addressed. Monetarist theory called for governments through their central banks to restrict firmly the growth of the money supply by setting targets for its growth. Interest rates and exchange rates should be allowed to float freely and to respond to changes in the stock of money. Such strenuous monetary discipline would drive inflation down.

A strongly restrictive monetary policy had been long resisted by Keynesians because it led to high levels of unemployment. But for governments with weak ties to the labour movement and a reduced commitment to the full-employment objective, the option was attractive. It promised, after all, the price stability preferred by the business community. As unemployment levels rose, individual trade unions would be forced to restrain wage demands in any event in order to prevent further joblessness. Such market-induced wage restraint would, in turn, raise profit levels and encourage further investment by business.

By the 1980s, the policy options outlined above were narrower than they had been in the 1970s. With national governments forced to follow a restrictive high-interest-rates policy in response first to U.S. monetarism and second to the Reagan-induced fiscal deficit, their capacity to deliver on their side of any bargain with labour was reduced. Other than fall in line with the monetarist solution, their only option was, as we have seen, to follow a highly expansionist fiscal policy to counter the restrictive monetary policy. Yet this option promised to raise debt levels exponentially because of the high interest rates. With governments increasingly hesitant and indeed unable to pursue an expansive fiscal policy, trade unions became unwilling to continue to practise collective wage restraint. Government guarantees to reduce unemployment became either unconvincing or were no longer forthcoming.

By the end of the 1980s, governments had opted either for monetarism or for non-Keynesian supply-side microeconomic policies. Canada's path was a direct one. After brief flirtations with alternative solutions, Canada opted for monetarism. In fact, the choice had already been made in the 1970s. Explaining this choice brings us again to institutions.

Institutional Conditions

Successful pursuit of either the Keynesian full-employment strategy or the monetarist price-stability strategy depends, in part, on sets of institutional conditions being met. In any given country, the institutional factors that come into play in the design and conduct of macroeconomic policy are numerous and complex. Hence it is somewhat hazardous to isolate some factors as being particularly crucial. Nonetheless, policy studies do indicate that four institutional factors play a consistent role in the decisions to be made on macroeconomic strategies:

- the level of organizational development of the labour movement;
- the fiscal weight of the central government;
- the independence of the central bank;
- the presence or absence of a labour-oriented social democratic party in the governing coalition.

These institutional conditions vary in their importance, depending on the strategy chosen. Figure 7.1 summarizes these variations and indicates that the institutional conditions for a Keynesian strategy are more strenuous than for a monetarist approach.

FIGURE 7.1
INSTITUTIONAL CONDITIONS AND MACROECONOMIC STRATEGIES

Institution	Keynesian Strategy	Monetarist Strategy
Labour movement at high levels of organizational development	Necessary	Largely irrelevant
High fiscal weight of central government	Highly useful	Helpful but less necessary
High central bank autonomy	Potentially harmful	Highly useful
Composition of governing party coalition	Inclusion of social democratic party with close ties to labour highly helpful	Business-oriented governing party helpful

Organizational Development of Labour

The organizational development of the labour movement is a crucial factor to the Keynesian full-employment strategy. To be an effective partner of the government, labour organizations must be able to articulate the common, collective interests of all workers. They must have the capacity to develop a vision of the future and to convince members that the sacrifice of present interests is essential to the realization of that future. Labour organizations are more likely to possess these capacities if they represent a high proportion of the labour force, if their internal organization ensures minimal competition for members among component unions or union federations, and if that organization is vertically integrated and centralized. Analysts of neocorporatism identified such characteristics as indicative of a capacity to participate with governments in macroeconomic policy-making with government and to ensure the adhesion of members to any agreements reached. Labour organizations with these qualities are more likely to be able to offer governments a credible policy of wage restraint. In addition, they can ensure that restraint holds long enough for governments to stimulate demand using fiscal and monetary instruments.

These characteristics of labour organization are largely irrelevant when a monetarist strategy is being followed. By raising unemployment in an attempt to attain price stability, monetarists hope to induce individual unions and locals to restrain their wage demands in order to preserve jobs. These pressures will be felt whether collective bargaining is highly centralized or takes place at a local level between individual companies and trade union locals. The organizational development of the labour movement is not normally a factor in monetarist policy-making (Scharpf 1991, 175).

Fiscal Weight

We noted earlier that the Keynesian approach placed a heavy emphasis on fiscal policy. If fiscal policy is to have its intended effects, then the government has to be capable of engineering a stimulus of sufficient volume relative to aggregate demand. This capability depends, in turn, on the political and administrative character of the budget and the room it affords for discretionary spending. In federal states with vertically differentiated fiscal constitutions, it hinges as well on the fiscal potential of the central government. The resulting fiscal capacity of the central government is crucial to the Keynesian full-employment accord with labour. If the government cannot deliver the fiscal stimulus needed to encourage demand and to lower unemployment, labour organizations will be hard-pressed to maintain wage restraint and the corporatist bargain will unravel.

But this fiscal capacity is less crucial to the monetarist approach. To be sure, if fiscal capacity is high and if it can be utilized in directions consistent with monetary policy, then monetary restraint can be less stringent. But if fiscal capacity is disabled, as gradually occurred in Canada and the United States during the 1980s, those following a monetarist approach remain highly willing to rely on monetary policy, a willingness not normally found among Keynesians.

Central Bank Autonomy

A third institutional condition, central bank autonomy, accordingly becomes more important for the monetarists than the Keynesians. Woolley writes that a central bank can be considered independent "if it can set policy instruments without approval from outside authorities, and if, for some minimal period of time, the instrument settings clearly differ from those preferred by the fiscal authority" (1985, 320). Assessing central bank independence proves to be a delicate and difficult task. Although organizational characteristics such as the length of tenure of the governor or board members, degree of openness to outside review, and level of financial autonomy may provide some guidance, they can also be misleading. These kinds of organizational attributes need to be complemented by the central bank's success in cultivating the support of a "sound finance" community (Woolley 1985, 338), a community whose core resides normally in the commercial and investment banking sectors. When its "credibility" with this community is high, the central bank's ability to promote price stability at the expense of other macroeconomic goals within government circles is enhanced.

A relatively independent central bank facilitates the pursuit of a monetarist strategy. Independence means that the employment of monetary policy instruments rests with an institution that is dedicated to price stability, that normally enjoys strong support from key sectors of the business community, and that is able to act at arm's length from the normal political process. Such independence may provide the government with a cover that will assist in weathering the political storms resulting from high unemployment.

In contrast, central bank autonomy poses a potential hazard to the Keynesian strategy. In its "contract" with organized labour, the government assumes that it can co-ordinate an easing of fiscal and monetary policies to stimulate demand. Yet, if the monetary policy instrument rests in the hands of an autonomous central bank, the monetary authority may decide that price stability requires monetary restraint and may take a contrary position to the government. In this situation, monetary and fiscal policy may work at cross-purposes, dampening in the process the willingness of labour to practise wage restraint.[5]

Strength of Social Democratic Parties

Before considering the final institutional factor—the presence or absence of a social democratic party in the governing coalition—it is useful to consider macroeconomic problems and their impact on the electorate. Scharpf (1990, 132ff.) divides the population into three strata:

1. those without property who depend for their livelihood on relatively insecure jobs in the secondary labour market and on government transfers;

2. those who derive their income from more secure jobs in the primary labour market and from substantial property holdings (skilled blue- and white-collar workers, professionals);

3. those who depend primarily on profits and the returns of real and financial assets and who are not directly affected by the labour market (self-employed professionals, managers, entrepreneurs, rentiers—a group that would subsume Woolley's sound finance community).

The first group will give high priority to fighting unemployment and be less concerned with inflation. The third group prefers price stability and is largely untouched by unemployment. The second group will be ambivalent: if unemployment worsens considerably, they may feel threatened; yet if prices rise too fast, the resulting economic instability may also prove worrisome.

How well the concerns of each stratum gain support in government depends, in part, on the electoral system. Proportional representation systems will tend to produce a more accurate weighting of the respective strata in government than will single-member-plurality electoral systems such as is found in Canada. In the latter system one of the three strata often gain's a dominant position in the legislature despite having a minority position in the electorate.

The Keynesian strategy is ambitious: it seeks to follow a direct path from high unemployment and inflation to low unemployment and price stability (see Path 1 in Figure 7.2). In contrast, the monetarist approach is more indirect, taking a path (Path 2) through a purportedly transitory stage of high unemployment and low inflation to economic stability. Choosing the Keynesian strategy becomes more likely when the governing party has considerable support from the propertyless stratum. Since social democratic parties target this stratum plus selected parts of the skilled and professional labour grouping, they normally will push to follow a Keynesian path when in government. Ties between such a party and the labour movement may enhance the possibilities for agreement on wage restraint.

FIGURE 7.2
PATHS TO ECONOMIC STABILITY

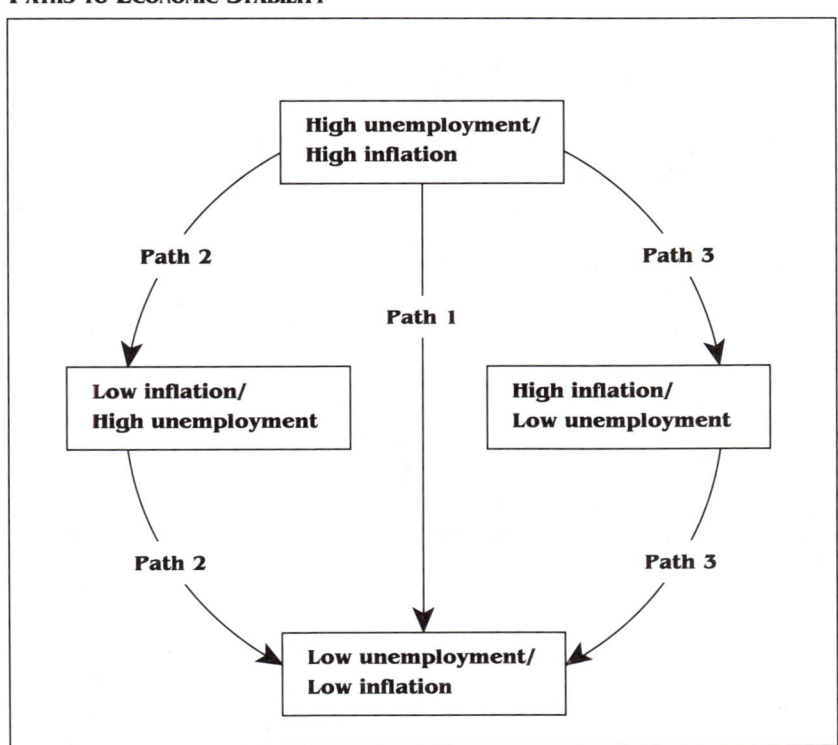

The social democratic Keynesian direct path to economic stability does contain some electoral dangers. The government may fail to follow the direct path and instead find itself in an intermediary situation of lowered unemployment but high inflation (Path 3). In these circumstances, when faced with an electoral choice between a social democratic party and a business-oriented party, voters in the second stratum may perceive the latter to be a more credible choice in the remaining fight for price stability.

Conversely, if the governing coalition falls to business-oriented parties without a core constituency in the propertyless stratum, the likelihood of a Keynesian full-employment strategy becomes very low. The business constituency of these parties strongly favours a return to price stability and suffers rather less from high unemployment. In fact, high unemployment may reduce aggressiveness by workers in labour markets, leading to a further rise in profits. The challenge for such a governing coalition arises when it finds itself in the other intermediate stage of low inflation and high unemployment. At this point, it must ensure that unemployment does not rise so high as to threaten the support it receives from the middle stratum of the electorate.

CANADA 1970–1990: THE ROAD TO MONETARISM

In the years following 1970, Canada moved gradually toward adopting a monetarist approach to macroeconomic policy. We shall trace the path Canada took, a path that involved wage and price controls in the 1970s, but that ended with price stability as the primary macroeconomic objective. The specific character of some institutions, we argue, made this path the most likely to be followed.

The Canadian economy was not spared any of the instability or problems faced by the advanced capitalist states in the 1970s and 1980s. As Figure 7.3 indicates, inflation began to rise after 1970, reaching a high of 10.8 after the first oil shock, and then after a slight fall, rising to a new high in 1981 after the second oil shock and the introduction of U.S. monetarism. Unemployment followed a similar path, reaching a peak of 11.8 percent of the labour force in 1983 but remaining stubbornly high throughout the two decades. The incidence of unemployment varied significantly by region, with levels approaching 15 to 20 percent of the labour force in the Atlantic provinces (Donner 1991, 33–34). Table 7.1 compares the Canadian performance with other countries in the Organization for Economic Cooperation and Development (OECD). The figures suggest that Canada held its own in the fight against inflation, remaining slightly below the OECD average throughout the 1970s and 1980s. In the fight against unemployment, Canada did less well. Its rate was consistently above the OECD average, with the departures being highest during the 1970s.

The Shift Toward a Monetarist Approach

The figures in Table 7.1 are consistent with a macroeconomic policy based on price stability. They show that Canada was more successful in fighting inflation than unemployment. When the Canadian record is compared with that of Austria and Sweden, two countries that attempted to follow a Keynesian full-employment approach in concert with labour in the 1970s, the difference is clear. Unemployment in both countries remained strikingly well controlled in the 1970s, and inflation did not exceed the OECD average in the 1973–79 period. Even in the more difficult circumstances of the 1980s, Austria and Sweden kept their unemployment levels well below the OECD average. Austria continued to hold its own against inflation, while Sweden had less success in this regard.

FIGURE 7.3
UNEMPLOYMENT AND INFLATION RATES, 1967–1989

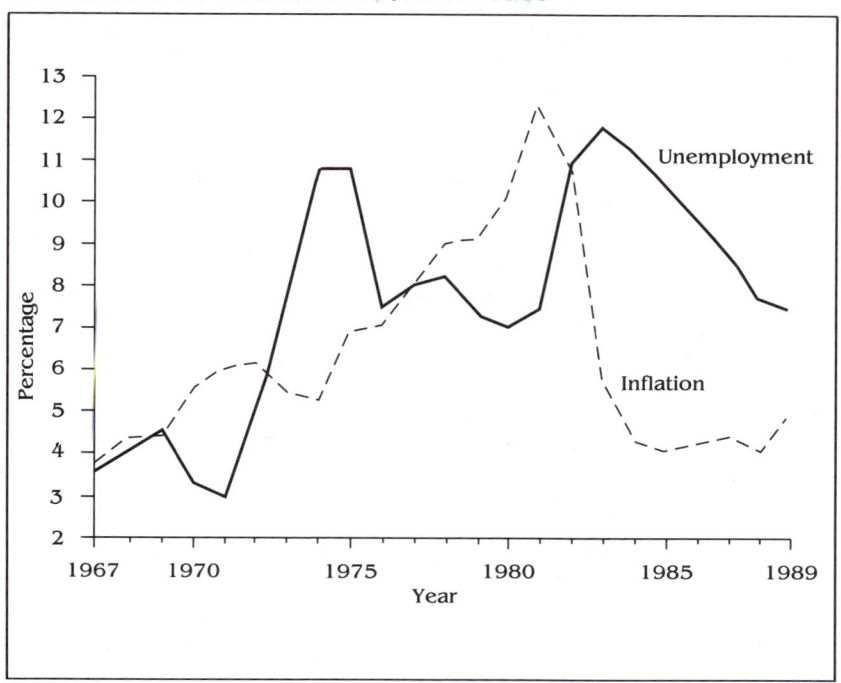

Source: Adapted from OECD (1991), *OECD economic outlook: Historical statistics, 1960–1989*. Paris: OECD

TABLE 7.1
COMPARATIVE ECONOMIC PERFORMANCE, 1960–1989

	Unemployment Rate 1960–1989				Consumer Price Increase 1960–1989(%)			
	60–67	68–73	74–79	80–89	60–68	69–73	74–79	80–89
U.S.A	5.0	4.6	6.7	7.2	2.0	5.0	8.5	5.5
U.K.	1.5	2.4	4.2	9.5	3.6	7.5	15.6	7.4
Austria	2.0	1.4	1.6	3.3	3.6	5.2	6.3	3.8
Sweden	1.6	2.2	1.9	2.5	3.8	6.0	9.8	7.9
Canada	4.8	5.4	7.2	9.3	2.4	4.6	9.2	6.5
OECD average	3.1	2.5	5.1	7.4	3.1	5.7	10.5	6.7

Source: Adapted from OECD (1991), *OECD economic outlook: Historical statistics, 1960–1989*. Paris: OECD.

During the early 1970s, the Canadian government practised the limited Keynesianism of the previous decades, focusing alternately on unemployment and inflation. But in the mid-1970s, faced with the growing intractability of stagflation, the government, led by the Bank of Canada, began to shift course. In October 1975, drawing heavily on the monetarist theories of such economists as Milton Friedman, the Bank announced that henceforth it would set targets for the growth of the money supply. It selected M1, cash and savings deposits in chartered banks, as its target aggregate and indicated that interest rates and the exchange rate would fluctuate freely in response to success or failure in reaching the target. In making this change, the Bank moved from a more activist, interventionist stance, consistent with Keynesian theory, to a less intrusive approach (Dufour & Racette 1986, 211). Its strategy was a gradual one: the Bank expected to reduce the target ranges for monetary growth over a period of years rather than administer a one-time shock. Already possessed of a reputation among central banks for being highly market-oriented (Courchene 1975, 266), the Canadian central bank was second only to the German central bank in adopting a monetarist targeting approach to monetary policy.[6]

Wage and Price Controls

A second step taken in a new approach to policy followed with the introduction of compulsory wage and price controls by the federal government. The extent of the policy shift became clear when the government stated its intention to move away from Keynesian fine-tuning and demand management in a budget speech early in 1976 (Doern 1985, 35). The government committed itself to keeping its own expenditures within the growth line of the GNP, and in doing so indicated its unwillingness to use fiscal policy in the future. Since these measures were coupled to limits on per capita dollar spending on such structural items as manpower training, they suggested a further retreat from the Keynesian goal of full employment (Doern 1985, 36).

The controls program appeared to have some success in restraining wages but less success in controlling prices (Canada 1985, 351–52). But the suspension of the collective-bargaining system precipitated significant protest in the labour movement. The leading labour central, the Canadian Labour Congress (CLC), reviewed its options, and its leadership proposed moving toward a more corporatist system for managing macroeconomic policy (McBride 1983). This attempt to promote some of the practices tried in Western Europe failed badly. It did not find favour among the CLC's autonomous affiliates, already angered by wage controls, and the central had little capacity itself to impose its ideas. What is more, with the government clearly moving away from the full-employment objective, policy-makers had little interest in concertation with labour and business on macroeconomic policy. In a proposal entitled *Agenda for Co-operation* published in 1977, the government proposed a multipartite rather than a tripartite forum and offered the new body an advisory rather than a decision-making role. The document reaffirmed the supremacy of Parliament in a thinly veiled attack on the CLC ideas (Fournier 1986, 299).

Decline in Fiscal Capacity

Traditional strategies for the use of macroeconomic policy instruments were gradually confounded further when, in 1975, the first in a now long-standing series of budget deficits materialized. At first blush, it is tempting to see these deficits as reflecting an expansionary fiscal policy based on government spending. But the deficits in the late 1970s did not result from wayward spending on social programs; in fact, the government had curbed these expenditures. Rather, they had their origins on the revenue side of the budget (Wolfe 1985). Beginning already in the early 1970s, the government had introduced a series of tax expenditures to incite business to increase investments, particularly in economically depressed regions (Savoie 1990, 326). The Trudeau government budgets of the mid-1970s reflected a growing disenchantment with Keynesianism. Finance minister John Turner accepted the argument that "taxes" had become essentially a cost consideration rather than an inducement. He believed that a tax cut would be anti-inflationary because it would lower costs, thereby leading consumers and producers to demand less in the form of higher wages and prices. The policy message was thus confused (Purvis & Smith, 1986): an apparently expansionary fiscal policy was now seen as a complement to a restrictive monetary policy under the central bank's monetary targeting.

When the second oil shock hit in 1979, the deficits of the preceding years compounded themselves into a new financial problem. The recession of 1981–82 led to a further increase in the deficit, as automatic stabilizers like unemployment insurance payments rose quickly. This increase, when costed out at the consistently high interest rates of the period, placed a heavy charge on the budget from which the government has been unable to recover. Servicing the deficit has come to absorb close to 30 percent of the expenditure budget, leaving virtually no room for the discretionary use of fiscal policy.

Consequently, by the early 1980s, monetary policy had to carry the brunt of government macroeconomic policy. Yet the Bank of Canada itself was facing difficulties in implementing its policy of monetary gradualism. Extensive financial innovations following the breakdown of the Bretton Woods system had made it increasingly difficult to define what money entailed and to find a clear relationship between a monetary aggregate and economic performance (Freedman 1986). In November 1982, the Bank abandoned its monetary targeting and began a search for a new policy approach. In subsequent years, it paid attention to interest rates and the exchange rate, and, in recent years especially, has placed particular emphasis on broader monetary aggregates (M2 and M2+) as "guides" to policy.

A Zero-Inflation Policy

Later in the decade, the Bank shifted again to a stronger public position, but this time emphasized a broad, longer-term objective. In his first major speech after becoming Governor of the Bank of Canada in 1987, John Crow (1987, 21–22) posed the question: "What should be the primary objective of Canada's monetary policy?" His answer was unequivocal: zero inflation or price stability. Since 1987, the Bank has elevated price stability to a pre-eminent position among the usual objectives of macroeconomic policy. Unless price stability is secured first, the Bank argues, other objectives—lower unemployment, higher growth, balanced trade—will not be achieved. As such, the Bank and implicitly the government have moved away from the preamble of the Bank of Canada Act, which simply groups price stability with the other goals of employment, productivity, and trade.

In his budget speech in the spring of 1991, the federal minister of Finance formally fell in with the Bank's strategy when he listed a series of steps over a period of years designed to bring inflation close to the zero level. Weeks later, a budget brought down by the NDP government in Ontario introduced a more classical expansionist fiscal policy. But this budget precipitated an intensive attack from the federal government and the threat of an investment strike by business. Evidently,

Keynesian ideas had clearly lost all legitimacy within the national governing coalition and the business community. By the autumn, the Ontario government too was attempting to cut expenditures. Simultaneously, as part of its constitutional proposals, the federal government proposed amending the Bank of Canada Act to confine its responsibilities to the achievement of price stability. The triumph of monetarism thus seemed complete.

Institutional Conditions

Social and political institutions structure collective behaviour by defining a restricted set of paths to policy formulation and implementation. In times of stability, these paths become well-worn and familiar, enabling decision-makers to design more complex strategies and approaches to problems. When a crisis occurs, these same paths may or may not be suitable for finding solutions, but they are the routes tried first of all. A country may be fortunate and find that its institutions can cope with the new circumstances. Or, if existing institutions cannot be adapted easily, a political crisis follows on the economic one until new institutions are crafted to deal with the economic difficulties at hand. When faced with the twin problems of rising unemployment and high inflation, Canadian decision-makers inherited an institutional path that allowed a rather smooth transition to monetarism. Macroeconomic policy-making did not in itself generate a deep political crisis. Rather, the consequences flowing from those policies precipitated a series of grave crises in another set of institutions, those of Canadian federalism (Jenson 1989a).

Let us review then the institutional conditions set out in Figure 7.1.

Organizational Development of Labour

The organizational development of the labour movement was comparatively low in Canada and a handicap to co-operation with governments on wage policy. The percentage of the civilian labour force belonging to a trade union rose gradually throughout the postwar period, reaching a high of 30.4 in 1981 (Canada 1996, xii). Despite this progression, the percentage of unionized workers remained rather low compared with many European countries. Austria and Sweden, the two countries that followed Keynesian policy prescriptions most closely, had unionization levels well above the Canadian figure. Hence, even if the Canadian labour movement were to have reached a Keynesian-like agreement on restraint with policy-makers, they could only have promised its implementation for one-third of the labour force.

If union density had been higher, the labour movement would still have lacked the organizational capacity for negotiating an accord with the government and for implementing such an agreement. Canadian labour organizations were highly fragmented. The Canadian Labour Congress represented only 58.6 percent of the unionized sector (Canada, 1990b, xiii). It had a weak position in Quebec, where the independent Confédération des syndicats nationaux had a long tradition of activity and where the CLC's own affiliate, the Fédération des travailleurs et travailleuses du Québec, had an exceptional degree of autonomy. The CLC itself is a decentralized organization with 52 international unions, 48 national unions, and 38 directly chartered unions as members (Canada 1990b, xx). Not surprisingly, then, in international comparisons, Canada ranks low in organizational centralization compared with such countries as Sweden, Austria, and Germany (Cameron 1984, 165).[7] The CLC plays primarily a co-ordinating role. It has difficulty articulating a common labour position and speaking for its affiliates. These, in turn, have considerable autonomy and occupy the collective-bargaining terrain. About 75 percent of collective agreements are still negotiated between local unions and individual companies (Fournier 1986, 324). Hence, centralized collective bargaining, another asset critical to labour–government co-operation, does not occur in Canada.

Fiscal Centralization

A second institutional factor highly crucial to a Keynesian full-employment strategy is fiscal capacity, the ability of the state to engineer an adequate fiscal stimulus in times of flagging demand. A review of comparative fiscal centralization and of federal–provincial relations in budgeting indicates that the Canadian federal government was not as strongly placed to create a fiscal stimulus as some other more centralized states. In addition, political and administrative difficulties have increasingly disabled the government's fiscal flexibility.

Table 7.2 presents several indicators of fiscal capacity. They show that the public spending of Canadian governments stands in a middle position, not as low as Switzerland or Germany, but higher than the United Kingdom and about the same as Austria. Given that the central government would normally engineer the fiscal stimulus, Table 7.2 shows that Canada may be handicapped in this regard. In comparison with the more centralized states of Britain, Sweden, and Austria, the Canadian federal government has less fiscal weight. As for federal systems, the central government in Canada has less weight than central authorities in Germany and only slightly more than the Swiss confederation.

How effectively a central government in a federal state can use its leverage depends, of course, on the relationships it maintains with subnational governments. In their review of these relationships in

Canada, Maslove, Prince, and Doern (1986, 240) find evidence for a significant amount of co-ordination between levels of government. They note a fair amount of independent action by the provinces but decide that much of this activity is relatively harmless in an economic sense. In a separate study, Courchene reaches similar conclusions: "There is, no doubt, room for improvement in the system, but in general, Ottawa retains enough scope and flexibility to pursue adequately its stabilization role on the expenditure side" (1986, 77).

TABLE 7.2
COMPARATIVE FISCAL CAPACITY, 1979–1980[1]

	Canada	Austria	Switzerland	Germany	U.K.	Sweden
Public-sector expenditure as a % of GNP	41.0	42.8	27.2	33.3	37.5	57.3
Central government share of total expenditures (%)	38.8	57.5	37.3	43.6	88.4	62.7
Degree of difficulty[2]	6.8	4.1	9.9	6.9	3.0	2.8
Net financing of government as a % of GDP, average 1980–89	−4.6	−3.0	—	−2.1	−2.4	−1.6

1. Canadian figures are for 1980. Transfer payments to the provinces are not included.
2. Budgetary changes by the central government that correspond to 1% of GNP.

Sources: For Canada, adapted from Canada (1985), Royal Commission on the economic union and development prospects for Canada, *Final Report* (vol. 2). Ottawa: Supply and Services Canada; G.B. Doern (1985), The politics of Canadian economic policy: An overview. In G.B. Doern (Ed.), *The politics of economic policy*. Toronto: University of Toronto Press; and author's calculations. Data for the other countries are from F.W. Scharpf (1991), *Crisis and choice in European social democracy* (p. 214). Ithaca, N.Y.: Cornell University Press. Data on net financing are adapted from OECD (1991), *OECD economic outlook: Historical statistics, 1960–1989*. Paris: OECD.

Scharpf (1991, 212–14) argues that these indicators of fiscal capacity must be interpreted in light of a third factor, the magnitude of budgetary change required in order to produce a stimulus. Table 7.2 contains the indicator he suggests for assessing this factor: the magnitude of change in the central government's budget that corresponds to 1 percent of GNP. Here again Canada appears somewhat weak: the change required in the budget is relatively high when compared with the centralized states of Great Britain, Sweden, and Austria. In short, a review of these first three indicators suggests that the activity of the central government in Canada provides some room for an effective fiscal policy, but less than that possessed by other, more centralized states.

Yet the matter cannot rest here. Some assessment must be made of the political and administrative difficulties in achieving budget change. Throughout the 1980s, Canada has lost flexibility for the pursuit of fiscal policy because of a rising deficit. This problem arrived to stay in 1975 when a deficit of $3.8 billion was recorded. In 1982, during the heart of the recession, the deficit rose to $21.1 billion, and has remained stubbornly in the $30 billion range through the 1980s (Savoie 1990, 321). By the late 1980s, debt servicing was absorbing 30 percent of the expenditure budget.

When compared with other countries on this dimension, Canada does not fare so well. Table 7.2 indicates that the financing needs of Canadian governments averaged 4.6 percent of GDP during the 1980s, a figure above those of the Keynesian states of Sweden and Austria and of the more monetarist Germany and U.K. In fact, the Canadian figure is the third highest in the OECD area following Italy (11.0) and the Netherlands (5.7). Even during the growth period of the mid- to late 1980s, the government was unable to reduce its deficit as Keynesian theory suggests. Savoie (1990) describes in detail the political and administrative problems besetting the Canadian expenditure process. His analysis suggests that an inability to discipline both tax expenditures and traditional spending by ministers undermines whatever fiscal capacity the federal government might otherwise possess. Such a weak fiscal capacity constrains a Keynesian approach more than a monetarist one.

Central Bank Autonomy

The third institutional factor, central bank autonomy, tilts policy strategy further to the monetarist side. If we take Woolley's definition of independence cited earlier—the ability to set policy without approval of outside authorities and the power to set a policy course at variance with that of the fiscal authority—then the Bank of Canada must be viewed as a rather independent central bank.

Formally speaking, the minister of Finance has "ultimate responsibility" for monetary policy. The minister's relationship to the Bank takes the following form: the responsibility for the formulation and implementation of monetary policy lies with the governor of the Bank. In the event of a disagreement between the governor and the government, the minister, with the approval of cabinet, may issue a directive to the Bank as to the monetary policy to follow. If such a directive were to be issued, it is most likely that the governor would resign. Hence the government retains ultimate responsibility.

In the absence of such a directive, the Bank of Canada is responsible for monetary policy (Coleman 1991). It is the governor who announces changes in interest rates or broader changes in policy, not the minister in the House of Commons as occurs in Britain. The government would only issue a directive under exceptional circumstances and would face highly volatile financial markets as a consequence. In fact, then, the directive power becomes a shield for the autonomy of the Bank. It means that, in the words of one official, "the Bank acts independently unless we formally tell it what to do." No government in the 24 years since the introduction of the directive power has seen fit to take this step.

When one moves beyond these structures, it is always difficult to establish how autonomous a central bank is. Too much decision-making takes place in closed forums. What can be said is that nothing in the policy history of the past twenty years contradicts the conclusion that the Canadian central bank enjoys considerable autonomy. Between 1970 and 1990, the Bank of Canada took three different decisions resulting in a basic shift in policy: the explicit adoption of monetarist targeting in 1975, the abandonment of formal monetary targets in 1982, and the adoption of price stability as its primary ultimate objective in 1987. Each of these changes was accompanied by an important change in the theoretical framework that guided the implementation of policy and each was controversial. Yet each change was announced by the Bank and everything indicates that the decisions were taken by the Bank. It is unclear how extensively the minister was involved.

Certainly, the adoption of targeting in 1975 preceded by several months the adoption of spending restraints. Similarly, it might be argued that the elevation of price stability to pre-eminence in 1987 was only partially consistent with government policy as reflected in the preamble of the Bank of Canada Act, which directs the Bank to concern itself with economic growth, trade, employment, and productivity as well as the level of prices. In addition, David R. Johnson (1990) has argued that the Bank's zero-inflation strategy ran counter to the inflation objectives set out in policy by the Department of Finance during the late 1980s.

To conclude, the relatively autonomous character of the Bank of Canada was a factor favouring a monetarist rather than a Keynesian approach to macroeconomic policy.

Strength of Social Democratic Parties

The final institutional factor—the presence or absence of social democratic parties in the governing party coalition—certainly reinforced the other conditions favouring a macroeconomic policy that stressed price stability over full employment. The postwar compromise between capital and labour over the character of the industrial-relations system and of social welfare was not brokered in the party system between a social democratic and a business party as occurred frequently in Europe. Rather, the compromise emerged out of a series of private struggles between labour and management in the workplace (Jenson 1989a). Even the first significant step to a comprehensive social-welfare net came in this forum, when the United Automobile Workers achieved such protections in collective agreements negotiated during the 1950s (Yates 1990, 275). Decisions taken on the advice of the Ottawa mandarinate, rather than as a consequence of partisan conflict, universalized social-welfare measures in the late 1950s and 1960s. In these circumstances, labour registered its demands as a normal pressure group and not through organizational ties to a social democratic party in a governing coalition (Yates 1990, 270).

The strongest proponents of full-employment policies in Europe in the 1970s and 1980s, social democratic parties remained largely absent from the national decision-making process in Canada. Partially, this absence arises from the Canadian "first past the post" electoral system that discriminates against third parties with a national electoral base. Most European countries have some elements of proportional representation in their electoral systems, an arrangement that increases significantly the likelihood of social democratic parties entering governing coalitions. The Canadian government thus stayed in the hands of the Liberal and Progressive Conservative parties, which assembled varying coalitions from across the electorate.

When in government, each of these parties had a strong core of support from the most advantaged economic stratum, which accumulated its wealth through profits and returns on financial and real investments. They added to this core by drawing varying support from the other two strata, with the Liberals perhaps slightly more successful with the propertyless stratum and the Conservatives with the professionals and skilled blue- and white-collar workers. Accordingly, the Liberals tended to favour redistributive and employment policies more than their Conservative counterparts, but these differences should not be overemphasized. When forced to choose, internal party pressures pushed both of these parties toward fighting inflation first and unemployment second. As long as unemployment did not reach crisis proportions—that is, did not seriously touch the middle, somewhat affluent, stratum—these parties retained an obvious electoral advantage when it came to macroeconomic policy. They could always appear to be more credible opponents of high inflation than could the New Democratic Party opponent with its ties to organized labour.

CONCLUSIONS

A macroeconomic policy that gives primary emphasis to price stability and relies heavily on monetary restraint as a policy instrument can take a heavy toll on the economy. The economists' Phillips curve traces the trade-off between unemployment and inflation. Examining that curve can indicate approximately how much unemployment must be suffered in order to lower inflation a given number of points. Fortin (1991) describes the Canadian Phillips curve as relatively flat: large increases in unemployment reduce inflation by only small amounts. He estimates that each one-point reduction in the inflation rate costs at least four percent of GNP, or about 26 billion 1990 dollars. When coupled with the deteriorating investment and declining human capital that such a policy brings in its wake, it is evident that the costs to the long-term development of the economy are potentially very high. What is more, the policy raises normative questions: the inflation battle is fought on the backs of the most vulnerable people in the labour force, people hardly responsible for the rise in inflation in the first place (Barber & McCallum 1980, 2).

In his analysis of policy options available to advanced capitalist states at the end of the 1980s, Scharpf (1991) observes that international developments have forced most countries to give increased emphasis to price stability in their macroeconomic policies. The policy question that arises is whether this emphasis inevitably means a serious loss in employment. Already we have seen that some states in the 1970s and 1980s enjoyed considerable success in maintaining employment while retaining a credible record in fighting inflation. The key to such success appears to lie in the nature of microeconomic policy.

In their assessment of Keynesianism, Matzner and Streeck (1991) note that Keynesians assumed that the processes of structural and technological adjustment on the supply side of the economy were market-driven and thus unproblematical. Certainly, it was believed, such processes did not require detailed public intervention. Yet not all countries were prepared to accept this assumption. Many did not believe that adjustment would be optimal when firms were asked simply to follow market signals as closely as possible.

Policy-makers in countries as diverse as Sweden, Germany, and Japan found state intervention on the supply side to be essential if rising unemployment was to be avoided. They believed that the harsh effects of monetarism could be cushioned if firms operated in settings where market pressures were mediated and institutional support promoting longer-term investment was forthcoming. In short, after observing these countries, Matzner and Streeck argue that demand-side intervention inspired by Keynes must be supplemented by "an advanced, sophisticated type of intervention centred around the gardening of institutions that induce and enable firms to choose a high productivity, long-term competitive adjustment path over its market-driven alternative" (1991, 7).

The capacity of the Canadian state to pursue a microeconomic policy along these lines is examined by Kenneth Woodside in the next chapter. When it comes to macroeconomic policy, Canada has the option of working toward greater international co-ordination of policymaking in forums like the Group of Seven (G7) countries. Theoretically, at least, some of the Keynesian objectives relative to full employment might be realized if the major capitalist states could co-ordinate their fiscal and monetary policies (Scharpf 1991). Within the G7, there is now an institutionalized dialogue and some efforts to develop common economic indicators and statistics, arguably a precondition for increased co-ordination. In addition, some co-ordination appears to have taken place in international monetary policy in the 1980s, albeit spasmodically (Funabashi 1988). Similarly, the 1991 decision by the European Community to move toward an economic and monetary union will lead those states to work much more in common when designing macroeconomic policy.

Canada can use what influence it has in promoting dialogue and serious policy discussions in the G7 and related forums. But results from such efforts promise to be slow in coming and restricted in impact. Hence microeconomic policies cannot be ignored. In this monetarist age, governments that abstain from active labour market and industrial policies jeopardize the jobs of the citizens who elect them.

NOTES

1. For a discussion of monetarism in Canada and Canadian monetary policy, see Courchene (1975, 1981, 1986). For a contrasting point of view, see Donner and Peters (1979).

2. The term "money market" refers to the arrangements by which "most non-equity fixed income securities maturing within three years are issued, traded and redeemed" and "short-term funds are borrowed and lent on the security of these obligations on an impersonal basis" (Sarpkaya 1984, 1). Capital markets, then, refer to markets for corporate and government debt issues with terms longer than three years and for corporate equity securities.

3. In July 1981, both the minister of Finance and the governor of the Bank of Canada asked the major chartered banks to limit their financing of takeovers by Canadians of businesses in Canada owned by nonresidents (Boreham 1988, 250–51).

4. The following discussion borrows heavily from Scharpf (1990, 1991).

5. Scharpf (1991, ch. 10) indicates that such a situation developed in the Federal Republic of Germany in the late 1970s and early 1980s.

6. The Bank's monetarist approach was highly controversial. Courchene (1981) attacked the policy for not following more closely the tenets of monetarist economics. Others such as Donner and Peters (1979) and Barber and McCallum (1982) criticized the Bank for being too focused on inflation. The debate is summarized well by Dufour and Racette (1986) and by Sparks (1986).

7. For example, in 1980, the ÖGB in Austria had 15 affiliates, the DGB in Germany 17, and the LO in Sweden 24 affiliates (Visser 1984, 63).

CHAPTER 8

Trade and Industrial Policy: Hard Choices

Kenneth Woodside

INTRODUCTION

Most Canadians have good reason to be satisfied with their present standard of living and the capacity of the Canadian economy to provide for their needs. The economy, for all its failings, has performed relatively well through much of the post–World War II period. In terms of the purchasing power of its currency, Canada's per capita gross domestic product (GDP) climbed from fourth among the member states of the Organization for Economic Cooperation and Development (OECD) in 1960 to second in 1989 (Porter 1991, 4). However, a strong sense of concern has emerged, along with the recession of the early 1990s, that these good times are now at risk.

There are many sources of these concerns and only a few can be raised here. In the first place, the world economy is undergoing considerable change and restructuring. Successive agreements under the General Agreement on Tariffs and Trade (GATT), the Canada–U.S. Free Trade Agreement (FTA), along with rapid technological change, deregulation of financial services, and many other developments are in the process of greatly liberalizing international trade and investment. Will Canada win or lose as a result of these changes?

Second, while Canadians remain relatively affluent, the low growth in productivity, especially in the manufacturing sector, is worrisome. During the 1980s not only did the gap between Canada and the United States in manufacturing productivity widen but some other advanced

---

The author wishes to express his appreciation to Michael Atkinson, William Coleman, and Kent Weaver for their thoughtful comments on earlier versions of this chapter.

countries such as Italy and France also overtook Canadian levels (Economic Council of Canada 1991, 8-9). Employment in the manufacturing sector continued to fall through the 1980s and unemployment remained disturbingly high relative to our major competitors (Cornell & Gorecki 1991, 39).

Third, many question whether Canada is well positioned to take advantage of the opportunities that will present themselves over the next decade. Will the high level of foreign ownership transform Canada into a warehouse economy, served largely by plants in the United States, or is the nationality of corporations losing much of its significance (Watkins 1988, 82; Reich 1991, 136-53)? And is continued reliance on natural resources (especially in the face of persistent price declines) a sound economic strategy? Canada's share of world trade in natural resources has grown from 5.0 percent in 1978 to 8.9 percent in 1989. At the same time, Canada's share of world trade in machine equipment has declined from 1.3 percent in 1978 to 0.7 percent in 1989 (Porter 1991, 10, 15-16).

The economic health of Canada is of crucial importance to the lives of its citizens. Among the governmental policies most closely associated with improving the performance of the economy are trade and industrial policy. In this chapter we will identify the principal features of these policies and explore the effect that political institutions have had on their evolution. The institutions we will focus on are the Westminster model of parliamentary government, political parties, the bureaucracy, and the federal system with its division of powers. In so doing we will consider why trade policy has gradually come to be the predominant preoccupation of the federal government, while industrial policy has increasingly been left to the provincial governments.

In the following sections we will discuss the meaning of the terms trade and industrial policy and the relationship between these two types of policy. This will be followed by a discussion of the general characteristics of the Canadian economy and its place in the world economy and a brief overview of the evolution of trade and industrial policy. Finally the impact of federal and provincial political institutions on trade and industrial policy will be described and assessed.

DEFINITIONS AND BACKGROUND: INDUSTRIAL POLICY

Industrial policy refers to the mix of government policies intended to enhance the productivity and growth of the economy. Given its broadest interpretation, there is virtually nothing that governments do that cannot be said to have some impact on the economy, if only indirect. However, a definition this broadly based excludes too little to be of much value. Thus, by convention, the term is used to refer to government policies that more directly attempt to affect economic performance. Within this narrower approach, industrial policy can be targeted at individuals—whether entrepreneurs or employees—or at firms or organizations. It can be well co-ordinated, organized, intrusive in private-sector decision-making, and possibly extensive in its coverage. In this form it might be described as an industrial strategy or an anticipatory industrial policy. It may also be less well co-ordinated or even unco-ordinated, unorganized, unintrusive, and responsive only to specific (often short-term) needs. In this case it might be described as a reactive industrial policy (Atkinson & Coleman 1989a, 23–27; Brooks 1989, 232–34; Morici, Smith & Lee 1982, 2–5). We will be referring to both of these approaches as industrial policy. They both focus on influencing domestic economic activity and attempt to resolve a potentially wide range of perceived domestic economic problems. We will focus on two broad categories of industrial policy. The first group are direct measures intended to subsidize specific activities in one way or another. The second group of measures—adjustment policies—are aimed at improving the general economic environment in which industry is situated.

Direct Industrial Policy Measures

Direct Spending

The first category of direct industrial policy measures are the many that involve direct spending by government to support actions by firms or individuals that satisfy specific governmental goals. One such granting program, which was very controversial, was the Petroleum Incentives Program (PIP) grants that were part of the National Energy Program introduced in October 1980. These grants replaced existing tax incentives available to all oil industry firms and were designed to provide larger benefits to firms that had higher proportions of Canadian ownership. In this way they were intended (along with other measures) to promote changes in the ownership structure of the oil industry at a time when many believed that high levels of foreign (especially U.S.) ownership along with high oil prices threatened Canada's economic independence (Doern & Toner 1985). A second example, introduced in 1962, is the Industrial Research Assistance Program (IRAP). The IRAP, run through the National Research Council, pays the salaries of researchers working on approved projects in industry. These projects must be judged to have the potential for commercial success but also be sufficiently risky that they might not be undertaken in the absence of financial support (Tarasofsky 1984, 57–61).

Use of Regulations

A second type of industrial policy measure involves regulating the behaviour of a sector or industry. One example of this occurred in the Canadian popular music recording industry. The Canadian Radio-television and Telecommunications Commission (CRTC), beginning with AM radio in 1971 and later with FM radio in 1975, established criteria that would define whether a particular musical recording was "Canadian" and mandated requirements as to how much of this Canadian music the licensed AM and FM stations had to play each day. In this way the CRTC helped to create a domestic market for Canadian recording artists. Singers such as Bryan Adams were given increased opportunities to have their recordings played and the CRTC helped to build up a domestic industry of popular recording stars (Canada 1986, 113-15, 124-26; Audley 1983). In the pharmaceutical industry another regulatory change had similar consequences. The 1969 amendments to Section 41(4) of the Patent Act introduced compulsory licensing of patented pharmaceutical products. This change gave a major boost to Canada's generic drug manufacturing industry. In exchange for a four percent royalty paid to the holders of these patents—almost exclusively large, foreign-owned companies—this measure allowed domestic generic (no-name) firms to develop a strong place in the Canadian drug market. In reducing the protection for intellectual property rights, there was also a substantial reduction in the cost of drugs in Canada. Eighteen years later, in 1987, a good part of this property rights protection was restored in exchange for a commitment from the pharmaceutical industry to invest a further $1.4 billion in research and development in Canada over the next decade (Ontario 1990, 16; Atkinson & Coleman 1989a, 122-41; Campbell & Pal 1989, 53-106).

Tax Incentives

A third type of industrial policy measure—tax incentives—are also extensively used to achieve a wide range of economic goals. In recent decades the tax system has been widely used to achieve goals other than just raising revenue. One such goal has been to promote scientific research and experimental development (R & D). Government involvement is regarded as desirable because of the overall importance of R & D to the economy and because of the high risk such investments pose. Government assistance can help to underwrite the risk. These tax measures have variously been in the form of either deducting specified expenditures from taxable income or providing a credit against the tax burden the company faced. Canada's incentives have generally been quite generous; one recent case—the Scientific Research Tax Credit—was excessively flexible and generous. However, despite these measures, levels of R & D investment remain low, about one-half the level of the United States and Japan (Sweeney & Robertson 1989, 315–20; McFetridge & Warda 1983).

Procurement Policies

Procurement or the purchase of goods and services by government is another potentially effective instrument of industrial policy. Procurement policies by their nature give some form of advantage to a designated group of producers. These policies can include preferences for local or domestic suppliers, tendering or bidding practices that favour these suppliers, and other provisions that encourage local or domestic sourcing. In a country like Canada, where foreign multinationals constitute a powerful force and may have their own foreign suppliers, government procurement policies can be an important stimulus. These protective practices provide a relatively guaranteed market for Canadian suppliers that can provide them with the longer-term leverage to enter other more competitive markets. They also allow a government to target sectors such as those in the high-technology area as the objects of these preferences.

Past initiatives, such as the National Energy Program (NEP), the Foreign Investment Review Agency (FIRA), and the megaprojects strategy all contained requirements for "industrial benefits" for Canadian suppliers (Morici, Smith & Lea 1982, 60–64). The preferred equipment supplier relationship between Northern Telecom and Bell Canada, which was sanctioned by the Canadian government, has undoubtedly been a positive factor in making Northern Telecom a strong competitor in the digital equipment world (Woodrow & Woodside 1986, 201).

One estimate suggests that governments and crown corporations in Canada purchased approximately eighteen percent of all goods and services in Canada in 1983 (Calvert 1988, 132). Clearly this is an area that, if carefully employed, can generate significant benefits for domestic producers. Indeed, over the past two decades, use of procurement has become an increasingly important approach for provincial governments seeking to concentrate benefits within their economies.

Crown Corporations and Agencies

Crown corporations and state agencies can facilitate the activities of private firms, sometimes by providing services or investment capital. One long-established example is Ontario Hydro. Initially created in 1906, but not a fully fledged provider of public power until much later, it has served many goals in the Ontario economy. In preventing the takeover of the last available undeveloped water power at Niagara Falls by unpopular monopolists in Toronto, Hydro ensured that this power could be used for the development of all of southern Ontario, not just Toronto (Nelles 1974). In later years it helped to create a nuclear industry in Ontario through its commitment to the use of nuclear power. For its part, Hydro-Québec has, since 1962, been an important force both in the economic development of the province and in the provision of good management jobs for aspiring Québécois (Courchene 1991b, 4).

State agencies can also play an important part in the provision and protection of investment capital. The Caisse de dépôt et placement du Québec plays just such a role in Quebec's economy. Established in 1965 to invest the contributions of the Québécois under the Quebec Pension Plan, it has sought to promote the development of Quebec's economy. Another body, the federal Export Development Corporation, provides loans, loan guarantees, and insurance to Canadian exporters to permit them to compete with foreign-based competitors (Morici, Smith & Lee 1982, 34-35; Brooks 1989, 221-23).

Adjustment Policies

Job Training

Among the various adjustment policies, we will discuss only three. The first is job training. These are policies that are aimed at easing transition costs in the workforce by training and retraining workers and even providing mobility or relocation allowances. These programs can be especially important in dealing with declining sectors of the economy. One such program has been the Canadian Jobs Strategy (CJS) introduced by the Conservative government in 1985. This program combines a focus on designated groups such as the long-term unemployed, women, youth and workers needing new skills, as well as employers facing a skills shortage. It attempts both to respond to market requirements and facilitate labour adjustment while focussing on the economically disadvantaged (Prince & Rice 1989).

A second program implemented under the umbrella of the CJS is the 1989 Labour Force Development Strategy (LFDS). Following the report of the Advisory Council on Adjustment in early 1989, the Conservative government introduced the LFDS with its focus on high-technology skills and on the preparation of workers for participation in the high value-added economy. The program encourages Canadian firms to invest in training through modest financial incentives to promote analysis of private-sector needs (Mahon 1990, 73-88).

Diffusion of Technology

A second group of adjustment policies involves those intended to speed the diffusion of technology. It is often assumed that once a research project has been successfully completed and the idea has been incorporated into equipment and processes the technology story is over. However, in Canada there has been considerable concern over how to make businesses and businesspeople more aware of available technologies and how they can use them.

One way in which governments have responded to this diffusion problem is by establishing technology centres. In Ontario six centres were established in 1981 to promote diffusion of a variety of technologies including some in microelectronics, robotics, and CAD/CAM. The federal government, in 1975, established the Program for Industry/Laboratory Products (PILP) whereby research projects in process could be transferred from government laboratories to private labs, once again to promote diffusion (McFetridge & Corvari 1985, 211–13). Federal and provincial governments have also sought to persuade multinationals that their Canadian branch plants could take on a world product mandate for a particular product. This means that the Canadian operation would be the worldwide supplier, for that firm, of the products based on a particular technology. The Canadian operation would then be in a position to develop the full potential of the associated technology (McFetridge & Corvari 1985, 217–21).

Labour Legislation

The third element of adjustment policy is the rules governing employee–employer relations. These rules are important in establishing the relative bargaining power of each party in wage determination, workplace conditions, job security, and a host of other decisions. Canada retains a relatively high level of unionization compared with the United States, and unionization has normally meant higher wages and a healthier workplace for employees (Mahon 1991, 320–29). The restructuring of industry in response to competitive pressures from foreign firms may be threatening the long-term viability of the trade union movement (Drache 1991, 249–65). While it is often argued that liberalized trade will produce better and higher-paid jobs, many of the new jobs generated in the 1980s were low-paid, part-time service-sector jobs (Economic Council of Canada 1990a).

One of the strategies available to management in unionized firms is to contract out the provision of goods or services to a non-union operation. In this way the firm can get around restrictions implied by its union contract and lower its overall labour costs. If this approach is widely followed, the union will suffer serious losses in membership and bargaining clout. Labour law can seek to limit and regulate this behaviour if the government has the political will, but there is also strong pressure to permit its use. In strike situations, if labour law includes so-called "anti-scab" measures to restrict the use of substitute workers, then union bargaining strength will be enhanced.

In each of these situations labour law can contribute to stronger or weaker unions, depending on the provisions imposed by government. Business management generally wants to maximize its flexibility to use and price its inputs, including labour, as circumstances warrant. Labour unions want security, stability, reasonable pay, and some control over the workplace. Legislation governing labour relations is the means whereby government sets the balance between the two parties, and this balance can be important in determining both the amount and the distribution of the gains and losses that result (Ontario 1991b).

DEFINITIONS AND BACKGROUND: TRADE POLICY

Trade among nations has become an increasingly important source of economic growth. In the years following World War II, a growing number of countries, through membership in the General Agreement on Tariffs and Trade (GATT), agreed to lower trade barriers to each other. The result has been a major increase in the amount of trade. The rate of growth of trade in products exceeded the rate of growth in the production of those products by several percentage points per year during the post-war period (Finlayson 1985b, 13). The expansion of trading relations has also meant that all countries are increasingly dependent on the health of their trade relationships (Lipsey & Smith 1985, 5–13). In this section we will first go over some of the principles of trade policy and then examine the issue of trade remedy laws.

The Principles of Trade Policy

International trade theorists are almost uniformly positive about the potential capacity of increased trade to raise living standards. Their optimism flows from the central principle of comparative advantage. Successful trade among countries depends on the relative or comparative costs of production. Countries have a comparative advantage when their costs are relatively lower because the relevant factors of production are in more abundant supply (Lipsey & Smith 1985, 34–36; Lazar 1981, 53). Countries should use trade to maximize their comparative advantage. This will raise the living standards of the population because citizens will be able to enjoy lower prices for products that are imported—due to the relatively lower costs for that product abroad—while earning good incomes producing the goods they export. The exchange rate acts as the central means of adjustment. If the dollar costs and prices in a country were to rise relative to those of its trading partners, the value of its currency would begin to fall. In the long run this would allow the previous comparative advantage to reassert itself. While the concept of comparative advantage may seem attractive, in reality governments have seldom been willing to depend exclusively on their comparative advantages to generate economic growth. Nor have they been willing to tolerate the political and economic pressures that emerge from these continuing adjustments. The result is that they develop trade policies to give their external economic relations more order.

Trade policy refers to the rules that govern the exchange of goods and services between countries. These rules are intended to protect domestic producers against foreign competitors (Stone 1984, 1-27). The major instrument that has been used to achieve this protection has been the tariff. Tariffs are taxes applied to the prices of imported goods. They are usually used where domestic producers require higher prices for their goods in order to make an acceptable profit or just stay in business. These tariffs are designed to raise the price of imported goods in order to make the price of domestic goods more competitive. Tariffs have several other consequences as well. Domestic consumers must pay higher prices, and foreign companies are induced to locate in Canada to avoid paying the tarrif. Thus branch plants of foreign firms will be established in Canada exclusively to compete with existing Canadian firms in their own market.

The GATT

As part of a move spearheaded by the United States to open up the world's economies to more international trade, the GATT treaty was signed in 1947. Its main initial goals were to eliminate quotas and reduce tariffs. The GATT also sought to establish acceptance of two principles of nondiscrimination that would form the basis for the regulation of trade relations. The first was most-favoured-nation (MFN) status wherein signatories of the GATT agreed to apply the same trade rules to all other GATT members (Stone 1984, 30-31). Thus, as the GATT succeeded over the years in negotiating, through a succession of "rounds" of consultation, a series of tariff reductions by its member countries, each GATT member would extend the same tariff reduction benefits to its fellow GATT members in accordance with the MFN principle.

The second principle was that of national treatment. This required that each member of the GATT treat the firms of fellow GATT members as if they were domestic firms (Stone 1984, 32-33). Thus Canada could establish any policy that it liked, but the government should treat foreign firms of GATT signatories just like domestic firms. This second principle has been less successfully implemented under the GATT—as a result of the many exemptions that have been permitted—but has emerged as a central principle in the Canada-U.S. Free Trade Agreement (FTA).

The FTA

Under the FTA, Canada and the United States have agreed to eliminate all tariffs between the two countries over ten years ending January 1, 1999. They have also agreed to extend national treatment to each other. The FTA is, in essence, a limited form of bilateral free trade but one that goes beyond previous agreements by including many, although not all, services. The agreement incorporated the existing Auto Pact, financial services, and trade in energy. The energy chapter includes a proportionality rule that effectively protects American consumers better than Canadian consumers in the case of Canadian production cutbacks. Continued government incentives for energy production were also given an explicit endorsement. Provision for the harmonization of rules of origin—which establish whether a good is Canadian or American—and of product standards were also included. Finally, the agreement established an elaborate dispute settlement process in which the trade panels that adjudicated disputes were only empowered to determine whether the U.S. or Canadian trade law had been properly applied by each country's trade agencies.

Trade Remedy Laws

When trade relations deteriorate, most countries employ trade remedy laws. These laws provide "contingent protection" for domestic industries, contingent because they cannot be invoked until certain conditions are met (Coughlin 1991, 4). There are two basic types of trade remedy law—those that require proof of "unfair" action by a foreign government and those that can be invoked in the face of hardship or "serious injury," regardless of the behaviour of the government or firms of the exporting country. The latter measures are those that are invoked under Article 19 of the GATT and involve safeguard measures. To justify these actions a nation need not establish that a foreign government is unfairly subsidizing its exports but only that the volume of those exports threatens serious injury to a domestic industry. If a safeguard action is involved, temporary tariffs will be imposed on all imports of the good in question for a specified period of time. These measures are essentially transitional in character, presumably allowing the domestic industry time to regroup and prepare for future competition at the end of the time period (Rugman & Anderson 1987, 14-15).

More widely used are measures directed at "unfair" trading practices. The two most commonly used measures are those alleging unfair subsidies by a foreign government or unfair pricing by a foreign company. If a government is accused of unfairly subsidizing its exports, countervailing duties may be imposed on the subsidized goods under Article 16 of the GATT (Stone 1984, 35). These duties can be levied up to the level of the value of the subsidy. In the United States, if an export subsidy exceeds 0.5 percent, it is judged to be subject to countervail action (Coughlin 1991, 14). It is the United

States that has been the prime user of countervail actions.

In the case of unfair pricing, firms are accused of selling their products in Canada, for instance, at prices lower than they charge consumers in their home market. In this case the measure is called an antidumping duty and it is equal to the difference between the price in the home and export markets. Antidumping actions are more common than countervail actions and even in the United States they have been more widely used since 1982 (Coughlin 1991, 11).

The United States also has available unique statutory provisions in Section 301 and Super 301 of the U.S. Trade and Tariff Act of 1984 and the Omnibus Trade and Competitiveness Act of 1988 respectively. These measures allow the U.S. government to unilaterally take action against any measure that hinders U.S. exports to a foreign country. Under the Super 301 provision the U.S. Trade Representatives Office must annually name those countries with the most restrictive barriers and take action if some resolution is not forthcoming. While these provisions have not as yet been much used, they could be important grounds for action in the future (Coughlin 1991, 8–11).

THE RELATIONSHIP BETWEEN TRADE AND INDUSTRIAL POLICY

There is no question that the distinction between trade and industrial policy is somewhat arbitrary. Trade policy can be considered a form of industrial policy, one that is less demanding of public institutions and more dependent on market incentives for its success. However the distinction between trade and industrial policy is a useful one because of the different emphasis placed on the international and domestic economies, and because of the different measures each type of policy employs.

There is another more theoretical reason for maintaining the distinction. In Chapter 1, Michael Atkinson distinguished two versions of the new institutionalism: rational choice and structural theory. Structural theory, with its emphasis on intervention and co-ordinated action, has much more relevance to an analysis of industrial policy than of trade policy. Industrial policy requires coherence and competence on the part of the state policy-makers, whereas trade policy does not require it to the same degree. The need to strengthen state institutions and cultivate public sector private sector relations is much more pressing in the case of industrial policy. On the other hand, rational choice theory, with its focus on incentive structures, has an obvious relevance for the study of trade policy in which the liberalization of policy restraints opens the door for decision-making by entrepreneurs.

Trade and industrial policy can work together in relative harmony with one or the other providing the lead role. Thus industrial policy might provide the overall framework and trade policy measures like tariffs might be used to make the industrial policy more effective. Alternatively, trade policy might provide the overall framework with industrial policy measures being used on an ad hoc basis as needed (Atkinson & Coleman 1989a, 191).

However, trade and industrial policy can also be adversaries, with the measures in one policy area creating problems in the other. Thus trade remedy laws aimed at export subsidies in one sector can provoke retaliation against goods benefiting from industrial policy measures in another. Many industrial policies do provide subsidies of one sort or another. If these policies help to generate exports, they may attract trade policy actions in the export market. Canadian exporters face their greatest test in the highly litigious U.S. markets and, as economic interdependence increases, their exposure to these measures is also increasing. Trade actions are used not only to combat allegedly unfair practices but also to harass competitors and domestic importers who may have to bear some of the liability for any assessed duties (Coughlin 1991, 14). Similarly, industrial policy actions that may make a lot of sense for the targeted industry can create instability in trade relations even if promoting exports is not an important part of the policy. Efforts to regulate foreign investment levels when they generate hostile political responses in unrelated areas, are a case in point. This may encourage hostile political responses that can affect exporters in other unrelated areas.

The growing importance of trade policy is reflected in the way proponents of industrial policy have moved to adopt and revise trade policy concepts. As already mentioned, comparative advantage is a central precept of trade policy. However, critics have argued that as a guide to policy-making it is a deeply flawed concept. The theory of comparative advantage assumes that factors of production are "found" not created and that cost increases discourage monopolies. Neither assumption is entirely realistic. The experience of the Japanese and other Asian high-growth economies suggests that comparative advantage can be created. It is not a given or static condition (Scott 1990). If there is some truth to this argument, there may be considerable long-run dangers associated with abandoning industrial policy and the possibility of creating new areas of comparative advantage.

THE CANADIAN ECONOMY AND ITS INTERNATIONAL ENVIRONMENT

The Canadian Economy

The Canadian economy is relatively small, prosperous, and open to international economic forces. As Table 8.1 indicates, Canada ranks very high among the countries of the developed world with a per capita gross domestic product (GDP) very close to that of the United States. When one considers purchasing power parity—in which the relative costs of similar purchases such as housing or appliances are taken into account—Canada's relative standing is even higher. Japan had a per capita GDP, based upon the weighted OECD exchange rate, almost 23 percent higher than that in Canada in 1988, but the purchasing power of this income was only 77 percent as much as the Canadian income. Finally, Canada's average annual growth rate for the period 1969–1989 compares favourably with that of other advanced countries, with the exception of Japan.

Structural Variations

The Canadian economy is also characterized by clear variations in the structures of the provincial economies. Over one-half of all manufacturing activity takes place in Ontario and almost 80 percent is located in Ontario and Quebec (see Table 8.2). The automotive sector is a particularly important component of manufacturing in Ontario, comprising over 26 percent of all manufacturing output (Wonnacott 1991, 31). Natural resource extraction and development is especially important in the other eight provinces. The logging and forestry industries are conspicuous components of the economy in British Columbia. Mining, especially oil and natural gas extraction, is a crucial

TABLE 8.1
CANADA'S AFFLUENCE COMPARED

Country	Per Capita[1] GDP, 1988	Purchasing[2] Power, 1988	Average Per Capita GDP Growth Rates (%) 1969–1989
United States	19 715	19 851	1.76
Japan	23 226	13 645	4.09
West Germany	19 560	14 621	2.50
France	17 107	13 584	2.46
United Kingdom	14 616	13 060	2.18
Italy	14 653	13 001	2.91
Sweden	21 545	14 941	2.06
Canada	18 969	17 681	2.91

1. Based on the OECD exchange rate using average daily rate for the year.
2. Based on the Penn World purchasing power parity formula.

Source: United States, Joint Committee on Taxation (May 1991), *Factors affecting the international competitiveness of the United States* (JCS–6–91), Table 1 (p.16). Figure 1 (p.17).

TABLE 8.2
Provincial Contribution to Total Canadian Production, 1986 (Current Dollars)

Selected Aggregates (Percentage Share of Total Canadian Production)

	Nfld.	P.E.I.	N.S.	N.B.	Que.	Ont.	Man.	Sask.	Alta.	B.C.	Yukon & N.W.T.	Total
Goods-producing industries	1.2	0.2	2.1	1.9	22.1	41.5	3.2	4.1	13.5	9.6	0.5	100
Agriculture	0.2	1.0	1.4	1.3	17.7	23.2	9.5	23.3	17.4	5.1	0.0	100
Fishing & trapping	14.6	4.4	30.0	7.2	7.6	4.7	1.8	0.8	0.7	27.6	0.6	100
Logging & forestry	1.7	0.1	2.9	7.1	21.8	19.0	1.0	1.2	3.1	42.1	0.1	100
Mining	2.0	0.0	0.9	0.8	5.4	12.4	1.7	8.2	57.8	8.0	2.7	100
Manufacturing	0.7	0.1	1.8	1.6	25.2	54.1	2.4	1.1	4.7	8.4	0.0	100
Construction	1.8	0.4	3.0	2.1	21.8	36.3	4.1	4.3	13.3	11.9	1.0	100
Other Utilities	2.3	0.3	1.8	3.6	29.1	33.3	4.3	3.1	11.8	10.1	0.5	100
Service-producing industries	1.4	0.3	2.8	2.0	23.4	37.5	4.0	3.6	11.9	12.4	0.5	100
Other	1.3	0.3	2.7	1.9	23.0	37.4	3.9	3.4	12.4	13.0	0.5	100
Nonmarket services[1]	1.8	0.5	3.2	2.3	24.6	37.6	4.4	4.1	10.6	10.3	0.6	100

1. *Nonmarket services include provincial and local government services, educational services, and health and social services industries. Federal government services are included in other services.*

Source: Adapted from Canada, Department of Finance (1991a), Economic linkages among provinces. *Quarterly economic review: Special reports.* Reproduced with the permission of the Minister of Supply and Services Canada, 1992.

part of the Alberta economy as is agriculture in Saskatchewan. In Atlantic Canada, fishing and trapping are important, as is the logging industry in New Brunswick.

Regional diversity in the provincial economies is mirrored by differences in the economic prosperity of Canadians who live in the different provinces. Table 8.3 presents data on the disparities in GDP per capita and income per capita across the provinces and territories of Canada over the years 1971 through 1989. Several observations about the data presented in this table warrant emphasis. First, the differences have been quite large and have persisted over time although there has been some significant movement in relative shares over the years. In terms of GDP per capita, the decade of the 1980s was particularly good for Nova Scotia, New Brunswick, Quebec, and Ontario and especially hard for Alberta, Saskatchewan, and British Columbia. Second, there have been some sharp changes in relative affluence among the provinces. As major downward shifts in economic fortunes tend to cause unrest, the turbulence in the fortunes of political parties in western Canada in the late 1980s may be in part a reflection of the sharp fall-off in economic performance. The changes in Alberta in particular were quite dramatic, reflecting the fluctuations in oil and natural

TABLE 8.3
REGIONAL DISPARITIES RELATIVE TO CANADIAN AVERAGE (CANADA = 100)

	1971 GDP/CAP[1]	1971 Y/CAP[2]	1981 GDP/CAP	1981 Y/CAP	1989 GDP/CAP	1989 Y/CAP
Newfoundland	56.0	63.5	56.0	65.7	59.5	71.0
Prince Edward Island	51.5	61.9	56.4	69.7	57.8	73.8
Nova Scotia	67.6	75.7	59.3	74.7	72.6	82.4
New Brunswick	64.3	71.6	58.5	70.7	70.4	77.2
Quebec	90.1	90.3	86.7	94.1	91.5	94.9
Ontario	117.8	117.4	104.6	105.9	113.6	112.0
Manitoba	89.1	92.1	87.8	91.0	85.5	88.0
Saskatchewan	83.3	78.5	101.4	94.9	80.1	80.7
Alberta	107.0	96.8	152.8	114.2	112.3	102.2
British Columbia	106.0	107.4	111.5	111.8	98.9	98.3
Yukon/Northwest Territories	118.6	97.9	122.1	104.2	146.9	113.9

1. *Gross domestic product per capita.*
2. *Personal income per capita.*

Source: Adapted from Canada, Department of Finance (1990a), *Quarterly economic review annual reference tables* (Table 8.2, p.16 and Table 16.2, p.31). Reproduced with the permission of the Minister of Supply and Services Canada, 1992.

gas prices in the 1970s and 1980s. Third, in the poorer provinces the relative levels of GDP per capita were almost always lower than the levels of income per capita. This reflected the impact of federal transfer payments on personal incomes.

The relative strengths of the provincial economies are also reflected in differences in rates of unemployment. From 1961 to 1989 Ontario's rate of unemployment was consistently below the national average. The Prairie provinces were equally blessed except for 1988 when unemployment reached the national average. In Atlantic Canada, on the other hand, the rates were persistently high, often four percent or more above the national average, and in Quebec and British Columbia the rates were also above the average with one brief exception in British Columbia (Economic Council of Canada 1990b, 34).

Trading Relationships

As for trading relations, Canada has especially close ties with the United States. The share of Canadian exports going to the United States rose from 69 percent in 1979 to about 75 percent in 1990 (Morici 1991, 11). All parts of Canada share in this relationship but it is Ontario, the principal beneficiary of the Auto Pact, that has the largest volume of trade with the United States. Exports to the United States constituted almost 18 percent of Ontario's gross provincial output in 1984 (Economic Council of Canada 1991, 37). There are also marked regional differences in the U.S. destinations of Canadian exports with the tendency being trade between contiguous parts of the two countries (Economic Council of Canada 1991, 37).

One important source of this close economic relationship has been the high degree of U.S. ownership of Canadian industry. While the proportion has been in decline since the 1960s, it still remains at about 45 percent of assets in manufacturing and at even higher levels in other sectors (Porter 1991, 14-15). Much of Canada's trade, therefore, takes the form of transfers between subsidiaries and their foreign head office. This high level of trade has created a substantial degree of interdependence between the two countries and has created considerable dependence on the part of the Canadian economy on decisions made by corporate leaders in the United States.

Sectoral Concerns

The various sectors of the Canadian economy each have their own special problems. The depressed level of natural resource prices in the late 1980s and early 1990s and the growing potential for substitution of synthetic materials are among such problems. However, for some time there has been particular concern for the future of manufacturing in Canada. This concern has centred, in part, on the impact that foreign ownership has had on the research and development effort, the export performance, and the growth potential of Canadian subsidiaries. Concern has also been expressed about the composition of manufactured goods. Table 8.4 indicates that, while Canada has a strong and relatively balanced trade in motor vehicles and parts, it is a major net importer of other manufactured products.

Trade in motor vehicles and parts has increased dramatically since the introduction of the Auto Pact in 1965—from 16 percent of imports and 6 percent of exports of manufactured goods in 1965 to 34.6 percent of imports and 36 percent of exports of manufactured goods in 1985 (Cornell & Gorecki 1991, 40). While Canada's exports in other manufactured products have also increased over the past two decades, so too have imports of these goods. Thus the overall improvement in the exports of manufactured goods has occurred largely under the auspices of the Auto Pact. As the U.S. auto industry continues to struggle, these gains may be increasingly threatened. Overall, the manufacturing sector's share of real GDP remained at around 19–20 percent from 1961 through to the late 1980s. However there has been a decline in person hours worked in manufacturing from 20.5 percent in 1971 to 17.1 percent in 1985 (Cornell & Gorecki

TABLE 8.4
MERCHANDISE TRADE: EXPORTS AND IMPORTS (PERCENTAGE OF TOTAL)

	1971 Exports	1971 Imports	1981 Exports	1981 Imports	1989 Exports	1989 Imports
Agricultural products	12.0	7.6	11.4	6.8	7.3	5.6
Crude petroleum and natural gas	5.9	3.5	8.2	10.3	5.3	2.8
Other crude materials	12.6	5.1	9.9	4.9	7.5	3.0
Fabricated materials	33.5	20.9	36.7	19.1	34.3	20.0
Motor vehicles and parts	23.4	26.3	16.0	20.4	23.7	23.8
Other end products	13.1	37.6	16.3	39.2	19.6	43.4
Residual1	–0.5	–1.0	1.7	–0.8	2.3	1.4
Total	**100.02**	**100.0**	**100.0**	**100.0**	**100.0**	**100.0**

1. A bookkeeping adjustment.
2. Numbers have been rounded.

Source: Adapted from Canada, Department of Finance (1990a), *Quarterly economic review annual references tables* (Table 8.2, p.16, and Table 16.2, p.31). Reproduced with the permission of the Minister of Supply and Services Canada, 1992.

1991, 39) and the overall share of manufacturing activity includes the increased activity in the automotive sector. The health of the auto sector therefore masks lost production in other areas of manufacturing.

The International Economic Environment

Reform of the GATT

The world economy has been getting increasingly competitive for some time. This increased competition derives from a number of sources, one of which is reform of the rules of international trade through successive rounds of negotiations under the GATT. These negotiations have resulted in a major reduction in tariff rates, thus increasing the access of foreign competitors to domestic markets. They have also generated a number of codes of conduct aimed at regulating national behaviour in such areas as subsidies and government procurement (Stone 1984, 185-87).

A second source of competition has been technological changes that have altered the prices and changed the composition of inputs into the productive process. Innovations in the computer and telecommunications industries have transformed production processes, reducing the importance of proximity to markets for some services and changing the demand for skills in other sectors. A third source of change has been the rapid emergence of new sources of economic power. Europe has been moving rapidly toward a much more liberalized and integrated trade regime with the passage of the Single European Act of 1987 (Cecchini 1988). In Asia, Japan's rise to economic power has been spectacular and a number of other countries like Taiwan and South Korea are following in its footsteps. The emergence of strong competition in North American markets from Europe and Asia has been reflected in the relative decline of both the Canadian and U.S. economies. In the United States this has sparked renewed interest in using trade remedy laws and in attacking the existence of so-called nontariff barriers (NTBs) in other countries — whether they be administrative practices, societal norms, or subsidy practices—that are said to impede or prevent U.S. exports (Kuttner 1991).

Liberalization of Capital Markets

Another aspect of the changing international environment has been the liberalization of capital markets in many of the more advanced economies. While trade in goods has grown more quickly than the rate of production of those goods, the volume of international capital flows has grown even more quickly. Most of this activity consists of commercial and government borrowing. Canadian offshore borrowing and lending grew by 30 percent per year through the 1980s (Brean, Bird &

Krauss 1991, 2-4). International capital flows have become enormous and, with the aid of new communications technologies, capable of rapid movement. The sudden loss of four cents in the value of the Canadian dollar in January 1990, as a result of a slight relaxation in Canadian interest rates at a time when other national rates (i.e., those in Japan and Germany) were rising, demonstrates the capacity of these markets to react and react quickly (Brean, Bird & Krauss 1991, 91-92). The net influence of these and other international developments has been to increase the influence on Canadian economic policy-making of international institutions and agreements.

Globalization

The concept of globalization is often used to describe how international developments are influencing domestic economic structures. Globalization refers to the increasing integration of many parts of the world economy (Reich 1991, 110-18; Kuttner 1991, 112-57). For decades, multinational firms have looked to the world rather than just domestic customers for their markets and factor inputs. Now, however, this pattern of behaviour is coming to characterize the behaviour of medium-sized and even smaller-sized firms. In North America the free trade agreement has encouraged firms of all sizes to begin thinking about the whole continent as one market. An important part of the impact of the FTA has been psychological in character, changing attitudes and orientations among businesspeople. One manifestation is the emerging pattern of corporate restructuring. This process sees firms becoming more specialized and producing for international markets. Restructuring even involves encouraging competition among subsidiaries of the same firm for the right to produce a particular product. By its nature this competition implies uncertainty and instability for both employees and management, generating political pressures on government to somehow mitigate its impact.

Competitiveness

With globalization has come extensive discussion of the need for Canadians and the Canadian economy to achieve greater "competitiveness." This is becoming a highly contested term. Does it imply the need to shed Canada's social programs as a means of lowering taxes and driving down the wages of Canadian employees to reduce corporate wage bills? Or does it mean maintaining these social programs— indeed possibly spending even more on education—and generally raising the skill level of the economy? Given the low levels of productivity increases in Canadian manufacturing over the last decade, it is not surprising that many observers feel that many Canadian businesses will press for lower wages and reductions in social services. (See Table 8.5.)

TABLE 8.5
OUTPUT PER HOUR IN MANUFACTURING: DECADAL AVERAGES 1960s–1980s
(AVERAGE ANNUAL PERCENTAGE RATE OF CHANGE)

Country	1960s	1970s	1980s	Average 1960–1989
United States	3.1	2.4	3.6	3.0
Japan	10.7	7.2	5.5	7.6
West Germany	6.2	4.5	1.8	4.1
France	6.8	5.0	3.4	5.0
United Kingdom	3.9	2.7	4.7	3.7
Italy	6.6	6.0	4.0	5.4
Sweden	7.0	3.7	2.2	4.1
Canada	4.7	3.0	1.5	3.0

Source: United States, Joint Committee on Taxation (May 1991), *Factors affecting the international competitiveness of the United States* (JCS–6–91), Table 3 (p.19).

In positioning his argument about Canadian competitiveness, Michael Porter states that governments can and must attempt to shape comparative advantage. However, unlike those who would see this as requiring a greater role for government, Porter stresses the need to promote competition among domestic firms as the route to excellence (Porter 1991). His approach would probably exacerbate regional inequalities— since there are large benefits from local networks of firms, suppliers, and customers—and would lead to reduced wages and social programs in the North American context. Paul Krugman places more weight on the decline in technological superiority, productivity, and reputation for quality as the sources of the loss of competitiveness (Krugman 1990, 15, 47). A 1991 Canadian government discussion paper, *Prosperity through Competitiveness*, focuses on a wide range of possible measures to enhance Canadian competitiveness (Canada 1991b). They include user fees to finance infrastructure investments, the reduction of interprovincial trade barriers, efforts to create foreign markets for Canadian goods, and improved business–labour relations.

One major focal point in the debate over competitiveness is the level of the Canadian dollar. The higher the dollar, the more expensive are Canadian goods and services. Traditionally it has been assumed that the exchange rate would adjust to reflect input cost conditions in the domestic market. Yet, in the late 1980s and early 1990s, the Canadian dollar was rising, vis-à-vis the U.S. dollar, despite rising labour costs and declining productivity. Why didn't the dollar decline? The volume of transactions in the international capital market—highly responsive to interest rates and perceptions of the stability of a currency's value—has been one factor. At the same time, the Canadian currency may not be valued at unrealistically high levels. The dollar in 1990 was at about the same level as it was in 1980 and not far off its average levels over the last three decades (Morici 1984, 9; Economic Council of Canada 1991, 23).

In this section we have tried to outline some of the features of the Canadian economy and changes in the international economic environment that are most relevant to a study of the impact of institutions on trade and industrial policy. We turn now to an examination of the trade and industrial policies that the Canadian state has pursued in the past to cope with changing economic circumstances.

THE EVOLUTION OF CANADIAN TRADE AND INDUSTRIAL POLICY

In this section we will describe how, through much of Canada's first century, trade and industrial policy were used to create a Canadian economy that was both relatively prosperous and characterized by a remarkable level of foreign ownership. The national policy that began to be implemented in 1879 combined trade policy instruments—especially the tariff—with a range of industrial policy instruments to create an affluent, if dependent, Canadian economy. At this stage in its economic development, Canada's trade and industrial policies were working in concert. Over the past several decades, culminating in the free trade agreement in 1989, these two policies have begun to pose difficulties for each another. The old Canadian economy based on the national policy was no longer viable for both domestic and international reasons, and a new Canadian economy based on increasing international integration and competition, especially with the United States, was emerging.

The National Policy in the Period to World War II

Canada's economic options in the nineteenth century were either closer economic ties with the United States through trade liberalization or the use of tariffs, subsidies, and immigration policy to establish a more autonomous Canadian economy. These two options vied for preeminence through much of the nineteenth century following the repeal of the Corn Laws by England in 1846. In 1854 an agreement providing tariff-free access to U.S. markets for many Canadian natural resources was negotiated but it was terminated in 1866, in the aftermath of the U.S. Civil War (Granatstein 1987, 4). In subsequent years the Canadian government continued to show interest in trade liberalization with the

U.S., even after the development of the national policy in 1879, but no agreements were forthcoming.

The national policy was to become the centrepiece of Canada's policy for economic development in the years that followed. Its central focus was to provide tariff protection for Canadian manufacturing—through an average tariff of 28 percent—and only later came to be associated with settlement of the West and the building of a national railway system (Granatstein 1987, 5; Laxer 1989, 158-98). The tariffs were relatively successful in promoting Canadian manufacturing but they also helped, after the turn of the century, to encourage massive U.S. direct investment in Canada and the establishment of a branch-plant economy. This infusion of U.S. capital and ownership is important, especially in retrospect, because concern over its impact and efforts to limit it became so important to industrial policy debates much later in the 1970s and early 1980s as well as during the debate over free trade.

A range of industrial policy measures were used. They included extensive and excessive subsidies and investment in railways, not only to open the West to settlement and development but also to Canadian sovereignty in the West against American encroachments. The Canadian state also sought to promote agricultural development and productivity, settlement of undeveloped lands, subsidies to attract industry (often with little concern or interest in its ownership), and the establishment of public utilities, especially in the area of electric power. The state also used regulations, such as the 1872 Patent Act, that required manufacturers holding a Canadian patent to begin manufacturing the patented product within two years or lose protection for the invention. These and other measures helped to generate increased economic activity in Canada with a substantial degree of foreign ownership (Bliss 1982; Laxer 1989).

Most of this foreign investment came from the United States. Unlike investment from British sources, which tended to be portfolio investment, the new investment from the United States was commonly direct investment involving the establishment or acquisition of firms in the Canadian market. Many reasons have been offered for this infusion of U.S. capital (Laxer 1989). A prominent explanation involves the tariff: U.S. firms would rather set up production facilities in Canada than pay the tariff on goods produced in the United States. (Granatstein 1987, 7-8). Another is the proximity of the U.S. economy, which, at the turn of the century, was beginning to expand into foreign markets. A third explanation focuses on the lack of domestic capital, a situation that arose because so much capital was targeted for railroad construction and because the Canadian banking system, conservative and risk averse, was unwilling or unable to fund Canadian industrial development.[1]

While the national policy was the dominant force shaping the Canadian economy in this period, there were continuing efforts to liberalize trade with the United States. In one particularly memorable effort, the Liberal government of Wilfrid Laurier negotiated a reciprocity treaty with the United States that eliminated tariffs on a range of natural resources and lowered tariffs on some others in an effort to appease unhappy farmers (Granatstein 1987, 8-11). The government was defeated in the election of 1911 on this and another issue, its naval policy, with Canadian manufacturers lining up against any change in the national policy and conducting a highly charged pro-nationalist campaign against the proposed treaty. Central Canadian manufacturing interests triumphed over those of the farmer. Later, there were a series of limited trade agreements with the United States in the 1930s and even closer economic ties during World War II that culminated in the secret negotiation of an extensive free trade agreement by the Liberal government in 1947-48 (Granatstein 1987, 13-26). The agreement was eventually rejected by Prime Minister King in part out of fear of a rerun of the 1911 campaign.

Postwar Adjustments and Industrial Policy

The period from the early 1960s through to the early 1980s saw renewed interest in industrial policy. Foreign ownership in mining and manufacturing had reached the level of about 60 percent by 1970, up from less than 40 percent just prior to World War II, as a result of open encouragement of this investment in the postwar years (Morici, Smith & Lea 1982, 37). Thus concern over the performance of the economy was increasingly associated with extensive foreign ownership.

The result was a number of new initiatives to strengthen the Canadian economy. Some of these were focused largely on performance, regardless of ownership. In 1958 a Defence Production Sharing Agreement (DPSA) was negotiated between Canada and the United States to ensure Canadian access to U.S. contracts for defence spending. In 1965 the Canada-U.S. Automotive Products Agreement (Auto Pact) was signed, allowing the three major U.S. auto companies to rationalize their operations in Canada and the United States while providing safeguards for the maintenance of production in Canada (Wonnacott 1987, 72-82). There were a host of other policy initiatives such as the 1969 establishment of the Department of Regional Economic Expansion, which was mandated to both co-ordinate and make more effective the government's policies on regional development; efforts to reform the Combines Investigation Act as a means of increasing competition; and programs to encourage research and development such as the Industrial Research Assistance Program (IRAP) and the Defence Industries Productivity Program (DIPP). Another program, the Enterprise Development Program (EDP) was introduced in 1977, absorbing and replacing a number of existing policies, to help small and medium-sized firms deal with risky investments and structural adjustment problems (Morici, Smith & Lea 1982; Bliss 1982).

There were also a number of initiatives that pursued the goal of increased Canadian control over the economy. Thus, in 1973, the Canadian Development Corporation (CDC) was established as an investment vehicle, and in 1974 the Foreign Investment Review Agency (FIRA) was set up to screen foreign acquisitions of Canadian companies to determine whether they brought significant benefits to Canada. In the face of large oil price increases in the 1970s, an energy policy was established to partially insulate Canadian consumers from world oil prices. In 1975 Petro-Canada, a national oil company, was created as a means of promoting Canadian interests in an otherwise largely foreign-owned industry.

These two concerns—enhancing the performance of the Canadian economy and encouraging more domestic control of the Canadian economy—reached their pinnacle in the early 1980s with the introduction of the National Energy Program (NEP) and, subsequently, the proposed megaprojects strategy along with a strengthened FIRA (Simeon & Robinson 1990, 231). The NEP was a very extensive and ambitious attempt to increase Canadian ownership in the oil and gas sector, keep Canadian oil prices below world price levels—it was hoped to give Canadian industry a comparative advantage—and make Canada self-sufficient in oil and to increase the federal share of oil and gas revenues (Doern & Toner 1985). The megaprojects strategy was intended to link the interests of manufacturers and natural resource development across the country. FIRA was to be strengthened to ensure foreign investment was bringing clear benefits to Canada. As it turned out, the overall policy was to collapse in the face of a very serious recession, the sharp decline in the world price of oil and other commodity prices, which had been the source of the initiative, and opposition from the western provinces (especially Alberta) where oil and gas reserves were concentrated. In the period following these initiatives, there was a move toward a reconsideration of the trade liberalization option.

The period of the 1960s through into the early 1980s also saw the emergence of a phenomenon later called "province building." This concept implies a conflictual and confrontational relation between the provinces and the federal government and, indeed, this was a period when intergovernmental relations were particularly strained (Simeon & Robinson 1990, 225–30). The focus on provincial development and diversification also reflects the fact that concern with overall aspects of the performance of the Canadian economy—such as weakness in the manufacturing sector—was increasingly seen in regional terms.

Manufacturing was a problem for Ontario and Quebec more than it was a Canadian problem. Energy policies were also regional in character, focused against the interests of the western provincial economies. Thus most of the provinces began to develop industrial policies aimed at diversification. In the western provinces, energy revenues were used to promote, for instance, petrochemical and medical research investments in Alberta and manufacturing and high-tech investments in B.C. Saskatchewan established a series of public corporations while Newfoundland sought to benefit from offshore oil and gas development. Quebec established and expanded the role of a number of publicly owned financial institutions to more carefully target growth in that province. While not all of these policies were in conflict with federal initiatives, they did reflect a growing preoccupation with regional economic differences and priorities (Jenkin 1983, 49-84; Simeon & Robinson 1990).

The Move to Trade Liberalization

Commencing in late 1981 there was a resurgence of interest in trade policy within the federal government. Canada had participated in successive rounds of negotiations under the GATT and tariffs had been substantially reduced. There were also several sectoral agreements in place with the United States such as those for automobiles and defence production. The initial emphasis was on negotiating an extension of the sectoral approach to other sectors but there were problems in agreeing upon the choice of sectors (Canada 1983, 45). Finally, following the 1984 election of the Conservatives with their greater emphasis on reliance on the market in economic decision-making and the report of the Liberal-appointed Macdonald Royal Commission in September 1985 advocating the desirability of trade liberalization, Canada, moved to initiate negotiations on a trade agreement. In December 1985 the U.S. president notified Congress of the U.S. administration's intention to enter negotiations with Canada, and in April 1986 the U.S. Senate's Finance Committee, by the barest of margins, granted the president so-called "fast-track" authority. The fast-track provision required that if the two sides could come to an agreement by early October 1987, the Senate could only approve or reject the result without amendment. As the agreement was of much less importance to the U.S. government, most of the key negotiations were left to the last several weeks and the Canadian side found itself a virtual captive of the U.S. fast-track deadline (Doern & Tomlin 1991). If the deadline were missed, this round of negotiations would likely fail.

As the 1980s unfolded it became increasingly clear that most Canadian business organizations and provincial governments supported the concept of a free trade agreement. Unlike in 1911, most of these organizations were supportive of the negotiations and their members participated actively in the fifteen sectoral advisory groups (SAGITs) that were set up to advise the Canadian government and establish sectoral policy consensus (Doern & Tomlin 1991, 103–25). Similarly, most of the provincial governments including Quebec saw free trade as potentially beneficial. Only Ontario offered serious opposition to the deal and this opposition was muted by concerns for national unity as well as considerable support for a trade deal among Ontario businesses (Doern & Tomlin 1991, 126–51, 228).

In the fall of 1988, the issue of support or defeat for the free trade option was joined in a federal election that saw the Conservatives re-elected with a majority of the seats, including 88 of 101 in Quebec and Alberta, although only 43 percent of the popular vote. The election was characterized by intense debate from both sides of the free trade issue. With the Conservative victory the acceptance of the FTA, was virtually assured.

Canada's main concern throughout the FTA negotiations was to guarantee access to the U.S. market. In the end, Canada and the United States agreed to establish a dispute-settlement process that provided for review of the application of trade remedy laws in each country. Although it has been argued that the Canadian trade representatives were outnegotiated by their U.S. counterparts (Doern & Tomlin 1991, 152–201), this concession must be evaluated within the context of the whole agreement and the nature of U.S.-Canadian relations. The relative disparity in economic size, the need to conciliate the U.S. Congress, and the relatively greater importance of the agreement to Canada ensured that the agreement would have to include important concessions to the United States.

But as the scale and scope of the FTA suggest, Canada had firmly moved to discipline many potential industrial policy measures through its nearly irreversible commitment to trade liberalization.

More recently, talks have been initiated to establish a trade agreement between the United States and Mexico. Canada has felt obliged to enter these negotiations as well to try to protect gains made under the FTA. The problem for Canada is that many Mexican exports to the United States compete directly with similar Canadian exports and they could undermine some of the potential gains obtained under the FTA (Morici 1991, 128–31, 158–59). Not only do many Canadians fear the potential competition from low-wage Mexico-based firms but also they believe a North American free trade agreement (NAFTA) might encourage further migration of industry and investment from Canada to Mexico. The movement for further trade liberalization by the United States has clearly forced Canada to embark on negotiations it might otherwise seek to avoid.

TRADE, INDUSTRIAL POLICY, AND POLITICAL INSTITUTIONS

Political institutions are important factors in determining how issues are defined, what issues receive consideration, and how effectively the decisions are implemented. The extent to which institutions help to shape policy is difficult to determine in any precise way but they clearly play a role. In this section we will consider the impact of four institutional factors on the making of industrial and trade policy in general and the growing emphasis on trade policy instruments in particular. The institutions we will focus on are the Westminster model of parliamentary government, the political parties that compete for power within that model, the bureaucracy which was charged with implementing industrial policy, and the federal system with its division of powers.

The Westminster Model of Parliamentary Government

In Canada, electors choose representatives in 295 constituencies using the single-member-plurality system. These representatives, or members of Parliament (MPs), belong to political parties, and the party that wins the most seats forms the government. If it wins a majority of the seats—an outcome made more likely by the rules of the electoral system—it forms a majority government. The leader of the winning party becomes prime minister and chooses a cabinet from among the elected MPs. A prime minister and cabinet with majority support have the capacity to initiate sweeping legislative changes because of the tradition of party discipline based upon the government's need to maintain the confidence or support of the House of Commons. Party discipline requires MPs to vote the party line—even if they personally disagree with the proposed policy. So while the Westminster model concentrates authority it also accentuates the adversarial relationship between the government party and the opposition parties. And because the electoral system also increases the possibility of regionally concentrated support, the possibility exists that governments will have a substantial capacity to act but will do so in a manner considered to be regionally biased.

One of the national initiatives that left a legacy of distrust and acrimony over the real agenda of industrial policy in the early 1980s was the National Energy Program. The NEP was implemented by a Liberal majority government with virtually no elected representatives from the West and yet the focus of the policy was on the oil- and natural-gas-producing provinces of that same region. Following a series of political battles between Alberta in particular and the federal government during the 1970s, the federal government sought to encourage the development of reserves in the northern territories, which were under federal control, and to deny the western provinces the full rents from their petroleum resources. While the NEP was popular among the Canadian people as a whole, its character gave it the image of a central-Canadian policy initiative intended to deny the western provinces their financial due. The weakness of representation from the West in the Liberal cabinet made it seem obvious that western concerns had not received their proper attention. The bitterness of this struggle was reflected in the speed with which the Progressive Conservatives, elected in 1984 with their own majority and also strong representation in the West, moved to terminate the NEP (Simeon & Robinson 1990, 236–49).

Similarly, in 1988, with a second majority win in the highly emotional and divisive federal election of that year, the Conservative government moved to pass the FTA that it had negotiated with the United States. The high symbolism expressed in the election and associated with the FTA reflected the enormous significance and divisiveness of the issue. Opponents described the FTA as the means by which Canada and its social programs would eventually be destroyed. While supporters of the FTA have argued that the election served as a referendum on free trade, election studies suggest that this argument is badly flawed (Doern & Tomlin 1991, 238–42). Once again the Westminster model provided majority governments with the capacity to defeat substantial opposition and implement its programs.

Political Parties: Their Ideologies and Strategies

In recent decades, Canadian governments have faced the problem of governing a regionally divided country through parties that were, themselves, regionalized in terms of electoral support. Their policies have had the potential to be destabilizing when they were perceived to have regional biases. The Liberals were the primary architects of this situation in their extended period of rule after 1963, winning large majorities in Quebec and very few seats in the West. The pattern of Liberal successes—concentrating on maximizing regional support to get a majority—was followed in the 1980s by the Conservatives with their solid support base in the West and in Quebec.

As the government began negotiating the FTA a potential new alliance of regional constituencies took shape. The Liberals had governed Canada for much of the twentieth century and the Conservatives sought to establish their own enduring alliance based upon Quebec and the West (Doern & Tomlin 1991, 34–35). The western provinces had long been strong sources of Conservative support and their provincial governments were very supportive of a FTA that would secure access to U.S. export markets and eliminate the possibility of any future NEP. Quebec was also supportive of a free trade initiative, especially after the election of the provincial Liberals in 1985. For Quebec an FTA promised a more secure relationship with the United States and, if Quebec were to achieve independence, a more favourable bargaining position with the rest of Canada (Doern & Tomlin 1991, 131–49). Ontario opposed free trade although some scholarly studies suggested it might have the most to gain over the long run (Harris 1985, 165–66). Ontario's opposition might have been more strident if it had not been for the success of the Auto Pact in Ontario in the mid-1980s. Production of cars and trucks and of Canadian value added both exceeded the safeguard requirements in this period by substantial levels (Wonnacott 1991, 33–35).

While the Conservative government negotiated and implemented the FTA, it is also true that the previous Liberal government was exploring various trade policy alternatives in the several years prior to its defeat in 1984. Might the Liberals have implemented the same program as the Conservatives? It seems unlikely. The commitment to market solutions was stronger in the Conservative party and the importance of Ontario in Liberal electoral calculations was greater. The Conservatives saw the possibility of long-term electoral gains by cementing a West–Quebec axis of support, and negotiation of a free trade agreement fit very nicely into this strategy (Doern & Tomlin 1991).

Many scholars have commented on the failure of class-based politics to emerge as a real force in Canada's party system. Inter-ethnic, religious, and regional divisions have generally been more important. The weakness of class-based politics is reflected in the overall weakness of partisan support for industrial policy-making. An effective industrial policy has required a measure of commitment to state intervention in Western countries. A strong class-based party system would tend to orient the parties and political system in that direction, providing an ongoing basis of support for intervention. In Canada this factor has been missing and its absence most likely made the new emphasis on trade policy easier to achieve.

The Bureaucracy and Industrial Policy

The Canadian bureaucracy, while a competent body in most respects, has received low marks by some observers as an agent of industrial policy (Atkinson & Coleman 1989a). Part of the problem stems from the dependence of Canadian politics on the adversarial political process enshrined by the Westminster model. Industrial policy-making within the bureaucracy has been hard to shield from partisan exchanges between political parties. Another part of the problem has been the absence of any continuing commitment to state-directed solutions, making it difficult to develop policies that involved substantial autonomy for the state machinery. Canadian industrial policy has remained largely firm-centred in its orientation, and government policymakers, for the most part, have lacked the independence to develop and sustain coherent policies (Atkinson & Coleman 1989a, 33, 185–86). The result has been a susceptibility to pluralist pressures—whether regional or sector—that undermined the capacity of the state to plan or orchestrate the co-ordination inherent in any successful anticipatory industrial policy.

Federal Policies

The largely reactive character of Canadian industrial policy can be seen in the lack of ongoing organizational focus in the mandates of responsible departments. Authority has been shared among a number of departments including not only the department directly responsible for industrial policy—in its various states of reorganization—but also with other departments. Over time, these have included, among others, the Department of Regional Economic Expansion (DREE), Energy, Mines and Resources (the source of the NEP), and the Department of Consumer and Corporate Affairs. The organization of the industry department has also been transformed a number of times, reflecting a longstanding uncertainty and instability as to its proper focus.

The Department of Industry was established in 1963 to improve co-operation between industry and government. In 1969 it was merged with the Department of Trade and Commerce and DREE was established to deal with regional development concerns. In 1982 the trade components of Industry, Trade and Commerce (ITC) were shifted over to External Affairs and the industrial components were merged with DREE to form a new, more regionally oriented Department of Regional Industrial Expansion (DRIE). Later, in 1987, the regional units were largely hived off with the creation of two explicitly regional industrial agencies, the Atlantic Canada Opportunities Agency (ACOA) and the Western Diversification Office (WDO). The nonregional sectors of DRIE were combined with the Ministry of State for Science and Technology (MOSST) to form a new department called Industry, Science and Technology Canada (ISTC) (Phidd & Doern 1978; Doern & Phidd 1983; Doern 1990c). The lack of organizational continuity and of continuing organizational focus reflects an ongoing dissatisfaction with the results of federal efforts to produce and sustain workable industrial policies.

Nonetheless there have been some industrial-policy success stories. Michael Atkinson and William Coleman have argued that when one focuses on the various sectors of the economy, rather than on the overall economy, one finds examples in which policy networks have evolved that permit industrial policy to be developed with some autonomy. Policy networks refer to the interrelationships that develop between the relevant parts of the government and the interest associations and economic actors of that sector (Atkinson & Coleman 1989a, 78–79). Those networks that successfully implement an industrial policy must have substantial autonomy at the sectoral level. This autonomy requires that bureaucrats have a clear understanding of their role and values, a separate professional identity from their clientele, a well-defined and distinct mandate, and an independent capacity to collect and monitor information (Atkinson & Coleman 1989a, 80–81). While this capacity has not generally existed in Canada, it has a presence in some sectors such as the dairy industry and the space subsector of the telecommunications equipment manufacturing sector (Atkinson & Coleman 1989a, 97–184).

Provincial Initiatives

Over the past few decades most provinces have also established industrial policies with varying degrees of coherence and success. The extent of these policies is such as to raise questions about whether they pose a threat—in the form of interprovincial trade barriers—to the economic benefits of nationhood in Canada (Economic Council of Canada 1991, 31–56). These policies are generally free from the pressures of regionalism, which are less well institutionalized within provincial politics. They also appear to benefit from the relatively greater local cohesion generated by the desire to defend provincial interests against national and international developments. However, these policies are more fragile because they are organized around a narrow base of leading firms and sectors of the economy.

One example that has received considerable attention, in part because of its association with the apparent willingness and self-confidence of the Québécois to "go it alone" and seek independence, is the so-called "market nationalism" of Quebec Inc.—that is, the state as catalyst rather than entrepreneur (Courchene 1991a, 4–7). Quebec's industrial policy is based upon a community of interest between business and government and gains much of its viability from the high degree of social homogeneity and consensual thinking among the Québécois. It is orchestrated by a number of financial institutions and crown corporations that seek to sustain local control over the Quebec economy as well as promote Québécois prosperity. The fact that many are public corporations makes them "take-over proof" (Courchene 1991b, 67). The Caisse de dépôt et placement du Québec has the responsibility of investing Quebec Pension Plan contributions and has served as a major provincial investment agency. Together with the Mouvement Desjardins, it controls substantial pools of investment capital. Mutual life companies like Laurentian and the National Bank also have investment roles. Quebec labour's solidarity fund and the

Quebec Stock Savings Plan—which provides tax benefits for Quebec residents who buy the stocks of Quebec-based corporations—are also part of this strategy. There is also the Société générale de financement, an investment and holding company, and the Société de développement industriel, which makes industrial development loans and grants. Hydro-Québec also has a role to play with its preference for local suppliers and subsidized rates for certain users such as the aluminum industry (Jenkin 1983, 75–84; Courchene 1991b, 63–73).

However impressive in appearance, like any provincial industrial strategy it has its vulnerabilities. In late 1991, the bankruptcy of Lavalin, a key Quebec engineering firm, raised some doubts about the durability of Quebec Inc. Moreover, in the event of Quebec's independence, the practices associated with Quebec Inc. might become the objects of U.S. trade remedy laws.

In early December 1991, the Quebec Liberal government introduced a new and revised industrial policy for the province. It is based on thirteen industrial clusters such as the aerospace and ground transportation clusters and it is hoped that their mutual interaction and cooperation will generate even greater opportunities and competitiveness for Quebec's goods and services. These clusters are intended to transform Quebec's economy from one based on mass production to one based upon value added. Within these industrial clusters, it is hoped that a synergy will emerge that will create more jobs and promote economic growth. The Quebec government's role in all this would be that of facilitator and catalyst, encouraging the formation and growth of these clusters. It would not take a direct role in organizing interaction within the cluster, leaving responsibility for that role within the private sector.

Overall, the capacity of the Canadian government to mount and sustain a successful industrial policy was called into question during the years leading up to the FTA. For a variety of reasons the Canadian bureaucracy was, for the most part, incapable of establishing the distance and collective purpose necessary to implement an anticipatory industrial policy. In the process, many politicians soured on the capacity of Canada's governmental institutions to engage in industrial policymaking. This made them more sympathetic to market solutions such as liberalized trade. While the provinces remain active in the area of industrial policy, their capacities are limited (the Quebec experience notwithstanding) and the potential implications of their failures are much greater.

The Federal System and the Division of Powers

The federal government's increased interest in market solutions, and thus in trade policy, can be traced in part to the division of powers between the provinces and the federal government. The division of powers have generated a series of ongoing political struggles in the area of industrial policy. The wide range of constitutional powers that are, in some way or another, involved in industrial policy solutions have produced never-ending problems and conflicts (Stevenson 1989, 177–209).

In trade policy the power of the federal government is more clear-cut. The trade and commerce power of the federal government had been interpreted narrowly by the Judicial Committee of the Privy Council (JCPC) when it was Canada's highest court of appeal. In the Labour Conventions Case of 1937 the JCPC had held that the federal government's treaty-making power was restricted to those areas of competence assigned to the federal government by the British North America Act, 1867. Each level of government had to respect the powers of the other in making treaties, and the federal government had no generalized treaty-making power (Russell 1988, 164–65). However, on a variety of occasions the Supreme Court has given some indication of its willingness to give a broader interpretation to the capacity of Canada's federal government to carry out its obligations as a sovereign state (Pilkington 1988, 95–97). Thus the federal government's powers over international trade and commerce are a relatively sound basis for its trade treaty-making power. That the federal government has not been more vigorous in moving to prevent provinces from discriminating against foreign imports (such as wine) is probably a reflection of its political sensibilities and an unwillingness to tug at the tiger's whiskers.

Thus, in a time of constitutional turmoil in the early 1980s—when the move to a free trade agreement first emerged—the trade-policy approach must have seemed particularly attractive. Not only could the federal government act, largely on its own, but the failures at industrial policy-making suggested that there were few alternatives. The provinces were given some opportunities to participate at arm's length—indeed seven supported the FTA—in order to enhance the legitimacy of the agreement, but the federal government had the requisite powers (Brown 1991, 81–145). As the negotiations on a subsidy code proceed, it is probable that a fuller level of provincial agreement will be necessary.

CONCLUSION

In this chapter we have argued that political institutions have played an important part in enhancing the role played by trade policy in federal economic decision-making. Industrial policy faced serious obstacles in its implementation—in part because of the liberalization of international trade over the postwar period—and trade policy gained supporters as an alternative option. Of course industrial policy initiatives will continue to be attempted particularly in the area of adjustment policies. Indeed, if Canada's economic performance continues to decline through the 1990s, there will be great pressure on the national and provincial governments to mount industrial policy solutions to the crisis. While indirect industrial policy measures, such as support for manpower retraining and infrastructive expenditures, will continue, direct industrial policies will meet increasing international resistance. As the twentieth century draws to a close, international economic changes are reducing the autonomy of the nation-state. This chapter has emphasized the role that state institutions have played in affecting policy choices, particularly the popularity of the trade policy option. Future analysis will have to incorporate, in a more complete manner, the role of international institutions.

NOTE

1. Might Canada have developed differently? For the argument that Canada might have retained more control over its productive assets were it not for the strength of big business, the weakness of the agrarian classes, and the structure of Canadian finance, see Laxer (1989) and Atkinson and Coleman (1989, ch. 2).

Chapter 9

Social Policy: Two Worlds

Carolyn Tuohy

INTRODUCTION

Canadian social policy presents a puzzle. On the one hand, it comprises a relatively niggardly set of policies directed at income security—notably public pensions and social assistance. The one relatively generous income-maintenance program, unemployment insurance, has been the focus of ongoing controversy. On the other hand, Canada has adopted a system of national health insurance that is both generous and outstandingly popular. Why have Canadians been so parsimonious and chary in protecting individuals and families against poverty, and so generous and enthusiastic in protecting them against the costs of health care?

To solve this puzzle — to understand the differences between these "two worlds" of the Canadian welfare state—we need to turn to the framework outlined in the Introduction. That is, we need to look to the intersection of ideas, interests, and institutions. *Ideas* or "public philosophies" (Manzer 1985) about the extent to which human needs ought to be met through state action have influenced the evolving agenda of social policy. Moreover, because they are explicitly intended to redistribute resources from some groups in society to others (from higher to lower income groups, from the young to the old, from the healthy to the sick), social policies are also shaped by the relative power of different *interests*—those who would benefit from different programs and those who would bear their costs. (Indeed, social policies often create certain categories of interest, such as groups of bene-

---

The author wishes to thank Keith Banting and Michael Atkinson for their insightful comments on an earlier draft of this paper.

ficiaries who come to view particular kinds of benefits as entitlements, and providers of service whose livelihood is tied to the existence of particular programs and modes of delivering service.)

But neither ideas about the role of the state in meeting human needs, nor the balance of social interests, translates directly into social policies. Those policies must be developed through authoritative *institutions*. The way in which those institutions are structured—for example, the extent to which authority is divided between levels or branches of government—will affect the way in which certain ideas are (or are not) brought to bear and certain interests are (or are not) channelled into the policy process. Equally important, social policies require organizations for their implementation, and over time these organizations take on an institutional life of their own that shapes subsequent policy development.

Looking at the relationships between ideas, interests, and institutions will help us to understand how the "two worlds" of health care and income-maintenance policy in Canada have evolved as they have. It can also help us to understand the responses of the Canadian welfare state to the challenges of the late twentieth century—responses that, as we shall see, present some further puzzles.

BACKGROUND AND DEFINITIONS
Three Welfare State Regimes

The centrality of institutions to the understanding of social policy is suggested by a term that is often used as virtually synonymous with social policy: the "welfare state." Some uses of the term "welfare state," it is true, emphasize functional aspects: the welfare state comprises those public policies directed at meeting basic human needs through the provision of "income and other consumption entitlements including health and social services" (Myles 1989, 1). Most definitions of the welfare state, however, insist on incorporating not only what it does but how it is structured (Esping-Andersen 1990; Quadagno 1988; Titmuss 1958). Such an approach to definition rejects the notion of a single ideal–typical welfare state that real-life systems approximate to a greater or lesser extent. Rather, this approach to definition recognizes the great variety of "welfare states," with different structures and different levels of generosity, and seeks to develop typologies to guide inquiry into this variety.

Esping-Andersen has categorized differences in the structure and generosity of social programs to identify three types of welfare state "regime." "Social democratic" welfare states have universal and generous programs whose benefits are available on uniform terms and conditions to all citizens. Fundamental to social democratic welfare states, moreover, is a commitment to full employment. "Conservative" welfare states offer differentiated benefits through social insurance for defined groups (usually occupational groups) within the population. These programs tend to be generous overall, but the level of generosity varies within "a labyrinth of status-specific insurance funds" (Esping-Andersen 1990, 24). Contributions and benefits are also related to earnings, with higher-income individuals making higher contributions and receiving higher benefits. Because of the occupational segregation of these funds, and because the funds are administered by representatives of contributors and beneficiaries themselves (usually employers and employees), "conservative" welfare states might also be termed "corporatist." Finally, "liberal" welfare states provide limited benefits primarily to those most disadvantaged in the market. Means-tested programs predominate, universalism is limited, and the middle and upper classes turn to the market, not the state, for insurance against income disruption and illness. These three "regimes" are in fact ideal types: most existing welfare states show elements of each, while corresponding most closely to one type.

Historically, corporatist welfare states were the first to emerge on the national level. In the 1880s, Germany under Bismarck established a set of occupationally-segregated social insurance funds that were to serve as a model for a number of its European neighbours such as Austria. Corporatist welfare states in France and Italy, however, were consolidated at the national level only after a considerably longer period of subnational experimentation. Universalistic welfare states began to develop in the Scandinavian countries in the early twentieth century, and were elaborated and merged with full-employment strategies under social democratic parties in the 1930s to create social democratic welfare states. "Liberal" social programs existed at the subnational level in Britain in the nineteenth century and in Canada and the United States in the early twentieth century, but it was not until the 1930s in the United States, the 1940s in Britain,[1] and the 1960s in Canada that liberal welfare states began to assume their present form at the national level.

Explaining Cross-National Differences in the Development of the Welfare State

A number of factors have been invoked to explain this cross-national variation in the development of welfare states. Explanations of differences in the timing of the adoption of welfare state programs, and the structure of the regime adopted have variously focused on the confluence of class forces (or "interests" in the terms used here) in individual nations (Esping-Andersen & Korpi 1984), on the development and diffusion of ideas about the role of the state in the provision of social benefits (King 1973; Ashford 1986; Collier & Messick 1975; Heclo

1974), or on institutional factors such as federalism (Leman 1977; Tuohy 1989). Differences in the level of generosity of social spending have been attributed largely to ideological differences as reflected in the relative power of parties of the left and the right, and to the organization of business and labour interests (Cameron 1984; Castles 1981), although federalism has also been suggested in this context as a brake on social expenditure (Castles 1981; Banting 1987).

Briefly, the following generalizations can be drawn. Corporatist welfare states developed under conservative regimes in nations where the state was inherently legitimate, as an explicit alternative to the social democratic agenda of the left. The power of the left in these nations has not been sufficient to transform corporatist structures to universalistic ones, but it has ensured that welfare state programs will be generous. Social democratic welfare states also developed in nations in which there was strong sociocultural support for the state. Although the seeds of these structures were sown by liberal regimes, their full flowering has occurred under the hegemony of parties of the left, in concert with a comprehensively organized labour movement. Finally, liberal welfare states developed where state activity was not inherently legitimate and where the left was weak, both ideologically and organizationally. Ideological factors and the balance of class forces, then, would appear to have had greater impact than institutional factors on the broad shape of the welfare state regime (social democratic, liberal, or corporatist) in particular nations.

Institutional factors, however, have intersected with these ideological and social forces to affect the pace and the shape of welfare state development. One set of institutional factors involves what might be called "macropolitical" institutions—the division of authority between levels and branches of government. Christopher Leman (1977), for example, argues that differences in Canadian and American political institutions have resulted in an incremental pattern of social policy development in Canada as opposed to the episodic "big bang" pattern of the United States. He argues that the relative strength of Canadian provincial governments in Canadian federalism has led to continual pressure on the federal system to accommodate provincial initiatives. In the United States, on the other hand, the division of powers within the national government makes policy change very difficult. Only when pressure builds to the extent that it explodes through these institutional barriers does change occur—and a newly entrenched status quo is the result.

By affecting the timing of opportunities for social policy initiatives, moreover, these institutional factors determine the climate of prevailing policy ideas in which those initiatives are developed, and hence affect their content. In the Canadian case, for example, the first major thrust toward a national program for financing health-care delivery occurred immediately after World War II, in a period in which there was a consensus among medical and hospital interests that a national governmental scheme was appropriate. The proposals were part of a larger package of federal–provincial financial arrangements, however, and foundered as a result of disagreement between federal and provincial governments. Federal and provincial governments did not reach agreement on a shared-cost program of hospital insurance until 1958, and on medical insurance until 1971.[2] Had federal–provincial relations favoured the development of these programs in the late 1940s, they would likely have been shaped by the policy ideas then prevalent, notably by the model of the state-organized National Health Service being put into place in Britain at that time (Tuohy 1989). As it was, the delay gave insurance models time to take root in the private sector in Canada, and the programs ultimately adopted were public-sector versions of these models.

Another set of institutional factors that has shaped social policies over time relates to the structure of welfare states themselves. As these structures become established, they develop an established repertoire of responses. They reinforce particular ways of thinking about social policy. And they come to be integrated with particular constellations of interests—beneficiaries, contributors, and service providers. That is, they not only entrench certain organizational patterns; they also crystallize certain ideas about social justice, and certain configurations of interests. Social democratic welfare states, for example, accustom contributors and beneficiaries to ideas of universal entitlement, and create broad groups of contributors and beneficiaries with shared interests in the system. Corporatist welfare states accustom people to the idea of entitlement on the basis of occupational status, and create narrower categories of interest and a complex administrative network. Finally, in liberal welfare states, where eligibility for benefits is on the basis of demonstrated need, the very concept of "entitlement" is contested; and a narrower base of the population than in either of the two other models has a "stake" in the benefits of social programs.

The "Crisis" of the Welfare State in the Late Twentieth Century

In the late nineteenth and early twentieth centuries, when welfare-state regimes were beginning to take shape, social policies in Western industrial nations were driven by the need to address the dislocations brought about by industrialization. In the late twentieth century, these nations are once again experiencing a period of rapid economic adjustment and concomitant social dislocations in response to the globalization of the international economy. And in the present context, these pressures are placing the structures established over the past century under great stress.

Changes in the Welfare State

The dramatic growth of social spending as a proportion of GDP in OECD nations in the 1960s and 1970s was followed by a sharp levelling off (and, in some nations a marginal decline) in social spending–GDP ratios in the 1980s.[3] In part, these changes over time and across nations reflect demographic differences.[4] But they also reflect policy changes, as what Tom Courchene (1990) has called the cushion of economic growth in the 1960s deflated under the pressure of international economic developments. In the context of lower rates of economic growth and increased capital mobility, the continued expansion of the welfare state implied increased rates of taxation or increased deficit spending. Neither of these options was politically attractive. As Klein and O'Higgins have pointed out, "the expansion of social spending has increasingly been financed by taxes that stretch further and further down the income distribution" (1988, 206). Although the tax tolerance of the middle class seems to vary widely across nations, most governments in the 1980s appeared to believe that they were operating very close to the limits of that tolerance. The scope for increasing the tax burden on upper-income individuals and corporations, in a context in which capital was becoming increasingly mobile internationally, was limited by the threat of capital flight. And increasing deficit spending, even apart from its effects on "business confidence," had the boomerang effect of increasing debt-service expenditures and further crowding the fiscal scope for welfare-state expansion.

Small wonder, then, that the question of the rolling back or retrenchment of the welfare state loomed large on the political agenda of the 1980s. Even among those who would defend the welfare state, attention turned to questions less of its expansion than its redesign (Heclo 1981; Marmor, Mashaw & Harvey 1990). But the responses of different welfare-state regimes to the "crisis" of the welfare state in the fiscal and economic climate of the 1980s and 1990s have been shaped by their institutional legacies. Although social spending as a proportion of GDP has actually fallen marginally in some social democratic welfare states such as Sweden, these nations remain generous social spenders. Spending reductions have been achieved largely through modifications to universal programs—for example, by extending waiting periods for benefits. The "purest" social democratic states, Sweden and Norway, moreover, have retained their commitment to the core of their welfare-state policies—full employment.

Corporatist welfare states have experienced little change. Germany managed to reduce spending on health care as a proportion of GDP through the use of "concerted action" techniques to achieve consensus among health-care providers, social insurance funds, and governments (Kirkman-Liff 1990), and has made technical changes in the calculation of pension benefits that reduced the value of those benefits for new and future beneficiaries. These policies represent only small increments of change, however, in an enduring corporatist system (Katzenstein 1987: 191–92; Pierson & Weaver 1992; Heidenheimer, Heclo & Adams 1990, 259–60). In France, the election of a socialist government in 1981 after the dominance of the right for most of the postwar period resulted in the enhancement of some social benefits, notably pensions. Later policy changes included experimentation with minimum-income programs to be implemented on a local basis. On balance, however, as Freeman reports, "the substitution of a government of the Left for one of the Right produced few innovations and no serious attempt at fundamental reform" (1990, 189).

In liberal welfare states, notably the United States and Britain, restraint measures have focused disproportionately on certain programs of public assistance and/or unemployment insurance. Changes to programs with predominantly middle-class beneficiaries, such as public pensions, have been less dramatic, and they have tended to affect future rather than present beneficiaries (Pierson & Weaver 1992; Weale 1990; Bawden & Palmer 1984).

The Role of Institutions

Institutional factors have played an important role in shaping these responses of established welfare states to the fiscal and economic pressures of the late twentieth century. This is true in two senses. In the first place, the institutional structures of welfare states themselves have delimited the range of possible responses. The heavy reliance of social democratic states on universal programs has meant that change, to be significant, must focus on such programs. But generous universal programs, with their broad clientele base, are politically very difficult to pare. Hence changes in these systems have been very limited. Corporatist welfare states add an element of complexity to the administration of middle-class entitlements, which make them even more resistant to change. Liberal welfare states, with their heavier emphasis on means-tested programs, which are less politically sacrosanct, offer greater potential for rolling back the welfare state. But these rollbacks have been selective, and their effects disproportionately borne by low-income groups.

Institutional factors, moreover, can also explain variation *within* regime categories. In particular, they can help us to understand the considerable variation among liberal welfare states. Pierson and Weaver (1992), for example, have examined reductions in public pension benefits in the 1980s in three liberal welfare states—Britain, the United States, and Canada. They find that reductions were greatest in Britain and least in Canada, with the United States in an intermediate position; and they attribute these differences to the different capacities of the political institutions of the three systems to "impose losses." Their argument relates to one of the puzzles of Canadian social policy—the difference between Canadian responses to the "crisis" of the welfare state in the late twentieth century and those of other nations. Before we consider that puzzle, however, we need to address a more central one: the contrast between the health-care and the income-maintenance arenas in Canada.

HEALTH CARE VERSUS INCOME MAINTENANCE IN CANADA

Esping-Andersen treats Canada's welfare state as "liberal"; and other students of Canadian social policy (Haddow 1990) accept this characterization. There is certainly evidence for this view: Canada does not have a generous welfare state in comparison with other advanced industrial nations. Canada's public spending on social programs (income maintenance, health, and education) as a proportion of GDP has consistently been below the OECD average—even below average for the seven major OECD nations, which include the low-spending United States and Japan. Canada's social spending–GDP ratio was estimated to be 22.3 percent in 1986, as compared with the OECD average of 24.7 and the average for the largest seven OECD nations of 23.3 (OECD 1989, 16–17).

Income Maintenance

It is Canada's parsimonious approach to income maintenance (other than unemployment insurance) that accounts for these relatively low social spending levels. Income transfers in general as a proportion of GDP are well below the OECD average (Banting 1987, 195). Furthermore, although the Canadian income-maintenance system has included some universal elements (notably old-age security pensions and family allowances), and some social insurance programs (the Canada and Quebec pension plans and unemployment insurance), Canada has relied much more heavily on means-tested social assistance programs than have most OECD nations (Smeeding, Torrey & Rein 1988).

Canada's system of income transfers to the elderly comprises three components: a flat-rate universal benefit (the old-age security pension, or OAS), a means-tested supplement to those whose income falls below a certain level (the Guaranteed Income Supplement, or GIS), and a contributory plan, in which benefits are related to contributions and both are related to earnings, up to a maximum (the Canada

Pension Plan, or CPP). All are federally administered, although, as noted below, changes to the CPP require provincial consent. Quebec administers its own contributory plan, the Quebec Pension Plan (QPP); and several provinces also administer their own means-tested supplements (see Figure 9.1).

Despite its universal and contributory components, this system is essentially "liberal." It is targeted at low-income groups, while encouraging middle- and upper-income earners to turn to the market for income replacement upon retirement. The system does well, in international perspective, in raising the low-income elderly out of poverty (Smeeding, Torrey & Rein 1988, 111). It performs relatively poorly, however, in replacing the income of the average worker upon retirement, and even more poorly in the case of upper-income earners.

Consider three fictitious single individuals who retired in Canada in 1980. One (Adams) was earning the average industrial wage before retirement, one (Black) was earning half that amount, and one (Cooper) was earning twice the average wage. Adams would have found that her OAS and CPP pensions, together with the GIS supplement, amounted to 33 percent of her preretirement income. If she had a spouse without income, this proportion would have been 54 percent. Black, however, would have found that the three components of the public pension system replaced 59 percent of his income—101 percent if he had a spouse without income. Finally, OAS and CPP pensions would have provided only 15 percent of Cooper's preretirement income—and only 23 percent if she had a spouse without income. In these circumstances, it is not surprising that Adams and Cooper would likely look to private sources to supplement their public pensions. Adams, Black, and Cooper would all receive more from public pensions if they lived, for example, in "social democratic" Sweden—and Adams and Cooper would be better off in terms of public pension payments even if they lived in the United States with its "liberal" welfare state (Myles 1989, 56).[5] Indeed, Adams could rely on public pensions to replace a higher proportion of her income in all but two of twelve industrial nations reviewed in a 1980 survey (Aldrich 1982, 5).

With regard to the nonelderly poor, the liberal character of Canada's income-maintenance system is even more apparent. Sixty-nine percent of income transfers to single-parent families in Canada are in the form of means-tested payments, as compared with 93 and 63 percent in the United States and Britain respectively, 16 percent in Germany, 45 percent in Sweden, and 4 percent in Norway (Smeeding, Torrey & Rein 1988, 111). Canada also ranks relatively poorly among advanced industrial nations in the extent to which its income-transfer programs move such families out of poverty. Public transfers close 75 percent of the "poverty gap"[6] in Canada, as compared with 58 percent in the United States, 90 percent in Britain, 84 percent in Germany, and over 200 percent in Sweden (Smeeding, Torrey & Rein 1988, 111).

FIGURE 9.1
Major Canadian Income-Maintenance, Medical, and Hospital-Insurance Programs

Program	Basis of Eligibility	Year of Adoption	Administration	Financing
Health Care:				
Hospital insurance	Universal	1958	Provincial	Cost-shared (general revenue)[1]
Medical insurance	Universal	1966	Provincial	Cost-shared (general revenues)[1]
Pensions:				
Canada Pension Plan (CPP)	Contributory	1965	Federal[2]	Federal (employer and employee contributions)[2]
Old Age Security (OAS)	Universal[3]	1951	Federal	Federal (general revenues)
Guaranteed Income Supplement (GIS)	Means- (income-tested)	1966	Federal[4]	Federal (general revenues)[4]
Other:				
Family Allowances	Universal[5]	1944	Federal	Federal (general revenues)
Canada Assistance Plan (CAP)	Means-(need-tested)	1966	Provincial	Cost-shared (general revenues)[6]
Unemployment Insurance (UI)	Contributory	1941	Federal	Federal (employer and employee contributions)[7]

1. Cost-shared between federal and provincial governments. As of 1992, two provinces funded a portion of these programs through "premiums," which were, in effect, earmarked taxes.
2. Quebec administers its own Quebec Pension Plan, financed through employer and employee contributions.
3. As noted in the text, old-age security pensions have been "clawed back" from upper-income earners, beginning with the 1989–90 federal budget.
4. Some provinces also administer and finance means-tested pension supplements in addition to the GIS.
5. As noted in the text, family allowances were "clawed back" from upper-income earners, beginning with the 1989–90 federal budget; and the 1992–93 budget proposed to eliminate universal family allowances entirely in favour of an income-tested cash benefit.
6. Cost-shared by federal and provincial (and, in some provinces, municipal) governments. Provinces also administer and finance some social assistance programs outside the CAP.
7. Until 1990, the federal government also financed some components of UI (notably regionally extended benefits).

Canada's unemployment insurance program, however, is relatively generous—largely because of its eligibility requirements and the duration rather than the level of its benefits. The unemployment insurance program, indeed, has come to play a redistributive role, both between income categories and between regions, beyond what might be expected of a contributory social insurance scheme (Banting 1987, 209). However, the burdening of the unemployment insurance plan with redistributive objectives (that the rest of the social security system is failing to address) has led to increasing controversy over the program in the 1980s, and changes introduced in 1990 reduced this redistributive role somewhat.

Health Care

In the area of health policy we find another tale. Indeed, health care is Canada's social policy success story. The Canadian national health-insurance program enjoys broad popular support and, increasingly, international acclaim. It provides universal, comprehensive first-dollar coverage of medical and hospital services. Although the proportion of total health-care spending in Canada that comes from public sources (about 76 percent) lies almost exactly on the OECD average, the structure of the Canadian health-care financing system is unusual in that the public and private sectors are segmented from, not parallel to each other. In other words, the vast bulk of medical and hospital services are financed entirely out of public funds—there are no private alternatives. The private sector comprises expenditures on drugs outside hospitals, dental services, eyeglasses and other prostheses, and amenities such as private rooms in hospital.

For almost all medical and hospital services, then, Canadians in all income categories face no out-of-pocket costs. The fictitious Adams, Black, and Cooper in our earlier example may participate in very different pension regimes, but they have access to the same medical and hospital care system. The single parent in poverty faces no greater financial obstacle to health care in Canada than does a person with ten times her or his income.

In terms of total health-care expenditures (public and private), Canada ranks with a group of European nations (including Germany, Austria, Sweden, and France) in which health spending accounts for between eight and nine percent of GDP. (This contrasts on the one hand with the case in Britain, in which total health-care expenditures amount to just over six percent of GDP, and on the other hand with the United States, whose largely private health-care system is also very expensive, with total health-care spending accounting for over 12 percent of GDP.[7]) A 1988 cross-national public opinion survey found Canadians to be more satisfied with their health-care system than are either Americans or Britons; and Americans saw a Canadian-style system as preferable to their own (Blendon 1989).

Explaining the Difference

Why is Canadian social policy characterized by a relatively generous and popular social program in the area of health care, but relatively niggardly and/or controversial programs in the area of income maintenance? In Esping-Andersen's terms, why does the health-policy arena evince a "social democratic" character, in its universalism and its generosity, while the income-maintenance arena remains distinctly "liberal" in its emphasis on means-tested programs and its limited benefits for the middle class?

The full answer would not appear to lie in the realm of ideas. As in Britain (and unlike the United States), the idea of universality took root in both the income-maintenance and health-care arenas in Canada. Universal family allowances were adopted at the federal level in 1944, and universal old-age security pensions in 1951, before universal hospital and medical insurance came into being. Threats to the "universality" of Canadian social programs (including medicare, but also including pensions) were invoked by opponents of the Canada–U.S. Free Trade Agreement, who recognized the potency of the symbol of universality. A focus on ideas alone cannot help us understand why universal benefits have been meagre and in need of supplementation in the income-maintenance arena but not in health care.

Nor do interests alone explain the difference. Public pensions remain at relatively low levels in Canada despite a significant constituency of support—manifested in a successful protest against proposals in the 1985 federal budget to de-index public pensions, to be discussed below. It might be that the existence of a powerful group of service providers (notably the medical profession) in health-care, and the absence of such a group in the income-maintenance arena, helps to account for the difference. As we shall see, this is indeed part of the explanation. But the impact of the medical profession has been different in Canada than it has in Britain or the United States. We need to turn to institutional factors for a fuller explanation.

Keith Banting has pointed out institutional differences between the health-care and income-maintenance arenas in Canada. Referring to Canada's "bifurcated," indeed "schizophrenic," welfare state, he draws attention to the greater institutional centralization of income-maintenance policy than of health-care (and social services, which are much less quantitatively significant). As will be discussed shortly, the federal government has sole discretion over key instruments in the income-maintenance arena (OAS, GIS, UI) but not in the health-care arena, in which it at best shares authority with the provinces over medical and hospital insurance. But, for our purposes here, it is not clear why greater centralization in the income-maintenance than in the health-care arena should have yielded less generous outcomes in the former—cross-national comparisons (and Banting's own work on

Canada) suggest that centralization is associated with more generous income-maintenance systems (Castles & McKinlay 1979). Furthermore, the most penurious income-maintenance programs (CAP and CPP) are precisely those that, like health care, are entangled in federal–provincial arrangements.

In order to understand the difference between these two worlds of Canadian social policy we need to consider other dimensions of federalism: its capacity to allow for subnational differentiation within a national framework, and its susceptibility to shifts in the climate of federal-provincial relations over time. And we need to consider not only the structures of government in this context, but also the way in which those structures have intersected with developing ideas and with the organization of interests in the health-care and income-maintenance arenas.

Constitutional responsibility for both health and welfare was lodged at the provincial level at Confederation, under a provision of the 1867 Constitution giving the provinces responsibility for "hospitals, asylums, charities, and eleemosynary institutions." The federal government has come to play a major role, however, through constitutional amendments giving it authority over unemployment insurance (1940) and old-age security (1951), and also through the use of its "spending power." This term refers to the federal government's ability to adopt programs of transfer payments—payments to provincial governments, institutions, and individuals—and to attach conditions to those payments, in areas of exclusive provincial jurisdiction. In practice, then, the federal–provincial balance in these arenas is always contested, although the federal government has gained sole authority over more significant instruments in the income-maintenance than in the health-care arena.

Ideas, Interests, and Institutions in the Health-Care Arena

Federal-Provincial Relations

The development of a national framework for financing health-care delivery can be explained in part in terms of the intersection between the structures of Canadian federalism and the development of ideas. The relative strength of provincial governments provided niches in which different ideas about health-care financing could be developed and implemented. Government hospital insurance, for example, was first adopted by the social democratic CCF government of Saskatchewan in 1944. The diffusion of ideas and programs, moreover, has depended heavily on the climate of federal–provincial relations, which in turn has affected the timing of policy changes. As noted earlier, federal proposals for cost-shared programs in the areas of both health care and income maintenance in the immediate postwar period foundered on provincial governments' suspicion of federal aggrandizement after a period of wartime centralization. It was not until the late 1950s and 1960s that the country entered into a period of federal–provincial "diplomacy" (Simeon 1972) sufficient to allow for a burst of policy-making that established some of the core programs of the contemporary Canadian welfare state.

By the time national hospital insurance was adopted in 1958, there had been considerable experience with governmental hospital insurance in several provinces. In 1962, the CCF/NDP government of Saskatchewan pioneered governmental medical insurance, in the face of a physicians' strike. The subsequent development of a national framework for governmental medical insurance, however, had more to do with federal–provincial political fiscal manoeuvring than with group–government relationships. In the mid-1960s, medical and insurance interests favoured government supplementation of private-sector programs over a universal program. There was, moreover, no "major outcry" for medicare on the part of the Canadian populace (Taylor 1978, 367). The adoption of medicare was nonetheless favoured by all parties at the federal level as a substantial assertion of federal authority to establish national standards in social policy. Conflict was channelled along federal–provincial fault lines, not along partisan lines within the federal or provincial governments. The Medical Care Act was passed in 1966 under a minority government, with only two dissenting votes in Parliament. But the provincial level was the locus of considerable opposition. Ontario, for example, protested that its entry into the program was practically coerced by the federal imposition of a supplementary tax introduced to pay for it (Taylor 1978, 375). Notwithstanding this opposition, the fiscal incentives of the scheme[8] were such that, between 1968 and 1971, all provinces entered the plan.

Financing the Health-Care System

The program established was one that essentially underwrote the costs of the existing health-care delivery system. Providers were to be remunerated (or consumers reimbursed) for care provided on a fee-for-service or per diem basis. Establishing a program of universal coverage, and making the federal and provincial governments responsible for its open-ended costs, guaranteed that the primary emphasis of the governmental agenda would shift from a concern with ensuring access to a concern with controlling costs. This shift was reinforced by cross-national trends. In virtually all advanced industrial nations (although to varying degrees) the increasing proportion of GDP devoted to health care became a matter of growing public-policy concern throughout the

1970s and 1980s (Schieber 1985). "Cost control" replaced "access" as the dominant theme of the international climate of policy ideas.

In Canada, the challenge of controlling costs was felt most strongly at the provincial level. Because provincial governments administered the insurance plans, it was they who had access to the primary levers of cost control. The federal government, although it shared the costs of the program, had virtually no leverage on those costs. In the mid-1970s the federal government moved unilaterally to cap the open end of its financial commitment. The Established Programs Financing (EPF) arrangements, negotiated in 1977 under the shadow of unilateral federal action, limited the rate of increase in federal cash contributions to provincial health insurance plans to the rate of increase in nominal GNP and population.[9] These arrangements left provincial governments 100 percent at risk for cost increases in health care over and above the rate of increase in the general inflation rate, GNP, and population.

Reaching Accommodations

The national framework for health-care financing, then, has been shaped largely by federal–provincial relations. The key to the success of the Canadian health system, however, has been the possibility of provincial-level accommodations between highly mobilized health-care providers and the state within this national framework. Within the overall framework established by these federal–provincial arrangements, the shape of the health-care delivery and financing system has been worked out between providers and governments at the provincial level. These relationships, and their policy outputs, have varied across provinces. British Columbia, for example, spends much more on physicians' services than the national average, while Quebec and the Atlantic provinces spend considerably less. This difference is largely attributable to B.C.'s relatively rich medical fee schedule; actual utilization of physicians' service is highest in Ontario and Quebec. Hospital expenditures per capita have been highest in Quebec. Spending on nursing homes, which is less constrained by the terms of federal–provincial cost-sharing, varies widely (Barer & Evans 1986, 69–82).

Canada's system of centralizing responsibility for health-care financing in "single payers"—the provincial governments—has often been credited with restraining cost increases. But the ability (or the willingness) to restrain costs has also varied across provinces. Indeed, as Barer and Evans have starkly pointed out:

> Had Canada as a whole followed the growth experience of the three western provinces, total health care costs in 1982 would have been ... from 9.3 percent to 9.6 percent of GNP—almost halving the difference with the U.S. Had Canada followed the growth pattern of Nova Scotia or

Newfoundland since 1971, we might now be spending as large a share as the U.S or more (1986, 72).

The Canadian health system, then, allows for different accommodations between provider groups and governments to be reached across provinces. But although they may differ on the specifics of policy, the interests of the major provider groups—physicians, nurses, and hospitals—are fundamentally similar across provinces; and, under medicare, they militate in favour of the diffusion of a relatively generous "national standard" around which provincial experimentation can take place.

Provider groups, notably physicians, have reached their accommodations with provincial governments in the shadow of two spectres: the British National Health Service (NHS) and the market-oriented U.S. model. In Britain, the institutional structures of the NHS as established in the 1940s provide fewer opportunities for physicians to press for generosity. The organizational structure of the NHS has sharply divided the medical profession between general practitioners and specialists or "consultants." It has also entailed more centralized budgetary control. In the United States, on the other hand, the absence of universal health insurance has allowed health-care providers considerable discretion. But, ironically, it has changed the organization of "health-care providers": it has given rise to large multi-institutional chains in which the clinical judgements of physicians are increasingly subject to detailed review by administrators. It has also led some "consumers" (large corporate employers who provide health-care benefits to their employees) and third-party payers (insurance companies) to scrutinize medical practice carefully as well. The limited structures of the U.S. welfare state, then, have by default given rise to a complex and dense population of interests in the health-care arena, in which the medical profession is no longer dominant, and in which individual physicians find their clinical discretion increasingly constrained.

The timing of its adoption was such that in Canada national health insurance avoided either the British or the American model. "Insurance" models (the underwriting of the costs of a system of private practice) had time to develop in Canada, but complex institutional networks on the American model did not. And the unattractiveness of either the British or the American alternative has rendered health-care providers in Canada open to accommodations with the state (Tuohy 1992). These provider groups, moreover, are relatively well endowed with the political resources to advance their interests: with well-established and well-staffed organizations and, in the case of hospitals, concentrated community support. The result has been a set of provincial-level arrangements that has allowed sufficient variation to accommodate the major provider groups while maintaining a generous and universal program nationwide.

Ideas, Institutions, and Interests in the Income-Maintenance Arena

The Programs and the Provinces

Circumstances in the income-maintenance arena are similar to those in health care in some respects. Certain key programs involve both federal and provincial governments. Legislation establishing the contributory Canada Pension Plan, for example, provides that any province may opt out of its provisions with compensation (only Quebec has done so); and that substantive amendments must be approved by two-thirds of the provincial governments representing two-thirds of the population. The needs-tested Canada Assistance Plan (the major social assistance program) is cost-shared by federal, provincial, and (in some provinces) municipal governments. Spending under CAP has also, until recently, been "open-ended," in that the federal government has borne 50 percent of the costs of assistance for all those qualifying for the needs-tested provincial public-assistance programs established under the plan.

The national framework established by CAP allows for substantial provincial discretion. In addition, provinces also operate income-maintenance programs outside the CAP umbrella. As a result, income-maintenance policies vary considerably across provinces. Welfare incomes as a percentage of average income for single employable persons varied from 17 percent in New Brunswick to 42 percent in neighbouring Prince Edward Island in 1989. For single-parent families with one child, this ratio ranged from 50 percent in Alberta to 60 percent in New Brunswick; and for two-parent, two-child families it ranged from 24 percent in New Brunswick to 34 percent in Saskatchewan. Furthermore, the profile of assistance (the relative treatment given to single employables, single parents, and two-parent families) varies considerably across provinces. Nowhere, however, do welfare incomes raise any type of family above the poverty line (National Council of Welfare 1990, 34). Different provinces, moreover, have adopted quite different treatment of the employment earnings of welfare recipients: the amount that a single parent receiving social assistance could retain from part-time net monthly earnings of $250 varied from $250 in Saskatchewan to $60 in Quebec in 1983 (Evans & McIntyre 1987, 108).

As in the health-care arena, then, we find open-ended programs cost-shared by federal and provincial governments and considerable cross-provincial variation in the arena of income maintenance. In contrast with the health-care arena, however, we find in this arena a relatively ungenerous set of programs.

The Organization of Interests

The reason for this difference lies in the different pattern of interests in the two arenas. The mobilization of "provider" groups in the income-maintenance arena is very limited. Benefits in this arena are overwhelmingly composed of income transfers as opposed to services. The political and economic role of service providers is accordingly much less. The interests of beneficiaries have been represented over time by middle-class advocacy organizations such as the Canadian Council on Social Development at the national level and various welfare and social-planning councils at the provincial and local levels. As Haddow (1990) notes, these organizations have had close ties to (and receive major funding from) the state, although their histories show some increasing autonomy. With the burst of welfare-state activity in the late 1960s, these middle-class organizations were joined by antipoverty groups drawn more directly from the ranks of the poor, such as the National Anti-Poverty Organization (NAPO), founded in 1971. At the provincial level, coalitions of local antipoverty groups, such as the Ontario Coalition Against Poverty, have formed over time.

The organizational and financial resources of the antipoverty groups have been very limited, however, and politically they remain distinct from (and in some cases suspicious of) middle-class advocacy organizations. Seniors' groups might be considered a source of political support for income maintenance for the elderly. But despite their success in mobilizing against the proposed de-indexation of OAS in 1985, to be discussed shortly, the elderly have not established an organizational structure to provide for an ongoing influence on policy (Prince 1991, 320–21).

The organizational pattern of interests in the income-maintenance arena, then, is fragmented; and the best-endowed groups are largely funded by governments themselves. Moreover, organized labour, which has played an important role in supporting generous income–maintenance policies in other nations (Cameron 1984; Castles 1987), is hobbled in its ability to play such a role in Canada. The Canadian labour movement is one of the most decentralized in the world. It has, moreover, traditionally been ideologically divided: between nationalist and continentalist perspectives, between "business" unionism and "social" unionism. And as Rod Haddow (1991) has demonstrated, even those "social unionists" committed to the enhancement of the welfare state face a dilemma: whether to work to enhance the generosity of the liberal welfare state whose very structure is incompatible with social democratic principles, or to risk a bolder insistence upon a restructuring of the welfare state along social democratic lines.

In the absence of cohesively organized political actors in the income-maintenance arena, the relative significance of the interests of "governments as governments" is correspondingly greater (Banting 1987, 43, 51). This phenomenon has at least three important implications. First, since change in a number of key income-maintenance programs entails a complex set of implications for the fiscal responsibilities of various levels of government, governmental interests have accordingly acted as a brake on policy development. Second, governments frustrated by federal–provincial entanglements will turn to those instruments over which they have exclusive control. Third, the way in which they use these instruments or others will be determined not so much by group pressure as by partisanship and ideology.

We can see these factors at work in the heavy reliance on unemployment insurance in the income-maintenance arena. The unemployment insurance program provides the federal government with a vehicle relatively unencumbered by federal–provincial jurisdictional conflicts. The absence of provincial government involvement is one of the reasons that unemployment insurance was seized upon in the early 1970s by social policy reformers in the federal Liberal government who had been frustrated in their attempts to gain broad cabinet support for guaranteed annual income or negative-income-tax proposals. The attractiveness of instruments relatively unencumbered by federal–provincial complexity also helps to explain changes in the Canadian welfare state in the 1980s and 1990s—the second puzzle of Canadian social policy, to which we now turn.

RESPONSES TO THE CRISIS OF THE WELFARE STATE

Income Maintenance

The response of the Canadian welfare state to the challenges of the 1980s and 1990s appears somewhat anomalous in cross-national perspective. In the income-maintenance arena, neoconservative governments in other liberal welfare states such as Britain and the United States were most successful in scaling back programs aimed at low-income recipients, and had very limited success in reducing middle-class entitlements. In Britain, for example, the unemployment insurance program bore the brunt of the Conservative attack on welfare-state spending after 1979, while a government proposal to abolish the State Earnings Related Pension Scheme (SERPS) in 1985 was abandoned in the face of widespread and vociferous opposition. (Instead, technical changes were made to SERPS, which were most deleterious to those with irregular work histories (Weale 1990, 207)). Under the Reagan administration in the United States in the early 1980s, much larger relative cuts were made to programs of assistance to low-income families and individuals than to social security retirement and disability pensions[10] (Bawden & Palmer 1984, 185).

In Canada, however, the thrust of the policy of the federal Conservative government since 1984 was to reduce benefits to upper-income groups under universal programs. Both implicitly and explicitly, the principle of universality was itself placed under attack. Furthermore, although reductions to federal transfers to provinces for public assistance have been made, these reductions have been confined to the three wealthiest provinces. Similarly, changes to the unemployment program in 1990 tightened eligibility requirements and reduced the duration of benefits in some regions, but left the program in regions of highest unemployment virtually untouched. If conservatives in the British and American "liberal" welfare states have reduced benefits to low-income groups, why have conservatives in Canada's liberal welfare state focused their cost-cutting instead on better-off groups and regions?[11]

Federalism and the Conservative Agenda

The answer to this question again lies in the structures of Canadian federalism and the interests of governments as governments. The changes in social policy adopted by the federal Conservative government in the 1980s came in two waves, at the beginning of the mandates gained in each of the 1984 and 1988 general elections. (Not surprisingly, the Conservatives sought to concentrate "loss-imposing" policies early in their mandates.) Upon coming to power in 1984, the Conservatives immediately began to search for ways to reduce the federal deficit (Carmichael, Macmillan & York 1989, 25-29). It is not difficult to identify the common characteristic of those social-policy instruments to which they first turned in this quest: they turned to those instruments over which they had exclusive control—family allowances, old-age security, unemployment insurance, and the federal income tax.

The 1985 federal budget announced a partial de-indexation of personal income tax exemptions and marginal rates, and of the two universal flat-rate benefit programs—family allowance and old-age security (OAS). (Previously, these provisions had been increased annually in line with price inflation; the federal budget proposed that they be increased by the rate of inflation minus three percent.) The proposed de-indexation of OAS immediately drew a storm of protest from federal opposition parties, premiers in economically disadvantaged provinces, seniors' groups, and even the Business Council on National Issues. The proposal was abandoned in little more than a month. The symbolism of achieving deficit reduction on the backs of the elderly had proved to be politically untenable. The partial de-indexation of family allowances and personal income tax, however, was adopted. The direct effect of these changes was to reduce the real value of family benefits over time, and to move taxpayers into higher income tax brackets as inflation raised the nominal value of their incomes.

At the beginning of their second mandate, the Conservatives turned again to universal transfers in their search for cost-cutting potential. Having learned from their earlier attempt at an across-the-board reduction in OAS, the government now moved instead to change its universal aspect. The budget established a graduated tax-back (or "claw-back") of OAS pensions (and of family allowances, which had proved less politically sensitive in 1985) from upper-income families and individuals. Above a specified income level, all of these benefits would be taxed back. It was estimated that about 4.4 percent of the recipients of OAS, for example, would pay back all or part of their OAS pensions under these changes (Prince 1991, 323). This percentage would increase over time, however, since the income thresholds triggering the partial and total claw-backs were only partially indexed to inflation. Over time, if inflation regularly exceeds three percent, more families and individuals will cross the threshold at which they are required to pay back some or all of these benefits. Having thus eroded the principle of universality with respect to these programs, the Conservatives later moved to eliminate it entirely for family allowances in their 1992-93 budget, which proposed to replace the family allowance program, as well as existing child tax credits, with an income-tested cash benefit.

Unemployment Insurance

A second set of changes introduced by the federal Conservatives in the 1980s related to another area of federal jurisdiction—unemployment insurance. In their first term, the Conservatives did little in this area. Rather than make immediate changes to the UI program, the government appointed a commission of inquiry, headed by a prominent Liberal, an economist and former social affairs minister in the Quebec cabinet, Claude Forget. The Forget Commission was appointed in July 1985 and reported in December 1986. It recommended a radical simplification of the UI program, treating it as an insurance program and shearing it of both its broader income support and its "developmental" components. The two labour representatives on the commission dissented vehemently from the report. The Forget report was sharply criticized, moreover, by the parliamentary Standing Committee on Labour, Employment and Immigration. In the face of this opposition, and already well into its mandate, the government announced that the program would not be changed.

Upon gaining a second mandate in 1988, however, the Conservatives acted quickly to reform UI. The changes, enacted in

1990, removed job-creation and training functions from the program, raised basic qualifying periods, and shortened basic maximum benefit periods. The basic qualifying period was raised from fourteen to twenty weeks, and the basic maximum benefit period was shortened from 38 to 35 weeks. Furthermore, the graduated unemployment-rate thresholds at which regional extended benefits would apply were also raised. Previously, for example, reduced qualifying periods and longer maximum benefit periods began to be available where unemployment exceeded four percent; the 1990 changes raised this threshold to six percent. Nonetheless, in areas of high unemployment, qualifying periods and benefit periods remained as they had been before the changes.

The changes to the UI program, sparing the regions of highest unemployment, reflect the regional sensitivity of the federal Conservative cabinet. Such sensitivity is endemic to the body that, bears the main responsibility for representing territorial interests in the federal government (Sutherland & Doern, 1985). Pending changes to the Senate, the formal institutions of Canada's federal government do not provide mechanisms of regional influence irrespective of population. Therefore, the most important mechanism of "intrastate" federalism (i.e., the representation of regional interests within the institutions of the central government) is one on which the Constitution is silent: the federal cabinet. It has been argued that the framers of the BNA Act paid such little attention to formal mechanisms of intrastate federalism because they took for granted that the nucleus of power, the federal cabinet (nowhere explicitly mentioned in this written version of a British-style Constitution), would be regionally representative (Mallory 1977, 18; Sabetti 1984, 15). In Chapter 2 Herman Bakvis and David Mac Donald describe the susceptibility of cabinet decision-making about various program expenditures—including unemployment insurance—to regional considerations. In the late 1980s, this sensitivity was heightened in a period in which the question of "national unity"—and particularly the relationship of Quebec to the rest of Canada—was foremost on the national agenda. Persistent high rates of unemployment, and long-term unemployment, are regionally concentrated in Quebec and the Atlantic provinces.

Shared-Cost Programs

The federal government also made changes to shared-cost programs, but these were across-the-board cuts that did not directly affect program structure.[12] And these cuts also were constrained by regional considerations. In 1989 the federal government moved to limit its fiscal liability for increases in transfers under the Canada Assistance Plan. The legislation establishing the CAP provided that the federal government would share the costs of qualifying provincial programs on a

50-50 basis. Agreements established under the plan could be amended by mutual consent or terminated on one year's notice by either party. In 1989, the federal government unilaterally and without notice limited the rate of increase in its CAP transfers to British Columbia, Alberta, and Ontario to five percent. Those three provinces, led by B.C., launched a legal challenge to this action. The federal government argued, at first unsuccessfully in the British Columbia courts and then successfully before the Supreme Court of Canada in 1991, that its obligation to share half of costs under CAP was established by its own CAP legislation, not by the subsidiary agreements with the provinces, and that it was within the sovereign authority of Parliament unilaterally to revise that obligation. The court challenge nonetheless served the provinces' purpose of highlighting the federal reductions, and required the federal government to expend both resources and political capital in defending its position. In Ontario, meanwhile, the social democratic New Democratic Party government elected in September 1990 raised basic welfare payments by seven percent and shelter allowances by ten percent despite the federal limits.

The five percent "cap on CAP" was a gross limit—it did not directly affect the structure of social-assistance benefits. The only structural changes to a program involving federal–provincial arrangements under the federal Conservatives related to the Canada Pension Plan; and they were modest changes. The multiple vetoes provided under the CPP have made it notoriously difficult to change (Banting 1987, 69–73). In 1986, the CPP was modified by federal–provincial agreement to provide for greater flexibility in the retirement age, improve the rights of surviving spouses, and enhance disability benefits to bring them in line with the Quebec Pension Plan. The most significant change was an increase in the contribution rate—a change that was in the interest of provincial governments who otherwise faced the prospect of paying back loans from the CPP (Prince 1991, 326–27).

Changes in federal policy toward income-maintenance in the 1980s, then, were shaped much less by a coherent set of ideas about social policy than by the overriding priority given to deficit reduction and by the constraints of the federal system. These constraints required the federal government to focus largely on those instruments within its sole jurisdiction, and to make blunt and unilateral changes to programs entangled in federal–provincial arrangements. And in making these changes, the government was kept sensitive to regional considerations through the central mechanism of intrastate federalism, the federal cabinet.

Health Care

In the health-care arena, policy changes in the 1980s were also largely shaped and constrained by the climate and the structures of Canadian federalism; but in this arena, as argued above, explanations also need to take account of the relationship between health-care providers and provincial governments. This intersection of factors can help us to understand why Canada has, in at least one sense, been even more "social democratic" than Sweden. While Sweden maintains "user fees" for physicians' services, Canada has banned medical "extra billing" and other forms of user fees.[13]

The Extra-Billing Issue

In 1983, the federal Liberal government, declining in popularity and facing non-Liberal governments in each of the provinces, seized upon the issue of medical "extra billing" (that is, the billing of patients by physicians at rates above those covered by governmental medical insurance). The Liberals attacked extra billing as eroding the "universality" of medicare, the country's most popular social program. The general climate of federal–provincial relations was extremely sour. The federal government developed and enacted, with only the most perfunctory discussion with the provinces, legislation reducing federal cash transfers to any province allowing direct patient charges to be made for insured services. The Canada Health Act of 1984 provided that federal transfers were to be reduced by an amount equal to the dollar amount of charges to patients for insured services above governmental insurance coverage—a "dollar for dollar penalty" for such charges. As Banting (1987) has pointed out, moreover, such an action imposed no fiscal costs upon the federal government. (Indeed, had provinces failed to comply, it would have saved the federal government a very small proportion—less than one percent of federal transfers for medical and hospital insurance—of transfers withheld from the provinces.)

True to the Canadian pattern in health care, however, these changes to the national framework resulted in different provincial-level accommodations between the medical profession and government. At the time of the passage of the Canada Health Act, extra billing was practised in six provinces. All of these provinces banned extra billing within the three-year grace period for compliance specified by the Act. The terms on which extra billing was banned, and the process by which the change was made varied considerably across these provinces (Heiber & Deber 1987; Tuohy 1988). But, in general (with one exception), the process of negotiating the ban was relatively nonconflictual, and the medical profession achieved substantial gains in the form of fee schedule increases and binding-arbitration mechanisms for future fee schedule disputes, in return for the sacrifice of extra billing.

The exceptional case was that of Ontario. There, the banning of extra billing was marked by a period of unprecedented conflict between the government and the Ontario Medical Association (OMA).

This conflict was marked by a legal challenge by the OMA and the Canadian Medical Association to the Canada Health Act, and culminated in a four-week doctors' strike in 1986. Over the next five years, however, an accommodation between the profession and government was gradually re-established; and by 1991 both provisions for the binding arbitration of fee disputes and a joint bipartite profession–government committee on the management of the health-care delivery system had been established.

The Decentralization of Authority

The capacity of the Canadian system to generate provincial-level accommodations in the health-care arena takes on even more significance in the context of the de facto decentralization of authority that appeared to be underway in this arena in the late 1980s and early 1990s. This decentralization was subtle. It began with the partial de-indexation of the personal income tax system in 1985, which had indirect effects on the composition of federal transfers to the provinces for health care and postsecondary education under the EPF formulas noted above. And it did so without explicitly raising the issue of EPF transfers at all.

Essentially, overall federal EPF transfers were calculated to increase, from the base year 1976, with increases in nominal GNP (that is, real GNP plus inflation) and population. These transfers were made up of an unconditional component, representing the value of a given number of "tax points," and a cash transfer conditional upon the province's compliance with federal standards. The cash transfer was the "residual" component—the difference between the amount owed to the province under the GNP-population formula, and the amount generated by the tax points. The de-indexation of personal income tax meant that the value of the tax point component would increase faster than nominal GNP, and hence faster than overall EPF transfers. Hence conditional tax transfers would constitute a smaller and smaller proportion of EPF transfers over time, and the federal government would become less and less capable of enforcing federal standards.

The rate at which conditional EPF transfers would disappear was further hastened by explicit and unilateral changes made to the EPF formula by the federal government in 1986, 1989, and 1991. In 1986, the rate of increase in per capita EPF transfers was limited to the rate of increase in GNP minus two percent. In 1989, the amount of the per capita transfer in each provinces was frozen (that is, transfers would increase or decrease only in line with population, not GNP); and in 1991 this freeze was extended. With overall transfers frozen (except for population change) and the value of tax points increasing, it would not be long before unconditional tax transfers made up the whole of EPF transfers, and the federal government lost the sanctions necessary to enforce national standards. In the wealthier provinces, it has been projected that this will occur in the mid- to late 1990s.

It is not clear that the federal Conservative government sought this loss of control, although its ideology is distinctly more decentralist than was that of federal Liberals under whose aegis the EPF arrangements had been established. But loss of control over provincial social spending was apparently a price that the federal Conservatives were willing to pay in order to reduce their own fiscal obligations.

In other jurisdictions, such technical changes might have remained fairly "invisible." As Pierson and Weaver (1992) note, governments seek relatively less visible ways of imposing losses. Under the Westminster model, with its concentration of power in the executive, technical changes have limited visibility, especially in arenas in which affected interests lack the resources to analyze policy. But in Canada, provincial governments are well endowed with the resources necessary to analyze the effects of technical changes to federal–provincial cost-sharing arrangements. Hence, opposition to the federal changes to tax indexation and EPF transfers, with their implied loss of federal authority to maintain national standards in medicare, was not long in developing. Provincial governments and federal opposition parties opposed to the reductions in transfers could tie their opposition to a threat to national medicare standards. In response to this opposition, the federal government in 1991 introduced legislation allowing it to deduct penalties for transgressing the Canada Health Act from federal transfers to the provinces under other programs. Thus the federal government has shown some concern for the erosion of its authority in the health-care arena.

CONCLUSIONS AND FUTURE PROSPECTS

The answers to the puzzles of Canadian social policy lie in the interrelationships of ideas, interests, and institutions. The idea of "universality" in social programs took root in Canada with the adoption of family allowances, old-age security pensions, and hospital and medical insurance from the 1940s to the 1960s. But "two worlds" of the Canadian welfare state have evolved as very different structures of interests have intersected with relatively similar structures of Canadian federalism in the health-care and income-maintenance arenas. In the income-maintenance arena, universal benefits remain limited, and must be supplemented by means-tested programs for low-income individuals and by private sources for those in middle- and upper-income groups. In the health-care arena, however, it has been in the interest of highly mobilized groups—health-care providers—to press for generous universal programs, especially since different preferences within and across these groups have been accommodated at the provincial level.

In the latter half of the 1980s, social policy at the federal level was shaped by the agenda of deficit reduction and the constraints of the federal system. The federal government made changes to the design of transfer programs over which it had sole authority—the two universal programs of family allowances and old-age security pensions, and unemployment insurance—and made unilateral cuts (with no direct implications for program design) to shared-cost programs. The federal Conservative government was severely constrained from following the lead of neoconservative governments elsewhere in making cuts to means-tested programs and unemployment insurance. Changes to the design of means-tested programs, which were cost-shared with the provinces, would have entailed federal–provincial negotiations. Changes to the unemployment insurance program were constrained by regional sensitivities as represented in the federal cabinet. A by-product of a number of these changes, however, was a de facto decentralization of authority to provincial governments.

A decentralist thrust was even more explicit in the federal government's 1991 constitutional proposals. The government proposed that the consent of seven provinces with 50 percent of the population be obtained before new federal shared-cost programs in areas of exclusive provincial jurisdiction could be introduced. (It also proposed that up to three provinces be allowed to opt out of such a program, and to receive equivalent compensation if they adopted their own programs consistent with the objectives of the national program.) Also on the agenda in the 1991–92 constitutional debate, however, was the issue of a "social charter" through which all Canadian governments would be held to certain standards in social policy. Such a charter was proposed by the New Democratic Party government of Ontario as well as by a number of advocacy groups in the social-policy arena. Their concern is to check the erosion of national social programs that they believe are threatened by the decentralist tendencies of the past eight years.

In the health-care arena the implications of further decentralization are likely to be very different. Even in the absence of national minimum standards (but assuming the continuation of equalization payments to poorer provinces), the broad popularity of medicare together with the interests of powerful provider groups are likely to operate in favour of the continuation of a generous program, even as attention turns to more cost-effective ways to provide care. In the late 1980s and early 1990s, task forces or commissions of inquiry were established in each province to give broad policy advice to governments in the health field. While their emphases varied, there were a number of common themes in the reports and documents issued by these bodies, including a focus on a broad set of determinants of health (beyond the health-care delivery system), a shift from institutionally-based to community-based care, a reallocation of functions among health-care personnel, and a decentralization of decision-making to regional councils representing a variety of interests in the health field. These themes echoed those of similar policy documents of the mid-1970s, and their incorporation into actual policy change is likely to be gradual and heavily conditioned by the existing accommodation of interests. Nonetheless, the existence of these various provincial commissions provided a mechanism and an opportunity for interprovincial communication, not only among the commissions themselves but among the groups involved in their deliberations.

In the income-maintenance arena, however, where policies on balance enjoy neither the popular nor the elite support accorded to medicare, the prospects for erosion and fragmentation in a decentralized system appear greater. Cost-shared social assistance programs are likely to be most vulnerable. Here the generosity and structure of programs could come to depend very much upon the partisan complexion of provincial governments.[14] With federal constraints loosened, partisanship could play a greater role in generating cross-provincial differences just as it does in generating cross-national differences (Cameron 1984; Castles 1981; O'Connor 1988).

Even if authority over social policy is not further decentralized, there is little reason to believe that income-maintenance policy in Canada will become much more generous. Barring a substantial change in the organization of interests in this arena, the complexities of federal–provincial relations are likely to continue to militate against substantial change in income-maintenance programs. Health-care and income-maintenance will remain two separate worlds.

NOTES

1. The British case does not fit neatly into Esping-Andersen's categories. The so-called Beveridge reforms to British social policy in the 1940s were premised on the idea of universality. The principle was one of universal flat-rate benefits for pensions, health care, or unemployment insurance. A system of means-tested "supplementary benefits" was put in place to fill gaps not met by the universal schemes, but it was intended to be a relatively minor dimension of the system. Over time, however, the meagreness of universal benefits in Britain meant that supplementary benefits assumed greater importance for low-income people, while middle- and upper-income people turned to the private market for pensions and, to a lesser extent, for health-care. Modest income-related components were added to unemployment insurance in 1966 and to the public pension system in 1973. The income-related component of unemployment insurance was abolished in the Thatcher government's first term. A proposal to abolish the income-related component of public pensions, as discussed below, was scaled back in 1985.

2. The federal Medical Care Act establishing the national framework for governmental medical insurance was passed in 1966; all provinces had joined the plan by 1971.

3. Social spending as a proportion of GDP increased from an average of 12.3 percent in OECD nations in 1960 to an average of 23.3 percent in 1980. By 1986, the average had increased only slightly to 24.7 percent. In some nations, notably the United States, Britain, and Japan, this ratio was virtually unchanged between 1980 and 1986; in some other nations, including the traditional welfare-state leaders Sweden and West Germany, it actually declined marginally.

4. The levelling off of the social spending–GDP ratio in Britain and West Germany, for example, reflects the fact that these nations were faced with the problem of an aging population in the 1970s, somewhat earlier than most other OECD nations. Hence their social spending–GDP ratios increased rapidly in the 1970s but stabilized in the 1980s.

5. If Adams lived in Sweden, her public-pension income would have been 60 percent of her former earnings, and 80 percent if she had a non-earning spouse. In the United States, the corresponding figures would be 41 and 61 percent. Baker would receive 70 percent (110 percent with a dependent spouse) in Sweden and 56 percent (82 percent with a dependent spouse) in the United States. Even the wealthier Cooper could rely on Swedish public pensions to provide 43 percent of her preretirement income and 54 percent if she had a dependent spouse. In the United States, the corresponding figures would be 22 and 35 percent.

6. This is the gap between pre-tax and transfer income and the poverty line.

7. In Britain, about 90 percent of health-care spending is public; in the United States, this figure is only about 40 percent.

8. Cost-sharing arrangements under medical insurance were even more regionally redistributive than those that had been introduced for hospital insurance in 1958, under which the federal share was calculated on a formula that included both actual provincial costs and national average costs. For medical insurance, no reference to actual provincial costs was made. The federal contribution was calculated as 50 percent of the average national per capita cost multiplied by the number of insured persons in the province. The federal government also instituted a two percent "social development" surtax on income in 1968 to launch the program: hence taxpayers were made aware that they were supporting the program whether or not their own provinces participated.

9. Under the EPF arrangements, federal contributions to the provinces were to be partly in the form of conditional per capita cash transfers and partly in the form of unconditional transfers of tax "points." The per capita amount of the cash transfer in each province was to be calculated on the basis of federal contributions in the base year, 1975–76, annually adjusted by the rate of increase in nominal GNP. In addition, block grants calculated on a per capita basis were made for "extended services" such as home care. Finally, the arrangements provided for transitional payments to ensure that the total transfers (cash plus tax points) increased by at least the rate of increase in population and GNP.

10. Social security benefits, however, did become subject to taxation for recipients above a specified income level.

11. We are focusing here only on income transfers. Tax changes between 1984 and 1988 were of benefit to the top one percent as well as the bottom 30 percent in income earners (Maslove, 1989). According to Banting (forthcoming), changes to the tax-transfer system of child benefits (including not only family allowances but also tax credits and deductions) left all but the poorest families (those with family incomes of $12 000 in 1984 dollars) worse off than they would have been in the absence of the changes. Furthermore, the combined effect of tax and transfer changes from 1984 to 1989 was more negative for lower-income than for upper-income families.

12. One area in which some modest changes to program structures were made through federal–provincial negotiation concerned programs allowing social assistance recipients to retain earnings to smooth their transition to employment. Federal administrative guidelines interpreting the CAP requirement that qualifying provincial programs be "needs-tested" had constrained the ability of provinces to develop such programs. In the 1980s, a number of provinces established work incentive programs for social assistance recipients outside the CAP umbrella, and in the latter half of the decade some programs designed to move social assistance recipients into employment were negotiated as federal–provincial agreements under CAP. Although a review of changes to social assistance programs at the provincial level in the 1980s and early 1990s is beyond the scope of this chapter, it should be noted that there was considerable variation across provinces, related largely to the ideological stance of the party in power. This variation encompassed programs of restraint under the Social Credit government of British Columbia and the Conservative government of Saskatchewan to programs of benefit enhancement and restructuring under the Liberal and NDP governments in Ontario.

13. Canadian extra billing differed from Swedish user fees, however. Swedish user fees are constant across providers, and are levied at set rates determined by government. Extra billing in Canada occurred at the discretion of individual physicians at rates that they themselves determined.

14. See note 12.

CHAPTER 10

Environmental Policy: Alternative Styles

George Hoberg

INTRODUCTION

In northwestern British Columbia, just below the Alaska Panhandle, nature has been reordered. To power its massive smelter at Kitimat, Alcan Aluminium Ltd. has dammed the Nechako River, which flows east from the coastal mountain range into the Fraser River watershed. To generate electricity, Alcan has bored a tunnel sixteen kilometres through the mountains, so that 60 percent of the water from the Nechako Reservoir now flows west into the Pacific Ocean near Kemano.

When Alcan sought to expand the Kemano project in the early 1980s, the federal government opposed the move because of the threat to salmon spawning grounds. The breeding habitat, already depleted by the initial project, is the final destination of salmon, which travel about 1000 km upriver from the Georgia Strait to perform one of nature's most spectacular rituals. Accordingly, Alcan agreed to alter its project somewhat to protect the salmon. In 1987, the corporation, the federal government, and the British Columbia government entered into a settlement agreement to allow the project to go ahead. Estimated to cost $1 billion, the project will divert about half of the remaining water from its natural eastern drainage through the mountains and west into the Pacific.

Research for this chapter was funded by the Social Sciences and Humanities Research Council. I would like to thank Greg Hein, Jeffrey Waatainen, Randy Hansen, and Shannon Leggett for their valuable assistance, and Michael Atkinson, Christopher Bosso, Stephen Brooks, Alan Cairns, Robert Paehlke, Jeremy Rayner, and Paul Thomas for comments on an earlier draft. I am particularly indebted to Kathryn Harrison, who has shared in the development of these ideas.

In May 1991, however, after Alcan had spent $500 million and the project was half complete, a federal court invalidated the 1987 agreement on the grounds that the federal government failed to comply with its own Environmental Assessment and Review Process. The court was responding to a lawsuit brought by native groups and environmentalists who were not included or even consulted in the 1987 settlement process. While the decision is being appealed by both Alcan and the federal government, work on the project has stopped and there is much speculation that it will never be completed (Wilson 1991).

In northern Quebec, nature is being reordered on an even greater scale, this time by Hydro-Québec, the provincially-owned utility. The enormous James Bay hydro-electric project reverses the direction of three major rivers. The Caniapiscau River, for instance, naturally flows north to Ungava Bay. In the 1970s, the river was diverted so that it now flows west into James Bay, where it is used to generate electricity that is then transmitted south to power industry and the lights of urban Quebec, and even parts of the northeastern United States. The environmental impacts of the project have been substantial. The flooding of vast amounts of vegetation led, through a complex chain of chemical reactions, to the release of toxic methyl mercury, contaminating the fish of the region, which are an essential constituent of the local native diet. When the Cree, native to the area to be flooded by Hydro-Québec, went to court in an effort to block the project in the mid-1970s their pleas were rejected. The province did enter into a settlement agreement with the Cree, providing some financial compensation, but the project went ahead more or less as planned.

When Hydro-Québec proposed to launch the second phase of the James Bay Project, known as "Great Whale," opposition was not so easily mollified. Having failed in previous legal battles, in 1991, the Cree, in coalition with the Inuit and environmentalists, convinced a court to issue an order requiring a comprehensive environmental assessment by the federal government. Claiming that the project was under exclusive provincial jurisdiction, the province at first refused to participate in the process, and stated that the project would continue. But faced with legal pressures from the courts, political pressure from the federal government, and market pressure from prospective American purchasers, the province surrendered to political reality, and postponed the project for one year pending satisfactory completion of a full environmental assessment (McCutcheon 1991).

Environmental Policy: A Changing Environment

The stories of these two megaprojects are symptomatic of profound changes in environmental policy in this country. Not so long ago, environmental policy decisions were made in closed, quiet meetings between the affected industry and government officials—federal, provincial, or occasionally both. No longer. Emboldened by growing environmental concern among the public, environmentalists have demanded to participate in the process, and governments have acquiesced. Some environmentalists, not satisfied with simply being consulted more regularly, have taken to the courts, and found a surprising amount of sympathy among judges for their demands for environmental action. Although they were virtually irrelevant to Canadian environmental policy-making until recently, the courts have begun to play a far more prominent role in environmental policy.

This chapter examines institutions for governance in Canadian environmental policy. The remainder of this overview will outline the concept of a "policy style" that will be used throughout the chapter—a package of interests, institutions, and ideas that characterize a particular policy domain—and describe the challenge to governance posed by environmental policy. A brief overview of the evolution of the environment as a political issue is then presented, as well as a survey of the policy style that emerged as a response by the Canadian political system to the first great upsurge in environmentalism in 1970.

Institutional Responses

The following two sections analyze the inchoate institutional responses to the second wave of environmentalism that arrived in the late 1980s. Thus far, two patterns of institutional response appear to be occurring. First, Canada has moved to expand traditional bargaining processes to include representatives of environmental interests and others (such as labour, consumers, and so on) in what are referred to as "multistakeholder" consultations. Second, in a potentially more dramatic departure from Canadian tradition, a series of court cases involving the federal government's Environmental Assessment and Review Process, including the Kemano and Great Whale projects described above, presage an increased judicialization of the Canadian regulatory process, and thus a potential to move down a path toward a more American-style system. Each section explores these two new policy styles, focusing on the different interests, institutions, and ideas that typify their operation.[1]

The conclusion explores the potential contradictions between these two emerging policy styles, arguing that they are based on quite different institutions and ideas. It also speculates about which is more likely to have a future in the Canadian system. This final section attempts to situate policy styles in their larger, macropolitical context. It focuses on how the structure of political institutions in Canada promotes certain forms of institutional change and discriminates against others. It argues that traditional Canadian political institutions create substantial obstacles to legalism, although the turbulent course of Canadian politics cautions against ruling out fundamental change.

Two general caveats are in order. First, this chapter analyzes rapidly changing developments and seeks to impose some conceptual order on a chaotic situation. But as the argument developed in the chapter will make clear, Canada confronts major choices about its governing arrangements in environmental policy, and it is important to reflect on the consequences of the different paths before such fundamental choices are made.

Second, this chapter focuses on the dynamics of environmental policy-making at the federal and provincial levels, but it does not address in any detail another essential ingredient to Canadian policy-making: federalism. Because many environmental problems cut across provincial and even national boundaries, Canadian federalism poses some special challenges to governance in this area. The environmental policy field is characterized by enormous jurisdictional overlap, creating confusion and conflict. As a result, a great deal of environmental policy-making in Canada is performed through mechanisms of intergovernmental relations (Harrison 1991; Lucas 1989; Dwivedi & Woodrow 1989; Nemetz 1986). While a detailed analysis of federalism and the environment is necessarily beyond the scope of this chapter, it is important to realize that the transformative dynamics analyzed here apply not only to decision-making at the level of federal or provincial governments, but also relations between governments in Canada. The chapter will highlight instances of this phenomenon.

DEFINITIONS AND BACKGROUND

Policy Styles

To describe the governing arrangements in environmental policy, this chapter develops the concept of "policy styles" (cf. Richardson 1982; Freeman 1985). A policy styles is essentially a package of interests, institutions, and ideas characteristic of a particular policy domain. First, the societal interests that participate in policy-making are a distinguishing feature of a policy style. Institutions are a second critical component. State organizations—including the rules that govern their operation and the capacity they embody—help to structure state-society interaction. The pattern of interaction that develops among societal and state actors has been characterized as a "policy network" (Coleman & Skogstad 1990).

The third component of a policy style consists of ideas, both about the substance of public policy and the process by which it is made (Manzer 1985). In essence, policy networks are delegated the authority for making policy in a particular sector (Pross 1986, 98). For this delegation to be accepted, policy must be legitimated by some guiding philosophy. If political values change, or if the distribution of power in society changes, a traditional policy style may be subjected to a crisis of legitimacy. As the analysis below makes clear, the Canadian style of governance in environmental policy entered such a crisis in the late 1980s.

While this concept of policy style gives a central place to state institutions, the concept is also designed to highlight the fact that the significance of institutions can be determined only in the context of interests and ideas. State institutions are not only critical actors in policy disputes, but institutional rules of the game are frequently a significant influence on the distribution of power between societal interests. These societal interests, understanding that fact, struggle over not only the substance of public policy, but also the institutional rules by which it is made. The complex interaction between interests and institutions occurs within an ideological and cultural context that, in periods of stability, provides the system with legitimacy in the eyes of the general public. But the ideas that legitimate a policy style are not necessarily taken as givens, and in periods of turmoil, such as the one affecting environmental policy in the 1990s, societal and state actors fight to reshape public philosophies in a manner that best suits their perceived interests.

Governing Functions

Environmental policy creates difficult governing problems. Environmental disputes frequently involve intense value conflicts, long time horizons, and immense factual uncertainty, greatly complicating government decision-making. Moreover, the diffuseness of interests in environmental protection creates organizational problems for groups attempting to represent environmental interests in the political process. A detailed examination of these dilemmas is beyond the scope of this chapter. What is necessary here is an outline of the governing tasks that the state must perform.

There are four different types of governing functions, distinguished by their relative level of generality (Doern 1990a). First, in what we will call the legislative function, the government must set the basic objectives of public policy and authorize the executive to carry them out. Second, in the regulatory function, the government has to translate these general objectives into specific policy measures to address specific pollution problems; for example, effluent standards for the pulp and paper industry. Third, in the project approval function, the government has to make decisions about discrete physical activities, such as the construction of a dam. And finally, in the enforcement function, the government is required to make decisions about how to achieve compliance with the regulations, usually at the level of the polluting facility.[2] As the following analysis demonstrates, distinguishing among these functions is important because the governing challenges and appropriate policy style may vary by function.

The Evolution of the Environmental Issue

As a political phenomenon, the environmental issue has gone through several distinct phases. The first major wave of environmentalism began to swell in the late 1960s, and crested with the first Earth Day celebration in April 1970. A 1970 opinion poll ranked pollution highest among issues deserving more attention from the government (Gallup Poll 1970, December 2). According to Kingdon's influential model of agenda-setting, issues reach the political agenda as a result of a combination of forces, or what he refers to as "streams." The two most important streams are the "problem stream," which consists largely of dramatic events that focus attention on a problem, and the "politics stream," which consists of public attitudes, electoral forces, and group pressures (Kingdon 1984). When an issue reaches the agenda, alternative policy solutions emerge from the "policy stream."

Between 1967 and 1970, several focusing events occurred that helped heighten public concern for the environment, particularly the *Torrey Canyon* and *Santa Barbara* oil spills, the Cuyahoga River fire, and in Canada, the grounding of the tanker *Arrow* in Chedabucto Bay, Nova Scotia, and the mercury scare (Woodrow 1978, 78a). In the political stream, deep-seated changes in values were occurring at the same time. As a result of a generation of people growing up in a period of sustained affluence, "post-materialist" values such as environmental preservation emerged to challenge previously dominant economic values (Ingelhart 1977).

Concern for environmental issues declined in the 1970s as the economy eclipsed the environment on the political agenda. (Ingelhart 1987). While public support for environmental protection continued, the problem ceased to be viewed as a major political priority. Indeed, by 1972 the environment had dropped down below economic issues to rank around fourth or fifth, and by 1973 and 1974, only three to four percent of the public ranked pollution as the top issue (Gallup Poll 1974, April 13).

By 1987 a second wave of environmentalism began forming and the salience of environmental issues surged. A series of dramatic events focussed attention on environmental problems.[3] The Bhopal chemical disaster occurred in December 1984, the scientific discovery of the ozone hole in 1985, and the Chernobyl nuclear accident in April 1986. The summer of 1988 was excruciatingly hot and dry across North

America, focusing attention on global warming and creating air quality problems in a many urban areas. In the same summer, medical wastes fouled the recreational beaches of the eastern United States, and a fire occurred at a Quebec PCB storage facility. The following summer witnessed the massive *Exxon Valdez* oil spill.

These focusing events occurred at the same time as a shift in the politics stream created fertile ground for the environmental issue to blossom again. The mid- to late 1980s witnessed the longest postwar period of economic expansion, diminishing the salience of economic issues. The energy crisis dissipated as the price of oil collapsed and the easing of cold-war tensions diminished psychological preoccupations with the threat of nuclear war.

This second wave crested in the early 1990s, and there are abundant signs that the environmental issue is dropping in salience as a result of the onset of recession. A 1991 CBC–*Globe and Mail* poll revealed that the percentage of the Canadian public that identify environmental problems as the most important issue facing Canada dropped from seventeen percent in 1989 to four percent by April 1991 (Windsor 1991; Miller 1991).

INSTITUTIONAL RESPONSE TO THE FIRST WAVE: BIPARTITE BARGAINING

When the first wave of environmentalism emerged around 1970, Canadian governments responded with new policies and new organizations. At the federal level, the twenty-eighth Parliament, which lasted from 1968–72, enacted nine new environmental statutes, including the Clean Air Act, Canada Water Act, and amendments to the Fisheries Act. A new federal department, Environment Canada, was created in 1971. Provincial governments also responded with a wave of new statutes, agencies, and regulations. Ontario passed its Environmental Protection Act in 1971, and Quebec its Environmental Quality Act in 1972. New environmental lobby groups were formed, including Greenpeace, Pollution Probe, and the Canadian Environmental Law Association (Woodrow 1980; Dwivedi 1974). The Canadian Council of Resource Ministers was expanded to include the environment portfolio in 1971, and renamed Canadian Council of Resource and Environment Ministers.

The Canadian political system adapted to the new pressures without any major changes in policy style. In sharp contrast, in the United States the first wave of environmentalism unleashed profound changes in policy-making institutions and procedures. The policy style that characterized the New Deal and the period prior to the late 1960s, was based on closed, co-operative relationships between government and business. This style was transformed into an open, adversarial, and legalistic system, in which administrative discretion was carefully restrained by both the legislators and the courts (Vogel 1986; Harris & Milkis 1989; Hoberg 1992). No such change occurred in Canada. New bureaucratic organizations were created and new policies enacted, but in the environmental policy area the core policy network of interest groups and institutions, and the public philosophy supporting them, marked no significant departure from either past patterns or patterns in other policy domains.

Bipartite Bargaining as a Policy Style

The Essence of the Environmental Regulatory Process

The interests and institutions that made up the "policy network" in this period worked together in a manner best described as "bipartite bargaining." This policy style is characterized by closed, co-operative negotiations between government departments and industry. According to Andrew Thompson, "bargaining is the essence of the environmental regulatory process as it is practiced in Canada" (Thompson 1980, 33; Schrecker 1984). For the most part, environmentalists were excluded from this bargain because they lacked the organizational sophistication and political clout to inspire state officials to invite them into the process. They also lacked the legal or procedural rights to pry the doors open. While they played a minor role in policy formulation, environmentalists remained on the periphery of the policy network (Wilson 1992).

Representation of Environmental Interests

In the realm of ideas, the ruling norm at the time was that environmental interests were to be represented in the policy process not by private interest groups as in the pluralist model, but by the relevant government agency headed by the minister. To the extent that environmental interests were to be balanced against other societal concerns, this occurred behind closed doors either in cabinet or the bureaucracy, depending on the political sensitivity of the issue.

Power relations within this policy style are best characterized by a relatively weak state, strong business interests, and weak environmental interests. Atkinson and Coleman (1989a) describe Canada as exhibiting a "weak state tradition," and nothing in the environmental policy sphere seems to contradict that characterization. The legislative responses to the first wave in the early 1970s provided the state with significant new regulatory authority, but in general it lacked the resources, knowledge, and will to make effective use of it (Conway 1990).

Fragmentation of Regulatory Authority

State capacity was also undermined by both vertical and horizontal fragmentation. Much of Canadian environmental regulation remained decentralized at the provincial level, and whatever assertions of federal authority took place were cautious and characterized by deference to the provinces. For instance, when the Canada Water Act was enacted in 1970, it was considered a major expansion of federal authority to protect the environment. Despite being on the books for more than two decades, the statute's potentially powerful planning and regulatory authority has never been used. In another example, while the federal government had clear authority to regulate pulp and paper mills under the Fisheries Act, it delegated much of its enforcement authority in the area to the provinces (Harrison 1991).

Even in areas of clear federal jurisdiction, bureaucratic fragmentation was pervasive. Automobile emission regulation is shared by Transport Canada and Environment Canada, toxic chemical regulation is shared by Environment Canada and Health and Welfare Canada, and pesticide control is shared by Agriculture Canada, Health and Welfare Canada, and Environment Canada. Despite the acceptance of a clear role for the federal government in these areas, in all three cases the provinces still claim a significant share of the responsibility, aggravating the problem of institutional fragmentation (e.g., Auditor General of Canada 1990, 444ff.).

Industry Resources

While state institutions are relatively weak, business has formidable power resources at its disposal (Schrecker 1984, ch. 1). In addition to large financial resources and control over vital information, business has clear organizational advantages. While Canadian business is not noted for its strong associational system at the macro level, there are some well-organized sectoral associations, the Canadian Pulp and Paper Association being a prominent example (Atkinson & Coleman 1989a, ch. 2; Coleman 1988). Since environmental regulation tends to be organized by sector—for instance, pulp and paper, mining, and automobiles—Canadian business has been well organized to influence the process. Moreover, where it really counts, where the regulator meets the polluter in the enforcement function—at the level of the firm—Canadian business is quite strong. On top of these organizational advantages, business control over investment is an extremely powerful resource, giving business the ability to threaten divestment if regulation becomes too stringent (Lindblom 1977; Block 1977; Schrecker 1990).

While the government possesses regulatory authority, and business has powerful financial, organizational, and structural assets, the power resources of environmentalists are minimal. The diffuseness of the environmental interests makes group mobilization difficult. While new groups emerged around 1970, they lacked adequate financial resources and organization to compete effectively with their business counterparts. They have no structural source of power comparable to business control over investment. Their only power resource resides in public opinion, in that they act as the organized expression of public demands for environmental protection. The problem with this resource is that it depends on the electoral salience of the environmental issue. If politicians fear electoral retribution for ignoring the environment, then this resource can be quite formidable, but if the environment is not politically salient, environmental groups are virtually resourceless.

The Bargaining Process

Under this system of bipartite bargaining, the essential dynamic was bargaining between business and government, with environmental groups playing only a peripheral role. And while there was no outright delegation of state authority, business had various organizational and resource advantages over government. While a surge in public interest in the environment forced government to respond, the rapid decline in salience of the issue, and the limited clout of environmental groups, meant that limited, relatively symbolic responses were sufficient to maintain legitimacy for the system. The imbalance in power relations within this system was in part masked by a traditional public philosophy that assigned the role of representing the public interest to the state. As time went on, however, challenges to this system and its supporting norms escalated, and pressures for reform forced more fundamental institutional changes.

INSTITUTIONAL RESPONSE TO THE SECOND WAVE: MULTIPARTITE BARGAINING

While the Canadian political system successfully adapted to the first wave of environmentalism without significant changes in form, the second wave of environmentalism posed a greater threat to the system's adaptive capacity. The renewed salience of environmental issues challenged the legitimacy of the dominant policy style (Howlett 1990). The system's ability to provide adequate levels of environmental protection was called into question, and the policy style itself was given a large share of the blame. After a decade and a half of experience, the idea that the state could adequately represent environmental interests now appeared to be a cloak concealing a system dominated by business interests.

Multipartite Bargaining as a Policy Style

The Concept of Sustainable Development

When the confluence of the problem and politics streams created the second wave of environmentalism, several critical ideas prominent in the "policy stream" emerged as solutions to the policy crisis in Canada. The first was the concept of sustainable development, popularized by the Brundtland Commission report, *Our Common Future*. The Commission defined sustainable development simply as development that "meets the needs of the present without compromising the ability of future generations to meet their own needs" (World Commission on Environment and Development 1987, 8). There was a great deal of Canadian participation in the Commission, and the Canadian environmental policy community has been strongly influenced by its deliberations. Despite, or more likely *because of*, its vagueness, sustainable development has emerged as the major policy objective advanced by a broad range of actors within the policy community. To environmentalists it offers the promise of sustainability; to industry it offers the promise of continued economic development that was frighteningly absent from the "limits to growth" concept popular in the early 1970s (Paehlke 1989, ch. 3).

Stakeholder Consultation

While sustainable development has provided Canadian environmentalism with a policy objective, there was also a process-oriented solution emerging in the policy stream at about the same time—the concept of multistakeholder consultations. By the early 1980s, both government actors and environmentalists had become dissatisfied with the existing policy style. Environment Canada contracted with the Niagara Institute, a firm specializing in negotiation, to develop a new consultation process for the agency to help resolve environmental policy conflicts. In 1984, the Institute brought together leaders from government, business, environmental groups, and labour and over the course of the year developed a proposal for a new process that would have a profound influence on Canadian environmental policy (Toner 1990). The proposed process, called the "Niagara process" by some and simply "multistakeholder consultations" by others, was defined as

> an ongoing dialogue among affected stakeholders, including government, aimed at obtaining all the relevant information, evaluating the available options and their related consequences, and providing an objectively balanced perspective to each stakeholder's decision making. A prime objective is to obtain consensus at each stage of the process (Niagara Institute 1985).

The Bargaining Process

In essence, the new process was an effort to expand the traditional bargaining system to include both labour and environmentalists as well as business and government. The objective was consensus, as stated in the proposed decision-making rule: "Decisions should be made through consensus and not through the democratic voting process" (Niagara Institute 1985).

While there is no necessary logical or causal relation between the ideas of sustainable development and multistakeholder consultations, there appears to be a strong elective affinity between the two concepts among core actors in the environmental policy community. Both are based on the idea that corporate interests in development can somehow be reconciled with interests in environmental protection. Political conflict over unavoidable trade-offs was perceived as unproductive, and consensus could be achieved only if a proper process was designed to allow the competing stakeholders an opportunity to communicate with each other. According to Toner, "this `constructively ambiguous' concept provided an intellectual rationale or conceptual framework for much of this newfound discourse between old foes" (1990, 8).

The first experiment with the process in federal policy-making was the development of a strategy to manage toxic chemicals, the first phase of discussions that eventually led to the enactment of the Canadian Environmental Protection Act in 1988. The next major use of the new process was Canada's response to the Brundtland Commission. As a result of the Commission's visit to Canada in 1986, the Canadian Council of Resource and Environment Ministers created the National Task Force on Environment and Economy (NTFEE), consisting of leaders from government, business, academia, and environmental groups. The most important part of the NTFEE report, issued in 1987, was the recommendation that the federal and provincial governments each form their own multistakeholder Round Tables. The linkage between the process of multistakeholder consultations and the policy goal of sustainable development was made clear by the NTFEE report: "Of all of our recommendations, we consider Round Tables to be among the most important. Their implementation and success are fundamental to the achievement of environmentally sound economic development in Canada" (National Task Force on Environment and Economy 1987). In other words, the key to achieving the substantive goal of sustainable development was to adopt a new process. By April 1990, ten jurisdictions had done so (Howlett 1990).

As governments began to feel more pressure to produce new environmental policies, multistakeholder forums became a standard operating procedure of the policy process at both the federal and provincial level. They have been, or are being, used in virtually every policy initiative, the most prominent being the Canadian

Environmental Protection Act of 1988, the pesticide registration review (Pesticide Registration Review 1990e), the federal pulp and paper effluent regulations, Ontario's overhaul of its water pollution control regime (the Municipal/Industrial Strategy for Abatement), and the federal government's showpiece "Green Plan."

Environmental federalism has also been influenced by this new concept. One of Canada's most important environmental initiatives in recent years was the development of a program to control urban smog, conducted under the auspices of the Canadian Council of Resource and Environment Ministers (Doern 1990b). In a significant departure from the pattern of executive federalism that traditionally dominated this area, a multistakeholder forum was used to develop the plan.

Multistakeholder Forums as a Policy Style

The new policy style can be referred to as multipartite bargaining. The range of relevant societal interests has been expanded as the traditional bipartite bargaining of the old style has been replaced by an expanded bargaining process including environmentalists and other groups. Significantly, the public philosophy underlying the policy process has also changed. The state is no longer trusted to represent environmental interests on its own—this task has devolved to organized environmental groups. While this new style solves some of the most important problems of bipartite bargaining, it creates some significant dilemmas of its own.

From one perspective, these multistakeholder forums represent only a minor modification of Canada's traditional regulatory style—the system is still based on bargaining. But from a different perspective, multistakeholder forums represent a fundamentally different policy style. Not only has the number of relevant societal participants expanded, but the relationship between the state and societal interests has changed. In bipartite bargaining, the state represented environmental interests (among others), and the conflict between environment and economy was internalized in the bargaining relationship between those two actors. But with the entrance of organized environmentalists, that conflict is now reflected in the relationship between environmental groups and industry groups.

This new process sounds a great deal like the pluralism that was so popular in postwar American political science, with the accompanying philosophical rationale. The relevant interests in a policy dispute are represented by groups, and the chimerical public interest emerges from a competition between those interests, with the state acting as a referee of the struggle, a codifier of the terms of the outcome into law, and an enforcer of that law.[4]

In fact, what is least certain about this new policy-making system is the role of the state, either in theory or practice. In the Niagara manifesto," government actors seem to be equated with other stakeholders. Principle #12 states:

> Governments, and different government departments and agencies, should recognize that they are stakeholders as well as decision-makers; and that other stakeholders are decision-makers too. It is recognized that government has special status as a decision-maker. This need not conflict with governments working co-operatively with other stakeholders, which is a fundamental tenet of consultation (Niagara Institute 1985).

One of the hallmarks of classic pluralist theory is the extension of group concepts to the institutions of the state. For example, Latham did draw an important distinction between state groups and private groups in that state groups were characterized by what he called "officiality," which established the "difference between the badge-wearer and the others" (Latham 1952, 389). But he emphasizes that groups within the state have much in common with groups outside the state. In striking similarity, the above-cited passage from the Niagara manifesto acknowledges government's "special status as a decision-maker," but it seems more intent on stressing what government actors have in common with other actors than what differentiates them.

Influenced by modern dispute-resolution techniques, however, the multistakeholder process does represent a departure from the stereotypical pluralist model. According to the Niagara manifesto, "consultation should, as a general rule, take place under the auspices of, and at all stages be chaired by, an independent facilitator who does not represent major stakeholder interests and is perceived by all as a neutral third party" (Niagara Institute 1985). The manifesto does mention that "in some circumstances, it may be appropriate for a government agency to play the facilitator role," but suggests that this would be the exception to the rule. In fact most multistakeholder processes have used professional, nongovernmental facilitators. The state is no longer even the referee, but merely one of many groups struggling to further its interests in the policy issue.

The Role of the State

Multipartite bargaining also differs from stereotypical pluralism in that the state plays an important role in organizing the bargaining process. Rather than the self-organizing free-for-all of the pluralist process, multistakeholder forums are typically organized by the government, and participation is by invitation only. While this state role is reminiscent of some characterizations of corporatism, the polycentric nature of the proceedings and the fragmentation of organized interests are antithetical to the concept of corporatism. Moreover, the process departs from corporatism in that it has yet to involve any formal delegation of state authority, as for instance occurs in occupational health and safety regulation in Britain, Sweden, and Germany, where regulations are made and enforced by boards made up exclusively of labour and business representatives (Kelman 1981; Badaracco 1985; Tuohy 1982).

While state authority has not been formally delegated, the Canadian state's increased reliance on multistakeholder consultations appears to reflect a predisposition for delegation where possible. When the potential for conflict exists, the state's instinct for blame avoidance (Weaver 1986) prompts officials to lock the warring parties in a conference centre and encourage them to resolve the conflict among themselves. But as the limited experience to date reveals, the process is hardly that clean and simple. In most cases the state has been forced to assume its traditional sovereign role of policy formulation and implementation. A telling case is the federal government's Green Plan, which involved what was certainly the most publicized and extensive multistakeholder consultation process to date. In the end, the decisions were made the old-fashioned way, in cabinet, where environmental concerns were represented by the Environment minister and competing concerns were represented—apparently quite effectively—by ministers with more business-oriented portfolios.

While the role of the state in this new policy style remains uncertain, what is clear is that the state uses multistakeholder forums to legitimate policy decisions (Howlett 1990, 580). In fact, they seem to provide the state with excellent opportunities for claiming credit and avoiding blame. If the process can achieve consensus, the state can claim legitimacy problems will not exist as long as all the major interests are included. Thus, the state can claim credit for a successful policy initiative. If consensus cannot be achieved, the state will have a good excuse for inaction—it can blame the major groups' participants for their inability to agree. If the state chooses to act despite disagreement, the fact that a variety of interests were provided the opportunity of participation in a bargaining forum will minimize legitimacy problems. In this way, the state uses multistakeholder consultations as a way of mobilizing consent for policies.

Perhaps the most difficult problem for the state will occur if the consensus solution of the multistakeholder forum is not acceptable to the state. For instance, the 1990 federal pesticide registration review recommended taking the authority for pesticide regulation away from the minister of Agriculture and vesting it in an independent regulatory agency (Pesticide Registration Review 1990e, ix). Understandably, the cabinet has rejected the recommendation. If the state ignores recommendations, when the consultation process it sponsored has produced a consensus, significant legitimacy problems may result.

Evaluation

The nascent regulatory style represented by multistakeholder forums is much closer to the ideal of pluralism than the pre-1987 style. The interest-group environment is more balanced, and the philosophy of representation is more group-centred than state-centred. But the problem with this new process is that it is vulnerable to some of the same criticisms to which academic pluralism was subjected in the 1960s and 1970s. First and foremost, it leads to a blurring of state authority and private interest (Lowi 1979). What are we to make of the concept of sovereignty when the state becomes a mere "stakeholder"? Second, it assumes the public interest more or less naturally emerges as an amalgamation of private interests. To the extent that the state has its own interests, they are merely equated with those of other relevant stakeholders. The state is no longer separate from the interest-group conflict within society, representing some larger public interest.

Third, the process assumes that the interest-group participants are representative of the balance of interests in society. Certainly the new system is more representative than its predecessor—at least environmental groups are at the table. But there is concern about the ability of environmental groups, and other groups representing diffuse interests, to compete effectively with their business counterparts in these forums. While environmental groups have become much more institutionalized and organizationally sophisticated since the early 1970s, environmental representatives still frequently lack the experience, expertise, time, and financial resources to match the business officials around the table (Gertler, Muldoon & Valiente 1990; Doern 1990b, 105). As one environmentalist lamented recently, "it is hard to play hockey when you don't have skates." As the number of consultation exercises grows, the scant resources of the environmental community will be stretched even more thinly. There is also the question of whether environmental groups can claim to represent "environmental interests," not to mention broad public interests. The extreme fragmentation and lack of organizational development of the Canadian environmental community undermines any representational claims.

Fourth, thus far multistakeholder forums have been applied to the legislative and regulatory functions. For the most part, the enforcement function seems to be characterized still by government–business negotiations, resulting in frequent concessions (Gibson 1983, 65–73). If business continues to dominate that process, environmental gains may be limited.

Fifth, using consensus as a decision-rule contains hidden biases. At first glance it may seem hard to argue with the objective of consensus decision-making. It is clear that a simple majority rule would be unworkable, since it would be easy to stack the number of representatives in the forum in such a way as to deny minority interests a meaningful role. But it must be realized that consensus as a rule has its own biases. Because it gives a veto to all the major participants, it is much easier to block action than to change the status quo. Thus, the consensus decision-rule favours those who benefit from the status quo. In contemporary environmental politics, where the major thrust of policy-making is to strengthen environmental regulation, this rule strongly favours those who oppose additional regulation.[5] In other words, in many cases the veto implicit in the consensus rule is an additional power resource for business interests.

Finally, the distribution of power resources within the policy network makes the environmental movement vulnerable in the long term. The principal source of environmental-group influence remains public opinion. The second wave of environmentalism has renewed the electoral salience of environmental issues, strengthening environmental interests. Moreover, the emergence of pluralist representational norms has increased the status of environmental groups within the policy network. But it is unclear how long public interest in the environment will be maintained; indeed, as mentioned earlier, there is already polling evidence that it has dropped off considerably. Widespread, intense public support is essential, because it is what gives business the incentive to participate in the bargaining forums. Business has yet to seize the advantage of its implicit veto because, in the current political climate, it fears that additional regulation is inevitable, so it might as well participate to ensure that it is done in an acceptable fashion. If public interest fades, the incentives of politicians to claim credit for protecting the environment will decline, and business may be less willing to co-operate in increasing its costs of production.

Multipartite bargaining appears to have produced some important policy changes in Canada: Ontario's system for controlling water pollution is being strengthened dramatically; major new regulations for the control of urban smog have been introduced; new legislation gives the federal government expanded authority to control toxic substances; and the Green Plan has increased the budgetary resources available to environmental programs. Still, the ultimate influence of multipartite bargaining remains to be seen. And while some environmentalists have been bargaining in conference rooms, others are challenging government actions in court, and finding surprising success there.

INSTITUTIONAL RESPONSE TO THE SECOND WAVE: LEGALISM

Multistakeholder consultations represent one possible solution to the crisis of legitimacy that confronted the Canadian state when the second wave of environmentalism swept the nation. Another potential solution is legalism, in which environmental interests would be represented not in the bargaining process, but in open, formal proceedings with a large role assumed by the judiciary.

Legalism as a Policy Style

As a policy style, legalism is profoundly different from even multipartite bargaining and a potentially much greater departure from Canadian traditions. While the societal interests involved are essentially the same as in multipartite bargaining, there are significant differences both in state institutions and public philosophy.

Distinguishing Characteristics

The distinguishing feature of legalism is the assertion of authority by the courts. In order for the courts to play a more prominent policy-making role, however, significant changes in the rules of the game are also required. In addition to an active judiciary willing to challenge executive decisions, legalism depends on the following three elements:

- formal administrative procedures, with widespread access to information and rights to participation for all affected interests;
- pro-regulatory interest groups with access to courts;
- nondiscretionary governmental duties, enforceable in court (Melnick 1983; Rabkin 1989; Hoberg 1992).

This final characteristic is essential, because it provides private litigants, working through the courts, a way to force the government to act. A classic example is the requirement in the U.S. National Environmental Policy Act that government agencies study an environmental-impact statement before undertaking a major federal action (Culhane 1978). If the government fails to perform an assessment, an environmental group can take it to court to force it to comply. If the statute were permissive rather than mandatory, if it merely stated that the government "may" perform an impact assessment—then the courts would have no legal basis for forcing the government to take action.

Some environmentalists had advocated the adoption of an "environmental bill of rights" since the mid-1970s (Swaigen 1981). While at first the idea received relatively little attention, it gained somewhat in legitimacy as a result of the emerging rights-consciousness in Canadian society that preceded and then was accelerated by the adoption of the Charter of Rights in 1982 (Cairns 1990, 331–39; Cairns & Williams 1985; Lucas 1989). In addition to this spillover of legalism from constitutional law, many Canadian environmentalists were envious of the legal rights their American colleagues had within their own environmental policy regime, a regime that has exerted persistent influence on Canadian policy-making (Hoberg 1991).

Origins

Legalism burst forth in Canadian environmental policy in disputes over environmental impact assessment. In 1989, in response to legal action by environmentalists, courts intervened in several controversies involving the construction of dams, forcing the federal government to perform impact assessments. While standard fare in the United States, these judicial decisions were unprecedented in Canada and sent shock waves through the environmental policy community. The 1990 Ontario election raised the possibility of even more extensive legalism. In its first throne speech, the New Democratic Party government promised to introduce an environmental bill of rights. The appointee for Environment minister, Ruth Grier, had been a long-time advocate of the concept, and in fact had introduced an environmental bill of rights as a private member's bill in the provincial legislature several times while in opposition. This section analyzes both of these developments and then examines legalism as a policy style.

The Judicialization of Impact Assessment

Ever since the Canadian federal government introduced its Environmental Assessment and Review Process (EARP) in 1973, it has explicitly tried to avoid the intense legalism associated with the National Environment Policy Act in the United States. Rather than embody the process into a statute, the government introduced EARP as a cabinet directive in 1973. The informality of this early process, and its reliance on self-assessment by initiating agencies, was widely criticized (Rees 1980, 357; Fenge & Smith 1986, 603). In response to such criticisms, the government issued a revised EARP as a "guidelines order" in 1984 under the authority of the Government Organization Act. The guidelines order helped to make the process somewhat more systematic and spelled out more clearly the responsibilities of those concerned with implementing EARP (Bowden & Curtis 1988). However, the 1984 changes failed to address many of EARP's perceived shortcomings. In particular, the legal status of the guidelines was questionable. It was generally assumed that they were not legally binding, that they "had no legal force to ensure compliance from intransigent departments" (Fenge & Smith 1986, 603; Lucas 1989, 179).

The EARP process came under increasing criticism, especially as public concern for the environment surged in the late 1980s. Consultations on a reform package began in 1987, and in October 1988 the federal Environment minister made a commitment to strengthen the process and enshrine it in legislation. Opposition within the government delayed the introduction of legislation until June 1990. In the interim, the process of reform was taken out of the government's hands, as dramatic developments in the courts transformed the nature of the EARP process.

Judicial Intervention

In a series of decisions, the Federal Court of Canada responded to requests by environmental groups to block the construction of dams because the federal government did not comply with the EARP guidelines order. These decisions transformed the guidelines order into a binding legal requirement, and demonstrated the courts' willingness to force the government to comply with the order. In the case involving the Rafferty and Alameda dams in Saskatchewan, the court ruled that the EARP guidelines order was legally binding, that "it is not a mere description of a policy or programme; it may create rights which may be enforceable by way of *mandamus*." Because the dam was on an international river, the federal government had jurisdiction over the project, and therefore was required to perform an impact assessment.[6] The trial court decision was subsequently upheld by the Federal Court of Appeal.[7] In addition, the Federal Court of Appeal made a similar ruling involving the Oldman River in Alberta.[8]

Environmentalists also experienced setbacks in their efforts to force the federal government to perform more extensive reviews. The Federal Court rejected an attempt to force a review of the cabinet decision to cut VIA Rail services, holding that EARP applied to departments but not the cabinet as a legal entity.[9] The Court also rejected an effort by environmentalists to force a public panel review of the Point Aconi power plant under construction in Nova Scotia.[10] British Columbia environmentalists failed in their effort to force a review of logging practices that may disrupt the habitat of the marbled murrelet.

After a period of considerable legal turmoil, the Supreme Court issued a landmark ruling on the issue in January 1992, upholding most of the Appeal Court decision in the Oldman River dam case. The Supreme Court agreed with the lower court interpretation that the EARP guidelines were binding, and also agreed with the court's expansive interpretation of federal authority over the provinces. The Supreme Court did narrow the scope of the Oldman River dam decision considerably, however. The Federal Court of Appeal had ruled that both the minister of Transport and the minister of Fisheries and Oceans had to perform assessments. The Supreme Court decided that Transport had to comply because it was required to issue a permit in this case, but that Fisheries and Oceans did not because it had no "affirmative regulatory duty," even though it has authority to protect inland fisheries.[11] While the Supreme Court did not go as far as some of the earlier decisions, it still provided a solid endorsement of legalism in Canadian environmental-impact assessment.

This new judicial activism has the potential to revolutionize the relationship between citizens and the government and between the courts and administrative agencies. It is also having profound implications for federal-provincial relations in Canada. As Kathryn Harrison argues, "the courts have empowered citizens to drive a wedge between the federal and provincial governments by granting them enforceable claims to federal actions" (Harrison 1991, 19). Just as multistakeholder forums have found their way into intergovernmental relations on the environment, so too has legalism exploded into the nexus of federalism and the environment, thrusting jurisdiction on a reluctant federal government and, especially in the recent case of Quebec's Great Whale project, generating intense conflicts that have reverberated throughout Canadian federalism.

The Canadian Environmental Assessment Act

As a result of the uncertainty generated by these cases, as well as strong public pressures for more rigorous environmental assessments, the federal government finally tabled legislation in June 1990 to incorporate environmental-impact assessment into a statute through the Canadian Environmental Assessment Act (Bill C-78).[12] Originally, the bill appeared to be an explicit attempt by the government to remove the nondiscretionary duties the courts have read into the guidelines order (Schrecker 1991). On the one hand, the bill clarified the legal status of the assessment process by giving it a statutory foundation, but on the other hand the government sought to remove the action-forcing aspects of the process. As one environmentalist lamented, "it is like polishing a car but removing the engine" (Vigod 1990).

From the perspective of the debate over legalism, the most significant aspect of the bill is that it substituted administrative discretion for the nondiscretionary language of the guidelines order. In essence, Bill C-78 inserted "in the opinion of the responsible authority" for every relevant "shall" in the guidelines order. It would seem that the government included the nondiscretionary language in the guidelines order only because it presumed that the guidelines order was not legally binding. When the courts declared that it was legally binding, the government's response was to reassert its autonomy by allowing the government to escape the legalism that has been creeping into environmental-impact assessment.

But as a result of environmental opposition, on the grounds that the bill weakens existing law, provincial opposition, on the grounds that it intrudes on provincial jurisdiction, and weak support within cabinet, the bill died on the order paper in May 1991. When the next session of Parliament convened, the government reintroduced the legislation, this time labelled Bill C-13. In response to political pressures from environmentalists, government-sponsored amendments that narrowed the scope of the discretionary language were adopted in committee. According to Environment Minister Jean Charest, the government removed "in the opinion of" in fifteen of the eighteen places it appeared in the original bill (Charest 1991, 9). Despite strong opposition from Quebec MPs, the bill passed the House of Commons on March 19, 1992. It appears as if legalism is here to stay. How far it penetrates other areas of environmental policy is another question.

An Environmental Bill of Rights

Mandatory environmental-impact assessment is just one small component of the larger strategy of judicializing environmental policy. The campaign for an environmental bill of rights goes beyond impact assessment to incorporate virtually all aspects of the environmental policy process. For instance, the Canadian Bar Association (CBA) proposal contains three basic elements: (1) a right to a healthy environment, (2) legal standing in environmental cases, including enforcement, and (3) public participation in administrative decision-making. While the CBA's ultimate goal is a constitutional right to a healthy environment, the short-term goal is a statute enunciating an environmental right that would supersede any law that is inconsistent with it (Gertler, Muldoon & Valiente, 1990).

Expansion of Standing for Environmental Interests

The key to enforcing this right is an expansion of "standing" for environmental interests. Traditional standing doctrine in Canada required that a party experience some "special," usually economic, damage to have access to the courts. Groups or individuals representing interests such as environmental protection found it difficult to bring cases to court. There are strong indications that barriers to standing are being relaxed, however. In the case *Minister of Finance of Canada v. Finlay*, the court granted "public interest standing" to a taxpayer who objected to a shared-cost program, on the basis that the citizen had a "genuine interest" in the matter and that "there is no other reasonable and effective manner in which the issue may be brought before the Court."[13] An indication of this more relaxed standing doctrine is the fact that the standing of the plaintiffs in the major environmental-impact assessment cases discussed earlier was not challenged (Lucas 1989, 177). The new standing doctrine is a dramatic example of how changing institutional rules of the game can have profound implications for the distribution of power among societal interests.

Greater Citizen Involvement

In addition to expanded standing, many environmentalists also argue for a greater citizen role in enforcement of environmental laws. While Canadian common law provides for "private prosecutions," their attractiveness to environmentalists is limited by the stringent requirement that violation be proved "beyond a reasonable doubt." In addition, the

Attorney General may intervene at any time to end the case. Many environmentalists advocate the adoption of American-style "citizen suits," which allow "any person" to sue polluters for violating the law or the government for failing to perform nondiscretionary duties (Gertler, Muldoon & Valiente 1990, 90–91).[14]

Formalized Public Participation in Administrative Proceedings

The third major element of the CBA proposal is formalized public participation in administrative proceedings. The CBA is critical of the informal nature of multistakeholder forums, and argues for American-style formal notice and comment procedures. These more formal procedures would involve formal regulatory proposals, a comment period, written submissions by interested parties, written responses by the government to the public comments, and the opportunity to request a full public hearing (Gertler, Muldoon & Valiente 1990, 95).[15]

While the NDP government in Ontario has committed itself to an environmental bill of rights, it has yet to formulate any specific proposals. But if something like Bill 13, submitted by Environment Minister Ruth Grier while in opposition, becomes law, it will involve radical changes in citizen access and judicial involvement (Muldoon 1988). For instance, the bill would give Ontarians the right to a healthy environment, allow any person to sue to stop activities that harm the environment, and empower the courts not only to impose injunctions and order damages, but also, more dramatically, to establish regulatory standards with which polluters must comply. Moreover, the bill provides that "if the activity complained of is not governed by any legally established standard, the Court may hear evidence as to the standard, if any, that should apply to the defendant ... and the Court may order the defendant to comply with such standard as it may determine" (Section 4(3)). This provision would grant the courts what is essentially an administrative or even quasi-legislative standard-setting authority!

U.S. Environmental Legalism

This bill of rights approach is quite different from the American version of environmental legalism. With the exception of several states (Michigan being the most prominent), there are no general environmental rights in the United States. Instead, relatively specific nondiscretionary duties are included in regulatory statutes (Sunstein 1990; Melnick 1989; Rabkin 1989). For instance, the 1990 Clean Air Act establishes a list of 189 toxic air pollutants, and requires the Environmental Protection Agency to promulgate technology-based emissions standards for 25 percent of them within four years, an additional 25 percent within seven years, and the entire list within ten years. If EPA fails to keep to this schedule, a citizen can sue the agency to force compliance. The U.S. approach relies a great deal on the judiciary, but it gives the judiciary far less discretion than would a bill of rights.

CEPA and Legalism

The language of rights first crept into the federal discourse on the environment when the Mulroney government introduced the Canadian Environmental Protection Act (CEPA). Environment Minister Tom McMillan claimed that the bill would be "in effect, if not technically, the country's first 'Environmental Bill of Rights'" (quoted in Schrecker 1990, 183). Even this qualified statement was an exaggeration, and the government was strongly criticized by the opposition and environmental groups for not proposing stronger rights measures.

Despite these criticisms, Environment Canada's public information package released after CEPA was passed claimed that CEPA provides for "the right to a healthy environment," and emphasizes the participatory and legal rights contained in the new statute. To symbolize the increased legalism of the new bill, the information sheet is sprinkled with pictures of gavels crashing down (Canada 1988a). Indeed, CEPA is far more legalistic than preceding Canadian regulatory statutes. For instance, "any person may ... request that a substance be added to the Priority Substances List" that is the focus of CEPA's scheme for regulating toxic chemicals. The minister must respond to the request within 90 days and explain "how the Minister intends to deal with the request and the reasons for dealing with it in that manner" (Chapter 16 (4th Supp), Section 12 (4), (5)).

Moreover, "any person" can request that a board of review be established in a number of circumstances. Curiously, in some cases the government may deny the request, but in others it is forced to establish a board of review if the request is made.[16] "Any two persons" can petition the minister to investigate alleged infraction under CEPA, and the minister is required to investigate the offence and report on the results within 90 days (Sections 108, 109). "Any person who has suffered loss or damage" as a result of a CEPA infraction can seek injunctive relief from the court or can sue the offender for damages (Sections 131, 136 (1), (2)).

An initial survey suggests that these provisions have had surprisingly little impact on the administration of CEPA. Formal petitions to add chemicals to the Priority Substances List are rare, and when they arrive they are responded to with a notice saying that the request will be considered when the entire list is re-evaluated, as required by statute. Enforcement officials were worried that citizen requests for inspections would absorb a great deal of resources, but in fact they have been virtually nonexistent. In the Pacific and Yukon region of Environment Canada, only one such request was filed between the time CEPA came into force in July 1988 and the autumn of 1991. Officials attribute the lack of utilization to lack of knowledge about the provisions, as well as the limited number of regulations that have been issued under CEPA thus far. Without regulations in force, there is little to investigate (personal interviews).

Legalism as a Policy Style

As a policy style, legalism is fundamentally different from both the bipartite bargaining that ruled environmental policy prior to 1987 and the multipartite bargaining that has emerged since 1987. Legalism transforms the institutional structure by introducing the judiciary as an important player. In addition, the relationship between other elements of the policy network also changes dramatically. Environmental groups gain some control over the governmental agenda by forcing the government to respond to their legal initiatives, raising the prospect of environmental groups, not government, determining which toxic chemicals should be regulated and which polluters should be prosecuted.

Legalism also involves a public philosophy that differs markedly from other alternative policy styles. Under legalism, the policy process is built on openness, distrust, and the assumption of conflict, a far cry from the consensus-building efforts of multistakeholder forums and the inclusive logic of sustainable development, not to mention the informal, closed style that has traditionally characterized Canadian regulation. Multilateral bargaining is built on a distrust of government's ability to represent environmental interests adequately, but legalism goes beyond that to a profound distrust of government's regulatory capacity generally. The rhetoric of advocates of environmental bills of rights embodies this distrust:

> The standing barrier assumes that the government is the sole and efficient protector of the public interest, and in particular, environmental quality. Yet this is suspect. Governments juggle competing demands and seek out politically expedient and popular solutions. History has demonstrated that governments trade off long-term environmental benefits for short-term economic or political gains. Governments may be reluctant to enforce existing laws or enact stricter ones because of lack or resources, the risks of jobs being lost, or simply because of some deal previously worked out with the polluter. Groups and individuals armed with legal rights, therefore, are needed to act as watchdogs for the trees, soils, and the waters of Canada that would otherwise remain unrepresented and unspoken for (Muldoon 1988, 35).

Citizen suits are an extreme example of the legalist public philosophy in action—they take the role of law enforcement away from the attorney general, acting for the state, and give it to private citizens. The courts are given special status within legalism—it becomes their task to ensure that all interests are adequately represented in government decision-making.

Were it to be actualized in Canada, legalism would represent a profound change in policy style. It would reject the closed, informal, cooperative style that traditionally dominated Canada in favour of an open, formal, adversarial style like that found in the United States. Moreover, legalism would give both interest groups and courts the ability to constrain Parliament, thus threatening the norms of responsible government outlined by Sharon Sutherland in Chapter 3. The Charter of Rights and Freedoms has already introduced legalism to Canadian constitutional law, but the extension of legalism to administrative law would be a dramatic new step.

The threat to government autonomy posed by legalism explains why the Canadian government has enthusiastically sponsored the multistakeholder process but generally opposed the emergence of legalism. Every important court decision challenging the government's discretion was appealed by the federal government. Bill C-78, the initial version of the Canadian Environmental Protection Act, was an obvious attempt to retreat from the legalism the courts have read into the EARP guidelines order. Protests by outraged environmentalists led to the reinsertion of some action-forcing language. While CEPA has a legalistic gloss to it, Conservative Environment Minister Tom McMillan strongly resisted opposition demands that the bill incorporate an environmental bill of rights, claiming that an environmental bill of rights "could very well undermine the capacity of elected and therefore accountable people to represent the public interest as they see fit" (quoted in Schrecker 1990, 183).

Evaluation

Legalism has some advantages over multipartite bargaining. In particular, by forcing the government to give more elaborate justifications for its actions, the increased openness and formality of legalism increases the accountability of the administrative process. Legalism also has the potential to solve some of the problems posed by multipartite bargaining. For instance, one of the concerns about the multistakeholder process is that environmentalists may lack the resources to represent their interests effectively. While business still retains significant resource advantages, legalism grants environmental groups a power resource that is absent in bargaining, which is of course why environmentalists find legalism so appealing (Muldoon 1988, 35–36; Schrecker 1990, 182). Legal rights enable environmentalists to force governments to take actions, such as enforcing regulations they might otherwise avoid.

In addition to this direct source of power, the existence of legal remedies also provides environmentalists with a source of leverage in the bargaining process, because the mere threat of a formal petition or a lawsuit might help persuade either government or business to their point of view. While the consensus decision-rule of multipartite bargaining gives business a de facto veto, legalism gives environmentalists an avenue to force actions to protect the environment. The additional power resource may also provide environmentalists a way of forcing government action when public interest in the environment subsides.[17] Finally, legalism allows environmental interests to penetrate the enforcement function that still seems insulated from multipartite bargaining.

Legalism is hardly a panacea, however. As a power resource, legalism may prove to be a double-edged sword. As courts become more comfortable challenging administrative discretion, business may find it easier to challenge pro-environment decisions. And while legalism might allow environmental groups to penetrate the enforcement process, it has little to offer in the more general regulatory and especially legislative functions involved in environmental policy.

In addition, legalism may actually aggravate some of the problems posed by the multistakeholder process. The partial delegation of state authority that exists in the multistakeholder process may in fact be extended by legalism. Citizen suits, for instance, surrender some of the enforcement function to private groups. Even when the delegation of state authority is not so transparent, the enlarged influence of private groups on government priority-setting constitutes a type of delegation.

In one sense, legalism shares with pluralism a rejection of the idea that the state embodies some collective interest that is distinct from the factional struggle within society. It actively militates against the administrative discretion and state autonomy that might provide that collective interest with an avenue of expression. To its credit, however, legalism does have the advantage of a functional substitute for responsible government: the rule of law. The judicial norms of impartiality and fairness help to provide legitimacy for a more legalistic process. However, the image of neutrality that is so essential to judicial legitimacy may become threatened as the policy-making role of the courts increases. In addition, while many are uncomfortable with shifting policy-making responsibility to an unelected judiciary, they would presumably be even more disturbed by the transfer of power to less publicly known and even less accountable interest-group representatives (Mandel 1989; Rabkin 1989).

There is some evidence that this creeping legalism is producing changes in policy. Certainly, environmental-impact assessment activity has increased dramatically since the Rafferty dam decision. Prior to that decision, the Federal Environmental Assessment Review Office performed an average of three panel reviews per year. Recently, the number of reviews has jumped to twenty (Charest 1991, 2). It is important not to overestimate the impact of this development. For instance, the construction of both the Rafferty and Oldman dams continued despite judicial requirements for environmental assessment. Nonetheless, it is likely that the increased emphasis on environmental assessment has fostered concern for the environmental impacts of projects, and the procedural burdens involved appear to pose serious threats to megaprojects like Great Whale and Kemano. Another indication of the impact of legalism is that the fines levied on polluters have increased dramatically in recent years. While part of this change results from more aggressive enforcement by regulatory authorities, it also results from changes in judicial doctrine, in that judges are interpreting cases now in ways far less sympathetic to recalcitrant polluters (Saxe 1989).

TENSIONS BETWEEN BARGAINING AND LEGALISM

Figure 10.1 provides a summary characterization of the interests, institutions, and ideas of the three policy styles surveyed here. Bipartite bargaining has been discredited, and new processes are emerging to take its place. The two tracks of reform analyzed here—multipartite bargaining and legalism—are evolving simultaneously. In some ways, the two developments may be complementary. For instance, environmental groups may be able to use their legal rights as a resource to strengthen their position in bargaining forums, diminishing some of the disadvantages environmentalists might have there. Moreover, the emphasis on different governing functions here raises the prospect of an efficient division of labour between the two policy styles: multipartite bargaining is strong where legalism is weak, in legislation and regulation; and legalism is strong where bargaining is weak, in enforcement. However, such a sanguine solution is unlikely, because the two emergent policy styles may be more contradictory than complementary.

The traditional bipartite system was based on the ministerial discretion characteristic of cabinet government. Bargaining between business and government was closed, informal, and co-operative. Multipartite bargaining maintains its reliance on ministerial discretion, but departs from the bipartite tradition by opening the process significantly, inviting environmentalists and other nonbusiness interests to sit at the bargaining table. But it retains the informal and co-operative aspects of the traditional style. Proposals are developed in face-to-face meetings, under the auspices of professional facilitators who attempt to guide the participants toward consensus. The product of such forums typically is a report representing the consensus of the participants. The reasons for particular decisions are not necessarily given, and as a result the essentially political nature of the process is obfuscated. The winners and losers, concessions made, and bargains struck are not revealed to nonparticipants.

FIGURE 10.1
COMPARING POLICY STYLES

Policy Style	Interests	Institutions	Ideas
Bipartite bargaining	Industry and government; industry dominant	Ministerial discretion	State represents the public interests, co-operation valued
Multipartite bargaining	Environmentalists and others included along with industry	Ministerial discretion	Public interest emerges from bargaining, co-operation valued
Legalism	Environmentalists and others included along with industry	Ministerial discretion constrained more by statutes and courts	Court supervises interest representation; open conflict encouraged

Legalism shares with multipartite bargaining an expansion in the types of societal interests involved, but it is based on significantly different institutional rules. Legalism is far more formalistic, and as a result, more open as well. Policy arguments are placed on the public record, whether it is a hearing open to the public, a legal brief in a case, or a written comment on a regulatory proposal. Written decisions are required, detailing the justifications for the action, including responses to comments made by interested parties. The resultant written record permits more careful external scrutiny of the process. While judges or ministers do not necessarily give the real reasons for their decisions, at least it is possible to determine readily who won and who lost by an examination of the written record.

In addition to different institutional rules, the two new policy styles are also based on quite different ideas. While multipartite bargaining is built on an ethic of co-operation, legalism assumes an adversarial relationship. Indeed, the two policy styles seem to express different world views (Amy 1990, 226–28). Multipartite bargaining rests on a world view that unites sustainable development as a policy objective with consensus through negotiation as a policy process. It assumes that industrial development and environmental protection are reconcilable. The world view of emerging Canadian legalism is fundamentally different. It tends to assume an inherent conflict between industrial development and environmental protection, and rejects the inevitable compromises essential to a consensual process in favour of authoritative decisions resulting from formal, adversarial proceedings.[18] Indeed, the very language of rights discourse militates against a compromising, consensus-building approach.

The formality, adversarial character, and, to a lesser extent, openness of legalism are antagonistic to the logic of multipartite bargaining. The concessions, trades, and deals that are an essential part of a successful bargaining process thrive on informality, and to a certain extent on exclusion (see Chapter 1 on "Access to the Policy Process"). If the terms of each compromise were publicized, the task of consensus building would probably be impossible (Webb 1990). Whereas consensus building relies on and promotes trust, an adversarial system feeds on and promotes distrust between interested parties. The apparent tensions between these two policy styles suggest that the Canadian regulatory process may face a future characterized by instability and turmoil.

CONCLUSION: POLICY STYLES AND THE MACROPOLITICAL SYSTEM

The two different logics of these policy styles strongly suggest that they have different futures in Canada. The fact is legalism is a greater departure from Canadian political institutions and traditions than multipartite bargaining. While multipartite bargaining departs from tradition in two out of the three elements of policy style, legalism differs in all three. The departure from ministerial discretion creates profound tensions between the legalism creeping into Canadian policy-making and the larger Canadian political system. For that reason, legalism faces a more precarious future.

Unlike the American system of government, in which the separation of power creates incentives for legislators to constrain executive discretion, the Canadian parliamentary system lacks the institutional incentives that promote legalism. Regulatory legalism in the United States is a tightly-coupled system consisting of three components: (1) environmental groups with access to courts, (2) a judiciary willing to challenge agency decisions, and (3) specific statutory standards (Melnick 1983; Harris & Milkis 1989; Hoberg 1992). Canada is now seeing the possibility of changes in the first two components. Standing seems to be opening up,[19] and courts are becoming more comfortable with an activist role as a result of the Charter of Rights and Freedoms.

However, with the exception of the Canadian Environmental Protection Act, there is little sign that Canada is moving toward what Americans call "action forcing statutes," containing specific goals and deadlines that severely restrict agency discretion. When American legislators write legislation granting regulatory authority to the executive, they do so in a way that will maximize the probability that their preferences are embodied in the regulatory decisions made by the executive (Moe 1989). In the United States, the separation of power between the legislative and executive branches magnifies the problem of controlling executive action. Because Congress does not trust the executive branch to implement its policies, it writes explicit statutes to force executive agencies to comply with congressional intent (Brickman, Jasanoff & Ilgen 1985, ch. 3; Nemetz, Stanbury & Thompson 1986). Environmental advocates of legalism outside government structures find powerful allies in legislators who are distrustful of executive discretion.

In parliamentary government, the fusion of the legislature and executive in cabinet government, combined with tight party discipline, virtually eliminates the incentives to limit executive discretion (Brickman, Jasanoff & Ilgen 1985). Because the executive (cabinet) belongs to the same party as the majority coalition in the legislature, the problem of ensuring that executive actions reflect the preferences of the majority in the legislature is not much of an issue.[20] Rather than write specific statutes, it makes more sense merely to provide the executive with adequate authority to pursue the government's policy goals. In stark contrast to the United States, Canadian regulatory statutes are largely enabling in character, with few if any nondiscretionary duties (Schrecker 1992). This pattern also has a deep resonance with Canadian political tradition. As a high-level civil servant intimately involved with environmental policy said recently, "you do not fetter Her Majesty" (personal interview).

An environmental bill of rights departs from the American model of an action-forcing statute in that it creates a vague citizen right, and a corresponding vague government duty. But the vagueness does not make it any less threatening to cabinet government, and thus to legislators in the majority party, because it would transfer a great deal of power to the judiciary to limit executive discretion.

For these reasons, legalism may not penetrate very far into Canadian environmental policy. Environmental assessment legislation may prove an exception, but legislatures can be expected to resist any more action-forcing statutes. And as experience in government teaches that the desirability of executive discretion is independent of political preferences, commitment to an environmental bill of rights by the government in Ontario could wane.

While it confronts formidable obstacles, it is too early to dismiss Canadian legalism, as the recent Supreme Court decisions on the Rafferty-Alameda and Oldman dams demonstrate. The problem is that because of the structure of parliamentary government, the "structural" interests of the majority coalition in the legislature and the external advocates of legalism are at odds. But there is a Canadian precedent for the government imposing legalistic limits on itself: the Canadian Charter of Rights and Freedoms. What is necessary for this sort of voluntary surrender of autonomy to occur is an overriding governmental motivation—in the case of the Charter, the desire to promote national identity to counter the centrifugal forces of federalism (Russell 1983; Knopff & Morton 1985).

It is conceivable that if external pressures for legalism intensify, the electoral incentives of the majority party may overwhelm its structural incentives. Environmental rights have powerful symbolic appeal, uniting the popular cause of the environment with the burgeoning rights consciousness in Canadian political culture. Not long ago it seemed reasonable to suggest that Canadian political culture was hostile to legalism. In the mid-1970s Kenneth McNaught wrote:

> Our judges and lawyers, supported by the press and public opinion, reject any concept of the courts as positive instruments in the political process... (P)olitical action outside the party-parliamentary structure tends automatically to be suspect—and not least because it smacks of Americanism (quoted in Lipset, 1989, 102).

But this hostility seems to have declined in the 1980s with the introduction of the Charter. According to Alan Cairns, "the Charter lessens deference to elites and governments, stimulates pressure for citizens' participation, and suggests that working the constitution and governing should be more of a partnership between office-holders and citizens than formerly" (1990, 339). Rather than being marginalized, advocates of environmental legalism are finding their arguments resonating more deeply within a society undergoing a transformation in relationships between the citizen and the state.

Concrete evidence of this change can be seen in the arguments made by federal Conservative Environment ministers. When the Canadian Environmental Protection Act was being considered in 1987 and 1988, Environment Minister Tom McMillan denounced legalism with a ringing defence of traditional Westminster-style responsible government: "Inevitably the interpretation is going to come from the courts, not from politicians who are accountable to the people. We would in effect abdicate to the courts the decisions affecting the environment, and the courts are not accountable" (quoted in Schrecker 1990, 183). By 1991, however, the ideological landscape of Canadian politics had changed, and government officials responded. In denying that government amendments were an attempt to court-proof Bill C-13, Environment Minister Jean Charest stated: "I think it is obvious to all that to 'court proof' legislation in the relatively new field of environmental assessment is simply impossible. Nonetheless we have eliminated as much discretionary language as possible. We have done so to maintain accountability of responsible authorities" (Charest 1991, 6–7).

In 1988, the Environment minister believed accountability was ensured by keeping courts out of policy-making. In 1991, the Environment minister—admittedly a different one, but an official of the same party—believed accountability was ensured by guaranteeing the courts a role. In the battle over ideas, environmentalists won an important victory, at the expense of business and traditional state institutions.

The Canadian policy style is clearly at a crossroads. Whichever road Canada chooses, it is important to realize that neither of the emergent policy styles addresses one of the fundamental problems underlying governance in this area: the weakness of the Canadian state. Both multipartite bargaining and legalism look outside the traditional executive apparatus of the state to solve the legitimacy problems that plagued the traditional bipartite policy style. While the state has been busy organizing consultative forums and resisting the encroachments of the judiciary, disturbingly little is being done to enhance the capacity of the regulatory state to formulate and implement policy in this complex, dynamic, and divisive policy area.

Canada confronts difficult choices in determining the governing arrangements for environmental policy. At present, the system appears to be evolving in two different directions at once, with remarkably little reflection on the consequences of choosing one path over another. Yet the two paths have fundamentally different implications for the role of the state; the allocation of authority between the legislative, executive, and judicial branches of the state, and the relationship between citizens, interest groups, and the state. The time has come for more careful deliberation and conscious choices.

NOTES

1. A third pattern of response may be occurring as well: a move to more decentralized community control over resource allocation decisions. In both Ontario and British Columbia, for instance, experiments are taking place with community-based planning on forest management issues. In these cases, the purpose appears to be to apply the principles of multistakeholder consultations at the local level.

2. A fifth governing function can also be identified: the allocation of governing authority between different levels of government, or what we can call the constitutional function.

3. The acid rain problem kept the environmental issue alive in the early 1980s, but public attention in that period did not compare with that of the late 1980s. Using the Canadian Newspaper Index as an indicator, the number of stories on the environment ranged between 600 and 800 between 1983 and 1988, but jumped to 1300 by 1989.

4. The classic statement is Earl Latham's: "The legislature referees the group struggle, ratifies the victories of the successful coalition, and records the terms of the surrenders, compromises, and conquests in the forms of statutes." Administrative agencies "are like armies of occupation left in the field to police the rule won by the victorious coalition" (1952, 390–391).

5. This point is made in reference to British workplace safety regulation by Wilson (1985, 44). An important exception to this pattern are project approvals that require the issuance of licences before activities that threaten environmental quality can go ahead.

6. *Canadian Wildlife Federation v. Canada (Minister of the Environment)*, 3 C.E.L.R. (N.S.) 287.

7. *Canadian Wildlife Federation v. Canada (Minister of the Environment)*, 4 C.E.L.R. (N.S.) 1.

8. *Friends of the Oldman River Society v. Canada (Minister of Transport)*, Action no. A-395-89, Federal Court of Appeal, March 13, 1990. The case that showed the most exacting standard of judicial review was a later case involving the Rafferty and Alameda dams, *Canadian Wildlife Federation et al. v. Minister of the Environment*, 4 C.E.L.R.(N.S.) 201. In a more recent case, a Federal Court judge ruled that the federal government has to perform an assessment on the Alcan Kitimat hydro-electric project, despite the fact that the cabinet passed an order-in-council explicitly exempting the project from the EARP process *(Carrier-Sekani Tribal Council v. The Minister of Environment*, T-2686-90, Federal Court of Canada, Trial Division, Vancouver, July 12, 1991).

9. *Angus et al. v. R. et al.*, 5 C.E.L.R. (March 1991) 157–91.

10. *Kantwell v. Minister of the Environment*, Federal Court of Canada, Trial Division, Court Number T-2975-90, January 18, 1991.

11. *Friends of the Oldman River Society v. Canada (Minister of Transport)*, Supreme Court of Canada, File no. 21890, January 23, 1991.

12. Canada, House of Commons, Bill C-78, An Act to establish a federal environmental assessment process, First reading June 18, 1990.

13. 2 S.C.R. 607 (1986). The Finlay case extended to administrative law an expanded standing doctrine that had emerged in a trilogy of constitutional cases: *Thorson v. Attorney General of Canada*, 1 S.C.R. 138, (1974); *Nova Scotia Board of Censors v. McNeil*, 2 S.C.R. 265, (1975); *Minister of Justice of Canada v. Borowski*, 2

S.C.R. 575, (1989). For more detail on standing law, see Ontario Law Reform Commission (1989).

14. Citizen suits are incorporated into every U.S. environmental statute except one (Boyer & Meidinger 1985).

15. While it has gone relatively unnoticed, the Canadian regulatory process has been increasingly formalized since the late 1970s as a result of the introduction of a socioeconomic-impact assessment requirement. Interestingly, this formalization of the rule-making process has been prompted by concern for the economic impact of regulations rather than for the environment (Canada 1988b).

16. The establishment of a board of review is mandatory if requests are made in the cases of regulations on international air pollution, nutrients, or the use of public lands, and if a determination on toxicity has not been made for a substance that has been on the Priority Substances List for five years. The decision is discretionary in cases in which the government declines to list a chemical as toxic, or when a regulation on toxic substances or ocean dumping is proposed (Section 89).

17. The presence of legalism has been credited with the success of American environmentalists in resisting the policy retrenchment attempted by the Reagan administration in the early 1980s (Hoberg 1990; Schrecker 1990).

18. Compare, for instance, Toner (1990) and Dorcey and Riek (1987), which reflect the multipartite bargaining world view, and the works of Ted Schrecker (1990, 1991), which reflect the legalist world view.

19. The advantages of greater standing are offset somewhat in Canada by the legal rules that require the losers in a case to pay the court costs of their opponents. The potential financial risk may serve as a powerful deterrent against environmental litigation. In stark contrast, in the United States losing litigants are not responsible for costs of their opponents, and many environmental statutes provide for payment of attorneys' fees for successful environmental litigants. Canada's, cost rules are evaluated in Ontario Law Reform Commission (1989, ch. 6).

20. The possibility that the current majority may lose power in the future does provide incentives to bind the executive more carefully, but those incentives are overwhelmed by the desire to avoid the short-term loss of discretion and autonomy that would be involved. This analysis is also greatly complicated by the possibility of minority governments, which at first glance would seem to

increase the prospects for nondiscretionary legislation because of the necessity of garnering some support from distrustful opposition parties to pass legislation. But the presence of a minority government increases the probability that the official opposition party will form the next government, reducing the desirability of checks on executive discretion for that party. A smaller third party, which may hold the balance of power, would have more incentives for seeking nondiscretionary legislation, but would have great difficulty getting the government party to go along.

BIBLIOGRAPHY

Alberta Court of Queen's Bench. (1984). *National Citizens' Coalition v. Attorney General of Canada*, (1984) 5 Western Weekly Reports 436.

Aldrich, J. (1982). The earnings replacement rate of old-age benefits in 12 countries, 1969-80. *Social Security Bulletin, 45*, (11), 3-11.

Amenta, E., and Skocpol, T. (1989). Taking exception: Explaining the distinctiveness of American public policies in the last century. In F. Castles (Ed.), *Comparative history of public policy*. New York: Oxford University Press.

Amy, D. (1990). Environmental dispute resolution: The promise and pitfalls. In N. Vig and M. Kraft (Eds.), *Environmental policy in the 1990s*. Washington, DC: CQ Press.

Ashford, D. (1986). *The emergence of the welfare states*. Oxford: Basil Blackwell.

Atkinson, M.M. (1984). On the prospects for industrial policy in Canada. *Canadian Public Administration, 27*, 454-67.

Atkinson, M.M., and Coleman, W.D. (1989a). *The state, business and industrial change in Canada*. Toronto: University of Toronto Press.

———. (1989b). Strong states and weak states: Sectoral policy networks in advanced capitalist economies. *British Journal of Political Science, 19*, 47-67.

Atkinson, M.M., and Nigol, R.A. (1989). Selecting policy instruments: Neo-institutional and rational choice interpretations of automobile insurance in Ontario. *Canadian Journal of Political Science, 22*, 107-35.

Atkinson, M.M., and Nossal, K. (1981). Bureaucratic politics and the new fighter aircraft decisions. *Canadian Public Administration, 24*, 531-62.

Atkinson, M.M., and Powers, R.A. (1987). Inside the industrial policy garbage can: Selective subsidies to business in Canada. *Canadian Public Policy, 13*, 208-17.

Aucoin, P. (1986). Organizational change in the machinery of Canadian government: From rational management to brokerage politics. *Canadian Journal of Political Science, 19*, 3-27.

———. (1988). The Mulroney government, 1984-1988: Priorities, positional policy and power. In A. Gollner and D. Salée (Eds.), *Canada under Mulroney*. Montreal: Véhicule.

———. (1991). Cabinet government in Canada: Corporate management of a confederal executive. In C. Campbell and M.J. Wyszomirski (Eds.), *Executive leadership in Anglo-American systems*. Pittsburgh: University of Pittsburgh Press.

Aucoin, P., and Bakvis, H. (1984). Organizational differentiation and integration: The case of regional development policy in Canada. *Canadian Public Administration, 27,* 348–71.

———. (1988). *The centralization-decentralization conundrum: Organization and management in the Canadian government.* Halifax: Institute for Research on Public Policy.

Auditor General of Canada. (1990). *Report of the Auditor General of Canada to the House of Commons.* Ottawa: Minister of Supply and Services.

Audley, P. (1983). *Canada's cultural industries: Broadcasting, publishing, records and film.* Toronto: Lorimer.

Axworthy, L. (1985). Control of policy. *Policy Options, 6,* (April), 17–20.

Axworthy, T. (1988). Of secretaries to princes. *Canadian Public Administration, 31,* 247–64.

Baar, C., et al. (1992). The Ontario Court of Appeal and speedy justice. *Osgoode Hall Law Journal, 30.*

Babe, R. (1990). *Telecommunications in Canada.* Toronto: University of Toronto Press.

Badaracco, J.L., Jr. (1985). *Loading the dice.* Cambridge, MA: Harvard Business School Press.

Baggalely, C. (1981). *The emergence of the regulatory state in Canada.* Ottawa: Economic Council of Canada.

Bakvis, H. (1989). Regional politics and policy in the Mulroney cabinet, 1984–89: Towards a theory of the regional minister system in Canada. *Canadian Public Policy, 15,* 121–34.

———. (1991). *Regional ministers: Power and influence in the Canadian cabinet.* Toronto: University of Toronto Press.

Banting, K.G. (1987). *The welfare state and Canadian federalism* (2nd ed.). Montreal: McGill-Queen's Press.

———. (forthcoming). Neoconservatism in an open economy: The social role of the Canadian state. *International Journal of Political Science.*

Barber, C.L., and McCallum, J.C.P. (1980). *Unemployment and inflation: The Canadian experience.* Toronto: Canadian Institute for Economic Policy.

———. (1982). *Controlling inflation: Learning from experience in Canada, Europe and Japan.* Toronto: Canadian Institute for Economic Policy.

Bardach, E., and Kagan, R.A. (1982). *Going by the book: The problem of regulatory unreasonableness.* Philadelphia: Temple University Press.

Barer, M., and Evans, R.G. (1986). Riding north on a south-bound horse: Expenditures, prices, utilization and incomes in the Canadian health care system. In R.G. Evans and G.L. Stoddart (Eds.), *Medicare at maturity* (53–164). Calgary: University of Calgary Press.

Bartley, A. (1988). The regulation of cross-media ownership: The life and short times of PCO 2294. *Canadian Journal of Communication, 13,* 45–59.

Bates, R.H. (1988). Contra contractarianism: Some reflections on the new institutionalism. *Politics and Society, 16,* 387–401.

Bawden, D.L., and Palmer, J.L. (1984). Social security: Challenging the welfare state. In J.L. Palmer and I.V. Sawhill (Eds.), *The Reagan record*. Cambridge, MA: Ballinger.

Birch, A.H. (1964). *Representative and responsible government*. London: George Allen and Unwin.

Blais, A., and Vaillancourt, F. (1986). The federal corporate income tax: Tax expenditures and tax discrimination in the Canadian manufacturing industry, 1972–1981. *Canadian Tax Journal, 34*, (5), 1122–39.

Blake, D. (1991). Party competition and electoral volatility in Canada. In H. Bakvis (Ed.), *Representation, integration and political parties in Canada* (Vol. 14, Research Studies of the Royal Commission on Electoral Reform and Party Financing). Toronto: Dundurn.

Blendon, R.J. (1989). Three systems: A comparative survey. *Health Management Quarterly, 9*, (1), 2–10.

Bliss, M. (1982). *The evolution of industrial policies in Canada: An historical survey* (Discussion Paper No. 218). Ottawa: Economic Council of Canada.

Block, F. (1977). The ruling class does not rule. *Socialist Revolution, 7*, 6–28.

———. (1987). *Revising state theory*. Philadelphia: Temple University Press.

Boothman, B.E.C. (1989). Strategic transformations among Canadian crown corporations. *Australian Journal of Public Administration, 48*, 291–311.

Boreham, G. (1988). *Money, banking and finance: The Canadian context*. Toronto: Holt, Rinehart and Winston.

Borins, S.F., and Boothman, B.E.C. (1985). Crown corporations and economic efficiency. In D.G. McFetridge (Ed.), *Canadian industrial policy in action*. Toronto: University of Toronto Press.

Bourgault, J., and Dion, S. (1990). *The changing profile of federal deputy ministers 1867 to 1988*. Ottawa: Canadian Centre for Management Development.

Bowden, M.-A., and Curtis, F. (1988). Federal EIA in Canada: EARP as an evolving process. *Environmental Impact Assessment Review, 8*, 97–106.

Boyer, B., and Meidinger, E. (1985). Privatizing regulatory enforcement: A preliminary assessment of citizen suits under federal environmental laws. *Buffalo Law Review, 34*, 833–964.

Brean, D.J.S., Bird, R.M., and Krauss, M. (1991). *Taxation of international portfolio investment*. Halifax: Centre for Trade Policy and Law and the Institute for Research on Public Policy.

Breton, A. (1985). Supplementary statement. *Report* (Vol. 3 of the Royal Commission on the Economic Union and Development Prospects for Canada). Ottawa: Minister of Supply and Services.

Brickman, R., Jasanoff, S., and Ilgen, T. (1985). *Controlling chemicals*. Ithaca, NY: Cornell University Press.

Brooks, S. (1987a). The mixed ownership corporation as an instrument of public policy. *Comparative Politics, 20*, 173–190.

———. (1987b). *Who's in charge? The mixed ownership corporation in Canada*. Montreal: Institute for Research on Public Policy.

———. (1989). *Public policy in Canada: An introduction.* Toronto: McClelland & Stewart.

Brown, D.M. (1991). The evolving role of the provinces in Canadian trade policy. In D.M. Brown and M.G. Smith (Eds.), *Canadian federalism: Meeting global economic challenges?* (81–145). Kingston: Institute of Intergovernmental Relations.

Brown-John, L. (1981). *Canadian regulatory agencies.* Toronto: Butterworths.

Brunelle, D. (1982). *L'état solide: Sociologie du fédéralisme au Canada et au Québec.* Montréal: Éditions Sélect.

Bryner, G.C. (1987a). *Bureaucratic discretion: Law and policy in federal regulatory agencies.* New York: Pergamon Press.

———. (1987b). Regulatory reform in the United States: A comparative perspective. *International Review of Administrative Sciences, 53,* 197–216.

Cairns, A.C. (1968). The electoral system and the party system in Canada, 1921–1965. *Canadian Journal of Political Science, 1,* 55–80.

———. (1971). The judicial committee and its critics. *Canadian Journal of Political Science, 4,* 301–45.

———. (1977). The governments and societies of Canadian federalism. *Canadian Journal of Political Science, 10,* (4), 695–725.

———. (1990). The past and future of the Canadian administrative state. *University of Toronto Law Journal, 40,* 319–61.

———. (1991). Constitutional minoritarianism in Canada. In R.L. Watts and D. Brown (Eds.), *Canada: The state of the federation 1990.* Kingston: Institute of Intergovernmental Relations.

Cairns, A.C., and Williams, C. (1985). Constitutionalism, citizenship, and society in Canada: An overview. In A.C. Cairns and C. Williams (Eds.), *Constitutionalism, citizenship, and society in Canada.* Toronto: University of Toronto Press.

Calvert, J. (1988). Government procurement. In D. Cameron (Ed.), *The free trade deal.* Toronto: Lorimer.

Cameron, D.R. (1984). Social democracy, corporatism, labour quiescence and the representation of economic interest in advanced capitalist society. In J. Goldthorpe (Ed.), *Order and conflict in contemporary capitalism* (143–78). New York and Oxford: Oxford University Press.

Campbell, C. (1983). *Governments under stress: Political executives and key bureaucrats in Washington, London, and Ottawa.* Toronto: University of Toronto Press.

———. (1985). Cabinet committees in Canada: Pressures and dysfunctions stemming from the representational imperative. In T. Mackie and B. Hogwood (Eds.), *Unlocking the cabinet: Cabinet structures in comparative perspective.* London: Sage.

———. (1988). Mulroney's broker politics: The ultimate in politicized incompetence. In A. Gollner and D. Salée (Eds.), *Canada under Mulroney.* Montreal: Véhicule.

Campbell, R.M. (1987). *Grand illusions: The politics of the Keynesian experience in Canada, 1945–1975.* Peterborough, ON: Broadview Press.

———. (1991). *The full employment objective in Canada, 1945–1985: Historical, conceptual and comparative perspectives.* Ottawa: Economic Council of Canada.

Campbell, R.M., and Pal, L.A. (1989). *The real worlds of Canadian politics: Cases in process and policy.* Peterborough, ON: Broadview Press.

Canada. (1912). *Report on the organization of the public service of Canada* by Sir George Murray (Sessional Paper No. 57a). Ottawa: Parmelee.

———. (1968). *Foreign ownership and the structure of Canadian industry: Report of the task force on the structure of Canadian industry.* Ottawa: Information Canada.

———. (1972). *Task force on foreign investment.* Ottawa: Information Canada.

———. (1979). Royal Commission on Financial Management and Accountability. (1979). *Final report.* Ottawa: Minister of Supply and Services.

———. (1983). Department of External Affairs. *Canadian trade policy for the 1980s: A discussion paper.* Ottawa: Minister of Supply and Services.

———. (1985). Royal Commission on the Economic Union and Development Prospects for Canada. *Final report* (Vol. 2). Ottawa: Minister of Supply and Services.

———. (1986). Department of Communications. *Report of the task force on broadcasting policy.* Ottawa: Minister of Supply and Services.

———. (1988a). Department of Environment. *The right to a healthy environment.* Ottawa: Minister of Supply and Services.

———. (1988b). Office of Privatization and Regulatory Affairs. *Regulatory reform: Making it work.* Ottawa: Office of Privatization and Regulatory Affairs.

———. (1990a). Department of Finance. *Quarterly economic review annual reference tables.* Ottawa: Minister of Supply and Services.

———. (1990b). Department of Employment and Immigration. *Directory of labour organizations in Canada, 1990/91* (Bureau of Labour Information). Ottawa: Minister of Supply and Services.

———. (1990c). *Public service 2000: The renewal of the public service of Canada.* Ottawa: Minister of Supply and Services.

———. (1990d). Public Service Commission. *Annual report.* Ottawa: Minister of Supply and Services.

———. (1990e). Pesticide Registration Review. (1990, December). *Recom-mendations for a revised federal pest management regulatory system* (Final Report). Ottawa: Supply and Services Canada.

———. (1991a). Department of Finance. Economic linkages among provinces. In *Quarterly economic review: Special reports* (34–54). Ottawa: Minister of Supply and Services.

———. (1991b). *Prosperity through competitiveness.* Ottawa: Minister of Supply and Services.

Canada Communications Group and Canadian Chamber of Commerce. (1990). *Organization of the government of Canada.* Ottawa: Minister of Supply and Services.

Careless, A. (1977). *Initiative and response: The adaptation of Canadian federalism to regional economic development*. Montreal: McGill-Queen's University Press.

Carmichael, E.A., Macmillan, K., and York, R.C. (1989). *Ottawa's next agenda*. Toronto: C.D. Howe Institute.

Carroll, B.W. (1991). The structure of Canadian bureaucratic elites: Some evidence of change. *Canadian Public Administration, 34,* (2), 359–72.

Carty, R.K. (1991). Three Canadian party systems: An interpretation of the development of national politics. In H. Thorburn (Ed.), *Party politics in Canada* (6th ed.). Scarborough: Prentice-Hall.

Carty, R.K., and Erickson, L. (1991). Candidate nomination in Canada's national political parties. In H. Bakvis (Ed.), *Canadian political parties: Leaders, candidates and organization* (Vol. 13, Research Studies of the Royal Commission on Electoral Reform and Party Financing). Toronto: Dundurn.

Castles, F.G. (1981). How does politics matter? Structure or agency in the determination of public policy outcomes. *European Journal of Political Research, 9,* 119–32.

———. (1987). Neo-corporatism and the "happiness index," or what the trade unions get for their co-operation. *European Journal of Political Research, 16,* 381–93.

Castles, F.G., and McKinlay, R.D. (1979). Does politics matter? An analysis of welfare commitment in advanced capitalist states. *European Journal of Social Research, 7,* 169–86.

Cecchini, P. (1988). *The European challenge 1992: The benefits of a single market*. Aldershot, England: Wildwood House.

Chandler, J.A. (1990). The United States. In J.E. Kingdom (Ed.), *The civil service in liberal democracies*. London: Routledge.

Chandler, W., and Bakvis, H. (1989). Federalism and the strong-state/weak-state conundrum: Canadian economic policymaking in comparative perspective. *Publius, 19,* 59–77.

Charest, J. (1991). *Notes for an address by the Honourable Jean J. Charest to the Legislative Committee on Bill C-13*. Ottawa: Minister of Supply and Services.

Clement, W., and Williams, G. (Eds.). (1990). *The new Canadian political economy*. Montreal: McGill-Queen's University Press.

Cohen, M.D., March, J.D., and Olsen, J.P. (1972). A garbage can model of organizational choice. *Administrative Science Quarterly, 17,* 1–25.

Coleman, W.D. (1984). *The Quebec independence movement*. Toronto: University of Toronto Press.

———. (1988). *Business and politics*. Montreal: McGill-Queen's University Press.

———. (1991). Monetary policy, accountability and legitimacy: A review of the issues in Canada. *Canadian Journal of Political Science, 34,* (4), 711–34.

Coleman, W.D., and Nossal, K.R. (1991). The state, war and business in Canada, 1939–1945. In W. Grant, J. Nekkers, and F. van Waarden (Eds.), *Organizing business for war: Corporatist economic organization during the Second World War*. Providence, RI: Berg.

Coleman, W.D., and Skogstad, G. (Eds.). (1990). *Policy communities and public policy in Canada: A structural approach.* Mississauga: Copp Clark Pitman.

Collier, D., and Messick, R. (1975). Prerequisites vs. diffusion: Alternative explanations of social security adoption. *American Political Science Review, 69,* 1296-1315.

Conway, T. (1990). Taking stock of the traditional regulatory approach. In G.B. Doern (Ed.), *Getting it green.* Toronto: C.D. Howe Institute.

Cornell, P.M., and Gorecki, P.K. (1991). Canada: Adjustment despite deficiencies in program design and execution. In H. Patrick and L. Meissner (Eds.), *Pacific basin industries in distress: Structural adjustment and trade policy in the nine industrialized economies* (33-87). New York: Columbia University Press.

Coughlin, C.C. (1991). U.S. trade-remedy laws: Do they facilitate or hinder free trade? *Federal Reserve Bank of St. Louis Review, 73,* (4) (July/August), 3-18.

Courchene, T.J. (1975). *Money, inflation and the Bank of Canada* (Vol. I: An Analysis of Canadian monetary policy from 1970 to early 1975). Toronto: C.D. Howe Institute.

———. (1981). *Money, inflation and the Bank of Canada* (Vol. II: An analysis of monetary gradualism, 1975-1980). Toronto: C.D. Howe Institute.

———. (1986). *Economic management and the division of powers.* Toronto: University of Toronto Press.

———. (1990). Social policy. In T.E. Kierans (Ed.), *Getting it right* (65-88). Toronto: C.D. Howe Institute.

———. (1991a). *The community of the Canadas.* Kingston: Institute of Intergovernmental Relations.

———. (1991b). Crumbling pillars: Creative destruction or cavalier demolition? In W. Block and G. Lermer (Eds.), *Breaking the shackles: Deregulating Canadian industry* (39-75). Vancouver: The Fraser Institute.

Crow, J.W. (1987). The Bank of Canada and its objectives. *Bank of Canada Review,* April.

Culhane, P. (1978). Natural resources policy: Procedural change and substantive environmentalism. In T. Lowi and A. Stone (Eds.), *Nationalizing government.* Beverly Hills: Sage.

Dawson, R. M. (1922). *The principle of official independence.* Toronto: S.B. Gundy.

de Cotret, R. (1990). Testimony. *Minutes of Proceedings and Evidence.* House of Commons. Special Committee to Pre-Study Bill C-78. 34th Parl., 2nd Sess. No. 3, November 1.

Dicey, A.V. (1885). *Introduction to the study of the law of the Constitution.* London: Macmillan.

Doern, G.B., (1977). *The Atomic Energy Control Board: An evaluation of regulatory and administrative processes and procedures.* Ottawa: Law Reform Commission of Canada.

———. (Ed.). (1978). *The regulatory process in Canada.* Toronto: Macmillan.

———. (1985). The politics of Canadian economic policy: An overview. In G.B. Doern (Ed.), *The politics of economic policy*. Toronto: University of Toronto Press.

———. (1990a). Canadian environmental policy: Why process is almost everything. Commentary (No. 19, July). Toronto: C.D. Howe Institute.

———. (1990b). Regulations and Incentives: The NOx-VOCs Case. In G.B. Doern (Ed.), *Getting it green*. Toronto: C.D. Howe Institute.

———. (1990c). The Department of Industry, Science and Technology: Is there industrial policy after free trade? In K.A. Graham (Ed.), *How Ottawa spends 1990-91: Tracking the second agenda* (49-71). Ottawa: Carleton University Press.

Doern, G.B., et al. (1975). The structure and behaviour of Canadian regulatory boards and commissions: Multidisciplinary perspectives. *Canadian Public Administration, 18,* 189-215.

Doern, G.B., and Phidd, R.W. (1983). *Canadian public policy: Ideas, structure, process*. Toronto: Methuen.

Doern, G.B., and Tomlin, B.W. (1991). *Faith and fear: The free trade story*. Toronto: Stoddart.

Doern, G.B., and Toner, G. (1985). *The politics of energy: The development and implementation of the NEP*. Toronto: Methuen.

Donner, A.W. (1991). Recession, recovery and redistribution: The three R's of Canadian state macro policy in the 1980s. In D. Drache and M.S. Gertler (Eds.), *The new era of global competition: State policy and market power*. Montreal: McGill-Queen's University Press.

Donner, A.W., and Peters, D.D. (1979). *The monetarist counter-revolution: A critique of Canadian monetary policy, 1975-1979*. Toronto: Canadian Institute for Economic Policy.

Dorcey, A., and Riek, C. (1987). Negotiation-based approaches to the settlement of environmental disputes in Canada (manuscript). University of British Columbia. March.

Drache, D. (1991). The systematic search for flexibility: National competitiveness and new work relations. In D. Drache and M.S. Gertler (Eds.), *The new era of global competition: State power and market power* (249-69). Montreal and Kingston: McGill-Queen's University Press.

Dufour, J.-M., and Racette, D. (1986). Monetary control in Canada. In J. Sargent (Ed.), *Fiscal and monetary policy*. Toronto: University of Toronto Press.

Dupré, J.S. (1986). Reflections on the workability of executive federalism. In R. Simeon (Ed.), *Intergovernmental relations* (Vol. 63 of the Royal Commission on the Economic Union and Development Prospects for Canada, Collected Research Studies). Toronto: University of Toronto Press.

———. (1987). The workability of executive federalism in Canada. In H. Bakvis and W. Chandler (Eds.), *Federalism and the role of the state*. Toronto: University of Toronto Press.

Dwivedi, O.P. (1974). Canadian governmental response to environmental concern. In O.P. Dwivedi (Ed.), *Protecting the environment*. Vancouver: Copp Clark Pitman.

Dwivedi, O.P., and Woodrow, R.B. (1989). Environmental policy-making and administration in a federal state: The impact of overlapping jurisdiction in Canada. In W. Chandler and C. Zollner (Eds.), *Challenges to federalism: Policy-making in Canada and the Federal Republic of Germany.* Kingston: Institute of Intergovernmental Relations.

Economic Council of Canada. (1979). *Responsible regulation.* Ottawa: Economic Council of Canada.

———. (1981). *Reforming regulation.* Ottawa: Economic Council of Canada.

———. (1986). *Minding the public's business.* Ottawa: Economic Council of Canada.

———. (1990a). *Good jobs, bad jobs.* Ottawa: Minister of Supply and Services.

———. (1990b). *Transitions for the 90s* (Twenty-Seventh Annual Review). Ottawa: Minister of Supply and Services.

———. (1991). *A joint venture: The economics of constitutional options* (Twenty-Eighth Annual Review). Ottawa: Minister of Supply and Services.

Elster, J., and Slagstad, R. (Eds.). (1989). *Constitutionalism and democracy.* Cambridge: Cambridge University Press.

Esping-Andersen, G. (1990). *The three worlds of welfare capitalism.* Princeton, NJ: Princeton University Press.

Esping-Andersen, G., and Korpi, W. (1984). Social policy as class politics in post-war capitalism: Scandinavia, Austria and Germany. In J.H. Goldthorpe (Ed.), *Order and conflict in contemporary capitalism* (179–208). New York and Oxford: Oxford University Press.

Evans, P.M., and McIntyre, E. (1987). Welfare, work incentives and the single mother. In J.S. Ismael (Ed.), *The Canadian welfare state.* Edmonton: University of Alberta Press.

Fenge, T., and Smith, L.G. (1986). Reforming the federal environmental assessment and review process. *Canadian Public Policy, 12,* 603.

Ferejohn, J., and Gaines, B. (1991). The personal vote in Canada. In H. Bakvis (Ed.), *Representation, integration and political parties in Canada* (Vol. 14, Research Studies of the Royal Commission on Electoral Reform and Party Financing). Toronto: Dundurn.

Finer, S.E. (1956). The individual responsibility of ministers. *Public Administration, 24,* 335–50.

Finlayson, J.A. (1985a). Canada, Congress and U.S. foreign economic policy. In D. Stairs and G.R. Winham (Research Co-ordinators). *The politics of Canada's economic relationship with the United States* (Vol. 29 of the Royal Commission on the Economic Union and Development Prospects for Canada, Collected Research Studies, 127–77). Toronto: University of Toronto Press.

———. (1985b). Canadian international economic policy: Context, issues and a review of some recent literature. In D. Stairs and G.R. Winham (Eds.), *Canada and the international political/economic environment* (Vol. 28 of the Royal Commission on the Economic Union and Development Prospects for Canada, 9–84). Toronto: University of Toronto Press.

Fletcher, F.J., and Wallace, D.C. (1986). Federal-provincial relations and the making of public policy in Canada: A review of case studies. In R. Simeon (Ed.), *Division of powers and public policy* (Vol. 61 of the Royal Commission on the Economic Union and Development Prospects for Canada, Collected Research Studies, 125–205). Toronto: University of Toronto Press.

Flora, P., and Heidenheimer, A.J. (Eds.). (1981). *The development of welfare states in Europe and America.* New Brunswick, NJ: Transaction Books.

Fortin, P. (1991). Credibility, controls or consensus: Is full employment without inflation out of reach in Canada? In J. Richards, R.D. Cairns, and L. Pratt (Eds.), *Social democracy without illusions: Renewal of the Canadian left.* Toronto: McClelland & Stewart.

Fournier, P. (1986). Consensus building in Canada: Case studies and prospects. In K. Banting (Ed.), *The state and economic interests.* Toronto: University of Toronto Press.

Freedman, C. (1986). Changes in the Canadian financial structure over the last decade. In Bank for International Settlements, *Financial Innovation and Monetary Policy.* Basel, Switzerland: BIS.

Freeman, G.P. (1985). National styles and policy sectors: Explaining structured variation. *Journal of Public Policy, 5,* 467–96.

———. (1990). Financial crisis and policy continuity in the welfare state. In P.A. Hall, J. Hayward, and H. Machin (Eds.), *Developments in French politics.* New York: St. Martin's Press.

Funabashi, Y. (1986). *Politics in hard times: Comparative responses to international economic crises.* Ithaca, NY: Cornell University Press.

———. (1988). *Managing the dollar: From the Plaza to the Louvre.* Washington, DC: Institute for International Economics.

Gertler, F., Muldoon, P., and Valiente, M. (1990). Public access to environmental justice. In Canadian Bar Association, *Sustainable development in Canada: Options for law reform.* Ottawa: Canadian Bar Association.

Gherson, G. (1990). Benoit Bouchard goes with the flow. *Financial Times* (November 19), 1.

Gibson, R. (1983). *Control orders and industrial pollution abatement in Ontario.* Toronto: Canadian Environmental Law Research Foundation.

Gormley, W.T. (1989). *Taming the bureaucracy: Muscles, prayers, and other strategies.* Princeton, NJ: Princeton University Press.

Gourevitch, P. (1986). Politics in hard times. Ithaca, NY: Cornell University Press.

———. (1989). Keynesian politics: The political sources of economic policy choices. In P.A. Hall (Ed.), *The political power of economic ideas: Keynesianism across nations.* Princeton, NJ: Princeton University Press.

Gowa, J. (1988). Public goods and political institutions: Trade and monetary policy processes in the United States. *International Organization, 42,* 15–32.

Graham, R. (1987). *One-eyed kings: Promise and illusion in Canadian politics.* Don Mills: Totem.

Granatstein, J.L. (1982). *The Ottawa men: The civil service mandarins, 1935–1957.* Toronto: Oxford University Press.

———. (1987). Free trade: The history of an issue. In M.D. Henderson (Ed.), *The future on the table: Canada and the free trade issue* (1–34). Toronto: Masterpress.

Greene, I. (1988). The doctrine of judicial independence developed by the Supreme Court of Canada. *Osgoode Hall Law Journal, 26* (1), 177.

———. (1989). *The Charter of Rights.* Toronto: Lorimer.

———. (1991). The administration of justice. In R.M. Krause and R.H. Wagenberg (Eds.), *Introductory readings in Canadian government and politics.* Mississauga: Copp Clark Pitman.

———. (forthcoming). Leave to appeal and leave to commence judicial review in Canada's refugee-determination system: Is the process fair? *Refugee Law Journal.*

Gruber, J.E. (1987). *Controlling bureaucracies: Dilemmas in democratic governance.* Berkeley: University of California Press.

Gunther, M., and Winn, C. (Eds.). (1991). *House of Commons reforms.* Ottawa: Parliamentary Internship Program.

Haddow, R. (1990). The poverty policy community in Canada's welfare state. In W.D. Coleman and G. Skogstad (Eds.), *Policy communities and public policy in Canada* (212–37). Toronto: Copp Clark Pitman.

———. (1991). The Canadian Labour Congress and the welfare state debate. [Paper presented at the annual meeting of the Canadian Political Science Association, Kingston, Ontario, June 2–4.]

Hall, P.A. (1986). *Governing the economy: The politics of state intervention in Britain and France.* Cambridge: Polity Press.

———. (1989). Introduction. In P.A. Hall (Ed.), *The political power of economic ideas: Keynesianism across nations.* Princeton, NJ: Princeton University Press.

Halpern, P., Plourde, A., and Waverman, L. (1988). *Petro Canada: Its role, control and operations.* Ottawa: Economic Council of Canada.

Harris, R.G. (1985). Summary of a project on the general equilibrium evaluation of Canadian trade policy. In J. Whalley (Research Co-ordinator), *Canada-United States free trade* (Vol. 2 of the Royal Commission on the Economic Union and Development Prospects for Canada, Collected Research Studies, 157–77). Toronto: University of Toronto Press.

Harris, R.G., and Milkis, S.M (1989). *The politics of regulatory change.* New York and Oxford: Oxford University Press.

Harrison, K. (1991). Federalism, environmental protection, and blame avoidance. [Paper presented to annual meetings of the Canadian Political Science Association, Kingston, Ontario, June 2–4.]

Harrison, K., and Hoberg, G. (1991). Setting the environmental agenda in Canada and the United States. *Canadian Journal of Political Science, 24,* 3–27.

Heclo, H. (1974). *Modern social politics in Britain and Sweden.* New Haven: Yale University Press.

———. (1981). Toward a new welfare state? In P. Flora and A.J. Heidenheimer (Eds.), *The Development of Welfare States in Europe and America* (383–406). New Brunswick, NJ: Transaction Books.

Heiber, S., and Deber, R. (1987). Banning extra-billing in Canada. *Canadian Public Policy, 13,* (1), 62–74.

Heidenheimer, A.J., Heclo, H., and Adams, C. Teich. (1990). *Comparative public policy: The politics of social choice in Europe and America* (3rd ed.). New York: St. Martin's Press.

Hiebert, J. (1989). Fair elections and freedom of expression under the Charter: Should interest groups' election expenditures be limited? *Journal of Canadian Studies, 24,* 72–86.

Hoberg, G. (1990). Reaganism, pluralism, and the politics of pesticide regulation. *Policy Sciences, 23,* 257–89.

———. (1991). Sleeping with an elephant: The American influence on Canadian environmental regulation. *Journal of Public Policy, 11,* 107–31.

———. (1992). *Pluralism by design: Environmental policy and the American regulatory state.* New York: Praeger.

Hodgetts, J.E. (1973). *The Canadian public service: A physiology of government 1967–1970.* Toronto: University of Toronto Press.

Hogg, P.W. (1985). *Constitutional law of Canada* (2nd ed). Toronto: Carswell.

Hogwood, B., and Gunn, L. (1984). *Policy analysis for the real world.* Oxford and New York: Oxford University Press.

Hogwood, B., and Peters, B.G. (1983). *Policy dynamics.* London: Wheatsheaf.

Hood, C. (1986). *The tools of government.* London: Chatham House. (First published in 1983.)

Horowitz, D. (1977). *The courts and social policy.* Washington: The Brookings Institution.

House of Commons. (1985). *Report of the special committee on reform of the House of Commons: Third report* (McGrath Report). Ottawa: Queen's Printer.

———. (1991). Annotated standing orders of the House of Commons. Ottawa: Minister of Supply and Services.

Howard, R. (1991). The greening of Jean Charest. *Globe and Mail* (May 11), D2.

———. (1991). Ottawa to give particle project millions in aid. *Globe and Mail* (September 20), A1.

Howlett, M. (1990). The round table experience: Representation and legitimacy in Canadian environmental policy-making. *Queen's Quarterly, 97,* 580–601.

Hult, K.M., and Walcott, C. (1990). *Governing public organizations: Politics, structures, and institutional design.* Pacific Grove, CA: Brooks/Cole.

Ingelhart, R. (1977). *The silent revolution.* Princeton, NJ: Princeton University Press.

———. (1981). Post-materialism in an environment of insecurity. *American Political Science Review, 75,* 880–900.

James, P., and Michelin, R. (1989). The Canadian national energy program and its aftermath: Perspectives on an era of confrontation. *American Review of Canadian Studies, 19,* 59–81.

Janisch, H.N. (1978). *The regulatory process of the Canadian Transport Commission.* Ottawa: Law Reform Commission of Canada.

———. (1979). Policy making in regulation: Towards a new definition of the status of independent agencies in Canada. *Osgoode Hall Law Journal, 17*, 46–106.

Janisch, H.N., et al. (1982). Reforming regulation. *Canadian Public Policy, 8*, 28–34.

Jenkin, M. (1983). *The challenge of diversity: Industrial policy in the Canadian federation* (Science Council of Canada, Background Study no. 50). Ottawa: Minister of Supply and Services.

Jennings, I. (1959). *The law and the constitution.* Oxford: Cambridge University Press.

Jenson, J. (1989a). "Different" but not "exceptional": Canada's permeable Fordism. *Canadian Review of Sociology and Anthropology, 26* (1), 69–94.

———. (1989b). Paradigms and political discourse: Protective legislation in France and the United States before 1914. *Canadian Journal of Political Science, 22*, 235–58.

———. (1990). Representations in crisis: The roots of Canada's permeable Fordism. *Canadian Journal of Political Science, 23* (4), 653–83.

Johnson, A. (1981). A minister as an agent of policy change: The case of unemployment insurance in the seventies. *Canadian Public Administration, 24*, 612–33.

Johnson, D.R. (1988). Regulatory agencies and accountability: A view from a small world. (Paper presented to the Canadian Political Science Association Annual Meeting, Windsor.)

———. (1990). An evaluation of the Bank of Canada zero inflation target: Do Michael Wilson and John Crow agree? *Canadian Public Policy, 16* (3), 308–26.

Johnson, N. (1977). *In search of the constitution: Reflections on state and society in Britain.* London: Methuen.

Johnston, C.C. (1980). *The Canadian Radio-television and Telecommunications Commission.* Ottawa: Law Reform Commission of Canada.

Jones, B., and Kavanagh, D. (1991). *British politics today.* Manchester: Manchester University Press.

Kaplan, H. (1989). *Policy and rationality: The regulation of Canadian trucking.* Toronto: University of Toronto Press.

Katzenstein, P. (1987). *Policy and politics in West Germany: The growth of a semisovereign state.* Philadelphia: Temple University Press.

Kelman, S. (1981). *Regulating America, regulating Sweden.* Cambridge, MA: MIT Press.

Kemp, P. (1990). Next steps for the British civil service. *Governance, 3*, 186–96.

Kent, T. (1988). *A public purpose.* Montreal: McGill-Queen's University Press.

King, A. (1973). Ideas, institutions and the policies of governments: A comparative analysis. *British Journal of Political Science, 3*, 291–314; 4, 409–23.

Kingdom, J.W. (1990a). Britain. In J.E. Kingdom (Ed.), *The civil service in liberal democracies.* London: Routledge.

———. (1990b). Canada. In J.E. Kingdom (Ed.), *The civil service in liberal democracies*. London: Routledge.

Kingdon, J.W. (1984). *Agendas, alternatives and public policies*. Boston: Little, Brown.

Kirkman-Liff, B.L. (1990). Physician payment and cost-containment strategies in West Germany. *Journal of Health Politics, Policy and Law, 15*, 1.

Kirsch, E. (1985). *Crown corporations as instruments of public policy: A legal and institutional perspective*. Ottawa: Economic Council of Canada.

Klein, R., and O'Higgins, M. (1988). Defusing the crisis of the welfare state. In T.R. Marmor and J.L. Mashaw (Eds.), *Social security: Beyond the rhetoric of crisis*. Princeton, NJ: Princeton University Press.

Knopff, R., and Morton, F.L. (1985). Nation-building and the Canadian Charter of Rights and Freedoms. In A. Cairns and C. Williams (Eds.), *Constitutionalism, citizenship, and society in Canada*. Toronto: University of Toronto Press.

Koerner, W. (1989). *Cabinet committees: Restructuring the system*. Ottawa: Library of Parliament, Research Branch.

Krasner, S.D. (1988). Sovereignty: An institutional perspective. *Comparative Political Studies, 21*, 66–94.

Krugman, P. (1990). *The age of diminished expectations: U.S. economic policy in the 1990s*. Cambridge, MA: MIT Press.

Kuttner, R. (1991). *The end of laissez-faire: National purpose and the global economy after the cold war*. New York: Alfred A. Knopf.

Lancaster, T., and Patterson, W.D. (1990). Comparative pork barrel politics. *Comparative Political Studies, 22*, 458–77.

Landes, R. (1991). *The Canadian polity: A comparative introduction* (3rd ed.). Scarborough: Prentice-Hall.

Langford, J. (1982). Public corporations in the 1980s: Moving from rhetoric to analysis. *Canadian Public Administration, 25*, 619–37.

———. (1983). The question of quangos: Quasi-public service agencies in British Columbia. *Canadian Public Administration, 26*, 563–76.

Latham, E. (1952). The group basis for politics. *American Political Science Review, 65*, 376–97.

Latouche, D. (1984). The organizational (counter)-culture of state owned enterprises: An exploratory study of the Quebec case. In R. Hirschorn (Ed.), *Government enterprises: Roles and rationale* Ottawa: Economic Council of Canada.

Laumann, E.O., and Knoke, D. (1987). *The organizational state*. Madison: University of Wisconsin Press.

Laux, J.K., and Appel Molot, M. (1988). *State capitalism: Public enterprise in Canada*. Ithaca, NY: Cornell University Press.

Law Reform Commission of Canada. (1980). *Independent administrative agencies*. Ottawa: Minister of Supply and Services.

———. (1985). *Report on independent administrative agencies: A framework for decision-making* (Report No. 26). Ottawa: Law Reform Commission of Canada.

———. (1986). *Towards a modern federal administrative law*. Ottawa: Minister of Supply and Services.

———. (1991). *The determination of refugee status in Canada: A review of the procedure* (Preliminary Study, consultative document). Ottawa: Law Reform Commission of Canada.

Laxer, G. (1989). *Open for business: The roots of foreign ownership in Canada*. Toronto: Oxford University Press.

Lazar, F. (1981). *The new protectionism: Non-tariff barriers and their effects on Canada*. Toronto: Lorimer.

Leman, C. (1977). Patterns of policy development: Social security in the United States and Canada. *Public Policy, 25,* 261–91.

Leslie, P.M. (1987). *Federal state, national economy*. Toronto: University of Toronto Press.

Lindberg, L. (1977). Energy policy and the politics of economic development. *Comparative Political Studies, 10,* 355–82.

Lindblom, C.E. (1959). The science of muddling through. *Public Administration Review, 19,* (2), 79–88.

———. (1977). *Politics and markets*. New York: Basic Books.

———. (1979). Still muddling: Not yet through. *Public Administration Review, 39,* (4), 517–27.

Lindquist, E. (1990). Even exorcists need theory: A new agenda for the literature on cabinet and budgetary systems. *Canadian Public Administration, 33,* 645–57.

Lipset, S.M. (1989). *Continental divide*. Toronto: C.D. Howe Institute.

Lipsey, R.G., and Smith, M.A. (1985). *Taking the initiative: Canada's trade options in a turbulent world*. Toronto: C.D. Howe Institute.

Louis, M.R. (1985). An investigator's guide to workplace culture. In P.J. Frost et al. (Eds.), *Organizational Culture*. Beverly Hills: Sage.

Lovink, J. (1973). Is Canadian politics too competitive? *Canadian Journal of Political Science, 6,* 341–79.

Lowi, T. (1979). *The end of liberalism* (2nd ed.). New York: Norton.

Lucas, A. (1989). The new environmental law. In A. Lucas (Ed.), *Canada: State of the federation, 1989*. Kingston, ON: Institute for Intergovernmental Relations.

Lush, P. (1991). Full review ordered on $1-billion project. *Globe and Mail* (May 17), A1.

Mahon, R. (1990). Adjusting to win? The new Tory training initiative. In K.A. Graham (Ed.), *How Ottawa spends 1990–91: Tracking the second agenda* (73–111). Ottawa: Carleton University Press.

———. (1991). Post-Fordism: Some issues for Labour. In D. Drache and M.S. Gertler (Eds.), *The new era of global competition: State power and market power* (316–32). Montreal and Kingston: McGill-Queen's University Press.

Mallory, J.R. (1957). Cabinets and councils in Canada. *Public Law,* (Autumn), 231–51.

———. (1977). Confederation: The ambiguous bargain. *Journal of Canadian Studies, 12*, (3), 18–23.

———. (1984). *The structure of Canadian government.* Toronto: Gage.

Mandel, M. (1989). *The Charter of Rights and the legalization of politics in Canada.* Toronto: Wall and Thompson.

Manitoba Court of Queen's Bench. (1986). *Badger et al. v. Attorney General of Manitoba.* [1986] 8 Charter of Rights Decisions 325–20–01.

Manzer, R. (1985). *Public policies and political development in Canada.* Toronto: University of Toronto Press.

March, J.G. (1988). *Decisions and organizations.* Oxford: Basil Blackwell.

March, J.G., and Olsen, J.P. (1984). The new institutionalism: Organizational factors in political life. *American Political Science Review, 78*, 734–49.

———. (1989). *Rediscovering institutions: The organizational basis of politics.* New York: Free Press.

March, J.G., and Simon, H. (1958). *Organizations.* New York: Wiley.

Marmor, T.R., Mashaw, J.L., and Harvey, P.L. (1990). *America's misunderstood welfare state.* New York: Basic Books.

Marshall, G., and Moodie, G.C. (1971). *Some problems of the constitution* (5th ed.). London: Hutchison University Library.

Maslove, A.M. (1989). *Tax reform in Canada.* Ottawa: Institute for Research on Public Policy.

Maslove, A.M., Prince, M.J., and Doern, G.B. (1986). *Federal and provincial budgeting.* Toronto: University of Toronto Press.

Matheson, W. (1977). The cabinet and the Canadian bureaucracy. In K. Kernaghan (Ed.), *Public Administration in Canada.* Toronto: Methuen.

Matzner, E., and Streeck, W. (1991). Introduction: Towards a socio-economics of employment in a post-Keynesian economy. In E. Matzner and W. Streeck (Eds.), *Beyond Keynesianism: Socio-economics of production and full employment.* Aldershot, England: Edward Elgar.

McBride, S. (1983). Public policy as a determinant of interest group behaviour: The Canadian Labour Congress' corporatist initiative, 1976–1978. *Canadian Journal of Political Science, 16*, (3), 501–17.

McCormick, P., and Greene, I. (1990). *Judges and judging: Inside the Canadian judicial system.* Toronto: Lorimer.

McCutcheon, S. (1991). *Electric rivers: The story of the James Bay project.* Montreal: Black Rose Books.

McDonnell, L.M., and Elmore, R.F. (1987). *Alternative policy instruments.* Santa Monica: Centre for Policy Research in Education.

McFetridge, D.G., and Corvari, R.J. (1985). Technological diffusion: A survey of Canadian evidence and public policy issues. In D.G. McFetridge (Research Co-ordinator), *Technological change in Canadian industry* (Vol. 3 of the Royal Commission on the Economic Union and Development Prospects for Canada, Collected Research Studies, 177–231). Toronto: University of Toronto Press.

McFetridge, D.G., and Warda, J.P. (1983). *Canadian R & D incentives: Their adequacy and impact* (Canadian Tax Paper No. 70). Toronto: Canadian Tax Foundation.

McKown, R. (1985). Legislatures. In T.C. Pocklington (Ed.), *Liberal democracy in Canada and the United States*. Toronto: Holt, Rinehart and Winston.

McRoberts, K. (1986). Unilateralism, bilateralism and multilateralism: Approaches to Canadian federalism. In R. Simeon (Ed.), *Intergovernmental relations*. (Vol. 63 of the Royal Commission on the Economic Union and Development Prospects for Canada, Collected Research Studies). Toronto: University of Toronto Press.

———. (1988). *Quebec: Social change and political crisis* (3rd. ed.). Toronto: McClelland & Stewart.

———. (1991). *English Canada and Quebec: Avoiding the issue.* Sixth Annual Robarts Lecture (Toronto: Robarts Centre for Canadian Studies, York University).

Melnick, R.S. (1983). *Regulation and the courts*. Washington, DC: The Brookings Institution.

———. (1989). The courts, Congress, and programmatic rights. In R. Harris and S. Milkis (Eds.), *Remaking American politics*. Boulder, CO: Westview Press.

Miller, D. (1991). Jurisdictional aspects of environment in Canada. [Presentation to Standing Committee on the Environment, September 26]. House of Commons, Ottawa.

Milne, D. (1991). Equality or asymmetry: Why choose? In R.L. Watts and D.M. Brown (Eds.), *Options for a new Canada*. Toronto: University of Toronto Press.

Moe, T.M. (1984). The new economics of organization. *American Journal of Political Science, 28,* 739-77.

———. (1989). The politics of bureaucratic structure. In J. Chubb and P. Peterson (Eds.), *Can the government govern?* Washington, DC: The Brookings Institution.

———. (1990). The politics of structural choice: Toward a theory of public bureaucracy. In O.E. Williamson (Ed.), *Organization theory: From Chester Barnard to the present and beyond*. Princeton, NJ: Princeton University Press.

Monahan, P. (1987). *Politics and the Constitution.* Toronto: Carswell/Methuen.

Morici, P. (1984). *The global competitive struggle: Challenges to the United States and Canada*. Washington, DC: C.D. Howe Institute and National Planning Association.

———. (1991). *A new special relationship: Free trade and U.S.-Canada economic relations in the 1990s.* Halifax: Institute for Research on Public Policy and the Centre for Trade Policy and Law.

Morici, P., Smith, A.J.R.,and Lea, S. (1982). *Canadian industrial policy.* Washington, DC: National Planning Association.

Morton, F.L. (1987). The political impact of the Canadian Charter of Rights and Freedoms. *Canadian Journal of Political Science, 18,* 31-55.

Morton, F.L., and Withey, M.J. (1986). *Charting the Charter, 1982–1985: A statistical analysis* (Occasional Papers Series, Research Study 21). University of Calgary: Research Unit for Socio-Legal Studies.

Mosher, F.C. ([1982] 1968). *Democracy and the public service.* New York and Oxford: Oxford University Press.

Muldoon, P. (1988). The fight for an environmental bill of rights. *Alternatives, 15,* 33–39.

Mullan, D.J. (1985). Administrative tribunals: Their evolution in Canada from 1945–1984. In I. Bernier and A. Lajoie (Eds.), *Regulations, crown corporations and administrative tribunals.* Toronto: University of Toronto Press.

Myles, J. (1989). *Old age in the welfare state* (rev. ed.). Lawrence, KS: University Press of Kansas.

National Council of Welfare. (1990). *Welfare incomes 1989.* Ottawa: Minister of Supply and Services.

National Task Force on Environment and Economy. (1987). *Report* (Submitted to Canadian Council of Resources and Environment Ministers, September 24.)

Nelles, H.V. (1974). *The politics of development: Forest, mines and hydro-electric power in Ontario 1849–1941.* Toronto: Macmillan.

Nemetz, P. (1986). The Fisheries Act and federal-provincial environmental regulation: Duplication or complementarity? *Canadian Public Administration, 29,* 401–24.

Nemetz, P., Stanbury, W.T., and Thompson, F. (1986). Social regulation in Canada. *Policy Studies Journal, 14,* 580–603.

Nevitte, N., Gibbins, R., and Bakvis, H. (1989). The ideological contours of new politics in Canada: Policy, mobilization and partisan support. *Canadian Journal of Political Science, 22,* 475–503.

Newman, P. (1963). *Renegade in power.* Toronto: McClelland & Stewart.

———. (1968). *The distemper of our times.* Toronto: McClelland & Stewart.

Niagara Institute. (1985). *The environment, jobs, and the economy: Building a partnership.* (Final Project Report).

Niosi, J. (1980). *La Bourgeoisie canadienne: La formation et le développement d'une classe dominante.* Montréal: Boréal Express.

Niskanen, W.A. (1971). *Bureaucracy and representative government.* Chicago: Rand McNally.

Noel, S.J.R. (1987). Dividing the spoils: The old and the new rules of patronage in Canadian politics. *Journal of Canadian Studies, 22,* 72–95.

Nordlinger, E.A. (1981). *On the autonomy of the democratic state.* Cambridge, MA: Harvard University Press.

Norrie, K., Simeon, R., and Krasnick, M. (1986). *Federalism and economic union in Canada.* (Vol. 59 of the Royal Commission on the Economic Union and Development Prospects for Canada, Collected Research Studies, 140–82). Toronto: University of Toronto Press.

O'Connor, J.S. (1988). Convergence or divergence: Change in welfare state effort in OECD nations 1960–1980. *European Journal of Political Research, 16,* 277–99.

Olmstead, R.A. (1954). *Decisions of the judicial committee of the Privy Council relating to the British North America Act, 1867 and the Canadian constitution 1867–1954* (94–124). Ottawa: Queen's Printer.

Ontario. (1989). *Review of Ontario's regulatory agencies.* Toronto: Queen's Printer.

———. (1990). Ministry of Health. *Prescriptions for health: Report of the pharmaceutical inquiry of Ontario.* Toronto: Ministry of Health.

———. (1991a). Ministry of Intergovernmental Affairs. *A Canadian social charter: Making our shared values stronger.* Toronto: Ministry of Intergovernmental Affairs.

———. (1991b). Ministry of Labour. *Proposed Reform of the Ontario Labour Relations Act* (Discussion Paper). Toronto: Ministry of Labour.

Ontario Law Reform Commission. (1989). *Report on the law of standing.* Toronto: Ministry of the Attorney General.

Organization for Economic Cooperation and Development (OECD). (1989). *OECD in figures.* Supplement to *The OECD Observer, 158,* (June/July).

Ostrom, E. (1990). *Governing the commons: The evolution of institutions for collective action.* Cambridge: Cambridge University Press.

Oziewicz, E. (1991). Refugee delays ruled unlawful. *Globe and Mail* (October 10), A1.

Paehlke, R. (1989). *Environmentalism and the future of progressive politics.* New Haven: Yale University Press.

———. (1991). Government regulating itself: A Canadian-American comparison. *Administration and Society, 22,* 424–50.

Page, E.C. (1989). Comparing bureaucracies. In J.-E. Lane (Ed.), *Bureaucracy and Public Choice.* London: Sage.

Painter, M. (1991). Intergovernmental relations in Canada: An institutional analysis. *Canadian Journal of Political Science, 24,* (2) (June), 269–88.

Pal, L.A. (1987). *Public policy analysis: An introduction.* Toronto: Methuen.

———. (1988). *State, class and bureaucracy: Canadian unemployment insurance and public policy.* Montreal: McGill-Queen's University Press.

Pal, L.A., and Morton, F.L. (1985). Impact of the Charter of Rights on public administration. *Canadian Public Administration, 25,* 221–43.

Parris, H. (1969). *Constitutional bureaucracy.* London: George Allen and Unwin.

Pennock, J.R., and Chapman, J.W. (1977). *Human nature in politics.* New York: New York University Press.

Perrow, C. (1986). *Complex organizations: A critical essay* (3rd ed.). New York: Random House.

Peters, B.G. (1989a). *The politics of bureaucracy* (3rd ed.). White Plains: Longman.

———. (1989b). Politicians and bureaucrats in the politics of policy-making. In J.-E. Lane (Ed.), *Bureaucracy and Public Choice.* London: Sage.

Phidd, R.W., and Doern, G.B. (1978). *The politics and management of Canadian economic policy.* Toronto: Macmillan.

Pierson, P.D., and Weaver, R.K. (1992). Political institutions and loss imposition: The case of pensions. In R.K. Weaver and B.A. Rockman (Eds.), *Do institutions matter?* Washington: The Brookings Institution.

Pilkington, M.L. (1988). Free trade and constitutional jurisdiction. In M. Gold and D. Leyton-Brown (Eds.), *Trade-offs on free trade: The Canada-U.S. free trade agreement.* Toronto: Carswell.

Poggi, G. (1990). *The state: Its nature, development and prospects.* Cambridge: Polity Press.

Porter, J. (1958). Higher public servants and the bureaucratic elite in Canada. *Canadian Journal of Economics and Political Science, 24,* 483–501.

Porter, M.E. (1991). *Canada at the crossroads: The reality of a new competitive environment.* Ottawa: Business Council on National Issues and Minister of Supply and Services.

Pressman, J.L., and Wildavsky, A. (1973). *Implementation: How great expectations in Washington are dashed in Oakland.* Berkeley: University of California Press.

Presthus, R. (1973). *Elite accommodation in Canadian politics.* Toronto: Macmillan.

Prichard, J.R.S., and Trebilcock, M.J. (1983). Crown corporations: The calculus of instrument choice. In J.R.S. Prichard (Ed.), *Crown corporations in Canada: The calculus of instrument choice.* Toronto: Butterworth.

Prince, M.J. (1991). From Meech Lake to Golden Pond: The elderly, pension reform and federalism in the 1990s. In F. Abele (Ed.), *How Ottawa spends: The politics of fragmentation, 1991–92.* Ottawa: Carleton University Press.

Prince, M.J., and Rice, J.J. (1989). The Canadian jobs strategy: Supply side social policy. In K.A. Graham (Ed.), *How Ottawa spends 1989–90: The buck stops where?* (247–87). Ottawa: Carleton University Press.

Pross, A.P. (1982). Space, function, and interest: The problem of legitimacy in the Canadian state. In O.P. Dwivedi (Ed.), *The administrative state in Canada.* Toronto: University of Toronto Press.

———. (1986). *Group politics and public policy.* Toronto: Oxford University Press.

Purvis, D.D., and Smith, C. (1986). Fiscal policy in Canada: 1963–1984. In J. Sargent (Ed.), *Fiscal and monetary policy.* Toronto: University of Toronto Press.

Quadagno, J. (1988). *The transformation of old age security.* Chicago: University of Chicago Press.

Qualter, T. (1986). *Conflicting political ideas in liberal democracies.* Toronto: Methuen.

Quebec Liberal Party (1991). *A Quebec Free to Choose* (Allaire Report). Report of the Constitutional Committee of the Quebec Liberal Party.

Rabkin, J. (1989). *Judicial compulsions.* New York: Basic Books.

Rainey, H.G. (1991). *Understanding and managing public organizations.* San Francisco: Jossey-Bass.

Reagan, M.D. (1987). *Regulation: The politics of policy.* Toronto: Little, Brown.

Rees, W. (1980). EARP at the crossroads: Environmental assessment in Canada. *Environmental Impact Assessment Review, 1,* 355–77.

Reich, R.B. (1991). *The work of nations: Preparing ourselves for 21st-century capitalism.* New York: Alfred A. Knopf.

Resnick, P. (1990). *The masks of Proteus: Canadian reflections on the state.* Montreal: McGill-Queen's University Press.

Richards, J. (1991). Playing two games at once. In J. Richards, R.D. Cairns, and L. Pratt (Eds.), *Social democracy without illusions* (107–31). Toronto: McClelland & Stewart.

Richards, J., and Pratt, L. (1979). *Prairie capitalism: Power and influence in the new West.* Toronto: McClelland & Stewart.

Richardson, J. (Ed.). (1982). *Policy styles in Western Europe.* London: George Allen and Unwin.

Riker, W.H. (1964). *Federalism: Origin, operation, significance.* Boston: Little, Brown.

———. (1980). Implications from the disequilibrium of majority rule for the study of institutions. *American Political Science Review, 74,* 432–46.

Robertson, G. (1971). The changing role of the Privy Council Office. *Canadian Public Administration, 14,* (4), 487–508.

Roman, A. (1982). Legal constraints on regulatory tribunals. *Queen's Law Journal, 9,* 35–61.

———. (1985). Governmental control of tribunals: Appeals, directives, and non-statutory mechanisms. *Queen's Law Journal, 10,* 476–97.

Roman, A. (1989). *Effective advocacy before administrative tribunals.* Toronto: Carswell.

Rose, R. (1987). Giving directions to permanent officials: Signals from the electorate, the market, laws and expertise. In J.-E. Lane (Ed.), *Bureaucracy and Public Choice.* London: Sage.

Roth, D. (1990). Innovation in government: The case of special operating agencies. *Consulting and Audit Canada,* (September), 1–7.

Rothbard, M. (1982). *The ethics of liberty.* Atlantic Highlands, NJ: Humanities Press.

Rugman, A.M., and Anderson, A.D.M. (1987). *Administered protection in America.* London: Croom Helm.

Russell, P.H. (1982). The Supreme Court decision: Bold statecraft based on questionable jurisprudence. In P.H. Russell et al., *The Court and the Constitution.* Queens University Press, Kingston, Ontario: Institute of Intergovernmental Relations.

———. (1983). The political purposes of the Canadian Charter of Rights and Freedoms. *Canadian Bar Review, 61,* 30–54.

———. (1985). The first three years in Charterland. *Canadian Public Administration, 25,* 367.

———. (1987). *The judiciary in Canada: The third branch of government.* Toronto: McGraw-Hill Ryerson.

———. (1988a). Canada's Charter of Rights and Freedoms: A political report. *Public Law* (U.K.), 385–98.

———. (1988b). The constitutional dimension. In J. Crispo (Ed.), *Free trade: The real story* (161–69). Toronto: Gage.

Russell, P.H., Knopff, R., and Morton, F.L. (Eds.). (1989). *Federalism and the Charter: Leading constitutional decisions* (5th ed.). Ottawa: Carleton University Press.

Russell, P.H., and Zeigel, J.S. (1989). Federal judicial appointments: An appraisal of the first Mulroney government's appointments. (Paper presented to the 1989 Annual Meetings of the Canadian Political Science Association and the Canadian Law and Society Association.)

Sabatier, P.A. (1987). Knowledge, policy-oriented learning, and policy change. *Knowledge, 8*, 649–92.

Sabetti, F. (1984). The historical context of constitutional change in Canada. In P. Davenport and R. Leach (Eds.), *Reshaping Confederation: The 1982 reform of the Canadian Constitution* (11–32). Durham, NC: Duke University Press.

Sarpkaya, S. (1984). *The money market in Canada* (3rd ed.). Toronto: CCH Canadian.

Savas, E.S. (1982). *Privatizing the public sector.* Chatham, NJ: Chatham House.

Savoie, D.J. (1990). *The politics of public spending in Canada.* Toronto: University of Toronto Press.

Saxe, D. (1989). Fines go up dramatically in environmental cases. *Canadian Environmental Law Reports, 3*, (N.S.), 104–21.

Scharpf, F.W. (1988). The joint-decision trap: Lessons from German federalism and European integration. *Public Administration, 66*, (Autumn), 239–78.

———. (1989). Decision rules, decision styles and policy choices. *Journal of Theoretical Politics, 2*, 149–76.

———. (1990). The political calculus of inflation and unemployment in western Europe: A game theoretical perspective. In R. Czada and A. Windhoff-Héritier (Eds.), *Political choice: Institutions, rules and the limits of rationality.* Frankfurt/Boulder, CO: Campus/Westview.

———. (1991). *Crisis and choice in European social democracy.* (R. Crowley and F. Thompson, Trans.). Ithaca, NY: Cornell University Press.

Schattschneider, E.E. (1960). *The semi-sovereign people.* New York: Holt, Rinehart and Winston.

Schein, E.H. (1985). *Organizational culture and leadership.* San Francisco: Jossey-Bass.

Schieber, G.J. (1985). Health spending: Its growth and control. *The OECD Observer* (13–19). November.

Schieber, G.J., and Poullier, J.-P. (1987). Recent trends in international health care spending. *Health Affairs,* (Fall), 105–12.

———. (1988). International health spending and utilization trends. *Health Affairs* (Fall), 105–12.

Schrecker, T. (1984). *The political economy of environmental hazards*. Ottawa: Law Reform Commission.

———. (1990). Resisting environmental regulation: The cryptic pattern of business-government relations. In R. Paehlke and D. Torgerson (Eds.), *Managing leviathan: Environmental politics and the administrative state*. Peterborough: Broadview Press.

———. (1991). The Canadian Environmental Assessment Act: Tremulous step forward to retreat into smoke and mirrors? *Canadian Environmental Law Reports, 5*, (March), 192–246.

———. (1992). Of invisible beasts and the public interest: Environmental cases and the judicial system. In R. Boardman (Ed.), *Canadian Environmental Policy*. Toronto: Oxford University Press.

Schultz, R. (1982a). Regulation and public administration. *Canadian Public Administration, 25*, 638–52.

———. (1982b). Regulatory agencies and the dilemmas of delegation. In O.P. Dwivedi (Ed.), *The administrative state in Canada: Essays in honour of J.E. Hodgetts*. Toronto: University of Toronto Press.

———. (1982c). Regulatory agencies and the political system. In K. Kernaghan (Ed.), *Public administration in Canada*. Toronto: Methuen.

———. (1988). Regulating conservatively: The Mulroney record. In A. Gollner and O. Salée (Eds.), *Canada under Mulroney*. Montreal: Véhicule Press.

Schultz, R., and Alexandroff, A. (1985). *Economic regulation and the federal system*. Toronto: University of Toronto Press.

Scott, B. (1990). Creating comparative advantage. In P. King (Ed.), *International economics and international economic policy: A reader* (78–90). New York: McGraw-Hill.

Searing, D.D. (1991). Roles, rules and rationality in the new institutionalism. *American Political Science Review, 85*, 1239–60.

Shepsle, K.A. (1986). Institutional equilibrium and equilibrium institutions. In H.F. Weisberg (Ed.), *Political science: The science of politics*. New York: Agathon.

———. (1989). Studying institutions: Some lessons from the rational choice approach. *Journal of Theoretical Politics, 2*, 131–47.

Simeon, R.J. (1972). *Federal-provincial diplomacy: The making of public policy in Canada*. Toronto: University of Toronto Press.

Simeon, R., and Robinson, I. (1990). *State, society and the development of Canadian federalism*. (Vol. 71 of the Royal Commission on the Economic Union and Development Prospects for Canada, Collected Research Studies). Toronto: University of Toronto Press.

Simon, H. (1956). *Models of man*. New York: John Wiley.

Skocpol, T. (1980). Political response to the capitalist crisis: Neo-marxist theories of the state and the case of the new deal. *Politics and Society, 10*, (1980), 155–201.

———. (1985). Bringing the state back in: Strategies of analysis in current research. In P.B. Evans, D. Rueschemeyer, and T. Skocpol (Eds.), *Bringing the state back in*. Cambridge: Cambridge University Press.

Skocpol, T., and Finegold, K. (1982). State capacity and economic intervention in the early new deal. *Political Science Quarterly, 97*, 255–78.

Skogstad, G. (1987). *The politics of agricultural policy-making in Canada.* Toronto: University of Toronto Press.

Smeeding, T., Torrey, B., and Rein, M. (1988). Patterns of income and poverty: The economic status of children and the elderly in eight countries. In I. Palmer, T. Smeeding, and B. Torrey, (Eds.), *The vulnerable* (89–119). Washington, DC: The Urban Institute.

Smiley, D.V. (1980). *Canada in question: Federalism in the eighties* (3rd ed.). Toronto: McGraw-Hill Ryerson.

———. (1983). Central institutions. In S. Beck and I. Bernier (Eds.), *Canada and the new constitution: The unfinished agenda.* Montreal: Institute for Research on Public Policy.

———. (1987). *The federal condition in Canada.* Toronto: McGraw-Hill Ryerson.

Smiley, D.V., and Watts, R.V. (1985). *Intrastate federalism in Canada* (Vol. 39 of the Royal Commission on the Economic Union and Development Prospects for Canada, Collected Research Studies). Toronto: University of Toronto Press.

Smith, B.C. (1988). *Bureaucracy and political power.* Sussex: Wheatsheaf Books.

Smith, D. (1985). Party government, representation and national integration in Canada. In P. Aucoin (Ed.), *Party government and regional representation in Canada* (Vol. 36 of the Royal Commission on the Economic Union and Development Prospects for Canada, Collected Research Studies). Toronto: University of Toronto Press.

Sparks, G.R. (1986). The theory and practice of monetary policy in Canada, 1945–1983. In J. Sargent (Ed.), *Fiscal and monetary policy.* Toronto: University of Toronto Press.

Stanbury, W.T. (1989). Privatization in Canada: Ideology, symbolism or substance. In P. MacAvoy et al. (Eds.), *Privatization and State Owned Enterprises: Lessons from the United States, Great Britain and Canada.* Boston: Kluwer Academic Publishers.

———. (1991). Controlling the growth of provincial governments: The role of privatization. In M. McMillan (Ed.), *Provincial public finances: Plaudits, problems and prospects* (Vol. 2). Toronto: Canadian Tax Foundation.

Stanbury, W.T., and Thompson, F. (1980). The scope and coverage of regulation in Canada and the United States: Implications for the demand for reform. In W.T. Stanbury (Ed.), *Government regulation: Scope, growth, process.* Montreal: Institute for Research on Public Policy.

Steinmo, S. (1989). Political institutions and tax policy in the United States, Sweden, and Britain. *World Politics, 41*, 500–35.

Stevens, D.F. (1991). Corporate autonomy and institutional control: The crown corporation as a problem in organizational design. *Canadian Public Administration, 34*, 286–311.

Stevenson, G. (1977). Federalism and the political economy of the federal state. In L. Panitch (Ed.), *The Canadian state: Political economy and political power* (71–100). Toronto: University of Toronto Press.

———. (1989). *Unfulfilled union: Canadian federalism and national unity* (3rd ed.). Toronto: Gage.

Stewart, J. (1977). *The Canadian House of Commons: Procedure and reform*. Montreal: McGill University Press.

Stewart, G. (1986). *The origins of Canadian politics: A comparative approach*. Vancouver: UBC Press.

Stewart, I.A. (1991). How much government is good government? In G.B. Doern and B.B. Purchase (Eds.), *Canada at risk? Canadian public policy in the 1990s* (91–100). Toronto: C.D. Howe Institute.

Stone, F. (1984). *Canada, the GATT and the international trade system*. Montreal: Institute for Research on Public Policy.

Struthers, J. (1983). *No fault of their own: Unemployment and the Canadian welfare state, 1914–1941*. Toronto: University of Toronto Press.

Sunstein, C. (1990). *After the rights revolution*. Cambridge, MA: Harvard University Press.

Supreme Court of Canada. (1976). *Reference re Anti-inflation Act*. [1976] 2 SCR 373.

———. (1981). *Attorney General of Manitoba et al. v. Attorney General of Canada et al*. [1981] 2 SCR 753.

———. (1985a). Re Manitoba Language Rights (*Order*). [1985] 2 SCR 347.

———. (1985b). *Singh et al. v. Minister of Employment and Immigration*. [1985] 1 SCR 177.

———. (1985c). *Regina v. Big M Drug Mart Ltd. et al*. [1985] 1 SCR 295.

———. (1985d). *Regina v. Therens et al*. [1985] 1 SCR 640.

———. (1986). *The Queen v. Oakes*. [1986] 1 SCR 103.

———. (1987a). *Reference re Bill 30, An Act to Amend the Education Act (Ontario)*. [1987] 1 SCR 1148.

———. (1987b). *Reference re Public Service Employee Relations Act (Alta.)*. [1987] 1 SCR 313 (Alberta Labour Reference).

———. (1988a). *Ford v. Attorney General of Québec* [1988] 2 SCR 712.

———. (1988b). *Regina v. Morgentaler*. [1988] 1 SCR 30.

Sutherland, S.L. (1987). Federal bureaucracy: The pinch test. In M.J. Prince (Ed.), *How Ottawa Spends 1987–88* (38–129). Toronto: Methuen.

———. (1990). The evolution of program budget ideas in Canada: Does Parliament benefit from estimates reform? *Canadian Public Administration, 33*, (2), 133–64.

———. (1991a). Responsible government and ministerial responsibility: Every reform is its own problem. *Canadian Journal of Political Science, 24*, (1), 91–120.

———. (1991b). The Al-Mashat affair: Administrative accountability in parliamentary institutions. *Canadian Public Administration, 34*, 573–603.

———. (1991c). Inexperienced ministers 1949 to 1990: The consequences of electoral volatility. In H. Bakvis (Ed.), *Representation, integration and political parties in Canada* (Vol. 14, Research Studies of the Royal Commission on Electoral Reform and Party Financing). Toronto: Dundurn.

Sutherland, S.L., and Baltacioglu, Y. (1988). *Parliamentary reform and the federal public service.* London, ON: National Centre for Management Research and Development, University of Western Ontario.

Sutherland, S.L., and Doern, G.B. (1985). *Bureaucracy in Canada: Control and reform* (Vol. 43 of the Royal Commission on the Economic Union and Development Prospects for Canada, Collected Research Studies). Toronto: University of Toronto Press.

Swaigen, J. (Ed.). (1981). *Environmental rights in Canada.* Toronto: Butterworths.

Sweeney, T., and Robertson, C. (1989). Income tax incentives for Canadian research and development. *Canadian Tax Journal, 37,* (2), 310–40.

Tarasofsky, A. (1984). *The subsidization of innovation projects by the government of Canada* (Study prepared for the Economic Council of Canada). Ottawa: Minister of Supply and Services.

Tate, C. N., and Sittiwong, P. (1989). Decision making in the Canadian Supreme Court: Extending the personal attributes model across nations. *Journal of Politics, 51,* 900–16.

Taylor, M.G. (1978). *Health insurance and Canadian public policy.* Montreal: McGill-Queen's University Press.

Thomas, P. (1991). Regionalism, parliament and party caucuses. In H. Bakvis (Ed.), *Representation, integration and political parties in Canada* (Vol. 14, Research Studies of the Royal Commission on Electoral Reform and Party Financing). Toronto: Dundurn.

Thompson, A. (1980). *Environmental regulation in Canada.* (Study prepared for the Economic Council of Canada by the Westwater Research Centre, University of British Columbia).

Thorburn, H.G. (1984). *Planning and the economy: Building federal-provincial consensus.* Ottawa: Canadian Institute for Economic Policy.

Titmuss, R. (1958). *Essays on the welfare state.* London: George Allen and Unwin.

Tobacco Advisory Council. (1992). Hear the other side. Advertisement in *The Times* (February 13), 8–9. London, England.

Toner, G. (1990). Whence and whither: ENGOs, business, and the environment (8–10). (Paper presented to a conference sponsored by the Department of Political Science, Carleton University, February 1990). Ottawa.

Trudeau, P.E. (1968). *Federalism and the French Canadians.* Toronto: Macmillan.

Tuohy, C. (1982). Regulation and scientific complexity: Decision rules and processes in the occupational health arena. *Osgoode Hall Law Journal, 20,* 562–609.

———. (1988). Medicine and the state in Canada: The extra-billing issue in perspective. *Canadian Journal of Political Science, 21,* (2), 268–96.

———. (1989). Federalism and Canadian health care policy. In W.M. Chandler and C.W. Zollner (Eds.), *Challenges to federalism: Policy-making in Canada and the Federal Republic of Germany* (141–60). Kingston, ON: Queen's University Institute for Intergovernmental Relations.

———. (1992). *Policy and politics in Canada: Institutionalized Ambivalence.* Philadelphia: Temple University Press.

Tupper, A. (1985). The Civil Service. In T.C. Pocklington (Ed.), *Liberal democracy in Canada and the United States.* Toronto: Holt, Rinehart and Winston.

Tupper, A., and Doern, G.B. (Eds.). (1981). *Public Corporations and Public Policy.* Montreal: Institute for Research on Public Policy.

———. (Eds.). (1988). *Privatization, Public Policy and Public Corporations in Canada.* Halifax: Institute for Research on Public Policy.

Turcotte, C. (1991). Québec axera le développement autour de 13 secteurs industriels, *Le Devoir* (December 3), A1, A4. Montreal.

United States. (1991). Joint Committee on Taxation. *Factors affecting the international competitiveness of the United States.* (JCS-6-91).

Vandervort, L. (1980). *Political control of independent administrative agencies.* Ottawa: Law Reform Commission of Canada.

Van Loon, R. (1983). The policy and expenditure management system in the federal government: The first three years. *Canadian Public Administration, 26,* 255–85.

Van Loon, R., and Whittington, M.S. (1981). *The Canadian political system: Environment, structure and process* (3rd ed.). Toronto: McGraw-Hill Ryerson.

Vaughan, F. (1986). Critics of the judicial committee of the Privy Council: The new orthodoxy and an alternative explanation. *Canadian Journal of Political Science, 19,* (3) (September), 495–520; A.C. Cairns, Comment, *Canadian Journal of Political Science, 19,* (3) (September), 521–30; P.H. Russell, Comment, *Canadian Journal of Political Science, 19,* (3) (September), 531–36; and F. Vaughan, Reply, *Canadian Journal of Political Science, 19,* (3) (September), 537–39.

Verney, D.V. (1986). *Three civilizations, two cultures, one state: Canada's political traditions.* Durham, NC: Duke University Press.

Vigod, T. (1990). Canadian Environmental Law Association, Testimony. *Minutes of Proceedings and Evidence.* House of Commons. Special Committee to Pre-Study Bill C-78. 34th Parl., 2nd Sess. No. 8 (November 20, 1990).

Visser, J. (1984). *The position of central confederations in the national union movement: A ten-country comparison* (EUI Working Paper No. 102). Florence: European University Institute.

Vogel, D. (1986). *National styles of regulation.* Ithaca, NY: Cornell University Press.

Waite, P. (1986). Becoming Canadians: Ottawa's relations with Maritimers in the first and twenty-first years of confederation. In R.K. Carty and P. Ward (Eds.), *National politics and community in Canada.* Vancouver: UBC Press.

Watkins, M. (1988). Investment. In D. Cameron (Ed.), *The free trade deal* (83–90). Toronto: Lorimer.

Weale, A. (1990). Social policy. In P. Dunleavy, A. Gamble, and G. Peale (Eds.), *Developments in British politics.* New York: St. Martin's Press.

Weaver, R.K. (1984). Government enterprises in competitive markets. In R. Hirschorn (Ed.), *Government enterprises: Roles and rationales.* Ottawa: Economic Council of Canada.

———. (1986). The politics of blame avoidance. *Journal of Public Policy*, 6, 371-98.

Weaver, R.K., and Rockman, B.A. (Eds.). (1992). *Do institutions matter?* Washington: The Brookings Institution.

Weber, M. (1922). *Economy and society* (2 vols.). G. Roth and C. Wittich (Eds.). New York: Bedminster Press, 1968.

Webb, K. (1990). Between rocks and hard places: Bureaucrats, law, and pollution control. In R. Paehlke and D. Torgerson (Eds.), *Managing leviathan: Environmental politics and the administrative state*. Peterborough: Broadview Press.

Weir, M. (1989). Ideas and politics: The acceptance of Keynesianism in Britain and the United States. In P. Hall (Ed.), *The political power of economic ideas: Keynesianism across nations*. Princeton, NJ: Princeton University Press.

Weir, M., and Skocpol, T. (1985). State structure and the possibilities for Keynesian response to the Great Depression in Sweden, Britain and the United States. In P.B. Evans, D. Rueschemeyer, and T. Skocpol (Eds.), *Bringing the state back in*. Cambridge: Cambridge University Press.

Whitaker, R. (1977). *The government party*. Toronto: University of Toronto Press.

———. (1987). Between patronage and bureaucracy. *Journal of Canadian Studies*, 22, 55-71.

Wilson, D. (1991). Mountains—and a hydro project—divide smelter town from native band. *Globe and Mail* (December 14), A1.

Wilson, J. (1992). Green lobbies: Pressure groups and environmental policy. In R. Boardman (Ed.), *Canadian Environmental Policy*. Toronto: Oxford University Press.

Wilson, G.K. (1985). *The politics of safety and health*. Oxford: Clarendon Press.

Wilson, J.Q. (1973). *Political organizations*. New York: Basic Books.

———. (1989). *Bureaucracy: What government agencies do and why they do it*. New York: Basic Books.

Wilson, J.Q., and Rachal, P. (1977). Can the government regulate itself? *Public Interest*, 46, 3-14.

Windsor, H. (1991). Canadians have turned a lighter shade of green. *Globe and Mail* (April 24), A6.

Wolfe, D. (1985). The politics of the deficit. In G.B Doern (Ed.), *The politics of economic policy*. Toronto: University of Toronto Press.

Wonnacott, P. (1987). *The United States and Canada: The quest for free trade*. Washington, DC: Institute for International Economics.

Wonnacott, R.J. (1991). Reconstructing North American free trade following Quebec's separation: What can be assumed? In G. Ritchie et al., *Broken Links: Trade Relations after a Quebec Secession* (20-44). Toronto: C.D. Howe Institute.

Woodrow, R.B. (1978). *The development and implementation of federal pollution control policy and programs in Canada, 1966-1974*. [Ph.D. Dissertation]. University of Toronto.

———. (1980). Resources and environmental policy-making at the national level: The search for focus. In O.P. Dwivedi (Ed.), *Resources and the environment: Policy perspectives for Canada*. Toronto: McClelland & Stewart.

Woodrow, R.B., and Woodside, K.B. (1986). Players, stakes and politics in the future of telecommunications regulation in Canada. In W.T. Stanbury (Ed.), *Telecommunications policy and regulation: The impact of competition and technological change* (101–288). Halifax: Institute for Research on Public Policy.

Woolley, J.T. (1985). Central banks and inflation. In L.N. Lindberg and C.S. Maier (Eds.), *The politics of inflation and economic stagnation*. Washington: The Brookings Institution.

World Commission on Environment and Development. (1987). *Our common future*. Oxford: Oxford University Press.

Yates, C. (1990). Labour and lobbying: A political economy approach. In W.D. Coleman and G. Skogstad (Eds.), *Policy communities and public policy in Canada: A structural approach*. Toronto: Copp Clark Pitman.

Young, R.A. (1991). Effecting change: Do we have the political system to get us where we want to go? In G.B. Doern and B.B. Purchase (Eds.), *Canada at risk? Canadian public policy in the 1990s* (59–81). Toronto: C.D. Howe Institute.

Zussman, D. (1986). Walking the tightrope: The Mulroney government and the public service. In M.J. Prince (Ed.), *How Ottawa spends 1986–87* (250–83). Toronto: Methuen.

Glossary

Accountability An obligation on the part of an individual or group to reveal, to explain, and to justify the discharge of responsibilities whose origins may be political, constitutional, statutory, or contractual.

Adjudication The decision-making process employed by courts demanding that judges be impartial and that they apply the law to the facts according to strict rules of procedure.

Bipartite bargaining A policy style that consists of closed, co-operative relations between business and government.

Central bank A banking institution owned by the state but autonomous from it. It has responsibility for monetary policy, acts as a lender of last resort to banks in the economy, and normally has a responsibility for the overall health of the financial system.

Contributory program Program in which eligibility for benefits is limited to those who have made contributions to the plan or on whose behalf contributions have been made to the plan (typically by employers).

Courts Government-sponsored dispute-resolution centres in which officials called judges or adjudicators have been given the power to decide controversies according to the whole body of relevant law.

Crown corporation A government-owned enterprise that has a structure similar to a private firm and that is intended to have a sufficient degree of freedom from political involvement to enable it to operate in a "businesslike" manner.

Decision-rules Rules that govern the transformation of preferences into binding decisions—that is, the way in which choices are made in the face of disagreement. At the most general level, these include hierarchical, majoritarian, and unanimity methods.

De-indexation See **indexation**.

Demand management Attempts by government to manage the demand for goods and services through the use of monetary and fiscal policy.

Exchange rate Refers to the price paid in one currency to buy units of another currency. **Exchange rate policy** refers to attempts to influence the price of a given country's currency, usually by its central bank.

Extra billing The billing of patients by physicians for an amount beyond that covered by governmental health insurance.

Fiscal policy Policy aimed at economic objectives through the use of taxes, government spending, and investment.

Globalization Refers to the increased integration of international markets as domestic impediments to trade are reduced, producing competition for domestic producers.

Governance structures The informal and patterned ways in which different institutions and actors interact within particular political and administrative settings to develop policy goals, select among means, cope with uncertainty and controversy, and foster legitimacy and support for policies.

Governing (or policy) instruments The methods by which public policy can be delivered. Although a variety of terms are current, instruments boil down to the direct use of money; direct action by officials (programs within bureaucracy); laws and regulation; and persuasion and information.

Gross domestic product (GDP) A measure of the size of a nation's economy, it measures the total value of goods and services produced in the economy in a given time period.

Gross national product (GNP) A measure of the size of a nation's economy. It differs from GDP in that it excludes income earned abroad by domestic residents. In 1990, Canada's GNP was equivalent to about 97 percent of its GDP.

Indexation The adjustment of benefits or payments to take account of inflation, either wage inflation or price inflation. **De-indexation** refers to the removal of such adjustments.

Judicial impartiality The principle that judges and adjudicators must decide cases showing no favouritism to the parties involved and with as open a mind as humanly possible, given the constraints of the rules of court and the evidence.

Judicial independence Pursuant to the impartiality principle, the rule that judges and adjudicators may decide cases without interference from anyone, especially from members of the legislature and cabinet.

Legalism   A policy style that is formal, open, and adversarial and that gives a prominent role to the courts in supervising interest-group conflict.

Mandarinate   A closely knit group of senior public servants whose common background and outlook allow them to exercise considerable influence over the direction of public policy. The term is used especially in reference to the immediate post-World War II period.

Means-tested program   Program in which the eligibility for benefits is limited to those whose incomes fall below a given level (an **income-tested** program), or to those who can demonstrate, according to established criteria, that their means (income and assets) are not sufficient to meet basic needs (a **needs-tested** program).

Ministerial responsibility   The principle that cabinet ministers are individually responsible to the legislature for actions by their departments and other administrative agencies within their portfolios.

Monetary policy   Policy that regulates the supply of money, usually through influencing short-term interest rates.

Multipartite bargaining   A policy style that is relatively open, consisting of co-operative bargaining between government and all the relevant stakeholders in a policy arena.

Neoconservatism   A term applied to an ideology that gained strength in the late 1970s and 1980s. This ideology, similar to nineteenth-century liberalism, emphasized the role of market forces in the allocation of resources and argued that the state should play a limited role in the allocation of resources or the redistribution of wealth.

New institutionalism   A broad-based intellectual movement concerned with incorporating institutions into the analysis of social problems. It employs micro-analysis, with an emphasis on rules affecting individual choice, meso-analysis, with its emphasis on organizations in systems, and macro-analysis, with its concern for constitutional frameworks.

Nontariff barriers   Such barriers include many policies or procedures, other than tariffs, that prevent or penalize imports and benefit domestic producers.

Order-in-council   An action based upon a written decision of the cabinet and proclaimed in the name of the governor-in-council.

Appointments to crown corporations and regulatory agencies may be made by order-in-council.

Organization for Economic Cooperation and Development (OECD) An international organization of 24 nations whose membership comprises the wealthiest industrial nations. The OECD is a source of relatively consistent data regarding various measures of the economic performance, government expenditures, and so on, of its member states.

Patronage Refers to the bestowing of positions of public responsibility on political friends of the governing party as a reward for past or future political services and without particular regard for the qualifications and competence of appointees to perform duties effectively.

Policy style A package of interests, institutions, and ideas that characterize a particular policy area.

Rational choice theory A branch of political science that employs some of the conceptual tools of microeconomics to address problems of collective choice.

Restructuring Refers to a process of reorganization by firms to take better advantage of their economic opportunities and to allow focus on markets beyond national frontiers or on specialization in international markets.

Reference questions Questions put to provincial courts of appeal by provincial cabinets or to the Supreme Court of Canada by the federal cabinet.

Regulation Government legislation or agency rules having the force of law and often administered by a semi-independent governmental agency, which restrict or require certain behaviour on the part of individuals or institutions, mostly in the private sector but sometimes in the public sector.

Rule of law The constitutional principle that citizens are governed by laws enacted by legislatures that they have elected, that public officials may do only what the law permits, and that the law must be applied equally to everyone unless the law itself permits unequal application.

Spending power Refers to the authority of the federal government in Canada to spend, and to attach conditions to its spending, in areas of provincial jurisdiction.

Standing A judicial doctrine determining the interests that have the right to go to court to file a lawsuit.

Stare decisis   A rigid version of the doctrine of precedent employed in common-law countries according to which judges and adjudicators must interpret the law in conformity with decisions of higher courts in the same jurisdiction, and should consider as persuasive the decisions of common-law courts of equal or higher status in other jurisdictions.

Structural heretics   Public-sector organizations that lie outside the regular departmental structure of government and enjoy some independent decision-making authority; so called because they are said to compromise to some degree the fundamental constitutional principle of ministerial responsibility, since cabinet ministers are not as fully involved in their operations as they are in their departments.

Trade remedy laws   Measures used against imports receiving unfair subsidies from their home government or sold at prices below those in the home market.

Universal program   One whose benefits are available to all those within a given jurisdiction who have satisfied basic residence requirements.

Value added   Refers to efforts to increase the market value of goods and services throughout the production and distribution process. It involves adapting technology for new uses, raising levels of quality, and targeting products for specific consumers.

Welfare state   In a given nation, the set of programs that provide entitlements to benefits in the form of income and access to health and social services, and the institutions through which those benefits are delivered. Depending on their level of generosity, the basis of eligibility for benefits, and their institutional structure, welfare states can be characterized as *liberal, conservative* (or *corporatist*), or *social democratic*.

CONTRIBUTORS' PROFILE

MICHAEL M. ATKINSON

Michael M. Atkinson is professor of political science at McMaster University and from 1986 until 1992 was chair of the department. He has co-authored two books: one on legislative politics, *The Canadian Legislative System* (with Robert Jackson), and the other on the political economy of industrial policy, *The State, Business and Industrial Change in Canada* (with William D. Coleman). He has published in a wide variety of Canadian and international journals, and in 1992 he became co-editor of *Governance: An International Journal of Policy and Administration*.

HERMAN BAKVIS

Herman Bakvis teaches political science and public administration at Dalhousie University. He is the author of *Regional Ministers: Power and Influence in the Canadian Cabinet*. During the period 1990–92, he was a research co-ordinator with the Royal Commission on Electoral Reform and Party Financing.

WILLIAM D. COLEMAN

William D. Coleman is professor of political science at McMaster University. He has written three books: *The Independence Movement in Quebec, 1945–1980*, *Business and Politics: A Study in Collective Action*, and (with Michael M. Atkinson) *The State, Business and Industrial Change in Canada*. In addition to these books, he has written articles dealing with Quebec politics, business–government relations, and the making of economic policy that have been published in journals in Canada, the United States, and Europe.

IAN GREENE

Ian Greene has taught political science at York University since 1985 and was co-ordinator of the public policy and administration program from 1989 to 1991. He specializes in the fields of law and politics, political ethics, and public administration. He has authored two books, *Judges and Judging* (with Peter McCormick) and *The Charter of Rights*. His articles have appeared in a number of law and political science journals.

GEORGE HOBERG

George Hoberg is associate professor of political science at the University of British Columbia. After attending the University of California at Berkeley and the Massachusetts Institute of Technology, where he received his Ph.D., he moved to Vancouver in 1987. He has published *Pluralism by Design: Environmental Policy and the American Regulatory State* and a number of articles on comparative environmental policy. He is working on a book comparing Canadian and American environmental policies.

DAVID Mac DONALD

David Mac Donald is a liaison and policy officer in the Federal-Provincial Relations Office of the government of Canada. Previously, he was a senior research analyst with the Royal Commission on Electoral Reform and Party Financing. He has graduate degrees in political studies and public administration from Queen's University and Dalhousie University respectively.

KENNETH McROBERTS

Kenneth McRoberts is professor of political science and director of the Robarts Centre for Canadian Studies, York University. His publications include *Quebec: Social Change and Political Crisis*, 3rd edition, and he is also editor of *The International Journal of Canadian Studies*. At present, he is completing a monograph on the constitutional crisis, tentatively entitled *Separate Agendas*.

SHARON L. SUTHERLAND

Sharon L. Sutherland is professor of political science at Carleton University. A professor and practitioner in Canadian public administration for more than fifteen years, she has also taught at Dalhousie University and the University of Essex. Her research interests include public policy and program evaluation, political institutions, and democratic theory. She has recently published articles on ministerial responsibility in the *Canadian Journal of Political Science* and *Canadian Public Administration*.

PAUL G. THOMAS

Paul G. Thomas is professor of political studies at the University of Manitoba. He is the co-author of *Canadian Public Administration*, and a former chairman of the Manitoba Telephone System. He is currently an associate editor of *Canadian Public Administration*.

CAROLYN TUOHY

Carolyn Tuohy is professor of political science at the University of Toronto. She received her undergraduate degree from the University of Toronto and her M.A. and Ph.D. in political science from Yale University. Her teaching and research interests are in the area of comparative public policy, particularly social policy. She is the author of *Policy and Politics in Canada: Institutionalized Ambivalence*, a treatment of Canadian public policy in a comparative international perspective.

KENNETH B. WOODSIDE

Kenneth B. Woodside is associate professor of political studies at the University of Guelph. His research interests include taxation policy, trade policy, the study of policy instruments, and telecommunications policy. He has published in various journals, including the *Canadian Journal of Political Science*, *Canadian Public Policy*, and *Canadian Public Administration*. Currently, he is working on a study of taxation policy in Canada, Britain, and the United States.

OREST W. ZAJCEW

Orest W. Zajcew is currently enrolled in the doctoral program at the University of Toronto, having completed his M.A. in political studies at the University of Manitoba. He is interested in Slavic studies and the comparative study of Canadian politics.

Index

Accountability. See ministerial responsibility
Acton, Lord, 151
Adams, Bryan, 244
Adjuciation. See also courts, 182–83, 186, 190
Administrative law, 108
Advisory Council on Adjustment, 246
Agricultural policy, 38, 64, 162
Agriculture Canada, 315
Alberta, 153, 166, 168, 172, 184, 185, 199, 255, 256, 265, 266, 291, 297
Alberta Labour Reference, 184, 186
Alcan Aluminum, 307–308
Alexandroff, Allan, 120
Atlantic Canada Opportunities Agency (ACOA), 58, 73, 74, 270
Atkinson, Michael, 117, 164, 181, 189, 198, 251, 270, 274, 314
Aucoin, Peter, 62, 78, 79
Auditor-General, 93
Auto Pact, 257, 263, 269
Austria, 227, 231, 232, 234, 239, 277, 285
Axworthy, Lloyd, 68, 115
Axworthy, Tom, 64, 79

Babe, R., 143
Bagehot, Walter, 83, 100–101
Bakvis, Herman, 10, 78, 79, 296
Bank of Canada, 64, 207–208, 209, 210, 228, 230, 234–35, 239
Bank of Canada Act, 230–31, 235
Banting, Keith, 160, 286, 298, 304
Barber, C.L., 239
Barer, M., 289
Bartley, A., 137
Bell Canada, 143–44, 245
Bennett, R.B., 161
Bercuson, David, 111
Bill of Rights, 201
Bird, Reg, 131
Blenkarn, Don, 103
Block, Fred, 171

Boothman, Barry, 132
Bouchard, Benoit, 74
Boundary rules, 39–40, 48, 65
Breton, Albert, 151
Bretton Woods, 208, 216, 218
Britain, 32–33, 186, 232, 234, 235, 279, 281, 283, 290, 293, 302, 303, 320
  political parties in, 70, 99
British Columbia, 71, 128, 190, 207, 255, 256, 265, 289, 290, 297, 307, 326, 339
Brundtland Commission, 317
Bureaucrats. See also mandarinate, 24
  and patronage, 53
  as advisors, 94–95
  classified, 105–106
  resignations of, 112
Bureaucracy. See also Canadian public service, 25, 37, 81–82
  and industrial policy, 269–72
  controls on, 97–110
  defined, 85
  performance of, 63, 96
  roles of, 85-86
  rules of, 24, 104–108

Cabinet. See also central agencies
  as a representative body, 48, 61
  as political executive, 83
  decision rules of, 48, 63–64, 74
  origins of, 50, 52
  policy impact of, 69–75
  Prime Minister in, 61–62
  size of, 49
Cabinet committees, 49, 56, 58
  Economic (and Regional) Development, 56, 57, 64
  Expenditure Review, 58
  Operations, 58, 59, 62
  Priorities and Planning (P&P), 55, 58, 59, 62, 78
  Social Development, 56
  Unity, 59

Cabinet ministers:
  backgrounds of, 67
  logrolling and, 66, 68, 74
  pressures on, 67–69
  regional responsibilities of, 52–53, 55, 75, 78
  resignations of, 98, 102
  turnover of, 77, 98–99
  types of, 66
Cabinet organization
  functional issues, 63, 64–65
  spacial issues, 63, 65–67
  stages of, 51–59
Cairns, Alan, 168, 338
Caisse dépôt et placement, 246, 271
Campbell, Colin, 49, 62
Campbell, Kim, 80
Campbell, Robert, 216
Canada Assistance Plan, 72, 73, 291, 296–97, 304
Canada Health Act (1984), 298–300
Canada Water Act, 313, 315
Canadian Bar Association, 188, 328, 329
Canadian Broadcasting Corporation (CBC), 125, 144
Canadian constitution, 9
  changes in, 4, 78, 155–57, 301
  patriation of, 64, 156, 183
  role of Crown in, 83, 111–12
Canadian Council on Social Development, 292
Canadian Council of Resource and Environment Ministers, 313, 318, 319
Canadian Development Corporation, 264
Canadian economy
  and the provinces, 253–57
  competitiveness of, 259–61
  foreign ownership of, 242, 247, 257, 262–63, 264
  productivity in, 241, 260
  status of, 253, 259
Canadian Environmental Protection Act (1988), 318, 319, 330–31, 332, 336, 338
Canadian Jobs Strategy, 246
Canadian Labour Congress (CLC), 229, 232
Canadian Medical Association, 299
Canadian public service. See also bureaucracy
  department types, 89–90
  merit system in, 105–107
  organization of, 86–94, 116
  size of, 86–89, 96, 100
Canadian Pulp and Paper Association, 315
Canadian Radio-television and Telecommunications Commission (CRTC), 137, 141, 144, 244
Canadian state, 116, 262
  ambiguity of, 10–12
  weak tradition of, 9–10, 314, 339
Canadian Transport Commission (CTC), 137, 140, 141, 142
Capital markets, 238, 258–59
Cartier, George-Etienne, 50–51
Carty, Ken, 79
Causality, 20–23
Central agencies, 49, 53, 55–57, 90
Central banks. See also Bank of Canada, 25, 210, 213, 223–24, 228
Chapleau, J.A., 51
Chapman, John, 44
Charest, Jean, 327, 338
Charter of Rights and Freedoms, 12, 24, 40, 63, 165–66, 179–80, 184, 185, 194–95, 198–99, 201, 202–204, 205, 324, 332, 336, 337
Civil servants. See bureaucrats; public servants
Clark, Joe, 56, 59
Coalitions. See public policy
Cohen, Michael, 43
Coleman, William D., 14, 270, 274, 314
Combines Investigation Act, 263
Comptroller-General, 56, 93
Confédération des syndicts nationaux, 232
Conservative Party, 1, 2, 50, 58, 188, 203, 215, 236, 265, 266, 268–69, 294–96, 297
Constitution Act (1982), 165, 170
Constitution Act (1867), 83, 150, 153, 176
Constitutions. See also Canadian constitution), 7–8, 31–32
Co-operative Commonwealth Federation (CCF), 160, 215, 287, 288
Cooper, Barry, 111
Courchene, Tom, 233, 239, 280

Courts. *See also* judges:
  and bureaucrats, 107
  and environmental policy, 324–335, 337–38
  and federalism, 156–57, 163
  and lawyers, 193–95, 196, 204
  capacity of, 195–96
  defined,180–81
  organization of, 186–89
  policy role of, 179–80
  rules of, 189–93
Crosbie, John, 74, 75
Crown corporations, 11, 116, 118–119
  accountability of, 121–22
  and industrial policy, 245–46
  and ministers, 126, 127, 132–33
  defined, 118
  leadership in, 125, 127–28, 129–32
  objectives of, 126–27
  regulating, 144–45
Crow's Nest Pass rate, 64

Dawson, R. McGregor, 105, 111
Decentralization, 81
Defence Production Sharing Argeement (DPSA), 263
Deficits, 229, 234, 297
Department of Agriculture, 40, 90
Department of Communications, 44, 137
Department of Consumer and Corporate Affairs, 40, 270
Department of Employment and Immigration, 196
Department of Energy, Mines and Resources, 126, 270
Department of External Affairs, 270
Department of Finance, 14, 24, 39, 58, 64, 90, 92, 107, 112, 235, 239
Department of Fisheries and Oceans, 112
Department of Indian Affairs and Northern Development, 22
Department of National Defence, 112
Department of Regional Economic Expansion, 263, 270
Department of Solicitor-General, 112
Department of Trade and Commerce, 270
Deutsch, J.J., 79
Dicey, A.V., 191
Diefenbaker, John G., 55, 78, 99

  cabinet organization, 54
Doern, G. Bruce, 233
Donner, Arthur, 238, 239
Douglas, T.C., 172
Dufour, J-M., 239
Dupré, Stephan, 53

Election Expenses Act, 202
Electoral system, 49, 67, 77, 224–25, 236, 267
Elster, Jon, 21, 31
Employment and Immigration Commission, 199
Energy policy, 64
Enterprise Development Program, 264
Environmental Assessment and Review Process, 309, 325, 326, 333
Environmental Assessment Act, 327
Environmentalism, 312–313
Environmental policy. *See also* policy styles, 15, 71, 311
  "bill of rights", 324, 330
  citizen participation in, 328–30
  legislation, 313
  role of courts in, 326–34
  role of state in, 319–21
Environment Canada, 71, 313, 315, 317, 330
Esping-Andersen, Gosta, 276, 282, 286, 302
Established Programs Financing (EPF), 73, 289, 299–300, 304
Evans, Robert, 289
Exchange rate policy, 211, 248, 259, 260–61
Extra-billing, 298–99

Federal Court of Appeal, 199
Fédération des travailleurs et travailleuses du Quebec, 232
Federalism. *See also* intergovernmental relations)
  and dispersion of power, 32, 108–109, 232–34
  and experimentation, 11, 159–60
  and policy diffusion, 11, 160, 172, 287
  and public policy, 149, 157–63, 231, 273
  and regionalism, 3, 152–53
  and society, 169–73
  assymmetrical, 153, 170, 174–75
  Canadian, 152–55

defined, 150
effects of, 167–73
"executive", 154–55, 157, 161, 164, 166, 174
interstate, 150, 163, 175
intrastate, 150, 153, 174–75, 296
purpose of, 151–52

Federal-Provincial Relations Office, 56, 93
Fielding, William, 51
Financial Administration Act, 107
Fiscal policy, 210–211, 212, 213, 223, 224, 229, 232
Fletcher, Fred, 160, 165, 176
Forget, Claude, 295
Fortin, P., 237
Foreign Investment Review Agency (FIRA), 245, 264
France, 242, 277, 285
Freeman, G.P., 281
Free Trade Agreement (FTA), 14, 69, 70, 241, 249, 250, 259, 266, 268–69, 272–73, 286
Friedman, Milton, 228

Gardiner, J.G. (Jimmy), 53, 54
General Agreement on Tariffs and Trade (GATT), 241, 248, 249, 250
Germany, 18, 232, 234, 237, 239, 283, 285, 303, 320
Godbout, J-A., 161
Goods and Services Tax (GST), 1–3, 9, 32, 64
Gouverich, Peter, 214
Governance structures, 117–118, 123
Goyer, Jean-Pierre, 79
Great Whale project, 308, 309, 327, 334
Green Plan, 321, 323
Greene, Ian, 12, 199
Grier, Ruth, 325, 329
Guaranteed Income Supplement (GIS), 282
Gunn, L.A., 181

Haddow, Rod, 292
Hall, Peter, 31
Hamilton, Alvin, 54
Health and Welfare Canada, 315
Harrison, Kathryn, 162, 327
Health care policy, 285, 287–91, 297–300, 301–302
Heclo, Hugh, 41, 42
Hoberg, George, 15, 194
Hodgetts, J.E., 116
Hogg, Peter, 84, 107, 112
Hogwood, Brian, 181
Horowitz, D., 193
Howe, C.D., 53, 54, 79
Howe, Joseph, 51
Hult, K.L., 123

Ideas, and public policy, 1–2, 4, 275–76, 311
Immigration and Refugee Review Board, 195
Immigration policy, 185, 201
Income maintenance policy, 216, 282–85, 291–97, 302
Industrial Research Assistance Program (IRAP), 264
Industrial policy. *See also* research and development, 14
and the provinces, 265, 271–72
and trade policy, 251–53
defined, 242–43
job training, 246
spending programs, 243, 264
types of, 243–48
Industry, Science and Technology Canada (ISTC), 270
Inflation, 226, 230–31, 237
Interest groups, 8, 292, 313, 315–16, 322–23
Interests
and public policy, 2, 3, 275–76, 311
Intergovernmental relations. *See also* federalism), 25, 154–55, 161–62, 167, 287–91, 293, 298–300, 301, 310
Institutions:
and industrial policy, 269–73
and macro-economic policy, 213–14, 221–26;
and organization, 6, 35–36, 44–45
and policy learning, 42–44
and public policy, 2–3, 5, 18, 20–26, 36–44, 163–66
and rules, 6, 24–25, 27–29, 30, 44–45
and social policy, 276, 278–79
and trade policy, 268, 272–73
as human creations, 4, 6;

constraining side of, 23–25, 231
creative side of, 25–26, 35–36
defined, 5–7, 123
political, 8
resources of, 24
state, 7–8
Italy, 234, 242, 277

Japan, 18, 22–23, 237, 245, 253, 258, 282, 303
Jennings, Sir Ivor, 191
Johnson, Andrew, 75
Johnson, David, 140
Johnson, David R., 235
Johnson, Nevil, 111–12
Judicial Committee of the Privy Council, 156–57, 161, 163, 179, 273
Judges, 12
  ability of, 202–03
  as adjudicators, 183–86, 199–200
  background of, 188–89, 199
  independence of, 195–96, 198

Kaplan, Harold, 124
Kent, Tom, 79
Keynesian policy, 14, 32, 208, 237–38
  and unemployment, 217–21
  dilemma, 217–218
  ideas behind, 212–213
  in Canada, 214–216
  institutional requirements for, 213–214
  retreat from, 227–28
King, William Lyon Mackenzie, 53, 78, 161, 263
Kingdon, John, 43
Kirsch, E., 127, 129
Klein, R., 280
Krasner, Stephen, 30
Krasnick, M., 176

Labour Force Development Strategy, 246
Labour legislation, 247–48
Labour, organized, 211, 215, 216, 222–23, 224, 231–32, 236, 292
Language policy, 39
Lalonde, Marc, 58, 62, 64
Lapointe, Ernest, 53
Latham, Earl, 320, 340
Latouche, Daniel, 131
Laughren, Floyd, 207

Laurier, Wilfrid, 51–52, 263
Law Reform Commission, 195
Laxer, Gordon, 274
Lesage, Jean, 172
Liberal party, 51, 98, 215–16, 236, 267, 268–69, 293
Lindberg, Leon, 38
Lindquist, Evert, 80
Lord's Day Act, 180, 183

Macdonald, Sir John A., 50–51, 53
Mac Donald, David, 10, 296
MacEachen, Allan, 62
Macroeconomic policy. *See also* Keynesian policy;
  and institutions, 213–14, 221–26
  and social democratic parties, 224–26
  defined, 208–209
  objectives of, 209–210
  monetarism, 14, 39–40
Major, John, 99
Mallory, J.R., 51
Mandel, Michael, 196
Managerial Authority and Accountability (IMMA), 79
Mandarinate, 54, 95
Manitoba, 68, 128, 129, 205
March, James G., 26, 35, 109, 123
Maslove, Allan, 233
Matzner, E., 237, 238
Mazankowski, Donald, 59, 75
McCallum, J.C.P., 239
McCormick, Peter, 199
McKay, Elmer, 68
McMillan, Tom, 330, 332, 338
McNaught, Kenneth, 338
McRoberts, Kenneth, 11, 177
Medicare. *See also*, health care policy, 69, 70, 288, 303
Meech Lake Accord, 30, 59, 64
Mexico, 266
Ministerial responsibility, 24, 75, 84, 101, 102, 108
Ministry of International Trade and Industry (MITI) (Japan), 23
Ministry of State for Science and Technology (MOSST), 270
Morton, F.L., 201
Moe, Terry, 29
Monetary policy, 38, 70, 210, 217, 224, 230, 235
Monetarism, 14, 209, 222–24, 225;
  in Canada, 226–31
Mosher, F.C., 111

Mullan D.J., 142
Mulroney, Brian, 49, 58–59, 62, 99, 100, 161
Murray, Sir George, 52

National Anti-Poverty Organization, 292
National Centre for the Judiciary, 203
National Citizens' Coalition, 185, 202, 203, 204
National Energy Program (NEP), 9, 64, 69, 70, 110, 112, 166, 172, 245, 264, 267–68
National Policy, 261–63
Netherlands, 234
New Brunswick, 74, 255, 291
New Democratic Party, 71, 207, 216, 230, 237, 288, 297, 301, 325
Newfoundland, 265
"New institutionalism", 26-36, 117
Niagara Institute, 317, 319–20
Noel, S., 79, 80
Nordlinger, Eric, 167
Norrie, Ken, 176
North American Free Trade Agreement (NAFTA), 266
Northern Telecom, 245
Norway, 280, 283
Nova Scotia, 256, 326

O'Higgins, M., 280
Oil crises, 208, 216–17, 218, 230, 264
Olmsted, Richard, 176
Olsen, Johan, 26, 109, 123
Ontario, 74, 153, 158, 207, 230, 245, 247, 253, 255, 256, 257, 265, 266, 268, 297, 298, 325, 329, 339
Ontario Medical Association, 298
Organization for Economic Co-operation and Development (OECD), 226-27, 234, 241, 280, 285, 303
Organization theory, 34–36, 123–25
Organizational culture, 123–25, 133
Ostrom, Elinor, 28

Paehlke, Robert, 144
Painter, Martin, 155
Pal, Leslie, 176, 201
Parris, Harry, 100
Patent Act (1969), 244
Patronage, 50–53, 58, 68, 128, 188
Parliament. *See also* Westminster model, 3, 24;
accountability to, 84, 93, 100–102
party discipline in, 4, 102–104, 267, 337
reform of, 103
"Peace, Order and Good Government", 191
Penal policy, 22
Pearson, Lester, B., 54, 79
Pensions, 43, 156, 246, 281-82, 282–83, 286, 294–95, 302
Canada Pension Plan, 69, 161, 283, 297
old age security (OAS), 282, 283, 286, 294
Quebec Pension Plan, 246, 271, 283, 297
Pepin, Jean-Luc, 64, 66
Perrow, Charles, 31
Peters, B. Guy, 123
Peters, D.D., 238, 239
Petro-Canada, 126, 264
pharmaceuticals, 244
Phillips curve, 237
Pickersgill, Jack, 54
Pierson, P.D., 281, 300
Planning-Programming-Budgeting (PPBS), 55, 96
Policy. *See* public policy
Policy networks, 314, 323
Poggi, Gianfranco, 30, 31
Policy styles, 309, 336–39
bipartite bargaining, 313–16;
compared, 334-36
defined, 310
legalism, 323–34
multipartite bargaining, 316–23
Political parties, 8
and coalitions, 77, 268–69
failures of, 97–98
Porter, Michael, 260
Prime Minister's Office (PMO), 55, 57, 62, 95
Prince, Michael, 233
Privy Council Office (PCO), 55, 57, 61, 90, 91–92, 107, 112
Procurement policy, 245
Program Expenditure Management System (PEMS), 56, 58, 78
Program for Industry/Laboratory Products, 247
Progressive Conservatives. See Conservative Party
Province-building, 3, 168, 174, 264
Provinces: and industrial policy, 242

equality of, 4
  in competition, 109–110
Public goods, 38
Public policy: and courts, 183–189
  and federalism, 157–63, 165–67
  and regulatory agencies, 135–36
  and theory, 19–20
  approaches to, 1–5, 168
  change in, 23
  coalitions, 38, 39, 214, 224, 226
  defined, 18–19, 95, 181–82
  domains, 37–39
  exclusivity of, 38–40
  problems, 17–18
  research, 95–97
Public policy process:
  access to, 36–40
  and networks, 270–71
  learning in, 40–44
  programs and decisions, 19
  role of bureaucracy, 85
  stages of, 40
Public Service Commission (PSC), 93
Public Service Employment Act (1967), 85, 107
Public Service 2000, 79, 91, 105, 108

Quebec, 24, 54, 70, 74, 153, 156, 158, 168, 169, 170, 172, 174–75, 193, 253, 255, 256, 266, 268
  environmental policy in, 308, 311
  industrial policy in, 14, 246, 265, 271–72
  labour movement in, 232
  social policy in, 162, 289, 291

Racette, D., 239
Rachal, P., 144
Rational choice, 26–31, 34, 35, 44–45, 107, 251
  and boundary rules, 39–40
  and contractarianism, 27–28, 29–31
  and principal-agent problem, 28–29
Rationality, 34–35
Reagan, Ronald, 218, 221
Research and development, 18–20, 41, 244
Regulatory agencies, 11, 140–41
  and industrial policy, 245
  and ministers, 133, 136–38
  capture theory of, 142–44

controls on, 122, 134, 140
culture of, 117
decision-making in, 141–42
defined, 119–120
in Manitoba, 130, 131, 144
in Ontario, 129, 135–36, 138, 140
leadership in, 117, 125, 138–39
mandates of, 135–39
role of, 134
types of, 145
Richardson, James, 79
Riker, William, 29, 176
Robertson, Gordon, 91
Rose, Richard, 95
Russell, Peter, 180

Saskatchewan, 128, 160, 168, 184–85, 255, 265, 287, 288, 291, 326
Savoie, Donald, 66, 67, 68, 234
Scharpf, Fritz, 6, 36, 48, 155, 212, 219, 234, 237, 239
Schattschneider, E.E., 21
Schein, E.H., 124
Schrecker, Ted, 341
Schultz, Richard, 120
Scientific Research Tax Credit, 19, 244
Senate, 4, 77, 174
Skocpol, Theda, 31, 42, 169
Simeon, Richard, 176
Simon, Herbert, 34, 35
Skogstad, Grace, 162
Smiley, Donald, 152, 153, 159, 168, 176
Smith, B.C., 111
Smith, David, 79, 80
Social democratic parties, 224–26, 236–37
Social policy. *See also* income maintenance policy; health care policy; welfare state, 15, 41, 42–43, 191, 275–76, 280–81, 286–87, 300–302
  universality of, 286, 288, 294
South Korea, 258
Sparks, G.R., 239
Stare decisis, 191–92
State, the. *See also* Canadian state, 7–8, 34, 311
  capacity of, 33, 278, 314
  critiques of, 13
  organization of, 21, 82
State theory, 31–34, 167
Steinmo, Sven, 32

Stevenson, Garth, 176
Stewart, John, 84
Streek, Wolfgang, 237, 238
"Structural heretics", 116–117, 120–22, 145–47
Structural theory, 31–36, 44–45, 83, 251
Struthers, James, 163
Supreme Court of Canada, 161, 183, 184, 186, 196, 197, 205, 297, 337
Sutherland, Sharon, 10–11, 332
Sweden, 18, 32, 227, 231, 232, 234, 237, 239, 280, 283, 285, 303, 305, 320
Switzerland, 232

Taiwan, 258
Technology, 246, 260
Thatcher, Margaret, 99
Thomas, Paul G., 11, 112
Thompson, Andrew, 314
Thompson, Sir John, 53
Tobacco Advisory Council, 186
Toner, Glen, 318, 341
Trade, Canadian, 242, 247–58
Trade and Tariff Act (USA), 251
Trade policy, 39, 253
  and comparative advantage, 248
  and federalism, 272–73
  and industrial policy, 251–53
  and trade remedies, 250–51, 266
  defined, 249, 251
  liberalization, 14, 265–66
  role of tariffs in, 249, 261–63
"Tragedy of the commons", 27
Treasury Board, 24, 88, 92–93, 108
Treasury Board Secretariat (TBS), 90, 93
Trudeau, Pierre Elliot, 55–57, 61, 62, 99, 151, 156, 159, 167, 229
Tuohy, Carolyn, 15
Tupper, Charles, 51
Turner, John, 57, 229

Unemployment, 216, 217, 224–26, 237
  in Canada, 215, 226–27, 256
Unemployment insurance (UI), 43, 73, 176, 285, 293, 295–96, 301, 302

United Automobile Workers, 236
United States, 293–94, 303
  administrative law in, 108
  and monetarism, 221, 226
  congressional system, 75, 82, 103–104
  environmental policy in, 324, 328–29, 332, 336–37
  industrial policy in, 245
  regulatory agencies in, 139, 142–43
  social policy in, 42–43, 277, 281, 282, 283, 285
  tax policy in, 32
  trade policy in, 250–51, 258

Van Loon, Richard, 78
Verney, Douglas, 108
Vietnam War, 208, 216

Wage policy, 211, 215, 219, 228–29
Walcott, C., 123
Wallace, D.C., 160, 165, 176
Weaver, R. Kent, 132, 281
Weber, Max, 81, 105
Weir, Margaret, 32
Welfare state: changes in, 277–82, 294–300
  defined, 27
  types of, 27679
Western Diversification Office (WDO), 58, 73, 270
Westminster model, 10–11, 12, 15, 40, 80, 82, 83, 102, 104
  and environmental policy, 337–38
  and industrial policy, 267–68
  and social policy, 300
  role of bureaucrats in, 107, 110–111
  role of cabinet in, 47–48, 59, 65, 70, 267
Wheare, K.C., 176
Wilson, Graham, 340
Wilson, James Q., 130, 143, 144
Wilson, Michael, 58
Woodside, Kenneth, 14, 208, 238
Woolley, John, 234

Young, Robert, 97, 98

Zajcew, Orest, 11

To the Owner of this Book:

We are interested in your reaction to *Governing Canada: Institutions and Public Policy* by Michael M. Atkinson. With your comments, we can improve this book in future editions. Please help us by completing this questionaire.

1. What was your reason for using this book?

   _____ university course

   _____ college course

   _____ continuing education course

   _____ personal interest

   _____ other (specify)

2. If you used this text for a program, what was the name of that program?

3. Which school do you attend?

4. Approximately how much of the book did you use?

   _____ 1/4   _____ 1/2   _____ 3/4   _____ all

5. Which chapters or sections were omitted from your course?

6. What is the best aspect of this book?

7. Is there anything that should be added?

8. Please add any comments or suggestions.

(fold here)

**Business
Reply Mail**
No Postage Stamp
Necessary if Mailed
in Canada

43652

POSTAGE WILL BE PAID BY
Heather McWhinney
Editorial Director
College Division
HARCOURT BRACE JOVANOVICH CANADA INC.
55 HORNER AVENUE
TORONTO, ONTARIO
M8Z 9Z9

(tape shut)